# Writing the

# NIH

## Grant Proposal

# Writing the NIH Grant Proposal

## A Step-by-Step Guide

## William Gerin

Columbia University Medical Center

**SAGE Publications**
Thousand Oaks ▪ London ▪ New Delhi

*For information:*

 Sage Publications, Inc.
2455 Teller Road
Thousand Oaks, California 91320
E-mail: order@sagepub.com

Sage Publications Ltd.
1 Oliver's Yard
55 City Road
London EC1Y 1SP
United Kingdom

Sage Publications India Pvt. Ltd.
B-42, Panchsheel Enclave
Post Box 4109
New Delhi 110 017  India

Printed in the United States of America

**Library of Congress Cataloging-in-Publication Data**

Gerin, William.
Writing the NIH grant proposal : a step-by-step guide / William Gerin.
    p. cm.
Includes bibliographical references and index.
ISBN 1-4129-1531-7 (cloth) — ISBN 1-4129-1532-5 (pbk.)
   1.  National Institutes of Health (U.S.)—Research grants—Handbooks, manuals, etc.
2.  Proposal writing for grants—United States—Handbooks, manuals, etc.
3.  Proposal writing in medicine—United States—Handbooks, manuals, etc.
4. Medicine—Research grants—United States—Handbooks, manuals, etc.  I.  Title.
RA11.D6G47 2006
658.15′224—dc22

                                    2005033265

This book is printed on acid-free paper.

06   07   08   09   10   9   8   7   6   5   4   3   2   1

| | |
|---|---|
| *Acquisitions Editor:* | Jim Brace-Thompson |
| *Editorial Assistant:* | Karen Ehrmann |
| *Typesetter:* | C&M Digitals (P) Ltd. |
| *Indexer:* | Rick Hurd |
| *Cover Designer:* | Michelle Lee Kenny |

# Contents

# Introduction

For a researcher in the biomedical or behavioral sciences, National Institutes of Health (NIH) funding represents the big leagues. It is very prestigious to have one's research sponsored by the NIH, and investigators with NIH funding are a force to be reckoned with. I presume that you are highly motivated to join this select group, and I congratulate you. I cannot imagine a more satisfying career than one in which a people get to pose interesting questions that they care about and have the wherewithal to go out and find the answers.

But there is a catch: You need funding to conduct your studies and to advance your career. Many of you are clinicians, and you can depend on income from seeing patients in the event that you are unsuccessful at obtaining research funding. Others work in academic institutions and have tenure—or hope to—as a safety net. But if you want to be able to carry on your research, most of you will have to find financial support.

The purpose of this book is to help you do this. The need to apply for NIH funding is a constant pressure for many of us in the field. If you are at a more junior stage of your career, there may be expectations that you will apply for, and obtain, a K (career development) award. If you are at a more advanced stage, there is a menu of investigator-initiated alternatives, with the R01 as a main entrée. Chapter 3 describes the various grant mechanisms and provides flow charts to help you decide which mechanism is most appropriate for you.

The prospect of applying for such funding, and the not inconsequential possibility of being turned down, is daunting. However, the more you know about the process, the less intimidating it will become. Moreover, you can eliminate much of the uncertainty. Thus, although you cannot control how NIH reviewers will react to your research idea, you can endeavor to write your proposal clearly; you can present a budget that requests neither too much nor too little money; and you can ensure that the margins are correct, the figures clear, and the type size within the specified limits.

I am a psychologist, not a physician. My specialty is the study of psychosocial determinants of cardiovascular disease. I am not trained in either the study of animal models or in basic research. Rather than doing a poor job of trying to use models with which I am unfamiliar so that the book will *seem* more broadly based than it is, I have mostly stuck with my expertise. I do believe that the pathways to good science, and to good grant writing, are common across disciplines, but if you spend most of your time at the bench, you may spot areas in the book that you wish had been better covered. The best I can do is ask you to e-mail me (wg131@columbia.edu) to let me know the gaps, and, in the event there is ever a subsequent edition, I will try to address them.

The philosophy behind this book is simple: I plan to take you through the entire grant-writing process one step at a time. The process involves both conceptual material—how, for example, do you convey your specific aims in a way that intrigues your reader right from the beginning—to such seemingly mundane questions as how to title your proposal (this is not a mundane question, by the way). The steps cannot easily be divided into larger philosophical and scientific issues versus smaller administrative and formatting issues, and I have decided that the best way to help is to target a piece of the problem—say, writing the Background and Significance section—and tackle both the larger and smaller questions in the order in which they arise. We are going to explore every aspect of the application process, including the writing of the science, the administrative details, developing and managing collaborative relationships, budgeting, building a research team, and so on.

There is more material that you need to master than I could ever cram into one volume, so I have been selective. I have assumed, for example, that you are a competent scientist and are in the ballpark in terms of having the goods to put in a proposal to the NIH. At any rate, this book is not intended to teach you research methodology or statistics or how to have an idea. We start with the assumption that you already *have* a potentially fundable idea, that you are in an institution that is eligible for NIH funding, that you have access to research partners and staff necessary to carry out the proposed research, and so forth. So, if you think you're ready, we'll jump in.

## HOW TO USE THIS BOOK

The material in this book can be (loosely) broken down into three categories:

1. Materials that have been abstracted and condensed from other primary sources, primarily the Web. I don't wish to reproduce the Web materials in full: You can find those yourselves (I will always provide the web addresses [URLs] in the chapter endnotes). Although the NIH and related Web sites are extraordinarily helpful and well designed, they are also extensive. I have tried to provide the most relevant materials all in one place, and to locate the materials and distill them. Please note that, although many of the NIH Web addresses have been unchanged, often for several years, they may change at any time. If you cannot find a Web page using the URL I have provided, you'll have to search by topic. Let me add that the NIH has generously given me permission to use these materials, including reproducing their forms.

2. Clarifications of instructions and suggestions provided by the NIH that I and others have found to be ambiguous, difficult to follow, or sometimes even misleading. You must understand that maintaining the massive amount of Web material (you will find thousands of Web pages once you start searching the NIH sites) is difficult, and inconsistencies are bound to slip through.

3. My own strategic hints and opinions. I will identify these as such.

Some of the chapters in this book are more general and are meant, therefore, to be read through (i.e., not merely used as a reference). Chapter 2, for example, discusses issues concerning relationships with your colleagues, as well as with NIH staff, and you should just read it. Other chapters, such as those dealing with budgets and form pages, will be more useful if you have your application in front of you while you refer to the text. The latter will, for the most part, consist of examples and annotations, with the intention that you should be able to generalize from the example to your own specific needs. This is true whether you are an epidemiologist, a clinical trialist, or a basic scientist. The annotations will provide clarifications, hints, warnings, and other information garnered by my colleagues and myself over our many years of writing proposals. The information is intended to be practical and immediately applicable to your needs. I have arranged the examples so that annotations will appear close to the original text, so you need not be scrambling about.

This book is not intended to be the repository of everything that can be known about the grant-writing and submission process, nor is it intended to supplant the wealth of information that is available on the Web, largely on the NIH Web site (http://www.nih.gov). It is intended, rather, to serve as your own, personal expert consultant.

# Acknowledgments

Several people provided consultation and assistance in writing this book. I particularly would like to thank Juhee Jhalani for her invaluable help in researching many of the more elusive facts. In addition, Juhee and Tanya Goyal read drafts of the manuscript and provided greatly needed criticism. Gabrielle Albanese helped with the budget research and checked over my figures. Karina Davidson answered innumerable questions concerning career awards, and Lynn Clemow helped me edit the proposal used in the example. I am grateful to the staff of the Starwich Coffee Shop, who allowed me to spend untold hours drinking coffee and working away on my laptop. Stacey Shimizu did the copyediting, and Jim Brace-Thompson, my editor, has been immensely supporting throughout this process. My brother, Barry Gerin, provided both emotional and instrumental support, and put up with my occasional grouchy moods. Many of my friends and colleagues, including Gbenga Ogedegbe, Matt Burg, Peter Kaufmann, and Daichi Shimbo, offered comments and suggestions throughout the writing process. In addition, I thank the reviewers who improved the manuscript tremendously, including

Sharon Thompson
The University of Texas at El Paso

Robert Strack
University of North Carolina at Greensboro

Juliana van Olphen
San Francisco State University

Gale A. Spencer, Director,
Kresge Center for Nursing Research, Decker School of Nursing
State University of New York at Binghamton

Tami Benham-Deal
University of Wyoming

Beverly L. Roberts
University of Florida

And, finally, I would like to acknowledge and thank the NIH and its member Institutes and Centers for allowing me to reproduce its Web-based forms and supporting materials.

# Foreword

I have spent the better part of the last two decades writing NIH research proposals. Some of them got nailed in review; fortunately, many of them have been funded. Having also sat on NIH review panels, I have had the opportunity to see the situation from the other side of the table, as well. In the course of things, I have learned a great deal about the process, and I am pleased to have the opportunity to share my experience.

I cannot promise that you will grow to love writing grant proposals, and there is no question that a good portion of the process can be painful. But I assure you that the pain lessens in direct proportion to the likelihood of success. I wish you success in your endeavors.

Bill Gerin

# The National Institutes of Health

## THE NIH MISSION

Probably the best overview of the purpose of the National Institutes of Health is given by its mission statement:

> Begun as a one-room Laboratory of Hygiene in 1887, the National Institutes of Health (NIH) today is one of the world's foremost medical research centers. An agency of the Department of Health and Human Services, the NIH is the Federal focal point for health research.
>
> NIH is the steward of medical and behavioral research for the Nation. Its mission is science in pursuit of fundamental knowledge about the nature and behavior of living systems and the application of that knowledge to extend healthy life and reduce the burdens of illness and disability. The goals of the agency are as follows: 1) foster fundamental creative discoveries, innovative research strategies, and their applications as a basis to advance significantly the Nation's capacity to protect and improve health; 2) develop, maintain, and renew scientific human and physical resources that will assure the Nation's capability to prevent disease; 3) expand the knowledge base in medical and associated sciences in order to enhance the Nation's economic well-being and ensure a continued high return on the public investment in research; and 4) exemplify and promote the highest level of scientific integrity, public accountability, and social responsibility in the conduct of science.
>
> In realizing these goals, the NIH provides leadership and direction to programs designed to improve the health of the Nation by conducting and supporting research: in the causes, diagnosis, prevention, and cure of human diseases; in the processes of human growth and development; in the biological effects of environmental contaminants; in the understanding of mental, addictive and physical disorders; in directing programs for the collection, dissemination, and exchange of information in medicine and health, including the development and support of medical libraries and the training of medical librarians and other health information specialists.

## BASIC NIH FACTS[1]

**Location:** NIH headquarters are located in Bethesda, MD, and the surrounding areas. Some of the offices and institutes, however, are located elsewhere; for example, the National Institute on Aging (NIA) is located in Baltimore, MD.

**Organization:** The NIH comprises the Office of the Director (OD) and 27 institutes and centers (I/Cs). The OD is responsible for setting policy for the NIH and for planning, managing, and coordinating the programs and activities of all NIH components (see Figure 1.1).

**Leadership:** The NIH Director is Elias A. Zerhouni, MD

**Staff:** The NIH has more than 18,000 employees.

**Funding:** Fiscal year (FY) 2003 Congressional appropriations totaled $27,066,782,000.

The NIH funds most of the biomedical and behavioral-medical research conducted in the United States, and a great deal more conducted in other countries. Most of the I/Cs are organized around a specific set of physiologic systems and the disorders that affect these systems.

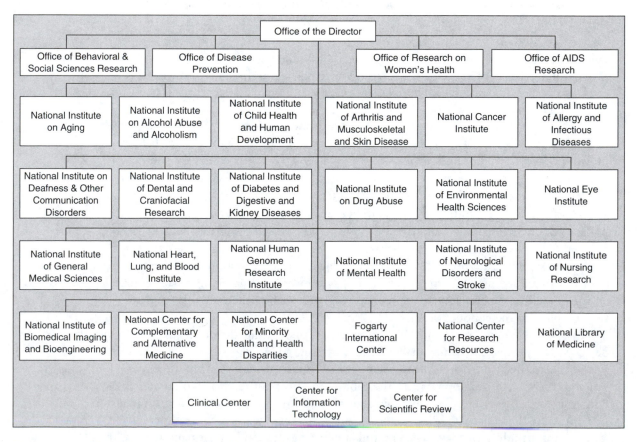

**Figure 1.1**    The Offices, Institutes, and Centers That Constitute the NIH

It may seem like an obvious point, but it is important that you identify the I/Cs that you think will be most interested in funding your research. And although it is usually fairly obvious, there are exceptions. For example, you have a hypothesis concerning the role of inflammatory markers in depressed patients with congestive heart failure (CHF). Is the emphasis of your study on depression (and the CHF population is just one model that allows you to pursue this question)? Or is the emphasis on CHF itself? If you focus on the psychiatric outcomes, the National Institutes of Mental Health (NIMH) may be interested in your proposal; but it is more likely, based on the title, that the National Heart, Lung, and Blood Institute (NHLBI) is the potential source of funding for such a project. It is important, then, that beginning with the title of your project (see Chapter 7 for more detail), you make the subject of your research clear.

Figure 1.1 shows an overview of the NIH organization, and Table 1.1 shows the names and URLs of the NIH offices, institutes, and centers.

**Table 1.1**     NIH Offices, Institutes, and Centers With Acronyms and URLs

| Office, Institute, or Center | Acronym | URL |
|---|---|---|
| Clinical Center | CC | http://clinicalcenter.nih.gov/ |
| Center for Scientific Review | CSR | http://www.csr.nih.gov/ |
| Center for Information Technology | CIT | http://www.cit.nih.gov/ |
| John E. Fogarty International Center | FIC | http://www.fic.nih.gov/ |
| National Cancer Institute | NCI | http://www.nci.nih.gov/ |
| National Center for Complementary and Alternative Medicine | NCCAM | http://nccam.nih.gov/ |
| National Center for Minority Health and Health Disparities | NCMHD | http://ncmhd.nih.gov/ |
| National Center for Research Resources | NCRR | http://www.ncrr.nih.gov/ |
| National Eye Institute | NEI | http://www.nei.nih.gov/ |
| National Heart, Lung, and Blood Institute | NHLBI | http://www.nhlbi.nih.gov/ |
| National Human Genome Research Institute | NHGRI | http://www.genome.gov/ |
| National Institute on Aging | NIA | http://www.nia.nih.gov/ |
| National Institute on Alcohol Abuse and Alcoholism | NIAAA | http://www.niaaa.nih.gov/ |
| National Institute of Allergy and Infectious Disease | NIAID | http://www.niaid.nih.gov/ |
| National Institute of Arthritis and Musculoskeletal and Skin Disease | NIAMS | http://www.niams.nih.gov/ |
| National Institute of Biomedical Imaging and Bioengineering | NIBIB | http://www.nibib.nih.gov/ |

*(Continued)*

**Table 1.1** (Continued)

| | | |
|---|---|---|
| National Institute of Child Health and Human Development | NICHD | http://www.nichd.nih.gov/ |
| National Institute on Deafness and Other Communication Disorders | NIDCD | http://www.nidcd.nih.gov/ |
| National Institute of Dental and Craniofacial Research | NIDCR | http://www.nidcr.nih.gov/ |
| National Institute of Diabetes and Digestive and Kidney Disease | NIDDK | http://www.niddk.nih.gov/ |
| National Institute on Drug Abuse | NIDA | http://www.nida.nih.gov/ |
| National Institute of Environmental Health Science | NIEHS | http://www.niehs.nih.gov/ |
| National Institute of General Medical Science | NIGMS | http://www.nigms.nih.gov/ |
| National Institute of Mental Health | NIMH | http://www.nimh.nih.gov/ |
| National Institute of Neurological Disorders and Stroke | NINDS | http://www.ninds.nih.gov/ |
| National Institute of Nursing Research | NINR | http://ninr.nih.gov/ninr/ |
| Office of AIDS Research | OAR | http://www.nih.gov/od/oar/ |
| Office of Behavioral and Social Science Research | OBSSR | http://obssr.od.nih.gov/ |
| Office of the Director | OD | http://www.nih.gov/icd/od/ |
| Office of Disease Prevention | ODP | http://odp.od.nih.gov/ |
| Office of Research on Woman's Health | ORWH | http://www4.od.nih.gov/orwh |

NOTE: See http://www.nih.gov/icd/ for a brief description of each unit.

## NIH FUNDING ALLOCATIONS

It's a good idea to be familiar with how the NIH distributes its money, and this changes somewhat from year to year. Figure 1.2 shows how funds were distributed in FY2004.[2]

## OTHER FUNDING AGENCIES

The NIH is not the only federal agency that provides research funding. There are several other agencies, centers, and programs that may be relevant for your research interests. Not all of these are funding agencies; however, you would do well to be familiar with the programs that tie in to your areas.

A comprehensive list of health-related federal agencies can be found at http://www.grants.gov/Health. Table 1.2 shows a list of the agencies and programs within the Department of Health and Human Services (HHS) that are most likely to concern you, along with the URLs at which more information can be found, and Table 1.3 provides a listing of the general research areas associated with each agency or program. Note that this is the last mention I shall specifically make of these other sources; from this point forward, I will focus exclusively on the NIH. However, much of the advice will be applicable to grant writing for other funding agencies.

One last word: Get on the Web, starting with the NIH home page (http://www.nih.gov), and let the links take you where they may.

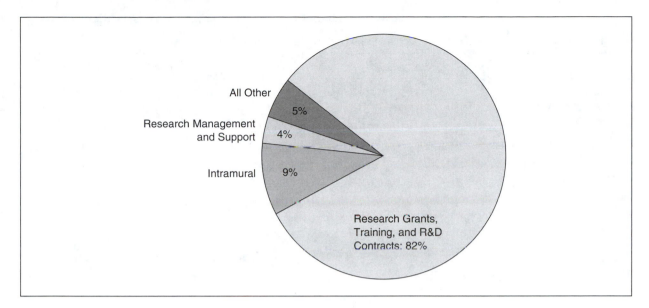

**Figure 1.2**      Distribution of NIH Budget, FY2004: $28.0 Billion

**Table 1.2**      Programs Within HHS Involved in Health-Related Research

| | | |
|---|---|---|
| Centers for Medicaid and Medicare Services[a] | CMS | http://www.cms.hhs.gov/ |
| Administration on Aging | AOA | http://www.aoa.gov/ |
| Administration for Children and Families | ACF | http://www.acf.hhs.gov/ |
| Agency for Healthcare Research and Quality | AHRQ | http://www.ahrq.gov/ |
| Agency for Toxic Substances and Disease Registry | ATSDR | http://www.atsdr.cdc.gov/ |
| Centers for Disease Control and Prevention | CDC | http://www.cdc.gov/ |
| Food and Drug Administration | FDA | http://www.fda.gov/ |
| Health Resources and Services Administration | HRSA | http://www.hrsa.gov/ |
| Indian Health Service | IHS | http://www.ihs.gov/ |
| National Institutes of Health | NIH | http://www.nih.gov/ |
| National Institutes of Occupational Safety and Health | NIOSH | http://www.cdc.gov/niosh/homepage.html |
| Office of Minority Health | OMH | http://www.cdc.gov/omh/ |
| Substance Abuse & Mental Health Services Administration | SAMHSA | http://www.samhsa.gov/index.aspx |

a. Previously known as the Health Care Financing Administration (HCFA)

**Table 1.3**    Research Areas Associated With HHS Agencies/Programs

| Topic | AOA | ACF | AHRQ | ATSDR | CDC | CMS | FDA | HRSA | IHS | NIH | NIOSH | OMH | SAMHSA |
|---|---|---|---|---|---|---|---|---|---|---|---|---|---|
| Alcoholism, Drug Abuse, & Mental Health | | | | | X | | | | | X | | X | X |
| Communicable Diseases | | | | | X | | | X | | X | | X | X |
| Education & Training | | X | | | X | | X | X | X | X | | X | X |
| General Health & Medical | X | X | X | X | X | X | X | X | | X | | X | X |
| Health Services Planning & Technical Assistance | X | X | X | X | X | | | X | X | X | | X | X |
| Indian Health | X | | | X | | | | | X | | | X | |
| Maternity, Infants, Children | | X | | | X | X | | X | | X | | | X |
| Mental Health | | X | | | | | | | | X | | | X |
| Occupational Safety & Health | | | | | X | | | X | | X | X | | |
| Physical Fitness | | | | | | | | | | X | | | |
| Prevention & Control | X | X | | X | X | | | X | X | X | | X | X |

# NOTES

1. These and other facts are available at http://www.nih.gov/about.

2. Information on the distribution of FY2004 funds can be found at http://grants2.nih.gov/grants/award/trends/distbud03.htm.

# Mentoring and Collaborative Relationships

## 2

From my point of view, collaboration cannot be separated from the grant-writing process. Science, for many of us, springs from the dialectic; science itself may be seen, after all, as an ongoing conversation that takes place in the journals. However, that is not where the conversation begins. There are some, admittedly, who can sit alone in a room, and conceive and draft an entire proposal or manuscript. I am not one of them, and I suspect most people aren't. It is impossible to overstate the value of having partners with whom you can brainstorm, colleagues who have skills that are complementary to your own, who can stimulate you to rise to higher levels than you otherwise might (and vice versa). Identifying collaborators and knowing how to sustain your relationships with them may be critical to the proposal and to your future career.

Collaborators may

- Help you "brainstorm" in the early stages of the proposal.
- Possess skills and knowledge necessary for the development and conduct of the proposal that are complementary to your own.
- Have conducted research that broadens the relevant experience of your team, and that can be incorporated into your "preliminary studies" section.
- Bring name-recognition value to the proposal.
- Take some of the burden of developing the proposal off your shoulders.
- Help you conduct the study and write papers.

These are all vital contributions, but the intangible aspects of such relationships are equally important. Writing a research proposal can be a lengthy and often stressful experience; having partners can make the process easier on you. Don't underestimate the importance of such support: One of the factors that will impact your chances of being funded is your staying power. In addition, the more eyes that review your proposal prior to submission, the better—many proposals are seen only by the principal investigator (PI), and the difference in quality is evident.

> Have a working draft of the science completed at least four weeks prior to the submission date, so that it can be sent to colleagues for critical appraisal!

Collaborations that work are priceless, and such relationships should be carefully nurtured. Unfortunately, this requires a social adeptness that is not often a strength of many scientists, either junior or senior. But you can learn.

# FINDING AND WORKING WITH A MENTOR

To an extent, identifying and collaborating with a mentor may be regarded as a special case of the more general issue of your relationships with colleagues. However, there are a few particulars that must be addressed when considering the mentoring relationship.

I am the grateful product of the mentoring model; there is no question that the mentors who took their role seriously and were conscientious about their responsibilities in helping me develop as a person, as a scientist, and as a professional in my field deserve a great deal of the credit for whatever success I have obtained. I am now fairly senior and have the lack of hair to prove it; I mentor my own students, many of whom, gratifyingly, have gone on to be successful researchers (and mentors) in their own rights. And I still have mentors whose advice and guidance I seek. Some of these are my seniors, persons who have been helping guide my career since I was a junior investigator; and some are considerably junior to me. I am not sure that I will ever be so senior as to not need advice about aspects of my professional career and the scientific endeavors I undertake. With that in mind, here are some things to think about.

## Why You Should Identify Potential Mentors

Mentors can help you in innumerable ways. They may provide advice concerning a particular career path you would be advised to take—or to avoid. They will have experienced some of the difficulties you will encounter: with other colleagues, for example, or coping with rejection (that is, of a manuscript; with reference to your personal life, you are on your own). They will know people in the field who may be helpful to you, and they may be able to provide introductions. They may be able to lend their name to aspects of your work early in your career to increase the likelihood of funding; however, you must be careful not to become overly reliant on this, or unfortunate attributions about the intellectual force behind your work may be made.

## Where to Look for Mentors

First, look close to home. Who is there in your department, or perhaps in your school or hospital, that has experience that would help guide you in your career and in your scientific endeavors? Is the person an expert in, or at least conversant with, your chosen area of research? Who has a manner with which you feel comfortable, and about whom you have a good gut feeling? Before you approach that person to establish a relationship, discreetly (discreetly!) check this person out unless you know her or him very well. Has she mentored graduate students, postdoctoral students, or fellows? Can you talk to any of these about their experience with this person? Can you find out—again, discreetly!—if any complaints have been filed about this person? What is this person's publication record, if that is relevant to your needs? (That is, you may be looking for mentoring in your specific scientific pursuits, such as developing an expertise in a particular assay, in conducting clinical trials, in analyzing simultaneous equation models. Such expertise may or may not be evident in publications.) Has the person ever served as a sponsor on a career award (NIH or otherwise), or on a training grant? Research a potential mentor with the same care you would devote to learning about a good school for your kids or a new experimental technique: It can have far-reaching implications for your career. Finally, go to your conferences; the sponsoring organization often will help arrange mentor-mentee pairings. I am always surprised at how many trainees don't do this.

> You will want to know quite a bit about a potential mentor before making a commitment. Thank goodness for the Web, which allows us to pry into other people's personal histories with just a key click. Log on to Medline and look at your potential mentors' publication records; look up their *curricula vitae* (cv)—they will be somewhere out there in cyberspace—and see whom they have mentored in the past. Then, look at their publication records; how many papers have they coauthored with mentees? Next, look to see that the mentees have gone on to productive research careers. Do you know any of the past or current mentees, or do you know anyone who might introduce you? A discreet conversation may help you to make up your mind one way or the other.
>
> I realize this all seems a great deal of trouble, but a mentor can have a tremendous impact on your life, for better or for worse. Choose carefully.

## What to Expect From a Mentor

I can tell you what you *should* be able to expect from a mentor, but you are often not going to get it. Being a good mentor takes a fearsome amount of energy and an intellectual and emotional investment, and many otherwise good folks just may not have that capital to spend. Let us agree, then, that I shall describe what you should expect from a hypothetical mentor. First and foremost, he or she should be looking out for your career interests. This can take many forms. A mentor should be actively looking for situations in which you can participate that will further your training and possibly your career. For example, when writing a grant, even one not in your area, a good mentor will invite you to the brainstorming sessions at which topics such as, "How do we approach this problem?" "What sort of design might we use?" "Who should serve as co-investigators?" and so on, will emerge. He or she might also include you in such activities as developing the budget, plotting out manuscripts, and other activities that will help you learn how one functions as a biomedical or behavioral scientist.

There is more, however. You should expect that when discussing your future, a good mentor is concerned with ensuring that you are on the right path for *your* needs, not his or hers. For example, I have heard of too many cases in which good graduate or postgraduate assistants, or medical fellows, get punished for their competence by not being trained for opportunities that would mean leaving the present mentor or institution. A good mentor prepares you to be independent, trains you to get ready to leave!

A good mentor is not jealous. I know of a senior investigator who does not permit her postdoctoral fellows *to speak to other faculty!* I believe that mentors should encourage their students to speak to and work on projects with other researchers. It benefits the mentees, because they acquire a divergent perspective about different areas. It may be gratifying, as a mentor, to have your mentees sit at your feet and take your instruction as gospel, but you leave the mentees defenseless when challenged as to why they have taken on a particular perspective. I urge you to work with various faculty and to acquire more than one mentor; this will increase your sophistication more than almost any other activity. A good mentor will encourage this as well.

## DEVELOPING NEW COLLABORATIVE RELATIONSHIPS

How do you find potential collaborators? Probably the best way to start is to choose from among your colleagues. You will have some knowledge about the people you work with; you already presumably know that you like and respect this person, and that he or she has skills and knowledge that are relevant to the enterprise. Of course, when you work with a friend, you take a risk that things may go badly and the relationship will suffer. There are ways to avoid this, for the most part at least, and we shall discuss these in later sections in this chapter.

Another way to select potential collaborators is to analyze your needs. These might include specific areas of the science, data analysis, clinical aspects, assay expertise, and so forth. In which of these areas do you not possess the necessary knowledge and skills? Next, identify persons who fill whatever gap or gaps you have found. This can often be accomplished by looking in your immediate vicinity, perhaps in your department or school, or by asking your colleagues for suggestions and introductions. Another possibility is to contact persons with whose work you are familiar through journals or conference presentations. These may not develop into full-fledged collaborations, but they may prove helpful. Sound like networking? Whether we like it or not, that's part of the deal. Many people, especially junior-level investigators, are reluctant to do this, fearing to impose on their senior colleagues. The fact is, the most well-regarded scientists in a particular area are as likely to welcome your approach as not. I prefer e-mail or regular post as a means of approach, because it allows me to carefully organize my thoughts before sending them off; I find it more difficult to do this in a phone call. Also, a phone call can be an abrupt means of introduction; an e-mail allows you to ease into it more gracefully. It is important to communicate that you are aware that this person's time is valuable, and that you are taking care not to waste it.

A small aside: I will be referring to *junior-level investigators* or *trainees*; please do not take offense or disdain allowing yourself to be lumped in with this group—and thus possibly denying yourself opportunities targeted to these groups. If you are just a few years out from your terminal degree, you are junior. Also note that if you have an MD or a PhD from several years back, and have only recently been awarded an MPH (master's in public health) or a research credential of some sort, it may be that your many years of clinical experience don't matter: You should still think of yourself as a junior investigator, although there may be certain awards for which you cannot qualify.

## MAINTAINING ONGOING COLLABORATIVE RELATIONSHIPS

As with any relationship, maintaining ongoing collaborative relationships takes work, judgment, and maturity, and there are any number of pitfalls that may occur. On the upside, such relationships can make the work infinitely more enjoyable, which is a major consideration. Do not take for granted that you already know all there is to know about how to manage these relationships.

### Your Role in an Ongoing Relationship

*Bear in mind that you are in this relationship for the long haul.* You want to find colleagues with whom your collaborative relationship will last a lifetime. These relationships may become one of your most important assets. Be aware that behavior that provides you a short-term advantage at the expense of your colleague is a poor trade. You may end up with, for example, an extra first-author publication, but you may lose your colleagues' trust and friendship. And that one paper will soon be forgotten.

*Maintain your ethics and honor.* We all know people who take the notion of "honor" seriously, persons who always do what they have promised and who obey a code of ethics about how they deal with others. Such persons are on time for meetings, they meet agreed-upon deadlines, they adhere to whatever commitments they have made, even ones that are not specifically stated; and they are proactive in taking actions that will benefit or protect their partners. Be that person: The compensations are invaluable.

> **A note regarding deadlines.** We all know people who tend to take a deadline as more of a suggestion of what might happen than a definite commitment. Don't let that be you. Be scrupulous about meeting agreed-upon deadlines, or you make life difficult for your collaborators. Also, it makes it easier for you to expect the same courtesy. I don't like to have to mention this, because most of you already know this stuff. But not all of you do.

*Protect your reputation.* Any particular scientific field tends to comprise a relatively small community. Your reputation, good or otherwise, will spread quickly. A small breach of ethics or trust can haunt you forever. And the person you anger today may very well be sitting on the study section or editorial board that is evaluating your work tomorrow.

*Do your homework—discreetly!* Before you dive into new relationships, discreetly learn about those persons. Look them up on the Web: Check out their publications and their funding history. Carefully and discreetly ask other colleagues what they know about these persons. If there is a potential problem, you may well hear about it, and thus avoid trouble.

*Lay out your mutual expectations up front.* Even if a collaborator is an old friend (perhaps especially so), work out a specific agreement about what each of you will do and by when. Bring up the possibility of violated expectations at the outset, and discuss how you will agree to resolve any that might arise. If none do arise, great; however, if problems occur, you will be very happy that you had this conversation. It isn't pleasant, but *do not avoid it.* You can make it easier by acknowledging to your colleague that this is an uncomfortable part of the process, but no reasonable person will argue that such a conversation should not occur. I suggest that you discuss authorship issues, for example, at the outset. Such considerations may be years off, but they will overtake you quickly.

*Be professional.* This means, first, that the job—that is, the quality and accomplishment of the work—takes precedence over individual egos. If the criticism delivered by your colleagues serves to improve the quality of the proposal, be grateful for it. When you get back a bit of writing from a colleague who gives you only a "Looks good!" in the margins, send it back. Demand that he or she slice away at your work, so that you can fix the problems *before they get to the reviewers.* Again, discuss this principle with your collaborators before starting the work and get consensus. Do *not* assume that everyone takes it for granted. Conversely, deliver criticism with sensitivity, but deliver it. *Develop an interpersonal discipline.* Stress brings out the worst in many people, and there will be stress at some point in the development of an NIH-quality proposal. Don't get mean or nasty, don't use sarcasm, don't do or say anything that you will later regret. If you do (it is human to err), repair the possible damage with a follow-up phone call or e-mail. You will not betray weakness by apologizing; instead, you will show strength and set an example. This seems awfully obvious, yet many fail to observe this when the going gets rough, especially those who are new to the process. This does not mean that you should never become annoyed or angry; all it does mean is that, if that occurs, you express your anger in an appropriate manner. (I have learned, for example, that before I send an angry e-mail, I first send it to one of my close colleagues, who will tactfully suggest that it should either be toned down or not sent.) Please remember, handling such situations appropriately is every bit as important a skill as knowing how to conduct a particular statistical analysis or a particular assay.

*Remember that collaborations don't always work.* You may regard the previous suggestions as idealistic, but they are, in fact, extremely practical and, not incidentally, they will make your work more fun. However, you will run into people who do not follow the same principles or encounter situations that render the principles inoperable. All one can do is to make the best of it, and then make it a point not to work with that person again. My own philosophy is that I only work with people I like and trust. However, I've been around for quite a while, and I have the luxury of picking and choosing. Follow the advice in all these points, and you'll be around for a while as well.

## When Problems Arise

Even if you follow these suggestions, things may go badly. Many persons have a lifetime of experience in which annoyance gets expressed through sarcasm or other childish behavior. (Let us be charitable and assume you are not one of the Scientists Behaving Badly.) Situations may arise in which a collaborative relationship begins to deteriorate. In addition, there may be other factors, such as the status of the other person: What do you do, for example, if the problematic person is your boss or a person who has control over your career? Obviously, these situations must be addressed on a case-by-case basis. However, here are a few general principles that may help prevent a bad situation from becoming worse.

*Avoid open warfare.* Don't give in to the temptation to behave badly yourself. Doing so may provide some short-term satisfaction, but the long-term consequences are rarely worth it.

*Make a sincere attempt to negotiate.* Attempt to have at least one good conversation about the problem, even if you are convinced that no good will come of it. At the least, you will feel that you did the best you could, and if you approach such a conversation with the right attitude (as in, *not* with the goal of humiliating the other person!), you may be surprised. In some proportion of cases, facts may come out that help to explain the other person's behavior and/or lead to an understanding between you so that the offending behavior will not reoccur.

*Know that sometimes it can get ugly.* Let's spend a moment discussing a particularly unattractive, but not uncommon, situation in which you feel that you have been sexually harassed. Your best response option may not be obvious, especially when the person who did the harassing is in a position of power over you. First, I urge you to tackle the issue head-on. Unless the situation absolutely forbids it, have a conversation with the person. He or she may actually not have understood that the behavior was indeed of a harassing nature and/or may apologize and promise it will not happen again. You may or may not, in those circumstances, let the incident pass, but it may affect what you decide to do (or not do) about it. If that does no good, have a private discussion with your department head or a person higher up (a dean, for example).

Do you risk acquiring an unfairly tarnished reputation if the person in question is vicious enough? Yes, I'm afraid you do. But giving in to highly inappropriate behavior is something you should not be able to tolerate. You may feel that it is easy for me to advise you to take such a risk, but my experience tells me that giving in because of fear of another person's power will haunt you later on. And there is a great deal less tolerance for inappropriate behavior than there was even a few years ago, so your colleagues will likely be supportive. However, this is clearly an area in which you must make the choices that you feel are best for you. I strongly urge you to find a trusted colleague, preferably a senior one, whom you trust and from whom you can ask for guidance.

*Do not treat negotiations as a zero-sum game.* The point of discussion is not for one person or the other to *win* anything. It is to open a line of communication that allows you to explain why you feel that trust has been breached and to collaborate on a productive solution. Very often, two people see the identical situation from different perspectives, which leads to conflict. If you cannot disclose your perception and/or the other person cannot disclose his or hers, problems are more likely to occur. However, you may both find that you have had incorrect perceptions of the *other's* motivations or perceptions, and that often removes barriers to negotiation.

*Do your best to avoid burning your bridges.* If you feel you have to terminate the relationship, do your best to keep your affect as neutral as possible. An ideal goal is that you both agree to disagree. That may not reflect your true resentment, but if things have gone so far that you desire to end the relationship, there is little use in having the last word, in bringing up all the things that have angered you in the past, or in detailing your colleague's or mentor's shortcomings. A somewhat rueful attitude ("I wish things had worked out differently between us, but it seems that our temperaments are too different to allow us to work together productively") is probably the best way to leave things. You must, however, also deal with the realities of such a situation. Is this person a co-investigator on your grant (or vice versa)? Is it someone with whom you have a half-finished manuscript? Is it a person who is in the office next to you, or who is likely to be reviewing your manuscripts and grant proposals? Worst of all, is the person in a position of power over you? Work out the details in a way that is optimally satisfying to both of you. Agree to put aside your difficulties in the limited context of your unfinished commitments. Be more generous than you may want to be, in service of your own peace of mind.

*There is a point at which you have to face the fact that the situation is unfixable.* What do you do when the situation has gone too far, and the person is someone who holds sway over your personal or professional life? Horror stories abound about advisers who misappropriate authorship, mentors who may seek personal favors outside the professional arena (whether it is sexual favors or picking up their dry cleaning), or department chairs who decide to take the role of primary investigator on an application you have conceived and written. Deciding what to do in such a situation is tough, because your sense of outrage (again, I am making the naïve assumption that you are truly in the right) must be balanced against your need to survive and thrive. One thing you should *not* do is be indiscreet; it is natural to want to complain and to seek social support and validation, but be very careful about whom you speak to, since you assuredly do not want this coming back to haunt you. You also do not want to develop a reputation as a negative, disaffected person in the eyes of other potential colleagues (perception, even if unfair, often supersedes objective reality). I suggest that you confide in a trusted senior colleague and seek advice. Anyone who has been a working scientist for many years has seen such situations and may have useful suggestions. In communicating the nature of the disagreements, take care not to allow your recital to become overly emotional. Be honest about what you may have contributed to the misunderstanding.

Some situations are just not destined to end peaceably. You must make the difficult decision as to whether to put up with it, in the interests of personal gain, or to risk the anger and possible abuse that may occur when you inform this person that you are leaving her lab, that you are withdrawing from his grant, that you no longer wish to work with her, or even that you are going to arbitration or bringing him up on charges of ethical misconduct (situations to be avoided if there is any way to do so). There is no formula to help with that decision: It must be a function of the specific situation (for example, nothing justifies remaining in a situation in which you are being sexually harassed), your temperament (some people have less tolerance than others for allowing a bad situation to continue), and the consequences (having your career ruined, missing out on important opportunities). Go slow, don't dash off an angry e-mail, don't rush into this person's office for a showdown. Cool off and seek advice before you act.

I have focused on the possible negative situations that may arise. However, let's dwell for a minute on the positive aspects. There are undoubtedly some people who enjoy working in isolation and who perhaps do their best work in that fashion. I do not. My best work has been a result of collaboration; I must have colleagues with whom I can air out my ideas and whose ideas I can listen to, perhaps taking the best of both to come up with a better idea. There are few things in life that are as rewarding as finding yourself on the same wavelength as a colleague concerning your research. Here's the fact: For most of us, research doesn't pay a whole hell of a lot; we do it for other reasons, and one of them is that it is the funnest game in town. And it's just that much more fun when you can share the experience.

Last comment: Just for the record, I am not being sanctimonious in this chapter, although it sometimes must sound it. I am describing an ideal, not, for example, my own behavior which often overlaps with the principles outlined above, but not always.

# Types of Award Mechanisms **3**

The NIH offers a wide menu of grant mechanism options. It is crucial that you understand the options so that you can pick the one most appropriate for your situation. Unless you are relatively senior, this should be done in collaboration with your department head or division chief, as there may be rules about what you can and cannot apply for. Thus, in some medical schools, you may not apply for a career (K) award until you have reached a certain year beyond the receipt of your degree. Then, there may not be rules, but may be career guidelines. So, in some medical schools you are *urged* to apply for a K award by your second fellowship year or else, you may be told, your career at that institution will be sidelined. I suggest you find senior faculty to consult before you launch yourself into the writing of any particular application.

## CLASSES OF GRANT MECHANISMS

At the broadest level, there are two major types of grants: project and career development grants. Project grants tend to support a discrete research project; typically, investigators, including the principal investigator (PI), do not allot most of their effort to such awards (see Chapter 7 for specifics). Career development grants, in contrast, typically provide most of the investigator's salary support and relatively less support for research. The two types of grant mechanisms are discussed in detail below.

Table 3.1 shows the classes of awards at the broadest level. These will be broken out into individual awards within each class later in this chapter.

You probably know that some award mechanisms are more or less suitable for you. In the following sections, details will be provided about the individual grant mechanisms; however, here are some of the criteria that may help you identify which sort of award you should be going for.

### Criteria for Identifying an Award Mechanism

*Your Career Stage. Career stage* relates to how many years out you are from your terminal degree; it may also relate, independently, to the number of publications you have and/or your record of accomplishment and experience in research or, depending on the mechanism,

**Table 3.1**       Classes of Grant Award Mechanisms

| Award Class | Description |
| --- | --- |
| Institutional Research Training Grants (T series; Table 3.2) | Awarded to eligible *institutions* to support predoctoral and postdoctoral research training to prepare scientists for careers in behavioral and biomedical research. Graduate students and postdoctoral trainees are appointed to the grant by the institution. |
| Fellowships (F series; Table 3.3) | All NIH awarding components offer individual postdoctoral fellowships, which provide support for doctoral-level research training in preparation for careers in behavioral and biomedical research. Several NIH I/Cs also offer individual postdoctoral fellowships to graduate students for research training leading to the doctorate. |
| Research Career Awards (K series; Table 3.4) | Various NIH I/Cs offer several types of career awards to research and academic institutions on behalf of scientists with clear research potential. Each award is part of an integrated program designed to foster the development of outstanding scientists and enable them to expand their potential to make important scientific contributions. |
| Research Grants (R series; Table 3.5) | Awarded to facilitate pursuit of a scientific focus or objective in the area of the principal investigator's interest and competence. |
| Program Grants (P series) | For more senior investigators only. Awarded to support a broadly based, often multidisciplinary, long-term research program with a particular objective or theme. Program Grants involve organized efforts of groups of investigators who conduct integrated research projects related to the overall program objectives. These grants tend to focus on mechanisms of disease. |
| Center Grants (P series) | For more senior investigators only. Awarded on behalf of program directors and groups of collaborating investigators; provides support for long-term, multidisciplinary research and development programs. The distinction between Program Grants and Center Grants is that the latter are more likely to have a clinical orientation and are usually developed in response to announcements of specific I/C needs and requirements. |
| Small Business Innovative Research Grants (SBIR)[a] | These grants are made to small business concerns that have the technological expertise to contribute to the biomedical or behavioral research mission of the NIH. |
| Small Business Technology Transfer Grants (STTR)[a] | The purpose of this program is to facilitate cooperative research projects that have the potential for commercialization of the subject of the research, between small business concerns and U.S. research institutions. |
| Conference Grants | The NIH provides funding for conferences to coordinate, exchange, and disseminate information related to its program interests. Generally, such awards are limited to participation with other organizations in supporting conferences rather than provision of sole support. |

a. See "The SBIR and STTR Award Mechanisms" section later in this chapter.

in clinical practice. Thus, for example, you may be senior enough to consider using the R01 (research) mechanism, but if you only have a few publications or if you have several publications but none in the area in which you plan to apply, an R01 is unlikely to be funded. You might consider that you are not yet at the appropriate stage for this application and, instead, should concentrate on getting manuscripts out the door.

In terms of your track record, if you are thinking about writing a research (R) grant, you really need to have two or three published manuscripts on an area related to the grant. Deans frequently suggest that new faculty, who may not yet have an appropriate publication record, write an R01 grant (which brings money directly into the institution, in a manner I will discuss in Chapter 7). However, often you would be better off writing the manuscripts than a grant at this juncture of your career. Remember, your dean (or division chief, etc.) may not have precisely the same goals for your career as you do; you need to be aware of your own agenda and the need to strike a balance between your career needs and those of your department.

*The Proposed Project's Stage of Development.* Do you have pilot data that convincingly demonstrate that (a) your hypotheses are on the right track and (b) you have the capability to carry out the proposed research? If the answer to both questions is "yes," and if you have the credentials and institutional support, you may consider an R01 research grant; if not, you might consider a mechanism that allows a more exploratory endeavor, such as the R21. But be careful: Not all I/Cs support the R21 mechanism.

*The Purpose of the Funding.* If you have a research project in mind and need funds to implement it, you should consider research mechanisms such as the R01 and R21; however, if, for example, the purpose is to provide structure and support for a set of ongoing funded projects, you might consider a Center Grant (P30, P50, P60); however, you should be fairly senior before you consider this.

*Commercial Ventures.* The NIH has specific mechanisms—Small Business Innovative Research (SBIR) Grants (R43, R44) and the Small Business Technology Transfer (STTR) Grants (R41, R42) that are designed to foster the development of commercial applications that require testing. There are many special considerations for such awards, and if interested, you should pay particular attention to the section devoted to them later in this chapter.

*Training of Predoctoral or Postdoctoral Fellows.* If the funding is for the training of fellows, either at the pre- or postdoctoral level, you should look into the T and F series of awards (see Tables 3.2 and 3.3).

The following decision trees (Figures 3.1 and 3.2) are designed to help you choose a mechanism that is most suitable for you. Please take note that these figures are meant to be a guideline to help you zero in on appropriate grant programs, but they should not be your only reference. Consult your mentor(s), experienced colleagues, department chair, and so on.

Once you have taken note of one or more mechanisms that might apply to your situation, details are provided about each of the mechanisms in the Tables 3.2–3.5.

## SPECIFIC GRANT MECHANISMS

The NIH Web site provides a great deal of detail on each grant mechanism, including who is eligible to apply, salary constraints, scope of work, and so on. I won't attempt to reproduce this level of detail; however, I *strongly urge* you to read every word you can find about your targeted mechanism on the various Web sites. Tables 3.2–3.5 provide many of the particulars about the various mechanisms to allow you to get an idea of which ones you should check out in detail.

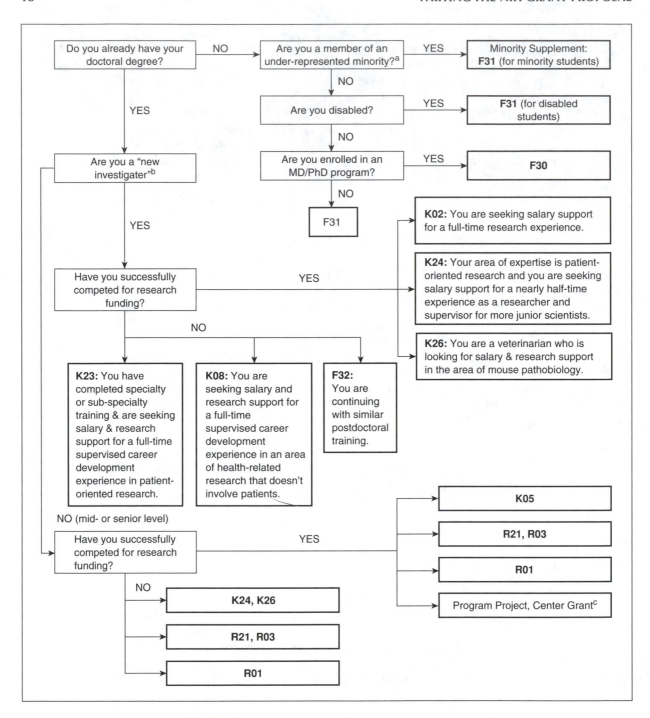

**Figure 3.1**      If You Hold (or Are Going for) a Health Professional Degree . . .

NOTES:

a. Defined by the NIH as African American, Hispanic, Native American, Alaskan Native, or Pacific Islander.

b. A new investigator is defined as PI on a competing R01/R29 award when he or she has *not* been a PI on any prior NIH research grant (except K01, K08, K22, K23, R03, R15, or R21). However, I/Cs may have their own criteria, so make sure to check.

c. There are several upper-level grant mechanisms available; I will not go into detail on these, however, since I assume most people reading this book are not yet applying for these.

Applicants for training awards (K, F, T) must be U.S. citizens, noncitizen nationals, or have been lawfully admitted to the United States for permanent residence (i.e., must possess a currently valid Alien Registration Receipt Card I-551 or other legal verification of such status).

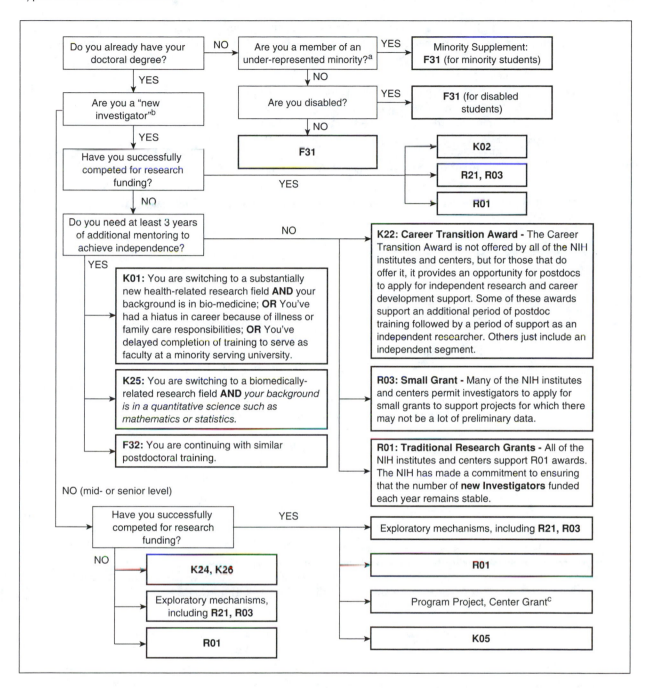

**Figure 3.2**     If You Hold (or Are Going for) a Research Degree . . .

NOTES:

a. Defined by the NIH as African American, Hispanic, Native American, Alaskan Native, or Pacific Islander.

b. A *new investigator* is defined as someone who has not previously served as such on any Public Health Services–supported research project other than a small grant (R03), an Academic Research Enhancement Award (R15), an exploratory/developmental grant (R21), or mentored career development awards for persons at the beginning of their research career (K01, K08, K22, K23, and K25). Current or past recipients of Independent Scientist Awards and other non-mentored career awards (K02, K05, K24, and K26) are not considered new investigators.

c. There are several upper-level grant mechanisms available; I will not go into detail on these, however, since I assume most people reading this book are not yet applying for these.

Applicants for training awards (K, F, T) must be U.S. citizens, or noncitizen nationals, or have been lawfully admitted to the United States for permanent residence (i.e., must possess a currently valid Alien Registration Receipt Card I-551 or other legal verification of such status).

A good place to begin is the NIH's own funding programs page.[1] This Web page provides links to each of the mechanisms, where you will find all the relevant information. Note that *not every mechanism is supported by every I/C*. Before writing a proposal for a particular mechanism, you should find out if the I/C that would be likely to fund your proposal does indeed support that particular grant mechanism. You will find, at the bottom of each of the linked Web pages, a list of the I/Cs that do and do not support particular mechanisms. These are also provided in Tables 3.2–3.5, but check anyhow. For example, at the bottom of the R01 page you will find the statement, "All Institutes and most Centers at NIH support the R01 grant mechanism." In contrast, at the bottom of the R03 (NIH Small Grant Program) page you will find the statement, "Listing of NIH Institutes and Centers that DO NOT accept investigator-initiated R03 applications includes the following: FIC, NCCAM, NCI, NCMHD, NCRR, NHGRI, NIAMS, NIDCD, NIDDK, NIGMS" (see Table 1.1 for the I/C abbreviations).

## TRAINING GRANTS

There are three types of training grant mechanisms: The T, F, and K programs. T is for training grants. You, as an individual, cannot apply to the NIH for these awards; you must apply to an institution that holds one of them. The T awards fund pre- and postdoctoral students and trainees in health professional schools. To a great extent, they support short-term research periods; for example, many students use T awards to fund summer projects between semesters. F refers to fellowship awards. They support pre- and postdoctoral trainees, as well as senior scientists who are looking to change the direction of their research careers or obtain new research skills. Finally, there are the K (for "career") awards. These represent the holy grail of training grants, and if you plan to be a successful, funded researcher, a K award launches your career (unless you skip right to writing a [funded] R01, in which case, you won't be hurt by skipping the K). However, there are good reasons to begin with a training grant. They provide structure, which is necessary for most scientists at the beginnings of their careers, as well as exposure to the administrative aspects of running a laboratory, where being a scientist is only one of a broad set of skills that is required.

Unlike research grants, all three of the training mechanisms have requirements concerning immigration and citizenship, as outlined by the NIH:

Individuals appointed to training grants must be citizens or non-citizen nationals of the United States, or must have been lawfully admitted to the United States for permanent residence (i.e., in possession of a currently valid Alien Registration Receipt Card I-551, or must be in possession of other legal verification of such status). Non-citizen nationals are generally persons born in outlying possessions of the United States (e.g., American Samoa and Swains Island). Individuals on temporary or student visas are not eligible.

*(Text continues on page 27)*

| **Table 3.2** | NIH Training Grant (T) Programs |
|---|---|
| *T32* | *National Research Service Award (NRSA) Institutional Research Training Grants* |
| Purpose | Support to institutions, *not* to individuals (you must determine if your institution has a T32) to develop or enhance research-training opportunities for individuals who are training for careers in specified areas of biomedical, behavioral, and clinical research. The purpose of the NRSA program is to help ensure that a diverse and highly trained workforce is available to assume leadership roles related to the nation's biomedical and behavioral research agenda. Accordingly, the NRSA program supports predoctoral, postdoctoral, and short-term research training experiences. |
| Eligibility | Predoctoral Training: Predoctoral research training must lead to the PhD or a comparable research doctoral degree. Students enrolled in health-professional training programs that wish to postpone their professional studies to engage in full-time research training may also be appointed to a T32. Predoctoral research training must emphasize training in areas of biomedical and behavioral sciences. |
| | Postdoctoral Training: For persons who have received a PhD, DVM, DDS, MD, or a comparable doctoral degree from an accredited domestic or foreign institution. Research training at the postdoctoral level must emphasize specialized training to meet national research priorities in the biomedical, behavioral, or clinical sciences. |
| Other | Short-Term Research Training for Health-Professional Students: Applications for Institutional Research Training Grants may include a request for short-term predoctoral positions reserved specifically to provide full-time, health-related research training experiences during the summer or other "off-quarter" periods. Such positions are limited to medical students, dental students, students in other health-professional programs, and graduate students in the physical or quantitative sciences. Short-term appointments are intended to provide such students with opportunities to participate in biomedical and/or behavioral research in an effort to attract them into health-related research careers. |
| | Normally, short-term positions are not to be used for individuals who have already earned a doctoral degree. Short-term research training positions should last at least 8 but no more than 12 weeks. Individual health professional students or students in the quantitative sciences selected for appointment should be encouraged to obtain multiple periods of short-term, health-related research training during the years leading to their degree. Such appointments may be consecutive or may be reserved for summers or other "off-quarter" periods. |
| Commitment | Trainees are required to pursue their research training on a full-time basis, devoting at least 40 hours per week to the program. Within the 40 hours per week training period, research trainees who are also training as clinicians must devote their time to the proposed research training and must confine clinical duties to those that are an integral part of the research training experience. |
| Stipend | Stipend: The NRSA provides stipends to graduate students and postdoctoral trainees. A stipend is provided as a subsistence allowance to help trainees defray living expenses during the research training experience. Stipend levels are adjusted nearly every year and current stipend levels are available at http://grants.nih.gov/training/nrsa.htm. |
| | For postdoctoral trainees, the appropriate stipend level is based on the number of *full* years of relevant postdoctoral experience at the time of appointment. Relevant experience may include research experience (including industrial), teaching, internship, residency, clinical duties, or other time spent in full-time studies in a health-related field following the date of the qualifying doctoral degree. |
| | Tuition, Fees, and Health Insurance: The NIH will offset the combined cost of tuition, fees, and health insurance (either self-only or family, as appropriate) at the following rate: 100% of all costs up to $3,000 and 60% of costs above $3,000. |
| | Other Trainee Costs: Trainee travel, including attendance at scientific meetings that the institution determines to be necessary to the individual's research training, is an allowable trainee expense. In addition, support for travel to a research training experience away |

*(Continued)*

**Table 3.2** (Continued)

| T32 | *National Research Service Award (NRSA) Institutional Research Training Grants* |
|---|---|
| | from the institution may be permitted. Under exceptional circumstances, which can include providing accommodations for a trainee with disabilities, it is possible to request institutional costs above the standard rate.<br><br>    <u>Training-Related Expenses</u>: Institutional costs of $2,200 a year per predoctoral trainee and $3,850 a year per postdoctoral trainee may be requested to defray the costs of other research training–related expenses, such as staff salaries, consultant costs, equipment, research supplies, and travel expenses for the training faculty. |
| Supported by | All I/Cs. |
| URL | http://grants1.nih.gov/grants/guide/pa-files/PA-02-109.html |
| T35 | *Short-Term Institutional Research Training Grants* |
| Purpose | To develop or enhance research training opportunities for individuals interested in careers in biomedical and behavioral research. Many of the NIH I/Cs use this grant mechanism exclusively to support intensive, short-term research training experiences for students in health professional schools during the summer. In addition, this mechanism may be used to support other types of predoctoral and postdoctoral training in focused, often emerging, scientific areas relevant to the mission of the funding I/C. |
| Eligibility | NRSA institutional short-term training grants are intended to introduce students and postdoctorate fellows to research that would not otherwise be available through their regular course of study. Short-term training is not intended, and may not be used, to support activities that would ordinarily be part of a research degree program. Funds may not be used for courses and study leading to an MD, DDS, DO, DVM, or other clinical, health professional degree, nor do they support residency training. The training grant positions should not be used in lieu of regular graduate stipends.<br><br>    Predoctoral trainees must have received a baccalaureate degree by the beginning date of the short-term appointment and must be training at the postbaccalaureate level. Predoctoral trainees must be enrolled in or considering enrollment in a program leading to a PhD in science or in an equivalent research doctoral degree program.<br><br>    Trainees in health professional schools must be enrolled and should have successfully completed at least one semester at an accredited school of medicine, optometry, osteopathy, dentistry, veterinary medicine, pharmacy (must be a candidate for PharmD), allied health professions, public health, audiology, or other accredited health professional schools such as schools of chiropractic or naturopathic medicine before participating in the program. Students enrolled at other institutions may be eligible, provided that a feasible plan for evaluating and monitoring the short- and long-term outcome of the students' research experiences is provided.<br><br>    Postdoctoral trainees must have received, as of the beginning date of the appointment, a PhD, MD, DDS, or comparable doctoral degree from an accredited domestic or foreign institution. Eligible doctoral degrees include, but are not limited to, the following: DMD, DC, DO, DVM, OD, Dpm, ScD, EngD, Dr. PH, DNSc, PharmD, ND, DSW, and PsyD. |
| Commitment | Trainees are required to pursue research training for 2–3 months on a full-time basis devoting at least 40 hours per week to the program. Within the 40 hours per week training period, research trainees in clinical areas must devote their time to the proposed research training and must confine clinical and other duties to those that are an integral part of the research training experience. |
| Stipend | <u>Stipend</u>: Stipends are provided as a subsistence allowance for trainees to help defray living expenses during the research training experience. Stipends for short-term trainees will be based on a monthly proportion of the annual NIH stipend level at the time of award. The FY2005 annual stipend level for a predoctoral trainee is $20,772; therefore, the monthly stipend is $1,731 per month. For postdoctoral trainees, the annual stipend is determined |

| T35 | *Short-Term Institutional Research Training Grants* |
|---|---|
|  | based on the number of years of prior relevant postdoctoral experience at the time of the trainee's appointment. The FY2005 range of annual postdoctoral stipend levels is \$35,568 (\$2,964 per month) to \$51,036 (\$4,253 per month). No departure from the established stipend schedule may be negotiated by the institution with trainees (see http://grants.nih.gov/grants/guide/notice-files/NOT-OD-05-032.html). |
|  | <u>Training-Related Expenses</u>: The institution may request the proportion of the NIH standard annual NRSA training-related expenses to help defray other costs of the short-term training experience, such as research supplies, tuition, fees, and certain types of travel and other expenses. The FY2005 amounts for training-related expenses are \$2,200 annually (\$183/month) for each predoctoral trainee and \$3,850 annually (\$322/month) for each postdoctoral trainee. |
| Supported by | NIA, NIBIB, NIAMS, NIDCD, NIDDK, NIDA, NEIHS, NINDS, NEI, NHLBI, NCCAM, NCRR, ODS, and OBSSR |
| URL | http://grants1.nih.gov/grants/guide/pa-files/PA-05-117.html |

| **Table 3.3** | NIH Training Grant (F) Programs: Issued by the Ruth L. Kirschstein–National Research Service Awards |
|---|---|
| *F30* | *Individual Predoctoral Awards for MD/PhD Fellowships* |
| Purpose | For research training in specified areas of biomedical and behavioral research, to help ensure that physicians/scientists will be available to meet the nation's mental health, drug abuse, alcohol abuse, and environmental health sciences research needs. |
| Eligibility | Applicants must have a baccalaureate degree and show evidence of high academic performance in the sciences and substantial interest in research in areas of high priority to the participating I/Cs. When the application is submitted, the applicant must be enrolled in an accredited MD/PhD program at a medical school, accepted in a related scientific PhD program, and supervised by a mentor in that scientific discipline. Applications are generally submitted during the first two years of medical school, but may be submitted at any stage of medical school provided that at least one year of dissertation-stage research training will remain at the time of the expected award date. |
|  | The applicant must identify a sponsoring institution and an individual who will serve as a sponsor (also called *mentor* or *supervisor*) and who will supervise the training and research experience. The sponsor should be an active investigator in the area of the proposed research, be committed to the research training of the candidate, and directly supervise the candidate's research. The sponsor must document the availability of sufficient research support and facilities for high-quality research training. |
| Stipend | <u>Stipend</u>: Kirschstein-NRSA awards provide stipends at the predoctoral level to fellows as a subsistence allowance to help defray living expenses during the research and clinical training experience. For the current stipend levels, see the NIH Web site at http://grants.nih.gov/training/nrsa.htm. |
|  | <u>Tuition, Fees, and Health Insurance</u>: The most recent program announcement indicates that the NIH will reimburse 100% of the cost of tuition up to \$3,000 and 60% of that cost above \$3,000 for the fellow. Tuition, for the purposes of this policy, means the combined cost of tuition, fees, and health insurance. |
|  | Self-only health insurance (for fellows without families) or family health insurance (for fellows with families) is an allowable cost at the sponsoring institution only if such health insurance is required of all persons in a similar training status, regardless of the source of support. |

*(Continued)*

**Table 3.3** (Continued)

| | |
|---|---|
| *F30* | *Individual Predoctoral Awards for MD/PhD Fellowships* |

<u>Institutional Allowance</u>: The most recent program announcement indicates that F30 fellows received an institutional allowance of $2,750 per 12-month period to nonfederal or nonprofit sponsoring institutions to help defray such awardee expenses as research supplies, equipment, books, and travel to scientific meetings.

For FY2005, the NIH will provide an institutional allowance of up to $1,650 for F30 fellows sponsored by federal laboratories or for-profit institutions for expenses associated with travel to scientific meetings, health insurance, and books.

<u>Other Training Costs</u>: Additional funds may be requested by the institution when the training of a fellow involves extraordinary costs for travel to field sites remote from the sponsoring institution or for accommodations for fellows who are disabled, as defined by the Americans With Disabilities Act. Such additional funds shall be provided only in exceptional circumstances that are fully justified and explained by the sponsoring institution.

<u>Stipend Supplementation</u>: See the Web page at the URL given below.

| | |
|---|---|
| Supported by | NIMH, NIDA, NIAAA, and NIEHS |
| URL | http://grants1.nih.gov/grants/guide/pa-files/PA-05-151.html |

| | |
|---|---|
| *F31[a]* | *NIH Predoctoral Fellowship Awards* |
| Purpose | Support for doctoral-level trainees who have successfully completed their comprehensive examinations or the equivalent by the time of award and who will be performing dissertation research and training. Candidates should be promising applicants with the potential to become productive, independent investigators in their scientific mission areas. |
| Eligibility | Applicants must have received, as of the activation date of the award, a baccalaureate degree and must be enrolled in a program leading to a research doctorate, such as the PhD or DSc. |
| Stipend | <u>Stipend</u>: For the current stipend levels, see the NIH Web site at http://grants.nih.gov/training/nrsa.htm. |

<u>Tuition, Fees, and Health Insurance</u>: The NIH will reimburse 100% of the cost of tuition up to $3,000 and 60% of tuition costs above $3,000 for the predoctoral fellow. Tuition, for the purposes of this policy, means the combined cost of tuition, fees, and health insurance.

Self-only health insurance (for fellows without families) or family health insurance (for fellows with families) is an allowable cost at the sponsoring institution only if such health insurance is required of all persons in a similar training status regardless of the source of support. Health insurance for predoctoral fellows who are eligible for this coverage is included in the calculation of the combined tuition, fees, and health insurance.

<u>Institutional Allowance</u>: The most recent program announcement indicates that predoctoral fellows received an institutional allowance of $2,750 per 12-month period to sponsoring institutions to help defray such expenses as research supplies, equipment, books, and travel to scientific meetings. The institutional allowance is adjusted from time to time. Prospective applicants are advised to check for the current institutional allowance in the most recent documentation related to NRSA stipends at http://grants.nih.gov/training/nrsa.htm.

<u>Other Training Costs</u>: Additional funds may be requested by the institution when the training of a predoctoral fellow involves extraordinary costs for travel to field sites remote from the sponsoring institution or for accommodations for fellows who are disabled, as defined by the Americans With Disabilities Act. Such additional funds shall be provided only in exceptional circumstances that are fully justified and explained by the sponsoring institution.

| | |
|---|---|
| Supported by | NIAAA, NIBIB, NIDCD, NIDA, NIMH, and NINDS |
| URL | http://grants1.nih.gov/grants/guide/pa-files/PA-04-032.html |

| F32 | *Individual Postdoctoral Fellowship* |
|---|---|
| Purpose | Supports postdoctoral trainees who have successfully completed their comprehensive exams or equivalent by the time of award and will be performing dissertation research and training. Candidates should have the potential to become independent investigators. The proposed training must be within the broad scope of biomedical, behavioral, or clinical research and must offer an opportunity to extend the Fellow's potential for a productive research career. |
| Eligibility | Before a Kirschstein-NRSA postdoctoral fellowship award can be activated, the applicant must have received a PhD, MD, DO, DC, DDS, DVM, OD, Dpm, ScD, EngD, Dr. PH, DNS, ND, PharmD, DSW, PsyD, or equivalent doctoral degree from an accredited domestic or foreign institution. Certification by an authorized official of the degree-granting institution that all degree requirements have been met is also acceptable.<br><br>Before submitting a fellowship application, the applicant must identify a sponsoring institution and an individual who will serve as a sponsor (also called *mentor* or *supervisor*) and who will supervise the training and research experience. The applicant's sponsor should be an active investigator in the area of the proposed research and should directly supervise the candidate's research. The sponsor must document the availability of research support and facilities for high-quality research training. |
| Commitment | Awardees are required to pursue their research training on a full-time basis, devoting at least 40 hours per week to the training program. Research clinicians must devote full time to their proposed research training and must restrict clinical duties within their full-time research training experience to activities that are directly related to the research training experience. |
| Stipend | Stipend: The stipend level for the first year of support is determined by the number of full years of relevant postdoctoral experience at the time the award is issued (not at the time of activation). Fellows with less than one full year of postdoctoral experience at the time of award will receive initial support at the zero level. Relevant experience may include research (including research in industry), teaching, internship, residency, clinical duties, or other time spent in full-time studies in a health-related field beyond that of the qualifying doctoral degree. The stipend schedule is updated nearly every year and applicants are advised to check for the posting of the current stipend schedule on the NIH Web site at http://grants.nih.gov/training/nrsa.htm.<br><br>Tuition and Fees: The NIH will offset the combined cost of tuition and fees at the following rate: 100% of all costs up to $3,000 and 60% of costs above $3,000. Costs associated with tuition and fees are allowable only if they are required for specific courses in support of the research training experience supported by the fellowship.<br><br>Institutional Allowance: The most recent program announcement indicates that fellows receive an institutional allowance of $5,500 per 12-month period to help defray such expenses as research supplies, equipment, health insurance (either self-only or family as appropriate), and travel to scientific meetings. Support for health insurance is allowable only if it is applied consistently for all individuals in a similar research training status regardless of the source of support. The institutional allowance is adjusted from time to time. Prospective applicants are advised to check for the current institutional allowance at http://grants.nih.gov/training/nrsa.htm.<br><br>Other Training Costs: Additional funds may be requested by the institution when the training of a fellow involves extraordinary costs for travel to field sites remote from the sponsoring institution or accommodations for fellows who are disabled, as defined by the Americans With Disabilities Act. Such additional funds shall be provided only in exceptional circumstances that are fully justified and explained by the sponsoring institution.<br>The sponsoring institution may provide funds in addition to the stipend. Such additional amounts may be in the form of augmented stipends (supplementation) or in the form of compensation, such as salary or tuition remission for services such as teaching or serving as a laboratory.<br><br>Stipend Supplementation: See the Web page at the URL given below. |

*(Continued)*

**Table 3.3** (Continued)

| F32 | *Individual Postdoctoral Fellowship* |
|---|---|
| Supported by | All NIH awarding components |
| URL | http://grants1.nih.gov/grants/guide/pa-files/PA-03-067.html |

| F33 | *Senior Fellowship* |
|---|---|
| Purpose | Support for experienced scientists who wish to make major changes in the direction of their research careers or who wish to broaden their scientific background by acquiring new research capabilities. |
| Eligibility | Applicants must be at least seven years beyond the qualifying doctoral degree, and can include a PhD, MD, DO, DDS, DVM, OD, Dpm, ScD, EngD, ND, DC, Dr. PH, DNS, Pharm D, DSW, PsyD, or equivalent doctoral degree from an accredited domestic or foreign institution and must have had at least seven subsequent years of relevant research or professional experience. The applicant will have established an independent research career and is now seeking support for retraining or additional career development.<br><br>Before submitting an application, an individual must arrange for acceptance by an institution and sponsor. The applicant's sponsor should be an active investigator in the area of the proposed research who will directly supervise the candidate's research during the period of the fellowship. The sponsor must document the availability of staff, research support, and facilities for high-quality research training. |
| Stipend | <u>Stipend</u>: Stipends are determined individually at the time of award. The amount of the stipend is based on the salary or remuneration from the home institution on the date of award. However, in no case shall the NIH contribution to the stipend during the fellowship exceed the NRSA stipend provided for individuals with more than seven years of experience. The current stipend schedule can be found on the NIH Web site at http://grants.nih.gov/training/nrsa.htm. For fellows on sabbatical, the level of the NRSA stipend award will take into account concurrent sabbatical salary support provided by the home institution and any other supplementation.<br><br>    <u>Tuition and Fees</u>: The NIH will offset the combined cost of tuition and fees, at the following rate: 100% of all costs up to $3,000 and 60% of costs above $3,000. Costs associated with tuition and fees are allowable only if they are required for specific courses in support of the research training experience supported by the fellowship.<br><br>    <u>Institutional Allowance</u>: The NIH will provide an institutional allowance of $4,000 per 12-month period to nonfederal, nonprofit, or foreign sponsoring institutions to help defray such awardee expenses as research supplies, equipment, health insurance (either self-only or family health insurance as appropriate), and travel to scientific meetings. This allowance is intended to cover training-related expenses for the individual awardee.<br><br>    <u>Other Training Costs</u>: Additional funds may be requested by the institution when the training of a fellow involves extraordinary costs for travel to field sites remote from the sponsoring institution, or accommodations for fellows who are disabled, as defined by the Americans With Disabilities Act. Such additional funds shall be provided only in exceptional circumstances that are fully justified and explained by the institution.<br><br>    <u>Stipend Supplementation</u>: See the Web page at the URL given below. |
| Supported by | NIA, NIAAA, NIAID, NIAMS, NCI, NICHD, NIDCD, NIDCR, NIDDK, NIEHS, NEI, NIGMS, NHLBI, NINDS, NINR, NHGRI, NCRR, and NCCAM |
| URL | http://grants1.nih.gov/grants/guide/pa-files/PA-00-131.html |

a. There are two other versions of the F31, specifically geared to (1) minority students and (2) students with disabilities. Find these at http://grants1.nih.gov/grants/funding/funding_program.htm.

## CAREER AWARDS

I know that many of you are specifically interested in career, or K, awards. A K award means that you are on your way to greater things. It is a highly prestigious award, and you can flaunt it to those colleagues who went off to private practice and are making more money than you—and always will (their loss, believe me). At some medical schools, if you *do not* receive a K award during your early years, your career is already off to a shaky start and perhaps worse—unless you happen to receive an R01 instead (which means you have leapfrogged the first stage and are a hero). In spite of my misgivings about general statements regarding the K awards, since procedures often vary by I/C, I shall provide a very general overview (Table 3.4). But check with the I/C by which you would likely be funded to see if it offers K awards and to examine the specifics concerning that award.

I am taking much of this information from the NIH's online K Kiosk.[2] The NIH uses a cute drawing to signify the "kiosk" part which I can't resist reproducing.

The NIH also provides a "wizard" that will walk you through a process to determine which K award you might qualify for, but, again, this is very general and I have found that it seems to misfire on occasion.[3] In Table 3.4, I have abstracted some of the information from the K Kiosk to give you an idea of the purpose of each award and for whom it is intended. I have also provided the URLs so that you can look at the entire document concerning that award.

## GRANT SUPPLEMENTS FOR UNDERREPRESENTED MINORITIES

PIs who already hold NIH research grants may apply for administrative supplements to the existing grant for the support and recruitment of underrepresented minority investigators and students.

If you are a PI (or if you *know* a PI and you are, yourself, of minority status, as stipulated by the NIH) on an active grant of any of the following types—R01, R10, R18, R22, R24, R35, R37, P01, P20, P30, P40, P50, P51, P60, U01, U10, U19, U41, or U42—and provided that the grant (the *parent grant*) has support remaining for two or more years of research,[4] you should absolutely consider a Minority Supplement.

First, the NIH has taken as a priority the recruitment of minority researchers very seriously and is anxious to increase the number of minority researchers that it funds. You may be cynical and suggest that this is due to politics; but I would say that it seems clear that the NIH has recognized that the playing field has not been level and is attempting to redress that, at least in part. Moreover, by failing to provide such opportunities to minority persons who might not otherwise have such an opportunity, the NIH and the field of science lose a great number of talented young scientists, a concern on the part of the NIH that drives these and other such initiatives.

Second, because of this, relative to other sorts of applications, Minority Supplements are relatively more available *to those who fulfill the requirements*. To begin with, the NIH does not necessarily define *minority* the way that you do. Students and researchers with an African American or Caribbean American background are eligible, as are those with a Latino background. This seems obvious; on the other hand, I know a physician who comes from Egypt who is not eligible. Asians are not eligible. You will need to check with the NIH if your alleged minority status falls outside the African American, Caribbean American, or Hispanic background.

*(Text continues on page 35)*

| **Table 3.4** | Overview of the Career (K) Awards |
|---|---|
| *K01* | *Mentored Research Scientist Development Award* |
| Purpose | Provides support for an intensive, supervised career development experience in one of the biomedical, behavioral, or clinical sciences leading to research independence. |
| Eligibility | Applicants must have a research or health professional doctorate and postdoctorate experience and must demonstrate a need for a 3-, 4-, or 5-year period of additional supervised research. |
| Commitment | Awardees must commit a minimum of 75% of their time to conducting research. The proposed award must be in a research area new to the applicant and/or one in which an additional supervised research experience will substantially increase the research capabilities of the applicant. Current PIs on NIH career awards are not eligible. |
| Salary | The NIH will provide salary and fringe benefits. No other NIH funds may be used for salary supplementation. |
| Supported by | NIA, NIAAA, NIAMS, NCI, NICHD, NIDDK, NIDA, NIEHS, NIMH, NINDS, NINR, NHGRI, NCCAM, and NCRR |
| URL | http://grants1.nih.gov/grants/guide/pa-files/PA-00-019.html |
| *K02* | *Independent Scientist Award* |
| Purpose | Provides up to five years of salary support for newly independent scientists who can show the need for a period of intensive research focus as a means of enhancing their research careers. |
| Eligibility | Applicants must have a doctoral degree and independent, peer-reviewed research support at the time the award is made. Some of the I/Cs require the candidate to have an NIH research grant at the time of application, while other I/Cs will accept candidates with peer-reviewed, independent research support from other sources, so check with your I/C. |
| Commitment | Applicants must be willing to spend a minimum of 75% of full-time professional effort conducting research during the period of the award. In addition, the candidate must be able to demonstrate that the requested period of salary support and protected time will foster his or her career as a highly productive scientist in the indicated field of research. Scientists whose work is primarily theoretical may apply for this award in the absence of external research grant support. |
| Salary | The NIH will provide salary and fringe benefits. No other NIH funds may be used for salary supplementation. |
| Supported by | NIA, NIAAA, NIAAD, NIAMS, NICHD, NIDCD, NIDCR NIDDK, NIDA, NIEHS, NHLBI, NIMH, NINDS, and NCCAM |
| URL | http://grants1.nih.gov/grants/guide/pa-files/PA-00-020.html |
| *K05* | *Senior Scientist Award* |
| Purpose | Provides stability of support to outstanding scientists who have demonstrated a sustained, high level of productivity and whose expertise, research accomplishments, and contributions to the field have been and will continue to be critical to the mission of the particular NIH I/C. |
| Eligibility | Candidate must be a senior scientist and a recognized leader with a distinguished record of original contributions, must have a record of support from a funding I/C, and must have peer-reviewed grant support at the time of the award. Scientists whose work is primarily theoretical may, depending on the policy of the I/C, apply for this award in the absence of research grant support. |
| Commitment | Must commit at least 75% full-time professional effort to the program and the remainder devoted to other research-related and/or teaching pursuits consistent with the objectives of the award. |

| K05 | Senior Scientist Award |
| --- | --- |
| Salary | The NIH will provide salary and fringe benefits. Supplementation may not be from federal funds unless specifically authorized by the federal program from which such funds are derived. |
| Supported by | NIAAA, NCI, NIDA, NIMH, and NCCAM |
| URL | http://grants1.nih.gov/grants/guide/pa-files/PA-00-021.html |

| K07 | Academic Career Award |
| --- | --- |
| Purpose | The K07 is used by the NIH I/Cs to support persons interested in introducing or improving curricula in a particular scientific field as a means of enhancing the educational or research capacity at their institutions. This award supports two types of activities: <br>(1) Development: Provides up to five years of support for junior candidates who are interested in developing academic and research expertise in a particular field. <br>(2) Leadership: The K07 can also provide from two to five years of support for more senior persons with acknowledged scientific expertise and leadership skills who are interested in improving the curricula and enhancing the research capacity within an academic institution. |
| Eligibility | K07 candidates must have a clinical or research doctoral degree. Candidates for the Development Award must demonstrate the potential to develop into an excellent academician in the fields of interest to the awarding I/C and must be able to identify a mentor who is an expert in the research field of interest and has a record of providing the type of supervision required by this award. Candidates for the Leadership Award must have sufficient clinical training, research, or teaching experience in the academic area of interest to the NIH to implement a program of curriculum development within the applicant institution and must have an academic appointment at a level sufficient to enable her or him to exert an influence on the coordination of research, teaching, and clinical practice in an emerging field. |
| Commitment | <u>Development Award</u>: Candidates must devote at least 75% of full-time professional effort to the research and developmental programs required for academic development. <br><u>Leadership Award</u>: Candidates must devote at least 25% but not more than 50% effort to the program, a portion of which may include research. |
| Salary | The NIH will provide salary and fringe benefits. Supplementation may not be from federal funds unless specifically authorized by the federal program from which such funds are derived. Research expenses and career development costs may be provided at the discretion of the NIH I/C. Applicants should contact the relevant NIH I/C staff for additional information. |
| Supported by | NIA, NIAAA, NCI, NIMH, and NCCAM |
| URL | http://grants1.nih.gov/grants/guide/pa-files/PA-00-070.html |

| K08 | Mentored Clinical Scientist Development Award |
| --- | --- |
| Purpose | To support the development of outstanding clinician-research scientists. This mechanism provides specialized study for individuals with a health professional doctoral degree committed to a career in laboratory or field-based research. |
| Eligibility | The candidate must have a clinical doctoral degree or equivalent. Examples include but are not limited to the MD, DDS, DMD, DO, DC, OD, ND, DVM, or PharmD. Those with the PhD or other doctoral degrees in clinical disciplines such as clinical psychology, nursing, clinical genetics, speech-language pathology, audiology, and rehabilitation are also eligible. Individuals holding the PhD in a nonclinical discipline but who are certified to perform clinical duties should contact the appropriate Institute concerning their eligibility for a K08 award. The candidate must be able to identify a mentor with extensive research experience. |

*(Continued)*

**Table 3.4** (Continued)

| | |
|---|---|
| *K08* | *Mentored Clinical Scientist Development Award* |
| Commitment | The candiate must be willing to spend a minimum of 75% of full-time professional effort conducting research and research career development. |
| Salary | The NIH will provide salary and fringe benefits for the career award receipient. Supplementation may not be from federal funds unless specifically authorized by the federal program from which such funds are derived. |
| Supported by | NIA, NIAAA, NIAAD, NIAMS, NCI, NICHD, NIDCD, NIDCR, NIDDK, NIDA, NIEHS, NEI, NIGMS, NHLBI, NIMH, NINDS, and NCCAM |
| URL | http://grants1.nih.gov/grants/guide/pa-files/PA-00-003.html |
| *K12* | *Mentored Clinical Scientist Development Program* |
| Purpose | This K is different from the others in that it is *awarded to the institution,* as a training grant, for the support of clinical scientists who wish to undergo research training. The calls from each I/C are so different from one another, however, that generalities cannot be given. Your best bet is to see the K Kiosk (http://grants1.nih.gov/training/careerdevelopmentawards.htm) for individual I/C URLs. |
| Supported by | NCI, NCRR, NEI, NIA, NICHD, NIDA, and NIDCR |
| *K18* | *Career Enhancement Award for Stem-Cell Research* |
| Purpose | To encourage investigators to obtain training to appropriately use stem cells in their research. Two types of applicants should consider applying: (1) independent junior faculty who wish to expand their research by the use of stem cells, and (2) more senior, established investigators who wish to redirect their research, in whole or in part, to include the use of stem cells. |
| Eligibility | Details not provided in the FY2005 calls for applications. |
| Commitment | Applicants must devote a minimum of 50% of their time to the research effort, although a full-time commitment for the 6-to12-month period is encouraged and up to 24 months is allowable. |
| Salary | The NIH will provide salary and fringe benefits for the career award recipient. For K18 awards used to support a sabbatical period, the award will take into account concurrent sabbatical salary support provided by the home institution and any other supplemental support. Recipients may hold independent research support, either federal or private, concurrently with this award and may derive additional compensation for effort from other federal sources or awards. |
| Supported by | NIDDK, NIAAA, NIAID, NHLBI, and NINR |
| URL | http://grants1.nih.gov/grants/guide/pa-files/PAR-02-069.html |
| *K22* | *Career Transition Award* |
| Purpose | Support to a postdoctoral fellow in transition to a faculty position. The particulars are specific to the awarding I/C, so few general statements can be made. See the K Kiosk (http://grants1.nih.gov/training/careerdevelopmentawards.htm) for individual I/C URLs. |
| Supported by | NCI, NHGRI, NHLBI, NIAID, NIAMS, NIDA, NIDCR, NIDDK, NIEHS, NIMH, NINDS, NINR, and NLM |
| *K23* | *Mentored Patient-Oriented Research Career Development Award* |
| Purpose | To support the career development of investigators who intend to focus on patient-oriented research. Provides support for 3–5 years of supervised study and research for clinically trained professionals who have the potential to develop into productive clinical investigators. |

| K23 | Mentored Patient-Oriented Research Career Development Award |
|---|---|
| Eligibility | The candidate must have a clinical doctoral degree or equivalent. Examples include but are not limited to the MD, DDS, DMD, DO, DC, OD, ND, DVM, PharmD, or PhD, or doctoral degrees in disciplines such as clinical psychology, nursing, clinical genetics, speech-language pathology, audiology, and rehabilitation. Persons holding the PhD in a nonclinical discipline but who are certified to perform clinical duties should contact the appropriate I/C concerning their eligibility for a K23 award. Candidates must have completed their clinical training, including specialty and, if applicable, subspecialty training, prior to receiving an award. However, candidates may submit an application prior to the completion of clinical training. |
| | Ineligible persons include current and former PIs on an NIH research project (R01), FIRST Awards (R29), comparable career development award (K01, K07, K08), subprojects of a program project (P01) or center grants (P50), and the equivalent. Former PIs of NIH Small Grants (R03) or Exploratory/Developmental Grants (R21) remain eligible. Current and former recipients of Clinical Associate Physicians Award (CAP) support may apply provided they have had no more than 3 years of CAP support by the time of the K23 award. The combined total of CAP plus K23 support must not exceed 6 years. A candidate for the K23 award may not have a pending CAP application or any other career development award, nor may the candidate concurrently apply for such awards. |
| Commitment | The candidate must spend a minimum of 75% of full-time professional effort conducting research career development and clinical research. |
| Salary | Most I/Cs will provide up to $75,000 in salary, plus fringe benefits. However, these limits are specific to the awarding I/C, so contact the I/C to get specifics. The I/C may supplement the NIH salary contribution up to a level that is consistent with the I/C's salary scale; however, supplementation may not be from federal funds unless specifically authorized by the federal program from which such funds are derived. |
| Research Support | The NIH will provide up to $25,000 per year for (a) tuition, fees, and books related to career development; (b) research expenses, such as supplies, equipment, and technical personnel; (c) travel to research meetings or training; and (d) statistical services including personnel and computer time. In exceptional cases, the research development support costs may be as high as $50,000. |
| Supported by | NIA, NIAAA, NIAAD, NIAMS, NCI, NICHD, NIDCD, NIDCR, NIDDK, NIDA, NIEHS, NEI, NIGMS, NHLBI, NIMH, NINDS, NINR, NCCAM, and NCRR |
| URL | http://grants1.nih.gov/grants/guide/pa-files/PA-00-004.html |

| K24 | Midcareer Investigator Award in Patient-Oriented Research |
|---|---|
| Purpose | To provide support for clinician investigators to allow them protected time to devote to patient-oriented research (POR) and to act as research mentors for clinical residents, fellows, and/or junior faculty. This award is primarily intended for clinician investigators who are at the associate professor level or are functioning at that rank in an academic setting or equivalent nonacademic setting and who have an established record of independent, peer-reviewed federal or private research grant funding in POR. |
| Eligibility | Candidates must have a health-professional doctoral degree or its equivalent. Such degrees include but are not limited to the MD, DO, DDS, DMD, OD, DC, PharmD, or ND, as well as a doctoral degree in nursing. Candidates with PhD degrees are eligible for this award if the degree is in a clinical field and they usually perform clinical duties. This may include clinical psychologists, clinical geneticists, and speech and language pathologists. Applicants should be at the associate professor level, or be functioning at that rank in an academic setting or equivalent nonacademic setting and must have an established record of independent, peer-reviewed POR grant funding and record of publications. This award is intended for individuals who are at a midcareer stage and have a record of supervising and mentoring patient-oriented researchers. |

(Continued)

**Table 3.4** (Continued)

| | |
|---|---|
| K24 | *Midcareer Investigator Award in Patient-Oriented Research* |
| | Candidates must be able to demonstrate the need for a period of intensive research focus as a means of enhancing their clinical research career and a need for protected time to enhance their mentoring activities. Candidates for the K24 award may not have pending or concurrently apply for any other Public Health Services career award. |
| Commitment | Candidates must commit 25% to 50% effort to conducting POR and mentoring. |
| Salary | The NIH will provide salary and fringe benefits for the career award recipient. The candidate may derive additional compensation for effort associated with other federal sources or awards provided the total salary derived from all federal sources does not exceed the maximum legislated salary rate and the total percent effort does not exceed 100%. Candidates may not receive additional compensation from another Health and Human Services award (specifically, AHRQ or SAMHSA) that exceeds the maximum allowable salary compensation. |
| Research Support | The NIH will provide up to $50,000 per year for (a) research expenses, such as supplies, equipment, and technical personnel for the PI and the mentees; (b) travel to research meetings or training; and (c) statistical services including personnel and computer time. |
| Supported by | NIA, NIAAA, NIAID, NIAMS, NIBIB, NCI, NICHD, NIDCD, NIDCR, NIDDK, NIDA, NIEHS, NINR, NEI, NHLBI, NIMH, NINDS, NCCAM, and NCRR |
| URL | http://grants1.nih.gov/grants/guide/pa-files/PA-04-107.html |
| K25 | *Mentored Quantitative Research Career Development Award* |
| Purpose | To foster interdisciplinary collaboration in biomedical research by supporting career development experiences for scientists with quantitative and engineering backgrounds. It is meant to attract NIH-relevant research investigators whose quantitative science and engineering research has thus far not been focused primarily on questions of health and disease. Examples considered appropriate for this award include, but are not limited to, mathematics, statistics, economics, computer science, imaging science, informatics, physics, chemistry, and engineering. It is intended for investigators from the postdoctoral level to the level of senior faculty. |
| Eligibility | Details not provided in the FY2005 call for submissions. |
| Commitment | Candidates must devote at least 75% effort to research and research career development activities of this award, and the remainder of the effort must be committed to other career development activities consistent with the overall purpose of the award. |
| Salary | The NIH will provide salary and fringe benefits. Supplementation may not be from federal funds unless specifically authorized by the federal program from which such funds are derived. |
| Research Support | The NIH will generally provide up to $40,000/year for (a) tuition, fees, and books related to career development; (b) research expenses, such as supplies, equipment, and technical personnel; (c) travel to research meetings or training; and (d) research support services including personnel and computer time. |
| Supported by | NHGRI, NCI, NHLBI, NIA, NIAAA, NIAID, NIAMS, NIBIB, NICHD, NIDCD, NIDCR, NIDDK, NIDA, NIEHS, NIGMS, NIMH, and NINDS |
| URL | http://grants1.nih.gov/grants/guide/pa-files/PA-02-127.html |
| K26 | *Midcareer Investigator Award in Mouse Pathobiology Research* |
| Purpose | The NCRR and NIA fund this award, to provide support for established pathobiologists to allow them protected time to devote to mouse pathobiology research and to mentor beginning investigators. The target candidates are outstanding scientists engaged in |

| K26 | *Midcareer Investigator Award in Mouse Pathobiology Research* |
|---|---|
| | pathobiology research who can demonstrate the need for a period of intensive research focus as a means of enhancing their research careers and who are committed to mentoring the next generation of mouse pathobiologists. |
| Eligibility | Most candidates for this award will have a DVM degree (or equivalent) from an institution recognized by the American Veterinary Medical Association (AVMA). In addition, persons holding other clinical or research degrees (such as the MD or PhD) may apply if they have been certified or have demonstrated the necessary expertise to perform funded research in mouse pathobiology. Candidates must have completed their specialty or research training within 15 years of submission, and there is no age limit. In exceptional circumstances, the eligibility period may be extended if it can be demonstrated that candidates had an interruption in their career progression due to personal circumstances. Candidates must be working in a research environment and conducting mouse pathobiology research and must have significant peer-reviewed research support. |
| Commitment | Candidates must be willing to spend up to 50% effort (at least 25%) conducting mouse pathobiology research and mentoring. |
| Salary | The NIH will provide salary and fringe benefits. The I/C may supplement the NIH contribution up to a level that is consistent with the I/C's salary scale. Institutional supplementation of salary must not require extra duties or responsibilities that would interfere with the purpose of the award. |
| Research Support | The NCRR will provide generally up to $25,000 per year for the following expenses: (a) research expenses, such as supplies, equipment, and technical personnel for the principal investigator and his or her mentored investigators; (b) travel to research meetings or training; and (c) statistical services including personnel and computer time. |
| Supported by | NCRR and NIA |
| URL | http://grants1.nih.gov/grants/guide/pa-files/PAR-99-065.html |
| K30 | *Clinical Research Curriculum Development* |
| Purpose | The NIH developed this program to attract talented individuals to the challenges of clinical research and to provide them with the critical skills that are needed to develop hypotheses and conduct sound research. The Clinical Research Curriculum Award (CRCA) is an *award to institutions*. It supports the NIH's efforts to improve the quality of training in clinical research. |
| | This award is intended to (a) support the development of new didactic programs in clinical research at institutions that do not currently offer them, or (b) support the improvement or expansion of programs at institutions with existing programs. |
| | There is a core of knowledge and skills common to all areas of clinical research that should form the foundation of the well-trained, independent clinical researcher. Formal course work includes the following: |
| | • Design of clinical research projects<br>• Hypothesis development<br>• Biostatistics<br>• Epidemiology<br>• Legal, ethical, and regulatory issues related to clinical research |
| | The Web site gives the names of all institutions that have obtained a K30 award and the PIs at those institutions. Check to see if your institution is listed. If it is, check with the contact person to learn specifics about eligibility, commitment, and salary/stipend. |
| URL | http://grants1.nih.gov/training/K30.htm |

| **Table 3.5** | NIH Research Grant (R) Programs |
|---|---|
| *R01* | *Research Project Grant Program* |
| Purpose | To support a discrete, specified, circumscribed project to be performed in an area representing the investigator's specific interest and competencies, based on the mission of the NIH. |
| Specifics | <ul><li>Budget ceiling of $499,999 per year (*not* $500,000!) for up to five years. If the budget is to exceed $499,999, permission must be granted prior to submission.</li><li>Applications renewable by competing for an additional project period (only two revisions of a previously reviewed application may be submitted).</li><li>Supplements and amendments are allowed.</li></ul> |
| Supported by | All NIH I/Cs. |
| URL | http://grants1.nih.gov/grants/funding/r01.htm |
| *R03* | *Small Grant Program* |
| Purpose | Supports small research projects that can be carried out in a short period of time with limited resources. Note that different I/Cs may have specific purposes for which they use this mechanism. Before applying, consult the list of participating I/Cs to determine if an R03 application is appropriate. |
| Specifics | <ul><li>Applicants may request a project period of up to two years and a budget for direct costs of up to $50,000 per year.</li><li>Small grant support is for new projects only; competing continuation applications will not be accepted. (Only one revision of a previously reviewed application may be submitted).</li><li>May not be used for thesis or dissertation research.</li></ul> |
| Supported by | NEI, NIA, NIAAA, NIAID, NIBIB, NICHD, NIDA, NIDCR, NIEHS, NIMH, NINDS, NINR, and NLM |
| URL | http://grants1.nih.gov/grants/funding/r03.htm |
| *R21* | *Exploratory/Developmental Research Grant* |
| Purpose | Intended to encourage exploratory/developmental research projects by providing support for the early and conceptual stages of development. Consultation with NIH staff contacts is encouraged. |
| Specifics | <ul><li>May request a project period of up to two years.</li><li>The combined budget for direct costs for the two-year project period may not exceed $275,000.</li><li>Exploratory/developmental grant support is for new projects only; competing continuation applications will not be accepted.</li><li>Two revisions of a previously reviewed exploratory/developmental grant application may be submitted.</li><li>No preliminary data is required but may be included if available.</li></ul> |
| Supported by | NCCAM, NCRR, NEI, NIA, NIAAA, NIAID, NIAMS, NIBIB, NICHD, NIDA, NIDCD, NIDCR, NIEHS, NIMH, NINDS, and NLM; in addition, FIC, NCI, NCMHD, NHGRI, NHLBI, NIDDK, NIGMS, and NINR accept investigator-initiated R21 applications only in response to their own initiatives (see Chapter 4). |
| URL | http://grants1.nih.gov/grants/funding/r21.htm |

NOTE: These are not the only R mechanisms; however, the others are less common and are usually quite specific to a particular purpose (e.g., organizing a conference). You can see all the mechanisms at http://grants1.nih.gov/grants/funding/funding_program.htm.

Here is the official NIH statement concerning eligibility:

For the purpose of this announcement, underrepresented minority students and investigators are defined as individuals belonging to a particular ethnic or racial group that has been determined by the grantee institution to be underrepresented in biomedical, behavioral, clinical or social sciences. Awards will be limited to citizens or non-citizen nationals of the United States or to individuals who have been lawfully admitted for permanent residence (i.e., in possession of an Alien Registration Receipt Card) at the time of application. Before submitting an application for a research supplement, applicants are encouraged to call their program administrator at the NIH to discuss any aspects of this program that need clarification. For general information about the program, minority candidates are encouraged to contact an appropriate awarding institute listed under "Inquiries" at the end of this document.[5]

The NIH anticipates that by providing research opportunities for underrepresented minorities at various career levels, the number of minorities entering and remaining in health-related research careers will increase. Accordingly, PIs are encouraged to consider administrative supplements under this program for minority individuals at the following career levels:

- High school students who have expressed an interest in the health-related sciences.
- Undergraduate students who have demonstrated an interest in the health-related sciences and wish to pursue graduate level training in these areas.
- Postbaccalaureate students and post–master's degree students who have recently graduated and have demonstrated an interest in health-related sciences and wish to pursue graduate level training in these areas.
- Predoctoral students who wish to develop their research capabilities in the health-related sciences.
- Individuals in postdoctoral training who wish to participate as postdoctoral researchers in ongoing research projects and career development experiences in preparation for an independent career in a health-related science.
- Minority staff and faculty who wish to participate in ongoing research projects while further developing their own independent research.

You should know that the amount of the stipends available is completely dependent on the stage of education. You may very well find it useful to have summer trainees (or to be one). Know also that it looks good for the PI of the parent grant to be supporting Minority Supplements.

There is no particular deadline for submission of a Minority Supplement application. You may submit at any time, and the NIH will try to turn your application around within eight weeks. In my experience, it has taken longer, but it is still a step up from the usual turn-around time. (See Chapter 9 for a grant timetable.)

Relative to a research proposal, such as an R01, the Minority Supplement is relatively brief. The NIH announcement for the Minority Supplement continues:

In all cases, the proposed research experience must be an integral part of the approved ongoing research of the parent grant and have the potential to contribute significantly to the research career development of the candidate. As part of this research experience, the principal investigator must describe a plan by which the minority individual will have the opportunity to interact with individuals on the parent grant, to contribute intellectually to the research, and to enhance her/his research skills and knowledge regarding the particular area of biomedical or behavioral science. Furthermore, the Principal Investigator must demonstrate a willingness and understanding that the purpose of the award is to enhance the research capability of the minority student or faculty member and that the research experience is intended to provide opportunities for development as a productive research investigator.[6]

This means that the candidate and the PI of the parent grant are expected to put their heads together to come up with a project that was *not* specified in the application for the parent grant but that can be piggybacked on the parent grant and that will both add to the knowledge provided by the parent grant and, at the same time, provide a legitimate, enriching experience for the trainee. This might include data analyses not named in the parent grant or the addition of new measures not originally included that speak to some question in which the PI, the candidate, and, presumably, the NIH will be interested.

As an example: I am currently conducting a trial in which the focus is on an intervention to improve blood pressure control and medication adherence in poorly controlled hypertensive patients. Pilot data have recently emerged from another study in our laboratory that post–myocardial infarction patients who are depressed are less likely to adhere to their prescribed aspirin regimen than those who are not depressed. This suggests a phenomenon that may generalize to other patient populations. We took on a Minority Supplement trainee who has now added self-report measures of depression to the trial and will analyze and presumably report on the results. Note that everyone benefits: The trainee receives a stipend, which is regarded as prestigious because it is funded by the NIH, and also learns new skills; I may see something interesting in my data that I might not have seen; and the NIH gets to sponsor a new minority trainee, as well as possibly having an additional paper, possibly an important one, published under their sponsorship.

Appointment of more than one person to a single grant depends on the nature of the parent grant, the circumstances of the request, and the program balance of the NIH awarding component. Minority persons may receive support from only one of these supplement programs at a time but may be supported by more than one minority supplement during the development of their research careers. Support under the supplement programs is not transferable to another individual or transportable to another institution:

The minority supplement programs have been designed to attract underrepresented minority individuals into research careers and are not intended to provide an alternative or additional means of supporting minority individuals who already receive support from a research grant or a research training grant or any other HHS funding mechanism. Minority graduate students or individuals in postdoctoral training who are supported by a National Research Service Award (NRSA) institutional research training grant may not be transferred to supplemental support prior to the completion of their appointed period of training. Individuals may not be transferred to a minority supplement to increase the availability of funds to the parent grant for other uses.[7]

So, if you are a PI, it is worth your while to actively search out possible minority candidates. You may even have assistants working for you right now who might qualify, and, if so, this would free up funds from the parent grant to be used elsewhere. If you are a candidate, it is worth your while to check into this. It is not always easy to find potential minority candidates, so if you think you are eligible, don't hesitate to find out who is funded in your substantive and geographic areas and contact them. It is possible that the PI you contact may not know about the program, so point out that your salary would not come out of the parent grant funds, but would be added to them.

This is a great program—see if you can take advantage of the opportunity.

| Table 3.6 | Success Rates for Different Grant Mechanisms for NIAID in FY2002 |
| --- | --- |
| *Grant Type* | *2002 Success Rate* |
| R01 | 31% |
| F32 | 25% |
| K02 | 63% |
| K08 | 66% |
| K22 | 59% |
| K23 | 39% |
| K24 | 27% |
| T32 | 60% |

## FUNDING LEVELS FOR DIFFERENT GRANT MECHANISMS

You may be wondering about the relative success rates of different grant mechanisms. The ways in which these rates are arrived at is discussed in Chapter 9. The National Institute of Allergy and Infectious Disease (NIAID) thoughtfully provides two tables that, taken together, provide an illustration of the different funding levels for different grant mechanisms within one I/C. The rates shown in Table 3.6 came from FY2002.

As you can see, success rates vary considerably, depending on which type of grant you apply for. Should you base your decision as to which type of grant to go for on success rates? Well, it would be nice to go for the low-hanging fruit, and sometimes you find yourself in a position to do that, but the career award mechanisms are very specific. If you are eligible for a K08, then, great, go for it; but if you are eligible for a K24, then you are *not* eligible for a K08, and so on. As to the R01 mechanism, you could actually find yourself in a position to make a choice between a K award and an R01, but that would not be typical. Mostly, you select the mechanism that best suits what you are trying to accomplish.

## THE SBIR AND STTR AWARD MECHANISMS

For those of you who have projects of a commercial nature, you should consider the Small Business Innovation Research (SBIR) program and the Small Business Technology Transfer (STTR) program (I will explain the difference between them later in this chapter). These programs should be considered when the focus of the proposal is to be on a particular *product* (this includes devices, services, software, etc.) that is or will be available for purchase or lease by the medical community or by consumers, including but not limited to patients (for example, a software program that helps patients quit smoking).

Often, however, your proposal is meant to focus on the science, and a particular product may be included in the service of that science. In that event, you should be looking at research awards, not at an SBIR or STTR. Here is an example: If the focus of your research were on computer-based products that helped at-risk patients change their risky behaviors, smoking cessation being one of those, the focus would be on the presumably generalizable effects of such interventions, not on that one in particular, and you would probably consider a mechanism such as the R01.

Alternatively, if you had established a relationship with the developers of the specific smoking cessation software and planned to test its effects on smoking cessation as a means of providing validation that may in turn be used as part of a marketing strategy, then you should be thinking about the SBIR or STTR mechanism.

## Structure of the SBIR and STTR Programs

The SBIR and STTR programs are structured in three phases:

- *Phase I.* The objective of Phase I is to establish the technical merit and feasibility of the proposed research/research and development (R/R&D) efforts and to determine the quality of performance of the small business awardee prior to providing further federal support in Phase II. Support under Phase I is normally provided for six months at $100,000 for an SBIR and for one year at $100,000 for an STTR.

- *Phase II.* The objective of Phase II is to continue the R/R&D efforts initiated in Phase I. Only Phase I awardees are eligible for a Phase II award. SBIR and STTR Phase II awards normally may not exceed $750,000 total. However, applicants may propose longer periods of time and greater amounts of funds necessary for completion of the project.

- *Phase III.* Phase III refers to work that derives from, extends, or logically concludes efforts performed under prior SBIR funding agreements, but is funded by sources other than either the SBIR or STTR program. Phase III work is typically oriented toward commercialization of SBIR or STTR research or technology.

*Fast-Track Applications.* You may submit both the Phase I and Phase II applications together, at the same deadline (deadlines given below). The advantage of the fast-track application is that, if you get funded, there is no gap between the end of Phase I and the beginning of Phase II. If you submit Phase I on its own, and it is funded, you will be submitting Phase II at a later deadline; depending on what that is, you will have several months of no funding between the two.

Why not, then, always submit a fast-track application? First, it takes a huge amount of work to prepare a fast-track application, as it comprises two separate applications. Second, the risk is greater: The competition is very tough for these applications (across I/Cs, fewer than 1 in 5 fast-track applications are funded). The funding of Phase I is less competitive and the feedback will give you a chance to see where the reviewers will expect to see your Phase II proposal heading. Also, what you do in Phase II may be dependent on how things come out in Phase I. If that is the case, it will greatly weaken a fast-track proposal, and if you submit a fast-track proposal that is turned down because the Phase II portion is weak, the *whole thing* gets turned down; they won't fund Phase I only. Fast-track your submission if you are very confident that you have a strong set of applications that work hand-in-hand. If you are tentative, get your feet wet with Phase I only, and take it from there. Finally, if you are contemplating the submission of a fast-track proposal, you are strongly encouraged to contact the I/C program staff to discuss the appropriateness of this mechanism for your project.

Here's the catch: You, the research scientist, cannot submit an application for these awards. In the case of the SBIR mechanism, it is the small business concern (in the above-mentioned example, the developer of the smoking cessation software) that applies and to whom, if the grant is funded, the money goes. An STTR award, however, is structured differently: You, the scientist may submit, via your home institution, and you will enter into a sub-contract with the business concern with whom you are collaborating. So, what is your role? Actually, that depends on whether you submit an SBIR or STTR: Again, we'll get to the fine points of the two programs in a bit, but essentially, the business will form a consortium with your institution (consortia will be discussed in detail in Chapter 7) and you, presumably, will be PI on a subcontract between the company and your home institution. You will claim some percentage of your effort (if you don't know what this means, refer to Chapter 7) and will receive, from the business, the percentage of your salary that corresponds to that effort. You may also be awarded funds for research assistants, other necessary staff, subject payments, and so on—in short, for anything for which you might have budgeted in any other type of research award.

The SBIR and STTR differ in their rules regarding the PI of the award. For the SBIR, someone from the company must be the PI on the main contract, and that person will devote some percentage of effort to overseeing the project and will draw salary based on the percentage effort and his or her salary. That person may be an engineer or even the CEO, or, if you can negotiate it, it can be you—but in that case you would be paid directly from the small business concern, not from your home institution, which your institution may not like. For the STTR, the scientist is the PI of the entire project; there still must exist, however, a subcontract between the company and your institution.

The SBIR award stipulates that the PI must work for the company at least 51% of the time. That does not, however, mean that he or she must be paid 51% salary on this particular grant: Note this, as it is a common source of confusion. As you will see a bit later on, the situation is different on this point for the STTR.

There are other restrictions, and we'll get to them, but to sum it up: You, the researcher, are most likely going to write the portion of the proposal that deals with the science; it is the company that officially submits the proposal, and if funded, the main contract is between the NIH and the company. Your institution must agree to a consortium arrangement with the company, and you will be paid from that consortium subcontract. There is still a great deal you may not yet know about these sorts of arrangements, so you will need to read Chapter 7 very carefully, but that is the substance of it. You might want to consider that the competition for SBIR and STTR funds may be less than that for R01s; often, these proposals are written by engineers in the company who may have little experience with writing a scientific grant proposal. Thus, if you are good at writing grant proposals (and, of course, once having finished this book, you will be), you should be able to outshine a great deal of other submitters, many of whom just may not have a good idea of what the game is. This might be considered some of that low-hanging fruit to which I referred earlier.

To return to the issue of research versus commercial types of awards: Might this research be appropriate for an R01? It might, but there would be several differences. In the SBIR and STTR programs, the device is the focus of the proposal. It is important to get this straight, because scientists often do not think this way. The idea behind the funding is that the product will *make money*. The NIH *wants* the business to make money. Why? Because if someone isn't making money, then the product will wither and die. The NIH recognizes this, and therefore is willing to back aspects of the testing of products it deems useful for the community.

If you were interested in writing an R01, however, you would focus on the issue of health behavior change in an at-risk population. Smoking cessation might be considered one facet of the broader issue, and the particular software you use to implement your intervention would be considered a useful tool, but one that could presumably be exchanged for a different brand, if it did the same thing.

Which should you write? It depends on several things, including your research interest (which should be first and foremost), your estimation of the fundability of each type of proposal, what is best for your career (the R01), what your department wants out of you (which can vary), and your connection to the company—and if you don't have one, call them up! Go visit them! They won't toss you out because you're trying to bring in more than three quarters of a million dollars to fund testing of their product! Just don't lose sight of the likelihood that the NIH will regard the development of this particular product to have the potential to address a public health need that the NIH will deem desirable and important.

A large amount of material is available on the Web concerning these mechanisms. I have distilled a bit of it for you in the following sections. You can see a great deal more by looking at the SBIR and STTR Web pages.[8] And, absolutely, get a copy of the application instructions and read them thoroughly.[9] Click on the line that says "Forms and Instructions."

Here is an edited version of the SBIR description given by the NIH:

The Small Business Innovation Research (SBIR) program is a set-aside program (2.5% of an agency's extramural budget) for domestic small business concerns to engage in Research/Research and Development (R/R&D) that has the potential for commercialization.

To date, more than $12 billion has been awarded by the SBIR program to various small businesses.

*Objectives.* The SBIR program includes the following objectives: using small businesses to stimulate technological innovation, strengthening the role of small business in meeting federal R/R&D needs, increasing private sector commercialization of innovations developed through federal SBIR R/R&D, increasing small business participation in federal R/R&D, and fostering and encouraging participation by socially and economically disadvantaged small business concerns and women-owned business concerns in the SBIR program. The STTR and SBIR programs are similar in that both programs seek to increase the participation of small businesses in federal R/R&D and to increase private sector commercialization of technology developed through federal R/R&D. The unique feature of the STTR program is the requirement for the small business applicant to formally collaborate with a research institution in Phase I and Phase II.

*Differences Between the SBIR and STTR.* The SBIR and STTR programs differ in two major ways. First, under the SBIR program, the PI must have his or her primary employment with the small business concern at the time of award and for the duration of the project period; however, under the STTR program, primary employment is not stipulated. Second, the STTR program requires research partners at universities and other nonprofit research institutions to have a formal collaborative relationship with the small business concern. At least 40% of the STTR research project is to be conducted by the small business concern and at least 30% of the work is to be conducted by the single partnering research institution. (See Table 3.7 for an outline of the differences.)

> This following information is very important, so please take note. Under the SBIR program, you, the scientist, can be the PI of the entire award, but you must be at least 51 percent employed by the company. Your home institution may or may not have something to say about more than half of your time being paid for by someone else. In addition, there may be implications for your health and retirement benefits. If your institution requires that you be employed there for more than 49% of your effort in order to receive benefits, this may be a major consideration as to whether it is worth being the PI of this award. As I mentioned previously, someone within the company can be the PI, and you can be the site PI, under a consortium arrangement (see Chapter 7). The STTR, however, is much less restrictive. What's the catch? There is none. The STTR is just structured differently, with the specific purpose of making such collaborations easier.
>
> Both the SBIR and STTR require that some portion of the work be done by the business or manufacturer who requests the award. Again, the SBIR is more restrictive: In Phase I, no more than one third of the monies can be paid outside the business (this includes subcontracts and consultants); in Phase II, no more than 50% can be so paid. This can represent a real problem when, as in the example I used earlier, almost all the work must be done at a scientific institution. Again, the STTR is less restrictive, but at least 40% of the work must be conducted by the small business concern. I have considered participating in SBIR and STTR projects that I had to give up because more of the work needed to be done outside the business than was allowed. This should be a major consideration.

Table 3.7 shows the differences between the SBIR and STTR. This table is part of an NIH document entitled Index.doc, available as a Word file or PDF document, that you can—and should—download from the NIH site.[10]

## In What Areas Is the NIH Interested?

The NIH welcomes SBIR and STTR applications from small businesses in any biomedical or behavioral research area that falls within its mission, which is to improve human health.

**Table 3.7** SBIR and STTR Comparison Table

| Requirements | SBIR | STTR |
|---|---|---|
| Applicant Organization | Small Business Concern | Small Business Concern |
| Award Period[a] | Phase I—6 months, normally<br>Phase II—2 years, normally | Phase I—1 year, normally<br>Phase II—2 years, normally |
| Award Dollar Guidelines[a] | Phase I—$100,000, normally<br>Phase II—$750,000, normally | Phase I—$100,000, normally<br>Phase II—$750,000, normally |
| PI | Employed by company more than 50% of his or her time *during* award.[a]<br>Minimum level of effort on the project not stipulated. | Employment not stipulated.<br>The PI must spend a minimum of 10% effort on the project and have a formal appointment with or commitment to the SBC. |
| Subcontract/ Consultant Costs | Phase I—Total amount of contractual and consultant costs normally may not exceed 33% of total amount requested.[a]<br>Phase II—Total amount of contractual and consultant costs normally may not exceed 50% of total amount requested.[a] | Phase I and Phase II—The small business concern must perform at least 40% of work and the single, partnering U.S. nonprofit research institution must perform at least 30% of the work.<br>Deviations are *not* permitted from these minimum requirements. |
| Performance Site | Must be entirely in the United States.[a]<br>Part of the research must take place in a company-controlled research space. | Must be entirely in the United States.[a]<br>Part of the research must take place in a company-controlled research space and part in that of the partnering U.S. research institution. |

a. Deviations permissible with written justification and approval.

Areas of interest are described in the solicitations reproduced below. You are encouraged, if you plan to apply to either of these programs, to read the NIH "Guide for Grants and Contracts" and to visit I/C Web sites for more information on emerging interests and areas of high priority.

## Receipt Dates

Receipt dates for SBIR and STTR applications are *not the same* as for most other grants, so please take note and check the NIH site:[11]

| SBIR and STTR Submission Dates[a] Phase I and Phase II | AIDS and AIDS-Related Application Submission Dates | National Technical Merit Review | Advisory Council/ Board Review | Estimated Award Date |
|---|---|---|---|---|
| April 1<br>August 1<br>December 1 | May 1<br>September 1<br>January 2 | June/July<br>October/November<br>Feb/March | September/October<br>January/February<br>May/June | November<br>March<br>July |

a. The NIH, CDC, and FDA now use the same three standard submission dates. The CDC and FDA do not participate in the STTR program.

Note that AIDs and AIDS-related applications have a different submission deadline, one month after the regular deadline. The Technical Merit Review dates are when the study section will evaluate the worth of your proposal and assign it a priority score; the Advisory Council date is when the council, which makes decisions that are strongly influenced by the Technical Review but which still operates independently, will make a funding decision. You will learn more about the review processes in Chapter 9.

> Rules involving the SBIR and STTR programs may change at any time, and I have observed that they change more often than with other programs. If you plan to submit an application, get on the Web and make sure that you have the latest information.

Remember that Phase II funding is based on three considerations: the results of Phase I, the scientific and technical merit of the project, and the commercial potential of the Phase II application. Applications not demonstrating sufficient results in Phase I may not receive a score in the peer review process. And note that you may *not* submit a Phase II application if you have not yet received your Phase I award.

> See Chapter 8 for information about how to submit the SBIR/STTR application. However, it is important to know that the Phase II grant application should be submitted no later than the first six receipt dates following expiration of the Phase I budget period.

*Receipt of Fast-Track Applications.* Fast-Track applications may be submitted on any of the three published receipt dates. The cover page of the application (the *Face Page*) for both the Phase I and Phase II portions should be clearly marked "fast-track," and copies of both portions should be assembled and submitted together, unless you are using the new SF (Standard Form) 424 forms, in which case this is not required (see Chapter 7).

## What Sorts of Businesses Are Eligible?

The Small Business Association (SBA) sets the definition of a small business concern and the eligibility criteria to participate in the SBIR and STTR programs. The eligibility criteria to receive an SBIR or STTR award are described in the grant solicitation. If you have questions beyond what is described in the solicitation, you should contact a specialist in the SBA's Office of Government Contracting.[12]

## Budget Information

Budgets are discussed in detail in Chapter 7. In that chapter, there is a separate section that discusses SBIR and STTR applications, but most of what I tell you about detailed budgets for the R01 grant is also true for the SBIR and STTR mechanisms.

*Unallowable Costs.* I will cover allowable and unallowable costs in general in Chapter 7; however, there are some differences for SBIR and STTR applications. You can find more details about unallowable costs on the NIH Web site.[13]

*Facilities and Administrative Costs.* I mention facilities and administrative costs (F&A; also called *indirect costs* or *overhead*) now because (a) you may have come across them and wondered what they referred to, and (b) it is very important you learn about them. I cover this topic in Chapter 7, with a separate heading for SBIR and STTR awards, so please make sure to check this out.

*Frequently Asked Questions (FAQs).* The NIH provides a FAQs page that provides a great deal of useful information. I strongly urge you to take advantage of it.[14]

*Tutorials.* The NIH provides very useful resources to help you write better grants, and you should definitely take advantage of them. The NIH site has two particularly useful PowerPoint presentations entitled "Overview of SBIR/STTR Program" and "Nuances of the SBIR/STTR program."[15]

# NOTES

1. See http://grants1.nih.gov/grants/funding/funding_program.htm.
2. The K Kiosk can be accessed at http://grants1.nih.gov/training/careerdevelopmentawards.htm.
3. See http://grants1.nih.gov/training/kwizard/index.htm.
4. There may be some give to this; if there is *almost* 2 years, you can try for it.
5. Available from http://grants2.nih.gov/grants/guide/pa-files/PA-01-079.html.
6. Available from http://grants2.nih.gov/grants/guide/pa-files/PA-01-079.html.
7. Available from http://grants2.nih.gov/grants/guide/pa-files/PA-01-079.html.
8. Contact information is available at http://www.sba.gov/size/indexcontacts.html, or from size-standards@sba.gov.
9. You will find them at http://grants1.nih.gov/grants/funding/sbir.htm#sol.
10. The file Index.doc can be found at http://grants1.nih.gov/grants/funding/sbir.htm under the heading "Instructions and Forms."
11. Receipt dates can be found at http://grants2.nih.gov/grants/funding/sbirsttr_receipt_dates.htm.
12. The SBIR page can be found at http://grants2.nih.gov/grants/funding/sbir.htm and the STTR page at http://grants2.nih.gov/grants/funding/sbirsttr_programs.htm.
13. See http://ocm.od.nih.gov/dfas/unallowables.htm.
14. You may download the FAQs document from http://grants1.nih.gov/grants/funding/sbirsttr_faqs.doc.
15. These presentations can be accessed at http://grants1.nih.gov/grants/funding/sbir.htm. In addition, you can access presentations from a 2004 conference on the SBIR at http://grants1.nih.gov/grants/funding/SBIRConf2004/presentations.htm.

# Preparation and Preliminary Steps

The primary driving forces behind the proposal of any research project are the investigator's convictions that (a) this is an important problem, (b) it is one that can be addressed using resources are at the investigator's disposal (with additional funding for direct costs), and (c) the project is one in which the NIH will be interested. All three are equally important. I suggest that it would be a poor strategy to base your proposal primarily on what you think the NIH wants to fund; something will inevitably trip you up if you take this path. It might as well be work about which you are passionate and in which you believe. However, there is little point in submitting a proposal on a topic that you are pretty sure the NIH will *not* fund, no matter how committed to it you may be. To address this, you must acquaint yourself with the NIH's priorities and goals. You will also want to know how the NIH communicates its desires, what applications have been funded in similar areas, and, in general, what information you need to usefully orient your proposal. All this information is readily available to you.

## ARE YOU READY?

In a way, you've been preparing for this challenge for most of your adult life. You presumably have a credential, usually a PhD, MD, or something comparable; you have mastered the core substantive material around which the proposal will be based; you have the skills to master additional material as the need arises; and you have other people lined up who will help you and whose areas of expertise presumably are not entirely the same as your own. That's a good start. You should also have permission from your department chair or the chief of your division; if you haven't solicited this permission, better do it first, or you may be wasting a lot of time. You know how to use the Internet; you can type, even if it is with two fingers. You know how to make coffee. So, next let's discuss your eligibility to apply.

As should be quite plain by now, there is no generic eligibility list that applies to all awards. Having said that, the following statement appears in many NIH requests for applications (RFAs; we will discuss these further later in this chapter):

Any individual with the skills, knowledge, and resources necessary to carry out the proposed research is invited to work with their institution to develop an application for support. Individuals from underrepresented racial and ethnic groups as well as individuals with disabilities are always encouraged to apply for NIH programs.

Caution: Your immigration status may play a role in terms of your eligibility. Again, it varies from mechanism to mechanism, so you have to check. Here is a standard statement taken from an RFA that applies to all training awards (T, F, or K awards; see Chapter 3 for a discussion of these mechanisms) but *not* for research awards such as the R01:

> Candidates must be U.S. citizens or non-citizen nationals, or must have been lawfully admitted for permanent residence by the time of award. Individuals admitted for permanent residence must be able to produce documentation of their immigration status such as an Alien Registration Receipt Card (I-551) or some other verification of legal admission as a permanent resident. Non-citizen nationals, although not U.S. citizens, owe permanent allegiance to the U.S. They are usually born in lands that are not states but are under U.S. sovereignty, jurisdiction, or administration. Individuals on temporary or student visas are not eligible for this award.[1]

Okay, we've talked about *your* eligibility; now let's talk about the eligibility of the institution at which you are employed. Remember, although it is you who are writing the proposal, it is *your institution* that must submit the application. If you are funded, your institution will regard it as *its* award and will take great pains to remind you of this. So, here is what the NIH has to say about your institution's eligibility to receive an R01 award:

> The NIH awards R01 grants to organizations of all types (universities, colleges, small businesses, for-profit, foreign and domestic, faith-based, etc.) and the R01 mechanism allows an investigator to define the scientific focus or objective of the research based on a particular area of interest and competence. Although the Principal Investigator writes the grant application and is responsible for conducting the research, the applicant is the research organization.[2]

Next, let's now focus on your qualifications. Presumably, you plan to be the PI of this application. Are you qualified in the eyes of the NIH? The reviewers will be equally interested in your ability to conduct the proposed research and in the quality of the science. Do you have a publication history in the area in which you are proposing research? How extensive this history must be depends on what grant mechanism you plan to use. Some mechanisms—the T and F awards, for example, and some of the K awards—don't expect you to have a lot of publications.

Let's discuss the R01. Is it appropriate for you to jump in? When you apply for an R01, even if you have checked the "new investigator" box on the Cover Page (see Chapter 7), you are competing in the basic research grant mechanism against the best minds and the best scientists in the toughest grant-writing environment that exists. I don't mean to discourage you, but you have to face reality: There is no point in doing this if you are not ready. So, how do you decide?

First, how many years out are you from your terminal degree? It is not unheard of for a brand-new PhD or physician to make the cut, but it is not typical. It would be more usual to go first for a K award. Of course, if you have had an R01 previously, this conversation is over: You're qualified. If you have been the recipient of a K award or one of the smaller R awards, such as the R21 or R03, you are, however, *not* necessarily automatically ready to apply for an R01. The reviewers will want look at your publication record. Have you published review papers, but no empirical studies? Have you published only a couple of small studies in not particularly prestigious journals? Have you published only one study, but it came out in *Journal of the American Medical Association*? (Even that doesn't necessarily qualify you.) There is no "correct" formula. Think about it from the point of view of the reviewers: Having a good publication record tells more about you than just your qualification in a particular area of endeavor. Publishing, especially in good journals (look up the journal's "impact factor," which relates to how often articles from that journal are cited by others, to help you evaluate how good it is), tells the reviewer that you are a sophisticated player in the game, that you are tenacious and ambitious, that you have research skills, that you can write, and that you can be responsive to criticism (most papers don't get accepted first time out). Are you that person? If not yet, focus your attention on publishing. Get those papers out—you know, the ones that are 95% finished and are just waiting for you to write those last few paragraphs. If you have a paper that came back with the recommendation to revise and resubmit, turn it around immediately, and get it back out. Beef up your *curriculum vitae* (cv).

> Do not list your conference presentations in with your papers on your cv. Don't list book chapters in there either. It is annoying to the reader. If you feel you have to list them, then there is a message: "Wait until you don't have to pad your cv."

Let's say you have a pretty good cv, but you haven't published anything on the topic of your proposal. This is a problem, no matter how experienced you are, no matter how many R01s you may have under your belt. Either (a) be content to be a co-investigator, which will be painful if it's your grant idea and you plan to do the writing, but it may be your best bet; (b) be a co-PI, a title that may soon gain legitimacy at the NIH; (c) have people who have a lot of experience in the area serve as your co-investigators; (d) go for a smaller grant, such as an R21 (but some I/Cs don't offer these); or (e) write some papers. I suggest the final option.

## TRY OUT YOUR IDEAS ON YOUR COLLEAGUES

We're now assuming that you have decided that your qualifications to submit a grant application are up to par, so let's move on to preparation. At the beginning of the process, *probably close to a year before your target submission deadline,* you need to test the waters. It is easy to fall in love with your own ideas; after a while, the story you would like to tell takes on a life of its own and it becomes difficult to see flaws. It can be painful, but before you get too far into the application process, you need to try out your ideas on colleagues.

### Two Strata of Colleagues

In regard to the proposal you plan to write, you have colleagues who you hope, or know, will serve as co-investigators on the proposal or serve in some other capacity. These constitute the inner stratum of colleagues. And then you presumably have colleagues whom you can ask to review your proposal as a courtesy—the outer stratum. If you do not have these types of colleagues, it is time to begin finding them. One difference is that you cannot ask as much of the outer stratum of colleagues as you can of those who will be listed on the proposal. Be very careful not to inundate them with drafts or, particularly annoying, to send them a new revision before you have received their comments (thus rendering their work possibly obsolete). I wouldn't recommend that you send more than two drafts unless you have a close professional relationship that will tolerate such a request.

> Develop a method for maintaining version control of the drafts you will be circulating. Designate one document as the master, and designate someone, possibly yourself, to be its keeper.

Whom should you ask to be in the inner stratum? Of course, you will think of others in your field, but also consider colleagues in other fields, so as to provide a broader skill base that is relevant to the project. A statistician should be included; you want your statistician in on the design of the project from the beginning, not *after* you have come up with a design. If there are procedures that require a special expertise that you don't have, try to have someone involved, as either a co-investigator or as a consultant who does; if the problem is circumscribed, you may include the person as a consultant, who will help with that specific issue. (See Chapter 7 for the distinction between *consultant* and *co-investigator*.)

I am an advocate of brainstorming sessions at the beginning of the process, in which you all meet and work together to produce a more refined product. Ideas tend to come out in conversation, as long as the conversation remains on track. This can be difficult: You, possibly the most junior person in the room, must lead the group and maintain discipline so that you accomplish your goals. At the beginning of the process, you want to avoid focusing on small details, but you also need to keep the discussion reined in so that you end the session having made progress. To increase the likelihood that this will happen, I suggest that you do the following:

- Prepare an agenda, photocopy it, and pass it around. The agenda should have action items you hope to accomplish by the end of that particular session. Don't make these items too ambitious. For example, in the early stages, an action item might be, "Decide on appropriate control conditions."
- If you think that your group would read materials ahead of time, then by all means send them; my own experience suggests that doesn't work. Instead, I suggest a brief slide presentation in which you lay out the idea, provide some rationale (but not too much), and give a preliminary design and provisional timeline. There may be other such areas, depending on what it is you plan to do, but the point is to lay out the major considerations.
- End with whatever action items have been decided upon, and make sure you agree on who is to do what, by when.
- Keep minutes and send them around just before the next meeting.

If the meeting just cannot be arranged because of scheduling or geographic barriers, use a conference call. Try not to include more than six people at most; after that, such calls become unwieldy.

> You will often find that one or more of your group will focus on small, usually methodological, details. If the discussion veers off to which reagent you are planning to use, or the amount you should pay subjects, the more important discussion can get sidetracked. The details have to be tackled, but not until you have an idea of what you want to study and how you want to study it. You have to be somewhat authoritative and not allow the discussion to become bogged down.

At the beginning of this process, you are interested in reality checking. Do the others think your idea is a good one? Is it innovative? Is the rationale strong enough to support it? Is it feasible? You have to go into this meeting prepared to hear that the answer to any of these is "no." Be very conscious of not being, or seeming, defensive; the point is to come up with a fundable study, not to make you feel better about yourself. If that is not your cup of tea—and I mean this with all sincerity—*get out of the business right now,* because to be a soft-money scientist means that for the rest of your life you will be inviting criticism. You will be offering your most cherished theories and your brilliant writing to colleagues and reviewers, and requesting that they tear it to pieces. If your colleagues don't, the reviewers most certainly will.

Be cautious that you don't fall into a "groupthink" pattern, first described by the psychologist Irving Janis, who, like many others in the early 1960s, had trouble understanding how the smart group of political analysts surrounding John Kennedy could come up with a plan like the Bay of Pigs. In some groups, people tend to agree with each other and to be insufficiently critical. Often, one person may overtly or covertly take on the role of the leader, and others may then abdicate the responsibility for original, critical thought. *You* must take on the leadership role, but not in a manner that discourages critical thinking by the others.

Having come up with a plan that you are all happy with, narrow the focus of succeeding sessions. There do not need to be many of these, unless the project is exceptionally complex. Instead, begin the writing. Possibly one or more of your colleagues, those who will be co-investigators or consultants, will write some portions. When you get far enough along in the writing, send it out to other colleagues for review. As I mentioned previously, don't abuse this by sending out repeated drafts, or your colleagues will begin refusing to read them. On the other hand, you don't want to wait until the entire thing is finished before you first get feedback.

Next, let us consider what you should know about the needs of the NIH. What is it looking for in a proposal? You need to understand the organization. It has needs; its representatives have to go before Congress and ask for money for the NIH budget, and they need to demonstrate *why* Congress should allocate increasingly scarce funds to medical research instead of other priorities, such as the military. The following sections will provide some insight that may help guide the direction and writing of your proposal.

## THE NIH WEB SITE: A USEFUL RESOURCE

If you haven't checked it out, log on to the NIH Web site at http://www.nih.gov. It is full of information you will need, and, in addition, the NIH has gone to a great deal of trouble to provide tutorials and supplementary information. It is an excellent resource, and I strongly urge you to spend a good deal of time paging through it. Let the links take you where they may: You will invariably wind up coming across things you'll be glad you learned. I borrowed liberally from it (with permission); direct quotes in this chapter are taken from the NIH Web site. URLs will be provided throughout the text where appropriate, and Appendix B provides a listing of all of them.

> The individual I/Cs provide information for beginning grant writers, and some provide better information than others. I have been very impressed by the materials I have found on the NIAID Web site (I will provide URLs for these sites when we come to specific topics). However, a word of caution: If the Web site you are reading is not from the I/C to which you will be applying, make sure the information you read is not specific to that particular I/C.

## HEALTHY PEOPLE 2010

The Healthy People 2010[3] (originally Healthy People 2000) initiative was developed by the NIH several years ago to address prevention needs:

> Healthy People 2010 is the prevention agenda for the Nation. It is a statement of national health objectives designed to identify the most significant preventable threats to health and to establish national goals to reduce these threats.

It has two major goals:

1. Increase quality and years of healthy life

2. Eliminate health disparities among different segments of the population

Both goals are taken extremely seriously by the NIH. The first goal may or may not be addressed in your proposal. However, the second goal should be incorporated into every proposal in which human subjects are to serve as research participants. This is not a suggestion or a guideline: It is mandated by law. Your research should document the existence of disparities, if they exist, in the outcomes you study; the base rates of affected populations in your catchment area and your sampling framework regarding these rates; and your recruitment and retention plans to ensure that you will be able to bring members of the affected population into your study. If you do not address these issues, you run the risk of receiving a lower score and possibly of having your proposal flagged for having human subject concerns. (Chapter 6 discusses human subject concerns and Chapter 9 addresses the NIH review process.)

In addition to these two goals, there are many more specific goals and agendas that you may want to investigate. While it is true that Healthy People 2010 specifically addresses prevention research, the caveats given above apply for any human research.

It is worth my spending an extra minute on the issue of health disparities and recruitment of persons who are disadvantaged and/or underserved due to gender, ethnicity or race, or economic circumstances. The NIH has taken an extremely progressive stance on these issues. Not only should you consider the imperative to represent such populations in your sampling scheme, you might also consider that such disparities represent a legitimate and important research opportunity. Many norms have been established based on majority populations—often on populations of white men. The extent to which these norms, or results of studies, generalize to other populations, however, is often unclear and may require studies developed specifically for the purpose of testing wider applicability. Similarly, an intervention that may be effective in one population may not be effective in a different population. You will not go wrong by addressing these sorts of issues in the eyes of those who will be reviewing your application.

## THE NIH ROADMAP INITIATIVE

In 2002, Elias A. Zerhouni, MD, became the new NIH director. In May of that year, Dr. Zerhouni organized a set of meetings that would plan for the future, that would generate a roadmap. The purpose of this Roadmap Initiative was "to identify major opportunities and gaps in behavioral or biomedical research that no single institute at NIH could tackle alone but that the agency as a whole must address, to make the biggest impact on the progress of medical research."

The Web site dedicated to the NIH Roadmap Initiative tells how the initiatives were developed and the rationale.[4] It also provides links to the related pages, including a page on grants and funding opportunities specific to the Roadmap. I shall highlight the main points here, but I recommend studying the document for the complete story.

Three themes are central to the Roadmap Initiative:

1. *New Pathways to Discovery.* The first theme addresses the need to understand the combination of molecular events involved in complex biological systems and urges the development of new technologies, including libraries of chemical molecules that may provide (a) probes of biological networks; (b) imaging probes for molecular and cellular events; (c) improved computational infrastructure for biomedical research; (d) nanotechnology devices capable of viewing and interacting with basic life processes; and (e) potential targets for new therapies.

2. *Research Teams of the Future.* The NIH recognizes the need for interdisciplinary groups to target specific research questions. A new award has been developed, the Director's Pioneer Award, which is designed to encourage investigators to undertake "creative, unexplored avenues of research that carry a relatively high potential for failure, but also possess a greater chance for truly groundbreaking discoveries." This theme also addresses the need for novel partnerships, such as those between the public and private sectors, with an eye to bringing research from "the bench to the bedside." In addition to the NIH Director's Pioneer Awards, NIH funds will be awarded to projects that are consistent with this theme. The list of possible funding opportunities is long, and rather than duplicating it, I refer you again to the Roadmap Web site.[5]

3. *Reengineering the Clinical Research Enterprise.* The third theme emphasizes the need for translation of basic research discoveries into clinical tools, such as drugs, treatments, and methods of prevention. Specific issues include the need for "new paradigms in how clinical research information is recorded, new standards for clinical research protocols, modern information technology platforms for research, new models of cooperation between NIH and patient advocates, and new strategies to re-energize our clinical research workforce." Strategies of interest to the NIH in this regard include "promoting the better integration of existing clinical research networks, encouraging the development of technologies to improve the assessment of clinical outcomes, harmonizing regulatory processes, and enhancing training for clinical researchers."

Reengineering the clinical research enterprise is a hugely important theme for the NIH: You will hear a great deal about "technology transfer," "bench-to-bedside," and "translational research," all phrases referring to the development of tools that will influence the way in which medicine is practiced. Even if you are conducting more basic or more theoretical research, do not fail to note the translational implications!

In addition to the funding that will be available via the Research Teams of the Future theme, the NIH has listed a number of initiatives that it plans to fund. Again, it is a long list, and you can find it at the Roadmap Web site.

The NIH has earmarked a substantial amount of money to fund Roadmap Initiatives. Look for RFAs and RFPs (requests for proposals) in the NIH "Guide for Grants and Contracts" to learn about these.

## THE NIH "GUIDE FOR GRANTS AND CONTRACTS"

The "Guide for Grants and Contracts" is the NIH's official publication for research grant policies, guidelines, and funding opportunities. It is published weekly online, and you will probably want to subscribe. To do so, send an e-mail to listserv@list.nih.gov with the following in the message body (not in the subject line):

Subscribe NIHTOC-L [your name]

*Example:* Subscribe NIHTOC-L Joe Smith

Once you have subscribed, every week, usually on Friday, you will receive an e-mail that contains the table of contents for that week's issue of the guide. The table of contents will include a link to the articles, as well as to each RFA, RFP, program announcement (PA), and notice of grant-related information published for that week.

### Program Announcement

A program announcement (PA) is a funding announcement for grants relating to areas of increased priority and/or emphasis for a specific area of science. PAs signal the NIH's interest in funding applications in these areas, but unlike RFAs and RFPs, there is no call for specific proposals at this moment and no set-aside funds.

### Request for Applications

A request for applications (RFA) is a funding announcement for grants that identifies a more narrowly defined area for which one or more NIH I/Cs have set aside funds for awarding grants. An RFA usually has a single receipt date, specified in the announcement. I discuss RFAs in detail later in this chapter.

### Request for Proposals (RFP)

A request for proposals (RFP) solicits *contract* proposals. An RFP usually has one receipt date, specified in RFP solicitation.

*Grants and Contracts.* Grants differ from contracts in several ways. Contracts are offered when the NIH wants to get something specific done: for example, developing and running an advanced program in a particular content area (such as clinical trials) or a scientific enterprise (such as testing the effect of a specific intervention in a specific population). The review process for contracts is very different from that of grants, and the NIH maintains much tighter control on contract details, where grants provide more leeway (for example, in rebudgeting). I am not going to say much about contracts in this book, but will instead focus on the grant process.

## REQUESTS FOR APPLICATIONS

Assuming you have a topic that you would like to research, you may submit an unsolicited application (the different types of applications are described in Chapter 3), or you may respond to an RFA if you see one that falls within your research interests and areas of expertise. An RFA is usually quite specific in terms of the type of research the NIH is looking for. The advantage to responding to an RFA is that you know that the NIH has an interest in it, that funds have been set aside for that purpose, and that a certain number of applications on that topic will be funded (assuming that a number of well-received applications are submitted). Usually, the RFA will tell how many applications will be funded, as well as how much funding will be made available for this purpose. RFAs usually have special deadlines, and often the interval between the announcement of the RFA and the deadline is quite short—say, six weeks.

A call for applications can be very seductive; often, it sounds as though it were written with you in mind . . . almost. That "almost," however, can be a deal breaker. I would exercise caution about jumping into an RFA. You may find yourself changing your focus or design to fall in line with its requirements. If the changes are minor, that may not be a problem; however, meeting the details of the RFA will often require substantive modifications to your proposal, and you may find yourself proposing research that is quite different from what you had intended or what you really wanted to do.

A second caveat concerning RFAs concerns the "hit rate"—the odds of any one proposal being funded. The problem is that you do not know how many people will respond to the RFA. What you *can* know, however, is the hit rate for unsolicited applications using a given mechanism: for example, the hit rate for an R01. This varies from year to year, depending on the NIH funding level as determined by Congress.

In FY2003, for example, the hit rate for R01 applications (which are *unsolicited*) was, depending on the I/C, around 28% or 29%, which means that a little less than one application in three was funded. It is lower in FY2005 (around 18%–19%, meaning that less than one in *five* will be funded). If you want to know the precise rates (and you do), the awards data are available to you on the NIH site.[6] However, what you really want to know is the hit rate that will likely be in effect when your application is reviewed. It is not always easy to find these. Go to your I/C homepage and look for the information. It is usually located somewhere, but many of the I/Cs (not all) do not make it easy to find this information. Be dogged, and find it.

As I mentioned, the success rate varies by I/C, but it also depends on the specific grant mechanism (R01 versus R15, for example) and other factors. The hit rate on an RFA, in contrast, can be much lower. A couple of years ago, for example, I learned (long after the deadline) that there had been 42 applications for an RFA in which I had been interested. I did know, because it was stated in the call, that six were to be funded, yielding a hit rate of one in seven. For other reasons, I avoided the RFA and submitted an R01 (there was a budget restriction on the RFA that allowed applicants to request considerably less money than the R01), which was subsequently funded (the success rate for an R01 at that time was around 26%; do the math).

## THE COMPUTER RETRIEVAL OF INFORMATION ON SCIENTIFIC PROJECTS (CRISP) DATABASE

CRISP (Computer Retrieval of Information on Scientific Projects) is a database that contains information on grants and programs supported by the Department of Health and Human Services (HHS).[7] Most of the research has been funded by the NIH; a small number of research grants are funded by the Centers for Disease Control (CDC), the Food and Drug Administration (FDA), the Health Resources and Services Administration (HRSA), and the Agency for Healthcare Research and Quality (AHRQ). CRISP also contains information on the intramural programs of the NIH and the FDA. The database is updated weekly.

Why should you bother going into the CRISP database? For one thing, it may serve you to be able to examine a successful proposal that is similar, at least structurally, to the one you want to write. In addition, knowing what has been funded can help you avoid duplication. You can search the database in much the same way you search for a paper in PubMed: by topic, by author, by number, and so on. Who are the people doing research in your area? What kind of research are *they* getting funded to conduct? What methodologies do they seem to favor? You get the idea. It is not a bad idea to look up the research of the people who sit on your study section (we'll discuss how you figure out who these are in Chapter 8). You can obtain a full grant proposal by contacting the PI directly or by contacting the NIH, which under the Freedom of Information Act (FOIA) is required to share funded proposals. Contact the NIH Freedom of Information Office Coordinator for the appropriate I/C at http://www.nih.gov/icd/od/foia/coord.htm or call (301) 496–5633. There is a processing and copying charge for the service.

The following tip comes from an excellent article published in *Annals of Internal Medicine* that I highly recommend you read. Researchers can customize searches for grant information on several Web-based services, including the Community of Science (http://fundingopps.cos.com/), Grantsnet (http://www.grantsnet.org/), and the Illinois Researcher Information Service (IRIS; www.library.uiuc.edu/iris/). Note that some of these databases charge a fee.

SOURCE: S. K. Inouye and D. A. Fiellin. (2005). "An evidence-based guide to writing grant proposals for clinical research." *Annals of Internal Medicine, 142*, 274–282.

## CONTACTING NIH PROGRAM STAFF

One way to find out if your research ideas will be viewed with enthusiasm at the NIH is to ask. I think there is a reluctance on the part of many investigators, especially those just starting out, to call the NIH program staff for advice and guidance. This is a mistake. While it is true that under some conditions, communication between investigators and program officers must be restricted concerning particular topics, most of the time you can and are encouraged to talk to them. You'll find most of them helpful and friendly, although you may run across a program officer who may be less welcoming than others. As to restricted communication, ask your questions; if they're not allowed to tell, they'll let you know.

How do you know which program officer to contact? The best way, I think, is to ask someone who does work in your field whom to contact. If that doesn't work (although I see no reason that it wouldn't), go to the Web page for the I/C most likely be interested in funding your research: Find the research page, then find the contacts page. The contacts page will be broken up into major topics; find the closest one to yours and try e-mailing the first one on the list. If it's the wrong person, he or she will most likely write you back with a suggestion of whom to contact.

When it comes to developing your proposal, the program officers can provide invaluable information. Moreover, they have every reason to want you to be on track and to succeed; *this is not an adversarial process.* After you have done the necessary legwork (described in many of the earlier sections in this chapter), contact a program officer (I suggest e-mail for this purpose), lay out the most basic elements of your proposal, and ask if this is a study that the I/C might be interested in funding.

Here is one possible example of an e-mail that an investigator might send to a program officer:

Dear Dr. Jones:

My friend Roberta Smith [a researcher with whom the program officer will presumably be familiar] suggested I contact you to request a bit of guidance concerning a proposal I would like to submit to the National Heart, Lung, and Blood Institute (NHLBI).

I am a new investigator, interested in studying the effect of an exercise intervention that has been found to be effective in post–acute coronary syndrome (ACS) patients and on improvement of symptoms in African American patients with congestive heart failure (CHF). The exercise intervention is somewhat novel in that it incorporates aspects of tai chi, which uses low-impact, moderate exercise (found to be well-tolerated in elderly populations) with an aerobic training program. In addition to the clinical outcome (CHF severity), I am also interested in examining one possible mechanism by which this intervention might operate, which is the improvement in endothelial function and release of nitric oxide. My colleague, Dr. Jeffrey Arnaz, is a cardiologist who has specialized in the assessment of endothelial function, and he would serve as a co-investigator on the project.

I would like to know if you think this is a topic in which NHLBI would be interested and if you have any specific suggestions concerning the development of the proposal. I would appreciate any guidance you can provide on this. Thanks in advance for your help.

Sincerely,

James Johnson

Note that the message provides just enough information to give a broad picture of what the investigator would like to propose. Specific features—such as the amount of time until follow-up, for example—are not mentioned (and should not be, unless one is an outstanding feature of the proposal: for example, because it is an especially long period) or what instrument the investigator plans to use to assess severity of symptoms. This level of detail would be inappropriate to discuss at this stage. On the other hand, the investigator has not given such a broad outline (e.g., "I am interested in studying congestive heart failure in African Americans") that the program officer could not possibly be expected to comment.

One thing you might keep in mind is that you may regard yourself purely as a supplicant to the NIH; however, the NIH does not see you as such. You have something of value to offer, and it is in the interest of the program officer to help you stay on the right track. You will of course run into NIH staff members who are less helpful—the distribution of personality factors is much the same at the NIH as anywhere else—but if that occurs, you look some more until you find someone who will be willing to provide guidance.

Do, however, be careful not to expect more in the way of advice than is reasonable. The last thing you want to do is become a nuisance. The program officer is not there to help you design your study, so exercise good judgment in terms of your communications. Finally, I would suggest that, once you have established a good relationship with someone at the NIH, you continue to be highly considerate of that person's time. (I apologize to those of you for whom this advice is unnecessary; however, my experience has been that some investigators may allow their enthusiasms to overwhelm their judgment.) If and when you do have questions for the program officer, hold off asking them one at a time; instead, try to batch them. As with any colleague, your manner should communicate that you appreciate the time that the program officer spends and that you are taking care not to abuse that.

Before you contact the program officer, *do your homework*. Is there a PA or an RFA on your topic? You'll look like an idiot if there is and you didn't know it. Is the issue addressed in the Roadmap? Is there someone at your institution who has submitted an application on a similar topic? You should know this. Anyhow, don't be afraid to talk to the NIH staff. When you go to conferences, make a point of meeting them. Go to the breakfast and lunch roundtables; go to the talks. Hang out and introduce yourself. You're shy? Don't allow yourself and your career to be penalized because of that. Get someone to go with you and introduce you, if that will help. But getting out there and meeting important colleagues can be as important to your career as knowing how to write a good proposal.

## STRANGE BEDFELLOWS: POLITICS AND SCIENCE

If you are not already paying attention to the changing political climate in the United States and the world, it probably is time to begin. The funds you are hoping to be awarded from the NIH depend on the state of the federal budget; the budget is recommended by the president, and passed, usually with a host of negotiated modifications, by Congress. Because of this, the various agencies clamoring for the budgeted funds participate in a zero-sum game: If one gets more, somebody has to get less. At this point—September 2005—the next budget calls for almost a zero increase in funding to the NIH. Much of the monies that would otherwise have gone to fund research have been diverted to fight the war in Iraq, among other interests. Knowing the state of the federal budget affects my decisions about when to submit applications. For example, 2007 looks to be even more poorly funded than 2006; thus, applications that my colleagues and I were planning for the long term, to be submitted a couple of years from now, will probably go in sooner. I want to make sure that my lab is as secure as an enterprise that exists almost solely on NIH funding can be over these next few years. So, as unpleasant a prospect as it may be, you might want to start watching the evening news.

## PILOT DATA

The last item we will consider before you actively begin your proposal by selecting your co-investigators, which will be discussed in the next section concerns data you have collected that lay part of the foundation. Must you have pilot data? As you know by now, the answer depends on which grant mechanism you are planning to use. If you are submitting an application for an exploratory grant (R21) or some of the K awards, you don't need pilot data. If you are planning to apply for an R01, however, the reviewers will definitely want to see data that show (a) that you have the capability of collecting such data both in terms of your and your team's skill base and in terms of the resources you have at your disposal (this includes, for example, access to the relevant subject population); and (b) that your hypotheses and power estimates to determine sample size are based on data you have collected.

So, what do you do if you have no pilot data?

The best thing to do, of course, is to go out and collect some. It doesn't necessarily have to be a lot of data; in fact, you don't want to collect so much data that the reviewers will wonder why you need funding to go any further. If there is *any way* to do this, then do it. It is your strongest ammunition. If you cannot, all is not necessarily lost, but you have to show some finesse. What data *have* you collected? Are they in the same subject population? Do they employ the same laboratory preparations? Are they in the same or a similar species of animal? Was a similar intervention used in the collection of the data? Citing these data will at least help with one of the aims of pilot data, which is to demonstrate feasibility, and that goes quite a long way. Put it this way: If the reviewers are *not* convinced you have the capability to carry out the proposed project, they will give it a poor score, no matter how good the idea or how innovative the science.

The second strategy is to ask, Have any of your putative co-investigators collected data that would legitimately be considered as useful preliminary results for the proposed project? If not, is there a person in your department or division who *has* collected such data, and might that person be interested in joining the team? You would certainly describe those data in the Preliminary Studies section of your proposal (see Chapter 5); after all, it is not solely you, but your research team, who will be designing and conducting the proposed study. The reviewers want to see that among the key players on the team the skills exist. Of course, you have to weigh that using your common sense: If *all* the expertise lies with others, you will be regarded as not particularly a good candidate for PI. And, usually, these data tend to address the first concern, feasibility, and not the second, which is preliminary support of your hypotheses.

However, let me be clear: Without very relevant pilot data, an R01 will not be funded. It is better that you wait a while and work on collecting pilot data before you submit.

It is far, far better to wait until you can present the best proposal you can than to get one in prematurely. *Do not* assume that there is no cost to submitting a less-than-outstanding application just to be able to say that you submitted, or just to get the reviewers' feedback, or just to get your department chair off your back. Some of the same reviewers will be there next time around and may have a poor impression of your work before they even begin reading!

## CHOOSING YOUR RESEARCH TEAM AND CONDUCTING INITIAL NEGOTIATIONS

The first concrete step toward developing the proposal is deciding who should be on the team. Every investigator should be there for a definable purpose, which you will present in a couple of places in the application, including the Preliminary Studies section of the proposal (discussed in Chapter 5) and the Budget Justification section (discussed in Chapter 7). You will want to decide early on who will constitute the *key personnel*, as defined by the NIH.[8]

The selection of personnel and the writing of the proposal may influence each other to some extent. As you begin working out the specifics of your design, you may realize that you need to include someone with expertise in an area that nobody on your team currently has. Conversely, your design may call for expertise that is just not available to you, for one reason or another, in which case you may decide to cut that part of the study or modify it.

However, you should be able to select the key personnel pretty close to the beginning of the process. Reason out the large elements of the design, and this will help you identify areas in which you need help. These may include such items as blood assays, particular diagnostic procedures, subject recruitment, and data management and analysis. Having done that, go through the process again, this time considering key personnel across other parameters, including demographics (Do you plan to examine health disparities in minorities? Is anyone on the team a member of a minority group?), education (Are you a basic researcher who is studying a clinical problem? Would it help to have a clinical investigator on the team?), and discipline (I assume this one is obvious).

> Be careful about approaching colleagues to be co-investigators or to serve in other capacities on your proposal too quickly. You may later change the design and find you no longer need a particular person, or you may run into budget problems. There are few things more embarrassing than having to explain to a person why she or he has been uninvited to the party.

Once you have approached a colleague and she or he has agreed to participate, you must establish a few ground rules immediately. (Immediately! Do not put this off.) You should agree on the nature of the contributions this person will make both in the writing of the proposal and, if funded, in the conduct of the grant. You are very likely to run into a problem somewhere along the line with this, no matter how careful you are, and it's a big pain in the neck. Problems are more easily dealt with, however, if you can point to an earlier specific agreement.

> Two different people who reviewed this book manuscript suggested having a written contract with each team member, spelling out what he or she has agreed to do. I don't hold with this, myself. It sounds good in theory, but in practice feels like a very awkward process that may be off-putting to the person you want to work with. Sort of like a prenuptial contract. In addition, if the person is your mentor, it becomes absolutely impossible, in my judgment. Yet there are people who swear by this technique, mentor or no. If it works for you, great, but be extremely careful about how you broach the subject.

Finally, once your colleague has agreed to collaborate on the proposal and grant with you, you must agree on the percent of effort this person will allot to the project and be paid for. One way to help determine how much of this person's time you think you will need is to break it down into days per week: An effort of 10% means the person plans to devote one-half day a week to the research.

> If the person is not at your home institution, you will first have to agree on whether he or she will serve as a consultant or as a co-investigator; the latter requires that a consortium be established between your two institutions, and the decision has important implications for both of you. This is discussed in detail in Chapter 7.

## SUMMARY

At this point, we've established that

- Your institution is qualified to submit a grant application to the NIH.
- Your division chief or department chair has no problems with your plan to submit.
- Your mentors and close colleagues think you are at a good stage in your career to submit for the particular mechanism you have selected and also think that your idea has a good chance to fly.
- Your experience and publication record are appropriate for the mechanism for which you plan to submit.
- You have researched areas relating to NIH priorities, such as CRISP and the "Guide for Grants and Contracts"; you've read up on Healthy People 2010 and the Roadmap Initiative; and you've checked around to learn if anyone in your institution is planning to submit a similar application (or, by the way, an application for a similar mechanism; sometimes—but only sometimes—they are limited to one person per institution).
- You've made contact with an NIH program officer.
- You have begun rounding up a research team, have begun trying out the basic thrust of the proposal on them, and have established who is doing what and by when.

You're off to a good start. In the next chapter, then, we can begin discussing the writing of the science.

## NOTES

1. See http://grants1.nih.gov/grants/guide/pa-files/PA-00-019.html for the eligibility statement.
2. From http://grants1.nih.gov/grants/funding/r01.htm.
3. The URL for the Healthy People 2010 program is http://www.healthypeople.gov/default.htm.
4. More information on the NIH Roadmap can be found at http://nihroadmap.nih.gov/.
5. Funding opportunities related to the Roadmap Initiative are listed at http://nihroadmap.nih.gov/grants/index.asp.
6. Hit rates for NIH programs can be found at http://grants1.nih.gov/grants/award/award.htm.
7. You can access the CRISP database at http://crisp.cit.nih.gov/.
8. The NIH defines *key personnel* in a specific way. See the PHS (Public Health Service) 398 instructions, available at http://grants1.nih.gov/grants/forms.htm.

# Writing the Application, Part I

## *The Scientific Content*

5

Let's review: You've established that both your institution and yourself are eligible for the grant mechanism for which you want to apply; you have selected a mechanism that is consistent with your experience and credentials; you have lined up your research team; you have an idea for a study that you believe might be funded; and your word processor is fired up. Now, all you have to do is write down your idea in a manner that will be clearly understood by the reviewers, and you have up to 25 pages, depending on the grant mechanism, in which to do it.

I'm going to use the R01 as a model, as this is the most common type of grant; when differences arise for other grant mechanisms, I'll note them. In Chapter 7, we shall get to the form pages you should use, how to fill them out, how to develop a budget, and so forth; here, we are going to concentrate on writing the science. The sections of your proposal narrative are lettered, A through K (again, this may vary according to the grant mechanism); in this chapter, we shall mostly concern ourselves with the science: Sections A (Specific Aims), B (Background and Significance), C (Preliminary Studies), and D (Research Design and Methods). We'll discuss Section E (Ethical Concerns) in Chapter 6. Some of the K awards require additional documents, and I'll address that separately.

## GENERAL NOTES CONCERNING SCIENTIFIC WRITING

How important is good writing? My mentor in graduate school, who was justly well known for his writing, once explained to me that "if your *bubba* can't understand what you've written, you've done a poor job." ("Bubba" is Yiddish for "grandmother," for those of you who have never been exposed to the joys of that melodic language.)

You can find a great deal of very useful guidance about writing the proposal on the Web sites of the NIH, Office of Extramural Research (OER), and individual I/Cs, and I recommend you take advantage of this advice. The NIH provides a Web page entitled "Resources for Grant Applicants," which contains links to several other Web pages that contain grant-writing help.[1] In the following section, I focus on what I can add as a result of my experience, and that of my colleagues, and have condensed much of this into a few rules.

*Rule 1: Write from the reader's perspective.* Don't write from your perspective as the writer, but instead do your best to place yourself in the role of the person who is going to be reading your proposal. In the case of NIH grant proposals, you are usually writing for an audience of two or three persons, at least one of whom probably is *not* an expert in your specific area. In addition, you must understand the context in which your proposal is being read. Assume that your readers have only begun reading their stack of proposals on the night before the review, and that yours is the last one in the pile, being read at, say, 3:00 a.m.

You can look up the names of all the people on the study section that will be reviewing your application with little difficulty (see Chapter 8). However, you will never know specifically which three of them will have your application assigned to them. As you scan the list of reviewers, you may come across one or two that you definitely feel will be on your panel, and you may guess correctly—or not. So, write from the perspective of the reader. For example, you sometimes need to explain what *you* might regard as obvious. Thus, if you have described a particular measure in the Background and Significance section, remind your reader what this measure is about when you bring it up again several pages later, say, in the Research Design and Methods section. *Make it as easy on your reader as you can!*

> You may find yourself short of space: 25 single-spaced pages sounds like it should be plenty, but you will most likely find in your earlier drafts that you are over this page limit and must cut the narrative. One easy temptation is to cut out the spaces between paragraphs, but I urge you to resist doing this. It is easier and less tiring to read material that has white space to break up the text, and it serves the dual purpose of highlighting the fact that a new thought is about to appear and making the text easier to read. Pictures and charts also help for this purpose. You can save space, however, by using a half-line space, rather than a full one, to separate paragraphs. I do, however, suggest using a full line space, or more, to set off major sections.
>
> Also, use headings (sacrifice the space; it is worth it) and be creative about making them stand out: Use boldfaced type, italics, all capitals—you get the picture. Make sure that you have a consistent hierarchy for headings; major headings could, perhaps, appear in bold capitals, and for a secondary heading you might then use bold lowercase letters.

*Rule 2: Clarity is key.* Each point you make should follow logically from the previous one. Your writing should proceed along a straight line, as much as possible. When you must veer off that line, be careful to bring it back again. Just tell your story without gumming it up with a lot of unnecessary material. Sounds easy, but I assure you it isn't. As a reviewer, I can tell you that only a small proportion of the proposals I have reviewed have met this goal. Get feedback on this from your colleagues.

> Avoid the use of jargon. Aim to have the proposal be understandable without anyone having to ask or look up what a particular expression (or acronym) might mean.

*Rule 3: Keep it simple.* As you write up your idea, you will begin to see other lines of thought that you could add, although they may not pertain to the main focus of the proposal. This is particularly true for the measures you propose: You may decide to add measures that are peripheral to your main hypotheses, but that would be easy and inexpensive to collect and might contribute something that would add to the depth of your proposed study. You will undoubtedly be able to come up with legitimate rationales for including them, which means you have to begin writing off of the main point. Your motivation is a good one: You're already doing the study, so it would be easy to tack on extra measures, and if you add these measures to the proposal, you can show the reviewers what a great bargain they are getting, since you would be giving them two or three studies for the price of one. But *resist the temptation to do this.* You'll find yourself saying things like, "You know, it would be easy to get bloods on these subjects. . . . We could assay for genetic markers . . ." or "It would be great to get depression measures, since we're already getting self-report measures; it would add another outcome. . . . Who knows?" When you hear yourself or your colleagues uttering these sorts of statements, beware. I'm not merely being a purist, although this is not the way good science is done. I'm giving you extremely practical advice. Think about the following: Every measure you include should be directly linked to

A hypothesis

A power analysis

A statistical analysis

We'll address some of these topics later. In the meantime, if you add a measure for which you are not adequately powered to detect effects, you can try to get away with using a sample size that will be adequate to detect an effect in your *primary* outcome, but not (necessarily) in other outcomes, and hope the reviewers won't notice, but I don't recommend it.

> Just because you aren't going to mention a particular measure in the proposal doesn't mean you might not go ahead and collect that measure in the course of the study. Just fight the temptation to mention it in the proposal! (And of course, you have to find funds to do it.)

*Rule 4: Tell a story.* Think of writing a screenplay. Each scene in a good movie is designed to move the story along. Your proposal should follow the same principal: The story must unfold in such a way that the reader can follow it; it should never violate the reader's sense of logic; and it must do this in a manner that makes the reader want to know what will happen next. Good science is *interesting*, and interesting reading will improve your chances of getting funded!

*Rule 5: Communicate your excitement.* Make no mistake, when you write a grant proposal, you are trying to sell something to a specific set of customers. Just like the guy on TV who sells that great rotisserie oven, you must communicate your excitement about this important research, and you must excite the readers as well about (a) the importance of the topic; (b) the innovative new methods you have devised for studying the topic better than previously; and (c) the broad implications and, more specifically, the *public health* implications of the study.

You must walk a tightrope when you write a grant application: Your proposal has to be ambitious in its scope, but must never appear unrealistic in terms of what your proposed study is meant to accomplish and in terms of your ability to carry it out. A grant proposal must do more than replicate previous work, such as your pilot study. It must move the field forward! *That* is what the reviewers want to fund.

Journal reviewers tend to look for what is *wrong* about a submitted manuscript. If you avoid major flaws and weaknesses, the manuscript will likely be published. In contrast, grant reviewers tend to look for what is *right* about an application. Why is the proposed work needed, important, and exciting? How does your application give the NIH an opportunity to move the science forward? Where is the originality and challenge? Give the reviewers a reason to believe that, 20 years from now, they will be proud that they funded your work.

*Rule 6: Get feedback early on.* You need to ask your colleagues and mentors to provide feedback on your proposal. Remember, however, you're asking a fairly large favor: If they're qualified to read your stuff, then presumably they have plenty of their own work, and a good reading of someone else's proposal can take hours. Presumably, you have done and/or are prepared to the same for them, but you still have to be careful to show that you understand the amount of effort they are providing on your behalf. The rules are different for co-investigators, of course. Set a deadline for yourself of six weeks before the actual deadline to complete your draft proposal. Give your colleagues at least two weeks for their reviews.

Right now, you're nodding your head in agreement with Rule 6, but in the end, most of you won't follow through on this. You'll get busy, you'll fall behind, and you will be writing up until the last overnight shipment goes out (or until you have to hit the "submit" button, when the NIH goes to fully electronic submission). All good reasons, but they don't do you any good if you want your grant to be funded.

Here are suggestions for specific questions you might ask your readers to address:

- Were you persuaded that this study should be done and that the results would help to answer the question or questions that it purports to ask?
- Did the writing communicate a sense of my excitement about this project?
- Did you find the story easy to follow? Were there parts that sidetracked the story line?
- Did you feel that the assertions made in the course of telling the story were adequately supported by the published literature and/or my own data?
- Do you consider the project innovative?
- Were the methods appropriate to the study questions?
- Did you find the power analysis convincing?
- What limitations do you feel I should have addressed?
- Was the manuscript adequately proofread?

## WRITING THE PROPOSAL

There are four parts to the main body of an NIH R01 research proposal (these will differ for other mechanisms, such as some of the K awards): Specific Aims (Section A); Background and Significance (Section B); Preliminary Studies (Section C); and Research Design and

Methods (Section D). We shall take each. section separately and will provide a checklist of the main items that should be included in each. A more extensive version of the checklist, also containing important reminders, is provided in Appendix C. It might not be a bad idea to photocopy this section and slip it into your proposal as a guide.

It is important that you understand that the writing of the proposal is not necessarily a linear process. Actually, it should be regarded as interactive, in that not only will some sections need to be written before others (and not necessarily in the final order), but also, as you modify a particular section, it often will influence other, previously written sections. For example, I always begin with the Specific Aims section, as having aims and hypotheses should dictate everything else: what background I will need to provide, what research strategy is required to test the hypotheses, what preliminary studies I will need to describe to demonstrate the particular skills required to employ that research strategy. As you develop the research strategy, you may find that one or more of your aims just cannot be carried out for some reason: Perhaps it is just too expensive, perhaps the power estimates require a sample size to which you do not have access, and so you will have to rewrite the parts of the proposal that relate to that particular aim.

Do not make the mistake of writing a piece and assuming that part has now been set in stone, unless it is fundamental to the entire basis of the proposal. And for that matter, some proposals just cannot be carried out. If that is the case, you have to be able to see it, no matter how enamored you are of your research idea.

You will also need to be writing the budget almost from the beginning (Chapter 7 describes this process). The research will of course influence the budget, but the budget in turn will influence the research you can carry out. Obviously, there are items you can revise later in the grant-writing process, but you do not want to have to significantly modify your specific aims late in the game, as that will likely require rethinking and rewriting the whole proposal.

In Chapter 8, I discuss the importance of looking on the Web to see precisely who will be on the study section that will be evaluating your proposal. One reason for this is to identify potential conflicts of interest (of which you will inform the NIH), as well as to identify one or more persons who, for some reason, you feel cannot provide an unbiased assessment of your work. You cannot know exactly which of the 20 or so panel members will be reviewing your proposal, although you can make guesses. I want to urge you to look at the study panel early in the writing of the proposal, however, not toward the end. You may find panel members whom you might not thought to have cited and, needless to say, if one of them were a reviewer on your proposal, that omission would sit poorly. If there are panel members who have worked in the area in which your proposal resides, it would be wise to take account of their particular points of view and to incorporate these in the proposal. You don't have to agree, of course, but you should address them. Chapter 8 provides detail on where to look for this information.

## Formatting Rules

Before we begin discussing the content of the four sections, I am going to describe the formatting restrictions, some of which (such as font size) apply to all the sections, not just A to D.[2] First, you have 25 pages for the R01 in which to tell your story. The rules state that the type height should be no smaller than 10 point and there should be no more than six lines of type in a vertical inch (2.5 cm). If constant spacing is used, there should be no more than 15 characters and spaces per inch. Margins should be at least half an inch on all sides.

Note that RFAs and PAs may have special page limits, so pay attention to the call. The NIH recently came out with an addendum, noting that the following typefaces, in a font size of 11 points or larger, are now acceptable: Ariel, Helvetica, Palatino Linotype, or Georgia.

Having done the measurements, I don't know why they specify a 10-point minimum; my measurements indicate that the font must be at least 11 point, and I strongly recommend you use that. *Do not* play games with any of these parameters in an effort to cram in a few extra words. It is not worth it. You might get away with it—or you might not. When you read the PHS (Public Health Service) 398 instructions, you will see, set off in its own box, the following statement: "Failure to comply with the formatting and page specifications will be grounds for the PHS to reject and return the entire application without peer review." I have a colleague who told me that one proposal she reviewed started out in 11 point, went to 10 point after a few pages, and continued in this vein until they reached 8 point! Even if you don't get busted and have your application returned, you don't want to annoy the reviewer.

Please note that formatting is pertinent even when you begin using the upcoming procedures for online grant submission, with the new SF (Standard Form) 424 forms. You will be instructed to write Sections A through D using your word processing software, convert it to a PDF (portable document format) document, and then attach it; so, the formatting restrictions must still be observed.

## THE NIH REVIEW CRITERIA

The NIH provides an excellent summary of the five criteria by which reviewers are instructed to review an application. These were recently revised and made public in a release dated October 12, 2004.[3]

Much of what follows is repeated, in greater detail, in Chapter 9; however, it is obviously useful to have these in mind as you are writing the proposal, so I present the criteria here as well. Thus, here is where your purchase of this book pays off big time, and I urge you not to share this valuable, secret information with others: The five NIH review criteria are:

1. *Significance.* Does this study address an important problem? If the aims of the application are achieved, how will scientific knowledge or clinical practice be advanced? What will be the effect of these studies on the concepts, methods, technologies, treatments, services, or preventative interventions that drive this field?

2. *Approach.* Are the conceptual or clinical framework, design, methods, and analyses adequately developed, well integrated, well reasoned, and appropriate to the aims of the project? Does the applicant acknowledge potential problem areas and consider alternative tactics?

> The first and second criteria, significance and approach, should be addressed in Sections A (Specific Aims) and B (Background and Significance).

3. *Innovation.* Is the project original and innovative? For example, does the project challenge existing paradigms or clinical practice? Does it address an innovative hypothesis or critical barrier to progress in the field? Does the project develop or employ novel concepts, approaches, methodologies, tools, or technologies for this area?

> The third criterion, innovation, should be addressed not only in Sections A (Specific Aims) and B (Background and Significance), but also in Section C (Preliminary Studies), if innovation in technique plays a major role in the application, and, correspondingly, in Section D (Research Design and Methods).

4. *Investigators.* Are the investigators appropriately trained and well suited to carry out this work? Is the work proposed appropriate to the experience level of the principal investigator (PI) and other researchers? Does the investigative team bring complementary and integrated expertise to the project?

5. *Environment.* Does the scientific environment in which the work will be done contribute to the probability of success? Do the proposed studies benefit from unique features of the scientific environment, or subject populations, or employ useful collaborative arrangements? Is there evidence of institutional support?

> "Investigators" will obviously be addressed mostly in Section C (Preliminary Studies), in the beginning, where you will describe the research team. Although you will presumably address the fourth and fifth criteria, investigators and resources, on the Resources page (see Chapter 7), you also will want to discuss them throughout Section D (Research Design and Methods).

I suggest that when you begin drawing up an outline of your research proposal, you review these five criteria and make sure that you not only address these points, but that you also *draw attention* to them. Remember, the reviewers must read several applications; they have the criteria in front of them while they do so. You want them to literally be able to check off each one as satisfied.

## Additional Review Criteria

RFAs, which are published in the NIH "Guide for Grants and Contracts," may list additional requirements specific to the RFA under each of the above criteria. In addition to the above criteria, the following items will continue to be considered in the determination of scientific merit and the priority score.

*Protection of Human Subjects From Research Risk.* The involvement of human subjects and protections from research risk relating to their participation in the proposed research will be assessed. See the Research Plan (Section E) on Ethical Concerns in the PHS Form 398.

*Inclusion of Women, Minorities, and Children in Research.* The adequacy of plans to include subjects from both genders, all racial and ethnic groups and subgroups, and children as appropriate for the scientific goals of the research will be assessed. Plans for the recruitment and retention of subjects will also be evaluated. See the Research Plan (Section E) on Ethical Concerns in the PHS Form 398, or in the SF 424, depending on which you are using. Note that the Ethical Concerns section is discussed in detail in Chapter 6.

*Care and Use of Vertebrate Animals in Research.* If vertebrate animals are to be used in the project, the five items described under the Research Plan (Section F) for Vertebrate Animals of the PHS Form 398 research grant application instructions will be assessed.

*Budget.* Reviewers will consider the reasonableness of the proposed budget and the requested period of support in relation to the proposed research. However, the priority score should not be affected by the evaluation of the budget.

> Though the budget review *should not* affect the priority score, reviewers, being human, tend to look at the budget and may penalize you if the budget seems notably too high or too low. If the latter, they may take that as an indication of inexperience.

*Foreign Applications.* In addition to the regular review criteria, reviewers rate foreign applications for their ability to bring in talent or resources not available in the United States or to augment U.S. resources. Foreign applications have a good chance of getting funded if either the expertise or resources are not available here: if, for example, the proposed project provides access to a unique study population. Reviewers will check whether a foreign application proposes research similar to that being done by U.S. investigators and whether there is a need for the research. If similar research is being done, the application will suffer in review.

*Title.* See Chapter 7 for suggestions concerning the title of your project.

## THE ABSTRACT

The abstract should be written with care, because, unlike the rest of the proposal, it is read by *all* the reviewers, not just the few that have been assigned your application. It is usually the first thing the reviewers will read, and it *must grab the reviewers' interest immediately.* In addition, if the grant is funded, the abstract becomes public information; it is what people will see when they look up your research in CRISP. Finally, the abstract will help guide the assignment of the proposal to a particular study section.

The abstract should describe the nature of the problem or research question, the long-term objectives, the need for and innovative features of the research, the specific aims, and the research design and methods. This is a place where clarity is crucial: Write the abstract only after you have gotten fairly far along in the writing process, and then ask colleagues and co-investigators to read it and provide critical feedback. Test it out on colleagues who have not read the proposal, to see if they can easily understand what you have proposed, and how you have proposed to carry it out.

## SECTION A: SPECIFIC AIMS

The Specific Aims section assumes a great deal of importance because, except for the abstract, it is often the first thing that reviewers read. Therefore, it is likely to influence their perceptions of the proposed research and, equally important, of your abilities. The Specific Aims must accomplish a great deal in a short amount of space. In fact, let's deal with the space issue first: I always make sure that this section is no longer than one page, that it does not spill over onto a second page at all. Perhaps this is superstitious, but I have found that many of my colleagues agree with this strategy. It is also the length suggested by the NIH, although it is not a formal restriction.

What do you need to accomplish in this page? First, you must, in only a couple of paragraphs, get across the main thrust of what the proposal is about: You must provide a context for the research question you are asking, and then describe the question and why the reviewers should care about it; you will want to explain why your study is innovative and necessary to push the field forward, and note the relevance to public health concerns.

Finally, you need to provide a brief summary of the strategy that you plan to use to conduct the study. You need to provide a statement of your specific aims and hypotheses.

> Do not propose overly ambitious aims. Reviewers will worry that the scope of the work is greater than your budget and/or that the amount of effort you have allocated to the project will be insufficient.

## Note on the Sample Proposal

I provide an example of the various sections using a proposal written by two of my colleagues (with their permission, of course). I have, however, changed a great deal of the proposal to suit the needs of this book: Thus, I have deliberately weakened parts of it so I could point out problems and possible solutions, and I have greatly simplified it, again for expository purposes. All names and places are fictitious.

The examples will be annotated using reference numbers (e.g., {1}), and these will be provided in the order in which they occur, not in order of importance. Annotations will always appear on the same page as or on the page facing the example, so you won't have to flip back and forth.

## Necessary Elements of the Specific Aims Section

- A clear statement of the problem or question you plan to investigate
- Background material, to provide context for your proposal
- Why your proposal is innovative, needs to be done
- Public health significance
- What you plan to do (i.e., basics of design, primary outcome(s), study conditions)
- Specific aims or hypotheses

### Section A: Specific Aims, Example

*Abbreviations {1}*

| | | | | | |
|---|---|---|---|---|---|
| **ANS** | Autonomic Nervous System | **HRV** | Heart Rate Variability | **RSA** | Respiratory Sinus Arrhythmia |
| **BP** | Blood Pressure | **HTN** | Hypertension | **SBP** | Systolic Blood Pressure |
| **CVD** | Cardiovascular Disease | **MAP** | Mean Arterial Pressure | **UC** | Usual Care |
| **DBP** | Diastolic Blood Pressure | **RCT** | Randomized Controlled Trial | | |

*A. Specific Aims {2}*

Although drug therapies have greatly improved blood pressure (BP) control, 50% of hypertensives on drug treatment have inadequately controlled BP, which leads to excess risk for morbidity, and mortality, and produces a huge economic burden on the United States. {3} Promising

## Notes: Specific Aims Example

{1} The authors have provided a key to the abbreviations. The first time the term appears in the text, spell it out, even if you have provided such a key, and put the abbreviation in parentheses.

{2} Use these or similar headings to signal that a new major section is about to begin.

{3} Make reference to the public health implications of the problem.

behavioral approaches to BP control include diet and exercise, as well as stress-response–focused interventions, including anger management therapy, tailored stress-reduction approaches, and device-guided breathing and other biofeedback techniques. This application proposes to add to the evidence base for guided breathing interventions, as these have high patient acceptability, promising initial evidence, and no known side effects. {4}

Guided breathing interventions which slow the breathing rate to the 6-10/minute range have shown substantial effects on BP reduction in several published studies. Although the sample sizes of the studies are small, the results are highly consistent, ranging from reductions in systolic/diastolic BP (SBP/DBP) of 5.5/3.6 to 15.2/10.0 mm Hg. These effects are surprisingly large, considering the relatively brief practice sessions (daily 15-minute sessions for 8 weeks), and may represent an effective, accessible, cost-efficient way to help control BP in hypertensives. {5}

Three limitations of the published studies must be addressed before guided breathing can be recommended for widespread use: (1) To what extent are the observed BP changes sustained throughout the day and night? The Food and Drug Administration (FDA) requires that effective antihypertensive treatment lower the BP over a full 24 hours. So far, only one small study (N = 13) has examined the effects on ambulatory BP (ABP) {6}. (2) Is there anything special about breathing at 6–10 breaths/minute, or is it a nonspecific relaxation effect? Analyses of behavioral methods of treating hypertension (HTN), such as relaxation training, have generally concluded that the effects are not specific to the treatment modality. (3) What is the effect duration? Only one study, of 6-month duration, examined the effects of guided breathing on BP for more than 8 weeks. {7} It is worth noting that one would not expect an 8-week period of anti-HTN medication to have an effect on BP a year later; however, the expectation has been that effects of behavioral interventions should be sustained for long duration, after the initial treatment regimen has ended. The development of behavioral interventions needs to take into account methods to sustain long-term effects, and that is one focus of this application. {8}

Our aim {9} is to conduct a blinded, randomized controlled trial (RCT) to test the efficacy of a guided breathing intervention in poorly controlled hypertensives. Twenty-four-hour ABP is the primary outcome, which allows inspection of the diurnal pattern. We will include two control groups, *usual care* (UC) and *placebo*, the latter using a device that is identical to the guided breathing device, except that it does not slow the breathing rate. There are two intervention conditions: The interventions are identical, except that in one (standard duration) the intervention lasts the usual 8 weeks, and in the other (extended duration) the intervention is continued throughout the 12 months of the study.

{4} Note that the introductory paragraph covers the problem (hypertension is poorly controlled in spite of drug therapy), the public health significance, a proposed solution ("guided breathing" provides a promising adjunct/alternative to medications), and a context (50% of hypertensives have inadequately controlled blood pressure but there are promising behavioral approaches). This paragraph also gives a lead-in to the main goal of the study (to test the effects of the intervention on blood pressure in hypertensive patients).

{5} The second paragraph provides support for the rationale by describing results from previous studies, indicating that there is reason to think the intervention works, but that these studies are based on small sample sizes. The paragraph also addresses a subtle point: On the one hand, it demonstrates the possible utility of the intervention by discussing reported blood pressure changes; on the other hand, these changes are larger than one might have expected from such an intervention, and by labeling them as "surprising," the authors are, in effect, saying, "You are probably somewhat skeptical about these effect sizes, but so were we; however, there are too many studies to dismiss." You will have different issues to contend with, but the important point here is this. *Talk* to the reviewers through the language of your proposal if you find yourself wanting to explain or to let the reviewer know that there is a problem, but that you are aware of it and are solving it in the following manner.

Note that this paragraph also addresses the idea of cost-effectiveness, a consideration that is important to the NIH and that should be addressed in any clinical trial. Finally, the paragraph foreshadows your methods, which are usually given toward the end of the Specific Aims section, as are here. There are two good reasons to do this. First, early on, you want your reader to already have an idea of what you are planning to do; this is true of both the Specific Aims and the Background and Significance sections. That way, readers have a context that allows them to better understand other material you are presenting. Second, it means you can provide somewhat less detail in the later paragraph on methods, which already will be detail-laden.

{6} Ambulatory blood pressure provides a highly stable measure compared with clinic blood pressure and is a better predictor of target organ damage. This is explained in the Background and Significance section, but the authors are presuming, probably correctly, that most cardiovascular scientists will know this. Note also that the authors get very specific here about the one ambulatory monitoring study; that is some of their most compelling evidence, and they wish to underscore it.

I have urged you to write from the point of view of your audience (the two or three reviewers who will score your application). However, keep in mind the larger audience, the NIH as an organization, and its agenda. The NIH leaders must convince Congress to allocate a great deal of taxpayer money for the funding of research. To do this, they must show that they are solving a problem for those representatives and senators; the NIH has to address the public health implications of the research it funds. Most congresspersons will not be particularly excited to learn that a particular inflammatory factor tends to stimulate platelet activation when passing through the artery of a pig. However, they *will* get excited when they hear that progress is being made in basic processes that will reduce morbidity and mortality, as well as the economic burden, in the United States. Hit the public health implications hard and emphasize how your study will address them, whether you are a basic or a clinical researcher.

{7} Again, the authors provide detail about a particular study they consider important. This is a good practice, but don't do much of this in the Specific Aims section. Of course, you will repeat it in the Background and Significance section, but try to legitimately provide detail, including statistical outcomes (which the authors in the present example fail to do), regarding particularly relevant studies in Specific Aims.

{8} The authors imply a rationale for the proposal, which the reader *probably* gets. However, this should have been spelled out clearly (i.e., "We plan to use 24-hour ABP monitoring, and to test the effect of the intervention over a longer duration; this will provide information that will help answer the question. . . . "). However, the authors have made a crucial point here concerning the unreasonable expectations of a behavioral intervention that would never be applied to a pharmaceutical one.

{9} The authors here move to general aims, including the fact that the study will be a randomized controlled trial (which provides a particularly strong test of intervention efficacy), and they describe the design (the control groups to be used are always an important issue in intervention studies), the patient population, and the study duration.

Primary hypotheses (based on systolic ABP at 8 weeks): {**10**}

1. Participants in the two intervention conditions (which are identical until 8 weeks) will have lower ABP compared to participants in both the UC and placebo conditions.

2. Participants in the placebo control condition will have lower ABP compared to participants in UC.

Secondary hypotheses (based on systolic ABP at 12 months):

1. Participants in both intervention conditions will have lower ABP at 12 months compared to participants in placebo and in UC.

2. Participants in the extended duration intervention condition will have lower ABP at 12 months compared to participants in the standard duration intervention condition.

Exploratory questions concerning putative mechanisms: We plan to evaluate potential mechanisms that may mediate the effects of the intervention on BP, including baroreflex sensitivity, heart rate variability (HRV), changes in ambulatory respiration, and self-reported changes in physical activity and anxiety.

{**10**} The general aims are followed by specific hypotheses. If the proposal is intended to be exploratory, as would be appropriate for a mechanism such as the R21, it is appropriate to use research *questions* rather than *hypotheses*. However, if you are submitting an R01, then presumably you have a strong rationale, based on theory and prior research, that allows you to make predictions about the outcomes. (If not, you might be considering the wrong grant mechanism.) Hypotheses should be worded carefully, in a manner that clearly specifies a relationship between an independent and a dependent variable and that relates to the proposed research, which is presumably an empirical test of that relationship. The hypotheses should be simple. If you have a compound prediction—for example, one that involves an interaction— break it down. Rather than saying,

We predict that both variables A and B will have main effects on variable C, and that further, variables A and B will interact to produce an independent effect on variable C . . .

it would be better to write,

Hypothesis 1: We predict a main effect of variable A on variable C.

Hypothesis 2: We predict a main effect of variable B on variable C.

Hypothesis 3: We predict an interaction effect between variables A and B on variable C.

The exploratory questions in the example were labeled as questions, not hypotheses, for a strategic reason: This study is meant to focus on *clinical outcomes,* not on *mechanisms,* and the authors want to emphasize this focus. However, they thought that testing these putative mechanisms was important and that their absence would raise questions in the reviewers' minds, so they included them, even though it makes the story more complicated.

You must tell the reviewers why you think your total body of work is new and important. Don't be bashful about this: Hammer home the strong points, and do it early and often. Your goal is to communicate your excitement about your proposal, and to get the reviewer excited as well.

## SECTION B: BACKGROUND AND SIGNIFICANCE

### Necessary Elements of the Background and Significance Section

- The problem your study will address
- Why the problem is a public health concern and therefore important to the NIH
- What others have done to address this problem, and why that wasn't sufficient
- What you plan to do that is different from previous studies
- How your research will have an impact on public health
- Why your plan is novel, cutting edge, and should excite the reader
- An overview of your methodology
- Study hypotheses

Notice that these points, in the order they appear, will tell a coherent story. I'm going to show annotated examples of each of them, using the sample narrative begun above. I have deleted the citation numbers that appeared in the original proposal, so they don't get confused with the annotation numbers.

As you see, the authors of the sample proposal begin the Background and Significance section by repeating some of what they described in the Specific Aims section. It's okay to do this, but if you find yourself repeating a lot of material, then this suggests that you may have included too much background in the Specific Aims.

---

**Section B: Background and Significance, Example**

*B. Background and Significance*

Overview: {1} Drug treatment has fallen short of getting most treated hypertensives to goal (BP below 140/90 mm Hg). A highly promising behavioral treatment is guided breathing, which involves a device that guides the patient to slow the breathing rate to 6 to 10 breaths/minute (the typical respiration rate is 16 breaths/minute or more). The guided breathing intervention is typically used 15 minutes a day for 8 weeks, and several small studies have reported that after about 4 to 8 weeks, a BP reduction was observed. However, the existing studies are not adequate to establish the efficacy of the treatment: We describe potential mechanisms that may mediate the effect of guided breathing on BP, which we plan to evaluate. We propose an RCT, powered to detect effects of the intervention compared to both placebo and UC at 8 weeks (the typical intervention period), and at 12 months. {2}

---

### Notes: Background and Significance Example

{1} Often, you will find yourself in the position where you need to describe A, but that to *understand* A you will have to have told your readers about B first. Simultaneously, it may be difficult to describe B if your readers have not yet been told about A. An overview is a device that allows you to introduce concepts that your readers will need to have heard about before you can tell them about other concepts. Here, many of the salient points you will want the reviewers to have in mind while they read are presented concisely.

{2} Break up the text. Solid blocks of text cause fatigue and thus interfere with the simple telling of the story. Use tables and figures for this purpose as well.

In the telling of your story, you will need to use redundancy; your reader, who is not necessarily an expert in your specific area, will need to be reminded of some of the elements of your story more than once. Find a balance between providing the necessary prompts and being overredundant. It may be difficult for you, the writer, to make this judgment, so ask your readers for feedback on this.

---

*B1. Background {3}*

- **Pharmacologic treatment of HTN is effective, but is limited in practice. {4, 5, 6}**

   Drug treatment for HTN has advanced considerably in recent years, and RCTs have demonstrated that it significantly reduces BP and, as a result, cardiac events and death. However, drug treatment alone has significant limitations. It is estimated that only 53% of hypertensives on drug treatment, and only 1/3 of all hypertensives, in the United States have controlled BP. Medications are often expensive and may have side effects that limit adherence. Adherence problems and patient reservations about long-term effects of medications are increased in the 2- and 3-drug regimens necessary to achieve control in most patients; thus, treatment guidelines recommend adjunctive behavioral treatments that may play an important role in improving rates of BP control.

- **Nonpharmacologic treatment of HTN provides a useful adjunct to drug therapy.**

   A number of nonpharmacological interventions have been tested as adjunctive treatment for HTN. In this review, we focus on interventions that involve relaxation, biofeedback, and guided breathing. {7}

---

{3} A numbering system is helpful because it allows you to refer backwards or forwards to a specific section, so that the reader doesn't have to search for it. However, don't go crazy with it. Don't number every single paragraph (you'll end up with notations like "B.4.7.112."

{4} In the Background and Significance section, I use a technique in which I set off the main point in bold type and with a bullet; the paragraph that follows the bulleted heading provides detail and support from the literature. Doing so means that the story could be followed by just reading the bulleted statements. Again, it makes it easier for your readers to follow your story line. (And the occasional reviewer may, while reading it at 3AM, be just as happy to absorb only the outline, and take your word for the supporting materials).

{5} In this paragraph, the story begins with a statement of the problem. The authors could have begun with a bullet point that might have read, "Hypertension remains a large problem in the United States in terms of morbidity and cost," but when you find that you are over the 25-page limit—and you will—you will have to look for places to cut. The authors decided that reviewers did not have to be convinced of the dangers of hypertension, and cut it out. Cutting is an important part of the process, and the inviolate rule is that when you are over the 25-page limit, *something* has to go. Obviously, look for stuff that doesn't undermine the story; but even after cutting out optional bits, you may still be over the page limit. Begin rewriting: Tighten up the narrative and give it to colleagues who will see places where this can be done. Finally, you have to be ruthless: If it's a choice between *the critical* and *the very important,* cut out the very important. Do not play games like reducing the font size.

{6} Note that I am not presenting the full text of this grant proposal here, only enough to illustrate the points I am trying to make; thus, the story will skip here and there.

{7} Provide a context for sections to come. You don't want readers to have to go through three paragraphs before they figure out *why* you have put in this material.

*Psychosocial Interventions.* {8} Several studies have examined the effects of behavioral or psychosocial treatments for HTN, {9} targeting the stress response. Overall, the results have been inconclusive, and the consensus of medical opinion does not favor the routine application of relaxation and biofeedback techniques for HTN at this time. Also, results have been mixed: early studies have sometimes failed to replicate, and interventions have failed to produce clinically significant BP reductions over placebo conditions. The consensus in the medical literature has been that the studies to date do not demonstrate the broad clinical utility of stress-focused interventions. *Specific Relaxation-Based Interventions.* A number of different relaxation training interventions have been reported to have beneficial effects on BP, with effect sizes in the range of 9.0–9.7 mm Hg SBP and 6.1–7.2 mm Hg DBP (raw changes). {10} Interventions have included autogenic training, progressive muscle relaxation, mindfulness and transcendental meditation, and biofeedback. However, it has been difficult to demonstrate replicable differences between any specific treatment modality and active control conditions (i.e., other relaxation techniques or placebo relaxation interventions). {11}

*Biofeedback Interventions.* The two most recent meta-analyses of biofeedback treatment to reduce BP arrived at similar conclusions. Both showed greater overall differences in BP reduction compared to inactive control conditions (6.7/4.8 and 7.3/5.8 mm Hg SBP/DBP; Ochre et al. and Umber et al., respectively). Both analyses showed that studies with active control conditions had smaller comparative effects (2.1/3.4 and 3.9/3.5 mm Hg SBP/DBP), which no longer reached significance when baseline BP levels were controlled for. {12}

{8} Use headings to signal that a particular event is about to occur: The bulleted headings, for example, herald the beginning of a new thought. Use different headings to signal that some sort of grouping will occur.

{9} Abbreviations and acronyms can save a considerable amount of space; however, stick mostly with standard ones. When there is a long word or phrase that you will be using repeatedly and that you want to abbreviate, (a) define it at the top of the Specific Aims page; (b) define it in the text the first time you use it; and (c) if it is really important, and hasn't been used in several pages, *redefine* it. Don't make your reader go searching for it.

{10} Provide data, for example means or effect sizes, for important studies you have cited.

{11} It is often the case that the results you are citing are mixed. This is a pain because (a) they don't completely support the point you want to make, and (b) they gum up what otherwise would be a nice, linear story, the kind I have urged you to tell. *Do not* confuse "linear," however, with the omission of facts that don't fit easily into the story. Report them, even when they go against you. The reviewers tend to be pretty knowledgeable, and you will annoy them if they think you are deliberately omitting studies that do not support your proposal or worse, if they think you are truly ignorant of those studies. If there is more to the story that you believe *does* provide a strong rationale for pursuing your research question in the way you plan, then it is your job to do a good job of writing so that this emerges. Use foreshadowing if you need to (e.g., "Although these results have been mixed, we will show that this is due in large part to an inconsistency in methodology . . ."). If you cannot reconcile or explain the mixed results in a convincing manner, perhaps you just don't have a strong enough case to put forward.

{12} I have put in more of this material than perhaps you wanted to know about to make the point that it leads up neatly to the next point the authors want to make. They have discussed the various types of nonpharmacological interventions that have been tested; have described the strengths and weaknesses, making the case that such interventions, as a group, show promise; and then begin a new section, focusing on the intervention *they* intend to use.

**Section B: Background and Significance, Example (Continued)**

- **Device-guided breathing shows promise for nonpharmacologic control of HTN.**

Advances in technology and increased interest in HRV as an index of cardiac health and a means of exploring autonomic nervous system (ANS) inputs to the cardiovascular system have led to studies that use HRV biofeedback coupled with devices that guide the breathing to the 6–10 breaths/minute (0.1 Hz) range. {13} It is this range at which respiratory sinus arrhythmia (RSA; the differences in heart rate during inhalation and exhalation) {14} has its greatest amplitude. Although much lower than the typical ~16 breath/minute respiration rate, breathing in the 6 breath/minute range has been extensively studied in the laboratory and is apparently safe. {15} It appears that people compensate by breathing more deeply, and pulse oximetry and end-tidal carbon dioxide ($CO_2$) indicate that there is little effect on blood gases. All the studies to be discussed here have in common that the patient is instructed in and guided by visual and/or auditory feedback to breathe in the 6–10 breaths/minute range. {16} The reason for using a device to guide the breath is that people often find it somewhat difficult to reduce the breathing rate to that range initially and the gradual pacing provided by the various devices makes the transition more comfortable. {17} The results of the studies of guided breathing effects on BP are summarized in Table A, and the studies are discussed in detail below. {18}

## Notes: Background and Significance Example (Continued)

{13} In addition to the clinical outcome, which is the main focus of this proposal, the researchers also plan to collect data on a mechanism by which the intervention might work to reduce blood pressure. It is always crucial to provide biologically plausible pathways by which your effect could occur. Here, the authors foreshadow events that will come later. In Section D (Research Design and Methods), for example, they will describe methods by which heart rate variability will be assessed; so here, they lay the groundwork and rationale for including those methods. You do *not* want to bring concepts late in the proposal for the first time; this is akin to the nefarious device of bringing a new character into a novel in the final chapter whom we discover to have been a secret lover of the murdered victim.

{14} Don't assume that your readers know about technical matters that you may consider commonplace.

{15} Anticipate reviewers' questions and deal with them immediately. If you wait, for example, until the Research Design and Methods section, the reader will read several pages with this question, or doubt, in mind. A particular mind-set can influence the way subsequent material is perceived, and by the time you set things straight, the reader may already have formed a negative impression which may then persist in spite of information that appears later on that explains your reasoning.

{16} Again, the authors have provided a context for what comes next.

{17} Again, the authors have anticipated a possible question that might arise.

{18} Previously, the literature concerning the interventions (e.g., biofeedback) was summarized in just enough detail to presumably convince the reviewer that the conclusions being presented are a fair representation of what is likely to be a huge literature. That won't do here. The authors need to provide substantial evidence (a) that this particular intervention has been shown to be effective in other studies and (b) that, in the present case, although the evidence is suggestive, the work you are proposing needs to be done.

| Table A | | Results of Studies on Guided Breathing Effects {19} | | | |
|---|---|---|---|---|---|
| Author, Year | N | Study Design | Control Condition | Dependent Measure(s) | Outcome |
| Meles, 2004 | 79 | Open label; Matched Controls Tx: Paced breath + home BP | Home BP monitoring | Office and home BP | BP reduction: 5.5/3.6 mm Hg vs. 2/0.9 control (office), DBP $p < 0.05$ 5.4/3.2 vs. 1.9/ 1.0 mm Hg (home BP), for both SBP and DBP: $p < 0.001$ |
| Schein, 2001 | 61 | RCT Tx: Paced breathing | Relaxation (Recorded music) | Office BP | BP reduction: 15.2/10.0 mm Hg vs. 11.3/5.0 mm Hg (control) for DPB & mean arterial pressure (MAP) $p < 0.03$ |
| McCraty, 2003 | 38 | RCT (not all HTN pts.) Tx: Paced breathing + other stress mgmt techniques | Wait list control | Office BP | SBP reduction ($p < 0.05$): 10.6 mm Hg vs. 3.7 mm Hg (control) |
| Herbs, 1993 | 91 | RCT Tx: Paced breathing + HRV biofeedback (clinic sessions only) | Finger temperature biofeedback | Office BP | SBP reduction (results not significant): 12.5 vs. 10.0 mm Hg HRV positively correlated with SBP |

*Randomized Controlled Trial.* The most recent RCT was a multisite study, in which the devices (the breathing device plus home BP for the treatment group; home BP only for controls) were mailed to the participants with no instruction other than a brief manual and videotape. (This is in contrast to previous studies, in which participants were instructed in the use of the device in person.) The intent to treat analysis did not show significant differences between groups, although in patients with isolated systolic HTN ($N = 129$), device-guided breathing led to significantly greater BP reductions compared to the control condition. There was strong evidence of a dose-response relationship between the number of minutes of practice for the treatment group and the amount of BP reduction ($p < 0.001$ for trend). {20}

{19} This table contained four additional studies that I have deleted to save space.

{20} Again, I have cut out much of this material. I did, however, want you to see the sort of attention to detail that must be provided when needed to make your case.

---

**Section B: Background and Significance, Example (Continued)**

*B2. Innovation and Significance* {21}

- **Guided breathing may be an effective intervention to lower BP in hypertensive patients.**

The results of the studies shown in Table A are overwhelmingly positive, but are limited by several factors: the sample sizes in many are small, two do not have control conditions, and only one small trial ($N = 13$) used ABP as an outcome. {22}

The consistency of the effect sizes across the studies suggests that guided breathing may be a useful intervention to test in an RCT that is adequately powered and that uses ABP as its main outcome. Some of the results seem larger than one might have expected from a relatively mild intervention {23} (the intervention involves breathing in time to feedback, such as a series of musical tones, that guide the breathing to a slower rate—6 to 10 breaths per minute—for 15 minutes a day for 8 weeks). {24} Of the eight published studies, four of them show SBP reductions of 12 mm Hg or greater, a very large effect. Potential advantages of the guided breathing intervention are that it is easy to learn, pleasant to engage in, and relatively inexpensive (Respirco monitors cost around $200). There are no known side effects, and it is accessible to a wide range of at-risk populations.

As impressive as the evidence shown in Table A is, only one small study used ABP; however, it is ABP that must serve as the gold standard for this intervention, as it is not susceptible to the so-called White Coat effect (a systematic BP elevation that occurs in the presence of the physician and that may lead to misdiagnosis of HTN), has been shown to be a superior predictor of target organ damage compared to office BP measurements, and provides a means to assess BP during sleep. A strength of the present study is that ABP will serve as the primary outcome. Although home BP is a more useful outcome than clinic BP, home readings cannot be taken during sleep though they are usually taken when the subject is relatively relaxed; moreover, it is critical to know if the treatment also lowers BP when the subjects are active. Only ABP can answer this question, and the only study to use this included only 13 subjects.

*The Proposed Study.* {25} We propose to conduct an RCT to evaluate the effects of the intervention in hypertensive patients, one adequately powered to allow us to detect between-group

---

## Notes: Background and Significance Example (Continued)

{21} It is useful to separate "background" from "significance" so that the reader knows exactly what point you are making and why; note that the authors have used a heading to set this section off, as was done with the background discussion.

{22} In the previous section, the authors demonstrated that there is good reason to think the intervention works to lower blood pressure; in the present section, the authors explain why that literature needs to be extended. In other words, here is why the proposed study is needed.

{23} The point being made here is a subtle one, as was pointed out in the section on Specific Aims: The results of the published studies are actually surprisingly large; the authors are anticipating that the readers will notice that and are addressing the point, and they are also letting the reviewers know that they (the authors) are sophisticated concerning the larger picture. This is very important! Insert your comments when you need to and *talk* to the reviewers about such points. Don't let them think that you are naïve or not knowledgeable about such things.

{24} Notice the gentle reminder of what the intervention will involve.

{25} This is the home stretch. The storyline has gone something like this: "HTN is still a problem and drugs don't do an adequate job of controlling blood pressure for enough people; behavioral interventions help, and a particular behavioral intervention—guided breathing— seems worthy of further investigation. . . ." Now, the authors are at the point at which they extend that storyline by adding, "Here is what *we propose to do* in the service of further investigation." The authors will explain a bit about what they will later describe in greater detail in the Research Design and Methods section because, once again, the authors want to provide a *context* for what will follow.

differences in ABP at 8 weeks and 12 months. The study will have two control arms, UC and placebo, and two intervention conditions, guided breathing for 8 weeks (standard duration) and for 12 months (extended duration). ABP will be measured at baseline, at 8 weeks, and at 12 months. Additional outcomes are ambulatory respiratory rate and HRV, baroreflex sensitivity, physical activity and other health behaviors, and anxiety. These outcomes are also assessed at baseline, 8 weeks, and 12 months.

Our primary hypotheses address the outcome at 8 weeks. It is this time period for which we have the strongest evidence and the strongest rationale. However, we regard the 12-month outcomes (secondary hypotheses) as very important, for obvious reasons. Unlike our rationale for the primary hypotheses, however, our rationale for the secondary hypotheses is not well supported. {26}

There are at least two models {27} that pertain to the 12-month outcomes: (1) that, following the example of aerobic conditioning or medication, the intervention must be maintained to be effective (Figure A, the "Exercise Model"); or (2) that several weeks of exposure to the intervention causes a resetting of some regulatory process, and this will affect the BP for a sustained period of time (Figure A, the "Set-Point Model"). The secondary hypotheses, regarding the 12-month outcomes, are designed as a comparison of these models. The study described in Table A, by Schein et al., collected data up until 6 months (the longest duration reported), and they found sustained effects on BP (approximately 7/5 mm Hg for SBP/DBP), but these were attenuated compared to the effects observed at 8 weeks (15.2/10.0 mm Hg). Thus, these data do not allow a clear inference as to which of the two models best describes the process.

**Figure A**    Two Models by Which the Guided Breathing Intervention May Maintain BP Effects Over Time

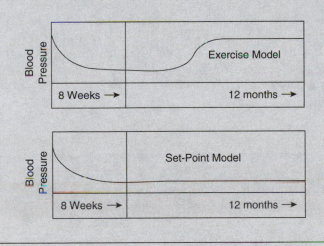

{26} Notice that, rather than trying to disguise a weakness in their design, the authors have laid it on the table. This was exactly the correct strategy, in part because they could afford to do it: It affects their secondary, *not their primary*, hypotheses, for which they have excellent support. Should you *ever* try to cover up an inconvenient fact? Well, yes, the situation may arise. However, it should be a minor point; if it is more than minor, and you feel you must disguise it, you have to consider whether you should be pursuing the question or the research strategy you want to propose.

{27} At all levels of science, from bench to clinical, reviewers like to see that you have thought about the alternative models that might hold for a given hypothesis, and that you have provided a thoughtful discussion concerning these. This is often a place where a figure or illustration will prove useful. The models provided by these authors are straightforward, uncomplicated, and tell their story clearly and simply. It is a good idea to provide a diagram, but do not make it overly complicated by dragging in variables or other physiological systems that are not necessary to the story you are telling.

*Mechanisms*

*Analyses Involving Potential Mechanisms Are Exploratory.* The main focus of this application is on the clinical outcome (i.e., ABP), and it is the measure on which our power estimates are based. However, because we will be seeing the participants over a sustained period of time (one year) and at several visits, we have the opportunity to collect data that will allow us to evaluate potential mechanisms at little additional cost or burden to the subjects.

It remains unclear why slowing the breathing rate for a few minutes a day should have these effects on BP. In addition to the clinical outcome, we will also collect data on potential mechanisms that may mediate the effect of the guided breathing intervention on BP. There is a specific physiological mechanism related to the controlled breathing that alters the regulation of BP. One candidate mechanism, suggested by Lehrer et al., is alteration of baroreflex sensitivity. Others include increased HRV and increased arterial compliance.

Let's discuss further an issue with which you will always have to contend: Inevitably, the science you are proposing (or are writing up for publication) is a simplification of what both you and your reviewers know to be a much more complex story. You should find ways to let your reviewers know that you are aware of these complexities, but you must not allow your proposals (or manuscripts) to get sidetracked by those complexities. I have seen this happen often and am occasionally guilty of it; it is difficult to avoid. Do not fall into the traps of (a) getting more complex than you need to in order to make your point, or (b) finding that your work never gets out the door because you have become frozen due to the innumerable pathways and systems, both inside and outside the body, that are genuinely relevant to your work but not necessarily to the specific issue you mean to address.

## Section B: Background and Significance, Example (Continued)

[Project narrative, continued.] {28}

Primary hypotheses (based on systolic ABP at 8 weeks): {29}

1. Participants in the two intervention conditions (which are identical until 8 weeks) will have lower ABP compared to participants in both the UC and placebo conditions.

2. Participants in the placebo control condition will have lower ABP compared to participants in UC.

Secondary hypotheses (based on systolic ABP at 12 months):

1. Participants in both the extended duration intervention condition (who continue the treatment throughout the 12-month study period) and in the standard duration intervention condition (in which the intervention ends at 8 weeks) will have lower ABP at 12 months compared to participants in placebo and in UC.

2. Participants in the extended duration intervention condition will have lower ABP at 12 months compared to participants in the standard duration intervention condition.

## Notes: Background and Significance Example (Continued)

{28} There are several pages of detail at this point, concerning the way in which, for example, guided breathing training might affect BP via the baroreflex sensitivity. I have cut this from the sample, but without knowing that it was actually present in the original proposal, the hypotheses, which come next and end this section, seem to appear somewhat abruptly.

{29} The authors have chosen to give the hypotheses here as well as at the end of the Specific Aims and beginning of the Research Design and Methods sections. It's a good idea, if you have the room, because it should fit logically into the story you have been telling so far. A useful technique is to end the Specific Aims section with a list of specific aims (which tend to be somewhat, but not much, less specific than hypotheses) and to end the Background and Significance section with the (presumably corresponding) hypotheses.

> The hypotheses given at the end of the Background and Significance section should relate directly to the specific aims given at the end of the Specific Aims section, and should be copied and pasted verbatim to the beginning of Section D (Research Methods).

## Summary

I have used the Background and Significance example to illustrate several principles or rules. First, the narrative here considers the reader: Terms are well defined, abbreviations explained, headings provided, and large blocks of type are broken up with white space. In addition, the section is written in a way that takes into account what the reviewers may be thinking as they read. So, new sections are set up with a preliminary statement explaining what is about to come and why, therefore, the authors have written this section and the reviewers are reading it. When issues arise that may be questionable or controversial in some manner, the authors explain their decisions. Note that they do *not* wait until the end of the proposal to discuss them; if they were to do so, by the time the reviewers would see the discussion, they may have already formed a negative impression. However, you should still include a limitations section near the end of the Research Design and Methods section; reviewers tend to expect it, and it is a good place to summarize your thinking about potential problems.

> Very often there is no correct answer to a particular problem, and every alternative has advantages and disadvantages. It is your job to select among them, make a decision, and explain your choices. A reviewer may or may not agree with the decision you have made, but at least will see that you are aware of the issues and have thought them through.

The story the authors are telling is a simple and clean one, and it is presented in such a way as to make the storyline easy to follow. The logic is explained, and no part of the storyline has been allowed to sag without the necessary supporting materials. When the study hypotheses are strongly supported in the published literature that is made clear; when hypotheses are less well supported and treated as exploratory, that is brought out as well. Again, the narrative was presented in such a way that the reviewers were made aware of the implications of having, or omitting, the more controversial hypotheses.

Finally, the authors really are telling a story. By now, you may feel that you know more about the potential effects of device-guided breathing on blood pressure than you ever wanted to, but you certainly were able to easily follow as much of the story as I provided. The authors actually gave a good deal more detail concerning the putative mechanism that may explain the clinical outcomes, but I omitted most of it because it wasn't necessary to my main points. You might also want to know, by the way, that the authors received a score that was *just* outside the fundable range, which means that the study section liked the proposal but wanted a few changes, and weren't ready to fund it first time out.

State concisely the importance and public health relevance of the research described in this application by relating the specific aims to the broad, long-term objectives. If the aims of the application are achieved, state how scientific knowledge or clinical practice will be advanced.

# SECTION C: PRELIMINARY STUDIES

The Preliminary Studies section is where you get to impress the reviewers with your capabilities to carry out the research you have proposed. Remember, the reviewers will be as concerned with this as with the quality of the science itself. Section C gives you a chance to tell the reviewers about the following:

- The names, degrees, and affiliations of the members of your team, and how long you have collaborated with them.
- The skills you and your team possess that are necessary to the project. For example, you may want to provide research abstracts that may not relate directly to the hypotheses or outcomes of the present study, but that demonstrate your competence, or that of a member of your team, in an area that will contribute to the conduct of the study. In the illustration, for example, the authors plan to measure heart rate variability and baroreflex sensitivity; presumably, at least one member of the team has that expertise and can provide abstracts or other support for the demonstration of those skills.
- Data that you and/or other members of the team have collected that *do* bear directly on the research question at hand (i.e., pilot data). Pilot data are more or less important depending on the mechanism you plan to use. For some K (career) awards or the R21 exploratory research mechanism, they are less important. For an R01 research award, however, they are crucial. Having gathered pilot data provides evidence concerning three important issues: (1) your experience in conducting research in the area in which you are requesting funding; (2) the feasibility of the project—that is, your ability, including appropriate institutional support, to carry out the proposed study; and (3) at least some support for your hypotheses, some evidence that you are on the right track.

Note that the Preliminary Studies section can be divided into two main areas: (a) Feasibility and Collaborative History and (b) Preliminary Studies.

Use the Preliminary Studies section to describe procedures that you have used in other studies and that you plan to use in the current study. This will demonstrate your expertise, and possibly that of your research team, as well as address the question of the feasibility of carrying out the proposed work.

## Necessary Elements of the Preliminary Studies Section

- Description of the team, including prior collaborations and relevant experience
- Studies conducted by the PI and key personnel that are relevant to the proposal
- Pilot data (for R01 and other applications that are not intended for [some] training awards or for exploratory research)

---

**Section C: Preliminary Studies, Example**

**C. Preliminary Studies**

*C1. Feasibility and Collaborative History*

This team has a great deal of experience in the conduct of clinical trials. Drs. Okata, Smith, and Ruggiero have successfully conducted many NIH-sponsored clinical trials over the past several years, including three that are currently ongoing, to test behavioral interventions and mechanisms through which they may operate. Drs. Smith and Ruggiero are both recognized experts in the measurement of BP. Dr. Smith pioneered the use of ambulatory devices for this purpose, and she and Dr. Ruggiero have instrumented several thousand patients over the previous 21 years of their collaboration. In summary, the team has the experience to address the requirements to successfully conduct the proposed trial. **{1}**

*Dr. Okata* (PI) is an internist with more than 10 years of experience working in primary care and subspecialty medical settings. He has experience as a co-investigator on several R01s and in developing and conducting multilevel behavioral interventions in primary care practices. Dr. Okata is currently a site PI on an NHLBI-funded RCT testing the effect of a stress-reduction intervention on BP. That trial, which will close before the currently proposed trial would begin, has studied the same population, using the same screening and recruitment methods, as those proposed for the current trial. **{2}**

*Dr. Smith* (Co-Investigator) is director of the New York Cardiovascular Health Program. She is a well-regarded HTN specialist and is currently the PI on an NHLBI-sponsored R01 that focuses on causes of essential HTN.

---

## Notes: Preliminary Studies Example

{1} Give an overview of the team, emphasizing their collaborative history, if any. I have used a fictitious PI who might not, on his own, have a record that would qualify him for an NIH R01. However, I have provided the PI with co-investigators who have a great deal of experience—enough experience between them to successfully carry off the proposed trial. Be careful, though, because this strategy can be a risk; you may still lose points on the qualifications of the PI (see Chapter 9 for the NIH review procedures).

{2} The authors have emphasized the fact that the proposed study will be carried out in a population (a) to which the team has access, and (b) with which the team has previous experience. This is especially important in terms of showing that you are able to *recruit* subjects into your study. Thus, the idea is not that you are going to get the same patients (most likely, you don't want them); it is that there is every reason to think that, if you were able to successfully recruit from this population before, you will be able to do so again. Note that the authors have been careful to explain that the previous study will have ended before the proposed trial would begin, so there is no worry that the two trials will be competing for the same subjects. This is precisely the kind of detail-oriented thinking you must do at the later stages of proposal development! Look ahead, anticipate difficulties that *might* arise, and address them immediately to forestall reviewers' concerns.

*Dr. Ruggiero* (Co-Investigator) is a top expert in the area of behavioral influences on autonomic control. His psychophysiological laboratory is set up to monitor electrocardiogram (ECG) readings for spectral analysis of HRV and continuous, noninvasive BP. With his staff, he has studied several thousand subjects, including healthy persons, heart transplant patients, and patients with implantable cardioverter-defibrillator (ICD) devices. In addition to his expertise in assessment of HRV, he has done extensive work in the assessment of baroreflex sensitivity.

*Dr. McBurney* is a recognized statistical expert with particular expertise in the areas of BP and HTN. Her work in the area of hierarchical models to study ABP has become a standard in the field. Dr. McBurney has worked with Drs. Smith and Ruggiero for more than 10 years. {3}

### C2. Preliminary Studies

Dr. Okata is site PI of a trial currently being conducted at the New York Medical Center (NYMC). This trial will complete patient accrual in October 2007. It is an RCT testing the effect of a multicomponent stress management intervention on BP in hypertensives. {4}

*RCT of a Stress Management Intervention (K. Okata).* The project focuses on patients at 10 community health centers, and in it, we have used several of the methods we are planning for recruitment in the currently proposed project. Thus far, this study has screened a total of approximately 6,000 people. We have seen an average of 460 persons at each screening and have found a 22% prevalence of HTN. Approximately 14% declined participation at the time of screening. Overall, of the eligible people we screened, we enrolled 55%. By the end of October 2007, we will have recruited a total of 400 hypertensives. We have, at this time, successfully retained approximately 90% of the participants

{3} Some studies or experiments will require little statistical analysis. In that event, you do not need to bring in a statistician, as you may have the skills to do the work yourself. Even with more complex designs, you don't need to have a statistician listed in the personnel so long as you or one of your co-investigators have documented expertise in the necessary statistics. If neither you nor the members of your team have the requisite expertise, however, you should consider enlisting the help of a statistician. For example, I am now involved in the conduct of multisite randomized clinical trials in which observations are clustered within sites—and this is just one of the more complex statistical issues that arises in such trials. I need to work with a statistician who has documented expertise in this particular area because there are subtleties that I am not qualified to address. A question that will arise is whether a statistician should join the project as *personnel* or as a *consultant*. In Chapter 7, I will talk about the difference. Briefly, though, a consultant is usually a person whom the PI lists on the proposal to help with a specific circumscribed aspect of the research, but who is not necessarily central to the science of the project.

As a rule, reviewers do *not* like to see that your statistical analysis will be handled by a consultant. For one thing, statistical analysis is an extension of the entire scientific enterprise, from the design phase onward, and needs to be an integral part of the study.

{4} Do not simply provide a list of several abstracts; an explanation about each should be given first, so the reviewers immediately understand why you are asking them to read this material.

whose 12-month evaluations have come due for one-year follow-up. Based on this experience, we feel comfortable that our accrual goals for this study are feasible. {5}

Dr. Ruggiero has published several studies concerning the relation between psychological factors and autonomic control, using spectral power analysis as the main outcome. He has examined these relationships both in the laboratory and in subjects' natural environments using 24-hour holter monitoring. He recently published the results of one such study in the *Journal of Important Psychophysiological Results*, 16:10–15, 2005. {6}

{5} Once again, the authors are taking the opportunity to showcase Dr. Okata's background, which, as I commented earlier, I have deliberately made somewhat thin in terms of what NIH reviewers might expect. It is possible that the authors are even overdoing it a bit, which might call attention to the fact that he has not yet been PI on an R01 (he is currently the *site PI* on a trial, which is a lesser distinction). However, they also are legitimately showing that Dr. Okata has experience crucial for running the study: He has conducted a randomized clinical trial, and has done so in the very environment he is proposing for the present study.

Dr. Okata's lack of experience places him at a disadvantage relative to other PIs who inevitably will possess far greater experience. However, the NIH is very interested in encouraging junior investigators, so they have acted to level the playing field a bit. There will be a place on the form, whether you are using the PHS Form 398 or the new SF 424, to note that you are—or are not—a *new investigator*. The NIH defines a new investigator as

someone who has not previously served as [an investigator] on any PHS-supported research project other than a small grant (R03), an Academic Research Enhancement Award (R15), an exploratory/developmental grant (R21), or mentored career development awards for persons at the beginning of their research career (K01, K08, K22, K23, and K25). Current or past recipients of Independent Scientist and other non-mentored career awards (K02, K05, K24, and K26) are not considered new investigators.

Being considered a new investigator is supposed to provide an advantage in terms of the standards to which the investigator's record and proposal will be held, although the enforcement of this policy has depended on who was leading a particular study section. However, the NIH recently announced that new investigators will be subject to less restrictive paylines (i.e., the score your proposal must receive in order to be funded; see Chapter 9). This is an amazing advantage as, very often, proposals fail by a couple of percentile points. Take advantage of this if you are eligible!

{6} Dr. Okata's data was a report of a study in progress. That is useful, but it is also useful to showcase peer-reviewed publications that demonstrate the investigators' expertise. The fictitious abstract shown here (note the publication information given) has little to do with the proposed study other than the fact that it, too, requires sophistication in the assessment of electrocardiograms for the purpose of assessing heart rate variability and baroreflex sensitivity. Thus, this paragraph is not intended to be pilot data, but is intended to testify to Dr. Ruggerio's expertise in this area. In the actual application, there were several more of these types of paragraphs—at least one for each of the investigators—but they did not add much more illustration than has already been shown, so I cut them in the example.

*Cardiovascular Autonomic Control and Hostility (R. Ruggiero).* We examined the relationship between anxiety and 24-hour HRV in 126 hypertensive patients who completed the Jones Anxiety scale and wore 24-hour ambulatory ECG recorders. We predicted that anxiety would be inversely related to the high frequency (HF) power response to psychological challenge. Support for this hypothesis would be consistent with the view that anxious persons engage in multiple episodes of anxiety throughout the waking day, with each episode causing a decrease in HF power. The cumulative effect of such episodes is lower levels of cardiac autonomic control in highly anxious subjects. As expected, there was a significant correlation ($r = 0.39$, $p < 0.05$) between anxiety score and HF power.

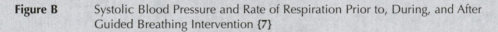

## Section C: Preliminary Studies, Example (Continued)

*C3. Pilot Data*

*Case Study.* We have examined the acute effect of the guided breathing intervention on the beat-to-beat BP in one subject, and simultaneously measured the breathing rate. The patient sat through a 10-minute resting period (baseline); the guided breathing intervention was then implemented for 15 minutes, and then the subject rested during a 12-minute recovery period. This patient had *not* been trained in the use of guided breathing; this had been his first session. Figure B shows the SBP and the breathing rate. Two things emerge: First, it is easy to see that the breathing rate, which averaged around 17–18 breaths/minute during baseline, quickly fell into the RSA-increasing range for this patient, averaging after the first few minutes slightly fewer than 5 breaths/minute during the intervention. As soon as the intervention ended, the breathing rate quickly climbed to approximately preintervention levels. The SBP averaged around 160 mm Hg during baseline, and fell during the intervention period (after the first 5 minutes) to less than 125 mm Hg. It climbed again once the intervention ended to a mean of approximately 150 mm Hg.

**Figure B**     Systolic Blood Pressure and Rate of Respiration Prior to, During, and After Guided Breathing Intervention {7}

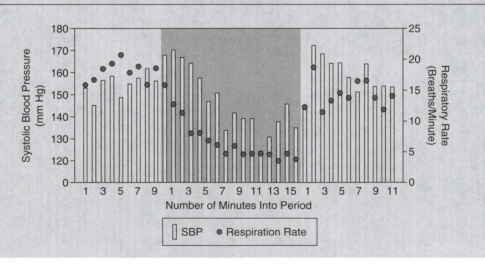

## Notes: Preliminary Studies Example (Continued)

{7} Note that a considerable amount of effort clearly went into this figure. Reviewers are just as human as anyone else, and a well-drawn picture catches the eye. Use figures when you legitimately can to break up the text, and find the person on your team who is best at configuring them.

While these data do not bear on the question of what will happen to the BP *after* having used the device for the 8-week training period, it does show what happens to the BP while using the device. The pattern seen here is similar to that seen in normotensives who use guided breathing techniques in the literature and who are able to change baroreflex sensitivity during slow breathing, but whose BP does not remain low in the immediate postintervention interval. Interestingly, in a small group of hypertensives that we tested in a similar manner, most continued to have BP that remained low immediately after the slow breathing and that was, in some cases, even lower in the post–guided breathing epoch than during the guided slow breathing. {8}

*Pilot Study.* We studied 5 hypertensive patients (3 male, 2 female) from our practice in an open-label trial with no control condition (approved by the institutional review board [IRB] and with informed consent for participation). All participants wore an ABP monitor for 24 hours at baseline, then were trained in the use of the guided breathing technique and instructed to practice 15 minutes daily for 8 weeks. ABP monitoring was then repeated. After 8 weeks of home practice, we found mean reductions of 11.6/5.4 mm Hg SBP/DBP in 24-hour ABP. We found that 3 of the 5 patients had a BP reduction that we would regard as clinically significant (> 5 mm Hg SBP). These results are in line with the one small, published study that measured ABP levels and support our primary hypotheses that the guided breathing procedure will reduce 24-hour BP at 8 weeks. {9}

{8} This is a nice little pilot study (of one person), but as you might guess, the authors are dancing as fast as they can. You can almost hear the conversation: "Well, it would be better if we had more pilot data. . . . What can we do that's quick and that will add to what we have?" The pilot data section would not have suffered unduly if this case study had not been shown. Obviously, it was a judgment call on the part of the authors to include it. After all is said and done, I agree with them: It is relevant and surely makes a pretty picture. (Incidentally, the reviewers did indeed see through the attempt; the main criticism of the proposal was that there were insufficient pilot data.)

{9} This is the real deal when it comes to pilot data. The number is very small ($N = 5$), but the results are in the predicted direction, and this little paragraph provides good support for going further with the study. Remember, you saw in the Background and Significance section that there were several small published studies (although not as small as this one), and only one that used ambulatory blood pressure monitoring—a much more convincing measure than clinic blood pressure for this purpose. So, all in all, this paragraph provides very important information. Also, the authors, having several months between the due date of the proposal and the reviews (Chapter 9 will discuss the timetables), are allowed to send in supplementary material, in which the sample size could be expanded.

## SECTION D: RESEARCH DESIGN AND METHODS

The Research Design and Methods section presents some particular challenges. It is the fussiest section, meant to be presented in what is often exhaustive (and exhausting) detail. In particular, you must address in detail how you plan to accomplish *each* of the specific aims. It can be difficult to write clearly, because you may need to present detail concerning one part of the methods so that the reader can understand a later portion, but the later portion needs to have been presented to provide a context for the former—and you can see the difficulties that must occur when you are violating the space-time continuum. Don't worry; there are ways around this, Einstein notwithstanding.

There is also the issue of precisely how much detail to present, and the example will address this question. Finally, this can be a section in which reviewers find points on which to downgrade your score. It is easier to ding an application on a solid methodological point than a more general or theoretical one, so this section must be crafted extremely carefully. Once again, you are going to learn more about how to conduct a clinical trial to evaluate the efficacy of guided breathing as a means of blood pressure control than perhaps you wanted to know, but it will serve as a means of illustrating these points.

Please note that, as with the previous sections, I have removed paragraphs that do not particularly illustrate any point I would like to make; thus, there may appear to be discontinuities in the section, but this is not due to the authors' lack of attention.

## Necessary Elements of the Research Design and Methods Section

- An overview of the methods you plan to use
- Hypotheses (identical to those given in the Background and Significance section)
- The study design, including strengths and advantages, and a discussion of possible alternatives and the reasons for not choosing them
- Subjects (population characteristics, inclusion/exclusion criteria)
- Informed consent procedures
- Recruitment and attrition information, including a flow chart (see Figure C) and a backup plan if recruitment is slower than expected
- Sample size and power calculations that address *each* hypothesis and each outcome measure
- Description of manipulation, intervention, independent variables, and control conditions
- Description of outcomes
- Procedures, including quality control measures to ensure high-quality data collection
- Randomization method and considerations (e.g., stratification, matching)
- Study timeline
- Measures used in the study
- Data management and missing values
- Statistical analysis
- Dissemination of results
- Potential limitations and solutions

---

### Section D: Research Design and Methods, Example

**D. Research Design and Methods**

*D1. Overview and Design*

We propose an RCT with two intervention conditions, standard duration ($N = 80$) and extended duration ($N = 80$), and two control conditions, placebo ($N = 80$) and Usual Care (UC) ($N = 80$). We will use a mixed design, examining the effects of the intervention on change in ABP (a within-subjects factor) across the intervention and control conditions (a between-subjects factor). {1}

---

## Notes: Research Design and Methods Example

{1} The Research Design and Methods section begins with an overview statement. By this time, the reader is vaguely familiar with much of this, so that it becomes easier to read and understand. However, you will also notice that each of the methodological points now become sharpened; that is, presented in finer detail. Thus, this is the first time a formal statement of the study design has been given.

Participants in the two intervention conditions are treated identically during the first 8 weeks (the typical period for this type of intervention); at 8 weeks, participants in the standard duration intervention discontinue the intervention, but continue in the study; those in the extended duration intervention continue the intervention throughout the 12-month period. A summary of the conditions follows:

Control 1: UC (no device given)

Control 2: Placebo (placebo device given, but only during first 8 weeks)

Intervention 1: standard duration (device used only during first 8 weeks)

Intervention 2: extended duration (device used for entire 12-month period) {2}

The intervention consists of the use of a device (Respirco in San Diego, CA) that guides the participant to reduce the breathing rate to 6 breaths/minute. The session lasts 15 minutes, and participants are asked to engage in sessions 4 days/week.

Participants in the placebo condition are provided with devices that are identical in appearance to those used in the intervention, with one exception: the placebo device does not guide to 6–10 breaths/minute. Instead, the participants listen to a set of random musical tones. The manufacturer has agreed to reprogram devices for this purpose (see letter). {3}

In the placebo condition, the device serves to create a 15-minute relaxation period, which provides a control that will allow us to evaluate (a) the effect of relaxation on BP; and (b) the effect of guided breathing on BP over and above that of relaxation. As in the standard duration intervention condition, the use of the placebo device ends at 8 weeks. {4}

The primary outcome is the difference between conditions in change in ABP between baseline (prior to randomization) and at 8 weeks; a secondary outcome is the difference between conditions in change in ABP between baseline and at 12 months. Additional outcomes are changes in ambulatory respiration rate, HRV, and baroreflex sensitivity, as well as in self-report measures of activity level and anxiety. {5}

*D2. Hypotheses* {6}

Primary hypotheses (based on systolic ABP at 8 weeks):

1. Participants in the two intervention conditions (which are identical at 8 weeks) will have lower ABP compared to participants in both the UC and placebo conditions.

2. Participants in the placebo control condition will have lower ABP compared to participants in UC.

{2} Although the conditions (or "arms") have been mentioned before, the authors now provide a summary to which readers can refer, making it easier for them.

{3} The authors specifically mention a letter from the supplier of the device to be used in the trials. It is easy for the authors to make claims about what will occur, but readers like to see evidence that such matters have actually been arranged. There is a separate section for letters (see Chapter 7).

{4} I think that this is a very creative and useful control condition. The authors carefully justify its inclusion: Without this control, the data would have been subject to an ambiguity that could not otherwise have been teased out. This is precisely the sort of detail that the reviewers will like.

{5} Once again, the authors give a very clear, straightforward statement, this time concerning the primary outcome.

{6} The hypotheses are repeated here to make it easier for the reader to match them up with the power analyses and statistical analyses.

Secondary hypotheses (based on systolic ABP at 12 months):

1. Participants in both the extended duration intervention condition (who continue the treatment throughout the 12-month study period) and in the standard duration intervention condition (in which the intervention ends at 8 weeks) will have lower ABP compared to participants in UC.

2. Participants in the extended duration intervention condition will have higher ABP at 12 months compared to participants in the standard duration intervention condition.

*D3. Design Considerations, Alternatives {7}*

*Why Not Use a Crossover Design.* We considered a crossover design. Such a design is useful when there is no possibility that the intervention will have carryover effects. Here, however, we are particularly interested in the possibility that the intervention will have carry-over effects (see the "Set-Point Model" in Figure A). Thus, a crossover design would not have allowed us to test the primary and secondary hypotheses in this study.

*UC Condition Is Not Really Usual Care.* An issue faced by all RCTs is the design of the control conditions. Usual care, in particular, presents a particular challenge, in that simply participating in the trial often affects patients' behavior. Our decision to use home BP monitoring in the UC condition was the result of a compromise: We must have comparable measures across conditions to allow us to understand the processes by which effects may be occurring; however, we do not wish to impinge on that effect. The main focus of the proposed trial is the clinical outcome; however, this is meant to be an efficacy, not an effectiveness, trial. {8} Thus, we felt that the current configuration was the best compromise possible.

{7} This portion of the Research Design and Methods section is very important. The authors provide explanations of methodological decisions they anticipate will arise in the readers' minds. Notice that these explanations are quite close to the beginning of the section, so that they are able to defuse those concerns as soon as they arise. Many authors put these in a section at the very end; by now you know why that may not be wise, although I recommend you do also include a limitations discussion at the very end of the Research Design and Methods section. Worse, many authors don't put them in at all, perhaps hoping they will not occur to the reviewers. Not a good idea.

{8} An *efficacy* trial tests whether a given intervention *can* have a clinical effect under controlled conditions; an *effectiveness* trial tests whether the intervention *will* have a clinical effect under naturalistic (less controlled) conditions.

## Section D: Research Design and Methods, Example (Continued)

*Potential Confounding Due to Changes in Medication, Especially in the Control Condition.* In an intervention in which the experimental group is predicted to show an improvement in the outcome measure, and in which participants in the control condition are predicted to show no change, there is always a concern that the attending physician may use other methods to control the illness, making it difficult to interpret the results. To minimize this possibility, we shall take the following steps.

At screening, potential participants will be informed that their BP is higher than recommended levels, and the research assistant (RA) will suggest that they see a physician. They will be told that if, as a result of the screening, they *do* plan to see a physician for possible treatment, they will not be admitted to the study immediately, but only after they have seen their physicians. If no new treatment has been prescribed at that physician visit, they may then be admitted to the study; if new treatment has started (either new medications or increased dosages of medications the participant is already taking), the participant will be told that, after 2 months, he or she may be rescreened (to allow the change in treatment to take effect and stabilize) and, depending on the results, may then be admitted to the study. We will recruit only persons with BPs of *no higher* than 165 mm Hg (SBP) or 100 mm Hg (DBP).

### D4. Participant Population

*Clinical Sites and Participant Population.* {9} The NYMC is a tertiary care teaching facility and medical school that draws its patients from the greater New York metropolitan area. There are 22 community health centers that fall under the NYMC umbrella, and the study will be conducted in 12 of these. Across the 12 centers, the patient population is very diverse, with 35% Caucasian, 29% African American, 19% Latino, and 16% Asian, and there are a total of 46,000 patient visits annually. (See the Letters of Agreement section.) {10}

To recruit patients, we will use a strategy that has proved successful in a trial that Dr. Okata is currently running in this population. {11} We estimate that approximately 30% will have a screening SBP greater than 140 mm Hg, or DBP greater than 90 mm Hg. More than 40% of those with hypertensive screening BP levels are African American, and this group is overrepresented in the hypertensive diagnostic group, as would be expected. Our experience with this population suggests that of those with screening BP in the hypertensive range, 15% will have normal BP when assessed using ABP. {12}

### D5. Screening, Recruitment, and Attrition

*Physician Referrals.* The 12 referring physicians (one at each site) have a total of > 52,800 patient visits/year with, between them, 15–20 new patients each week. We estimate that we must recruit 692 patients over the 4-year recruitment period. Assuming a 20% refusal rate, and 15% who are normotensive by ambulatory monitoring, that total will yield 400 patients to be randomized for the study. Given the patient flow, we anticipate that we should easily be able to recruit the required number. Figure C shows the screening and recruitment goals.

## Notes: Research Design and Methods Example (Continued)

{9} Whether you are proposing basic or clinical research, you must persuade the reviewers that you have the capabilities to carry out the research. If you can't do that, no matter how good or innovative the science, your score will suffer. Give specifics about the sites, the patient flow, the patient demographics, and so forth or, in the case of basic research, provide details concerning the laboratory space and equipment and, if appropriate, facilities for maintaining animal subjects.

{10} Whenever you are claiming that resources outside of your control (in this case, outside clinical sites) will provide some sort of service or product necessary for the conduct of the study, it is a good idea to provide letters. Also, in this instance, the authors are implying that, if you look in the Letters of Agreement section, you will find 12 letters from these sites (that is, from someone who has the authority to provide access); however, if you were missing a couple of them, that would probably pass without comment.

{11} Note the reminder that the researchers have experience in this particular patient population, which will increase the reviewers' confidence that recruitment will go as planned.

{12} The researchers begin giving the breakdown that leads to the number of subjects that will need to be screened so as to end up with the number they want to end with.

*Screening.* Based on the prevalence of hypertension in this population, and our experience with the proportion of persons who will remain hypertensive using ABP monitoring, we anticipate that we will need to screen a total of 1,960 participants (there will be 12 screening periods, with an average of 163 persons screened at each). Based on our current study, which uses the same techniques, we anticipate that we should be able to recruit the required number of patients.

*Attrition.* We will overrecruit by 20% to allow for dropout, so we will begin with $N = 100$ and end with $N = 80$ in each of the conditions. This means that, beginning at Month 6, we will need to recruit 11 participants per month throughout the recruitment period. To enhance retention, we are offering a financial incentive for study completion. Further, we will request the names, addresses, and telephone numbers of three friends, neighbors, or relatives who would know how to get in touch with the participant in the event of a missed appointment. **{13}**

**Figure C**          Flow Chart of Screening and Recruitment Needs **{14}**

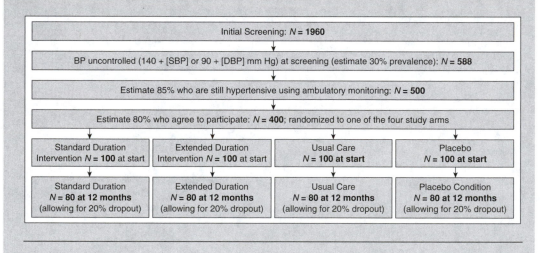

{13} Give a good amount of detail concerning issues of recruitment and attrition. Explain your plan to overenroll, and by what percentage, to allow for dropout; explain what procedures you will institute to retain subjects.

{14} Provide a chart like this one that summarizes the assumptions at each stage and that clearly shows how many subjects you need to screen. Note the extreme attention to detail the authors provide. Also, on a separate note, the more exclusion criteria you have, the lower your yield, and the more screening you have to do. And, of course, you pay a penalty in terms of the generalizability of your results. Just something to keep in mind.

Describe in detail your plans to sample—or oversample, if necessary—in different minority populations. Chapter 6 describes the NIH requirements to recruit women and minorities; it is incumbent upon you to describe outreach efforts, in the event they are needed, to recruit from populations that may not necessarily be represented in what you might consider your main population or populations. You do not want the reviewer experiencing doubt about your ability to recruit not only the absolute number of participants, but the appropriate composition, by sex and minority status, as well.

**Section D: Research Design and Methods, Example (Continued)**

*D6. Sample Size and Power {15, 16}*

We propose a design in which there are four arms, with 80 subjects *completing* the 12-month study in each arm. **{17}** ABP is assessed at baseline. In addition to the baseline measures, ABP

## Notes: Research Design and Methods Example (Continued)

{15} In the course of laying out the Research Design and Methods section, there is no set "correct" order in which to place the sections, and the order may vary in different proposals. It is clear, however, that some parts of the methods need to be explained before you can go on to other parts. Thus, it makes sense to begin with hypotheses, and then go on to explain the study design. Although you may not want to provide details concerning the independent variables at the very beginning of the Research Design and Methods section, you need to provide some information early on so that your readers have some context for the later sections. I usually put the discussion of sample size and power after my description of the sample. However, you may sometimes prefer to put it just before the discussion of statistical analysis, which often comes much later. As with every section, where you place it in the narrative should be a function of how the story unfolds, such that each section advances the storyline, even here in the Research Design and Methods section.

{16} The discussion of power is very important. If you are not intimately acquainted with this topic, I advise you to take the trouble to learn about it. If you cannot find a course at your institution, then look for workshops given at conferences, and, of course, there are any number of texts that will provide the basics. If you are not a sophisticated statistician, I advise you to hook up with one who is well versed in power calculations. You can find programs that will allow you to perform simple power calculations in many lower-level statistics texts or on the Web. However, these are usually appropriate for only the most basic and straightforward of designs. Once you move into more complex realms, you need someone who really knows this topic to help you. The reviewers pay close attention to the power calculations.

You probably know that there are different approaches to power estimates. You can begin with an effect size, gleaned from the literature or, preferably, from your own pilot data, and this can lead to a sample size. Often, however, you will—for various reasons, including economy or limited access to subjects—have a sample size in mind when you begin. Researchers can and often do fool a bit with the effect sizes so that they end with the sample sizes they want. There is some give, here, if it will really help you, but be careful about getting carried away. Do not fall into the trap of saying whatever you think you must to *get the money*, although you will be tempted. If you underpower your study, you are likely to fail to see significant effects, may end up wasting years of your time, and have little to show when you apply for your *next* grant. If you find yourself sorely tempted in this regard, rethink your research strategy.

Most researchers agree that it is desirable to have a minimum of 80% power for a given effect (although 90% is the standard for clinical trials); sometimes, you may end up with *greater* power than that, as in the example. The only reasons to *avoid* very high power levels, like those we see in the present study, are (a) that you may end up with more subjects than you needed, and therefore greater expense; and (b) that you may, ironically, end up finding statistical significance in comparisons that fail the test of clinical significance. Be aware of the controversy over the value of statistical tests. The course I take is to have a high regard for statistical significance, but also to have an equally high regard for effect size. In the sample study, I have saved space by omitting the power estimates for the secondary measures in which the power declines to just above 80%; you may need to provide yourself with very high power for some variables when the power declines for other analyses.

{17} The authors make a clear distinction between *assignment* of participants ($N = 100$ in each arm) and the anticipated *completion* ($N = 80$ in each arm) of the program by those participants—and note that the authors highlight the distinction by using italicized type. These are precisely the kind of details that you do not want to miss.

outcomes are assessed at 8 weeks (i.e., at the end of the intervention period) and at 12 months. The power estimates are broken into two sections, corresponding to the two follow-up assessment points. Primary outcomes are change in SBP from pretreatment.

*ABP Comparisons at 8 Weeks.* Based on previous studies, we hypothesize the ABP changes shown in Table B. We further assume a homogenous within-group variability corresponding to a standard deviation of 13 mm Hg. Based on these assumptions, our standardized effect size (f) for the overall analysis of variance (ANOVA) is 0.26, which is conventionally characterized as a medium effect size. With 80 patients in each of the two intervention conditions and 80 patients each in the placebo and UC groups, we will have a power of 0.98 to detect an overall effect using a nominal alpha level of 0.05. The planned orthogonal comparisons that reflect the specific study hypotheses and that will follow up the overall ANOVA are described below. {18}

The first comparison tests the effect of the device (whether guided breathing or placebo) relative to UC; the second and most critical comparison establishes the effect of the intervention relative to the placebo device. (See Table B.)

**Table B**          ABP Comparisons at 8 Weeks {19}

| Comparison | Expected SBP Change at 8 Weeks | Standardized Effect Size (Cohen's d) | Power to Detect Effect |
|---|---|---|---|
| Intervention (standard + extended) plus placebo vs. UC | Intervention + placebo: 8 mm Hg UC: 2 mm Hg | 0.46 | 0.95 |
| Intervention (standard + extended) vs. placebo | Intervention: 10 mm Hg Placebo: 5 mm Hg | 0.38 | 0.91 |

*ABP Comparisons at 12 Months*: In these analyses, the placebo and UC groups are each expected to have a 2 mm Hg (SBP) change at 12 months relative to baseline. Thus, participants in the placebo condition (those who gave up the device at the end of 8 weeks) will be combined with the UC group (N = 160), and the main focus will be on the standard duration and extended duration intervention groups. We expect that the extended intervention group will continue to maintain a 10 mm Hg decrease in SBP at 12 months relative to baseline, whereas we anticipate that the standard duration group will only partially maintain the treatment effect, showing a decrease of 6 mm Hg after 12 months relative to baseline. Based on these hypothesized effects and a homogenous within-cell standard deviation of 13 mm Hg for the SBP change, our overall ANOVA will have an effect size of f = 0.19 and our power will be 0.86 (using a nominal alpha level of 0.05). {20}

The two more critical follow-up orthogonal planned comparisons are summarized in Table C.

{18} Note the clear explanation of how the power estimates were arrived at.

{19} A table is a good way to present the estimates that pertain to each of your hypotheses. The authors here give specific contrasts, with estimated differences between them.

{20} Recall that the hypotheses were broken into primary and secondary hypotheses. However, the authors do not use this split to avoid powering the study to be able to detect effects in the secondary hypotheses (the smallest estimate is still around 80%). Thus, this section, and the second table, address those hypotheses.

**Table C**      ABP Comparisons at 12 Months

| Comparison | Expected SBP Change at 12 Months | Standardized Effect Size (Cohen's d) | Power to Detect Effect |
|---|---|---|---|
| Intervention (standard + extended) vs. UC plus placebo | Intervention + placebo: 8 mm Hg UC: 2 mm Hg | 0.23 | 0.81 |
| Extended vs. Standard intervention | Extended intervention: 10 mm Hg Standard intervention: 3.3 mm Hg | 0.51 | 0.90 |

As discussed earlier, you may have framed your predictions as "specific aims" or as "hypotheses," or both. In addition, you may have "primary aims" and "secondary aims," and "primary hypotheses" and "secondary hypotheses." To which of these must you power? Here is a general rule: Power to primary aims, and to any hypotheses, primary or secondary; do not power to secondary aims. This rule may have an impact on what you make the focus of your study; that is, if you plan to study a particular (primary) outcome, but will *not* be able to claim sufficient power to detect effects (possibly due to budgetary constraints or patient flow constraints, etc.), do *not* keep that outcome as your primary. This may mean you have to go back to the drawing board, or it may mean that you can identify a different outcome for which you *will* have sufficient power, and possibly you may treat your original aim as secondary. Of course, do not select an outcome solely for that reason. It must be one that is germane to your research question, and that the reviewers will regard as a worthy target.

## Section D: Research Design and Methods, Example (Continued)

*D7. Eligibility Criteria* {21}

Inclusion criteria:

- Aged 18 years or older
- Screening SBP of 140 *or* DBP of 90; in patients with documented heart disease or diabetes, SBP of 130 *or* DBP of 80
- Fluency in English or Spanish

## Notes: Research Design and Methods Example (Continued)

{21} Think out your eligibility criteria carefully. When the rationale for a particular criterion is not obvious, make sure to provide it. This is a point on which reviewers will fault you if you do not provide sufficient and clear information. Finally, you should copy this section in its entirety and paste it into Section E (Ethical Concerns; see Chapter 6).

Exclusion criteria:

- Being deemed unable to comply with the protocol
- Having a significant uncorrected hearing or visual impairment that would make it impossible to correctly use the intervention and BP monitoring devices
- Having an arm circumference of > 47 cm (oscillometric BP cuffs do not give accurate readings for arms of this size)
- Participation in any other HTN-related clinical trial

*D8. Description of the Intervention*

The device (by Acme, Inc., Paramus, NJ) consists of. . . . {22}

*D9. Description of the Control Conditions* {23}

*D10. Procedures*

*Personnel.* The research assistants (RAs) will conduct the screenings, patient scheduling, consent, enrollment procedures, and chart reviews. The RAs will be supervised by Dr. Okata.

*Screening and Recruitment.* . . . {24}

*Reminder Telephone Call.* Persons who are eligible at the initial screening and who desire to participate in the study are given an appointment for the initial visit and are told that they will receive a phone call the night before the appointment. {25}

*D11. Randomization Procedures* {26}

We shall follow the Consolidated Statement of Reporting Trials (CONSORT) guidelines wherever appropriate in this application, including in the description of the randomization procedures.
Unit of randomization: Individual.

*Method Used to Generate the Allocation Schedule.* Dr. McBurney, the project statistician, will create the randomization allocation by generating random numbers and placing subject assignment in sealed envelopes.

---

{22-24} Omitted to save space.

{25} This discussion of the reminder call illustrates the level of detail you need to consider. Try to anticipate *every* problem you could conceivably run into, and incorporate a methodological procedure to address it at the outset. Probably no reviewer would have criticized you for failing to have included this section; but they will certainly note your attention to detail because you *did* include it.

{26} Not all studies involve randomization, but most do, and this is an issue to which reviewers pay close attention. In a simple study, simple procedures are appropriate, but sometimes they need to be more elaborate. The present example is of a clinical trial, concerning which several journals have endorsed the CONSORT (Consolidated Statement of Reporting Trials) guidelines. CONSORT seems like a very neat method of breaking down the procedures, so I suggest using it for your clinical trial proposal, and it sets the stage for the later publications to come.

*Method of Allocation Concealment and Timing of Assignment.* Assignments will be generated within randomly sized blocks, so it is impossible for project staff to anticipate the likely group assignment of an individual at the end of a block by process of elimination.

*Method to Separate the Generator From the Executor of Assignment.* The sequence of assignments will be held by Dr. McBurney or a data manager in his office in Queens, New York, off site from the project, and they will be contacted by phone by project staff when the staff are ready to randomize a participant. Nobody who is connected with the conduct of the trial will have access to the records.

Dr. McBurney's office will keep a record of who was randomized to which group and will check that those randomized are analyzed in the correct group.

### Section D: Research Design and Methods, Example (Continued)

*D12. Visits* {**27**}

*D13. Timeline* {**28**}

Table D outlines the screening and visit schedule. Each screening contains $N = 163$ and each cohort contains $N = 33$ subjects. {**29**} The start-up period covers Year 1, months 0–3, and the tailing-off period is Year 5, months 6–12.

## Notes: Research Design and Methods Example (Continued)

{27} Omitted to save space

{28} Always provide a timeline. It may not look like this one, but it should provide the reviewer with a clear sense of when the major milestones are meant to occur. Note that this timeline leaves 3 months at the beginning of the proposal for start-up—in this case, going into the various health centers and working with the personnel there to ensure they understand and will cooperate with the procedures, developing a database, and so on. In a complex trial, such as this one, I might have left 6 months for start-up at the beginning. The reviewers will not balk at this; they would prefer to see that you are truly ready when you begin and that you will have had time to iron out the wrinkles *before* you begin studying actual subjects. Note, also, the tailing-off period, which provides time to get the database organized and to analyze data.

{29} A general point regarding both Table D, the timeline, and Figure C, in which the authors showed how they arrived at the screening numbers: In both cases, note the attention to detail, which allows the reviewers to easily follow the logic and understand the decisions that are being made. Obsess over the details; have someone else look at your tables and figures and see if they can draw the correct conclusions from them without having to expend a great deal of effort. I have seen several proposals in which the math was left ambiguous, leading to the inference that the author was either unaware of the proper methods or was careless; neither of these inferences help your cause. There will be other such issues that require close attention, depending on the specific proposal you plan to write. Note that, in the timeline, you can clearly see when any given cohort of subjects begins and when that cohort ends. You can also easily see the rate of recruitment that must occur for the study to remain on schedule.

**Table D**      Screening Timeline

|  | Months 0–3 | Months 3–6 | Months 6–9 | Months 9–12 |
|---|---|---|---|---|
| Year 1 |  | Screening #1 | Screening #2<br>Visit 1, Cohort 1 | Screening #3<br>Visit 1, Cohort 2<br>Visit 2, Cohort 1 |
| Year 2 | Screening #4<br>Visit 1, Cohort 3<br>Visit 2, Cohort 2 | Screening #5<br>Visit 1, Cohort 4<br>Visit 2, Cohort 3 | Screening #6<br>Visit 1, Cohort 5<br>Visit 2, Cohort 4<br>Visit 3, Cohort 1 | Screening #7<br>Visit 1, Cohort 6<br>Visit 2, Cohort 5<br>Visit 3, Cohort 2 |
| Year 3 | Screening #8<br>Visit 1, Cohort 7<br>Visit 2, Cohort 6<br>Visit 3, Cohort 3 | Screening #9<br>Visit 1, Cohort 8<br>Visit 2, Cohort 7<br>Visit 3, Cohort 4 | Screening #10<br>Visit 1, Cohort 9<br>Visit 2, Cohort 8<br>Visit 3, Cohort 5 | Screening #11<br>Visit 1, Cohort 10<br>Visit 2, Cohort 9<br>Visit 3, Cohort 6 |
| Year 4 | Screening #12<br>Visit 1, Cohort 11<br>Visit 2, Cohort 10<br>Visit 3, Cohort 7 | Visit 1, Cohort 12<br>Visit 2, Cohort 11<br>Visit 3, Cohort 8 | Visit 2, Cohort 12<br>Visit 3, Cohort 9 | Visit 3, Cohort 10 |
| Year 5 | Visit 3, Cohort 11 | Visit 3, Cohort 12 |  |  |

## Section D: Research Design and Methods, Example (Continued)

*D14. Measures Used in the Study {30}*

All study measurements obtained from patients will be assessed by trained RAs. Study measures are divided into three categories: (a) self-report measures, (b) physiological measures taken in laboratory, and (c) ambulatory physiological measures. Table E summarizes the measures (by modality) and notes which measures will be given at screening, baseline, and 12 months.

**Table E**      Measures Used in the Study at Specific Visits {31}

| Measure | Screening | Baseline | 8 Weeks | 12 Months |
|---|---|---|---|---|
| *Self-Report Measures* |  |  |  |  |
| NYMC demographic form | X |  |  |  |
| Branson self-reported adherence questionnaire |  | X | X | X |
| Current medications (from patients' medication vials) |  | X | X | X |

## Notes: Research Design and Methods Example (Continued)

{30} Always include a section about each of the measures you plan to use. Explain the purpose of each (e.g., is it meant to be an outcome, to provide a basis for stratification, to be used as a statistical control?). I have actually cut out most of the measures in the example to save space, but I'm sure you get the point with these few.

{31} It is not always necessary to include such a table doing so depends on the complexity of your design. In the example, I have simplified the table: There were actually several more visits than I have mentioned, and several more measures as well. You can see, however, how the table helps to avoid any possibility of ambiguity concerning the timing of the measures.

| Physiological Measures Taken in Laboratory | | | | |
|---|---|---|---|---|
| Height/weight | | X | | |
| Casual BP | X | X | X | X |
| Respiration rate | | X | X | X |
| ECG/(HRV) | | X | X | X |
| Beat-to-beat BP (for baroreflex sensitivity) | | X | X | X |
| *Ambulatory Physiological Measures* | | | | |
| ECG/respiration | | X | X | X |
| BP | | X | X | X |
| *Chart Measures* | | | | |
| Co-morbidities, antihypertensive medication changes | | ⟵ (retroactive) | | X |

*D14a. Self-Report Measures* {32}

*NYMC Demographic Form (SDF).* We have developed an instrument to collect sociodemographic data to allow us to properly describe the cohort and examine effects of these factors on BP control. Variables include age, gender, household income, education level, marital status, employment status, and health insurance status.

{32} If you are going to use self-report measures, use standardized, validated measures whenever possible. If no measure that does the job exists in the literature with which you are familiar, search on the construct to see if a measure has been developed for use with, say, a different patient population; you may be able to modify such a measure and still retain some of its reliability/validity. If you must make up a measure from scratch, try to keep it simple—preferably, one that requires self-report of a set of behaviors rather than items from which you attempt to infer, say, a personality construct or a patient's self-rating of symptom severity. Doing the latter just gives the reviewer an easy opportunity to criticize your proposal. In addition, when you do use self-report measures, acknowledge the limitations on the interpretation of such data.

> Be careful regarding patient burden. It is tempting to pile on measures and visits, but reviewers will consider whether they believe that patients will actually do all of it. Pilot data regarding this aspect of the study will provide important ammunition; if you don't have your own pilot data, data from a different study using a similar population and with a similar patient burden may suffice.

## Section D: Research Design and Methods, Example (Continued)

*Branson Medication Adherence Questionnaire.* Data on medication adherence will help us to interpret the effects of the intervention on BP control. Adherence to prescribed antihypertensive medications will be assessed using the well-validated 6-item scale developed by Branson that specifically addresses adherence to a prescribed medication regimen. It has been utilized in other studies of hypertensive patients and found to have a Cronbach's alpha of 0.9. {33}

*D14b. Physiological Measures Taken in Laboratory {34}*

*D14c. Ambulatory Physiological Measures*

*ABP.* We will use the well-validated Kaplan (Pomona, CA) model 1234 ABP monitor. {35} Monitors are validated for each person. BP readings will be taken simultaneously by the monitor and the RA, who has been trained in these procedures by Dr. Smith. The RA uses a T-connector and a mercury sphygmomanometer and stethoscope; readings are then compared. For validation to be considered successful, the mean agreement between the two sets of readings must be within 5 mm Hg. Subjects are instructed about reading failures, which are usually attributable to arm movement. In the event of a failed reading, the monitor will make one attempt, 2 minutes later, to obtain a valid reading. Subjects are also given a telephone number that they can call to speak to an investigator or technician if a problem with the ABP monitor occurs. {36}

*D14d. Chart Measures*

At discharge, the RA will conduct a chart review to abstract data on co-morbidities and antihypertensive medication changes. The purpose of these data is to assist in the interpretation of the BP outcome. A random sample of 20% of the charts will be reviewed by a second coder, who is blind to the first coder's ratings, and interjudge ratings will be calculated to ensure reliability.

## Notes: Research Design and Methods Example (Continued)

{33} Here, the authors provide a measure of reliability, Cronbach's alpha. (If you are not familiar with these and other measures of reliability and validity, you should be. I strongly advise you to learn about them. They are relevant for all types of measures, not just self-report.) Is alpha sufficient? I would say not. Cronbach's alpha gives you an estimate of one type of reliability (the extent to which the items tend to cluster), but most reviewers will want to see an estimate of test-retest reliability (the extent to which a score remains stable over time). Also, reliability is necessary, but by no means sufficient: Why should we believe that a score on this measure, even if it is stable over time, is actually indicative of the "true" underlying construct (for example, self-report of adherence to prescribed medications)? We also want to see evidence of validity of the measure. Such data should be available in the literature; if they are not, find a new measure, if one exists.

{34} In the interests of saving space, I am only showing you particular sections on which I wish to comment. Of course, a paragraph should be provided for each measure, including physiological measures. The next section provides an example.

{35} I have removed the reference numbers from the example because I didn't want them getting confused with my annotation references. However, the authors provided several published references to support their assertion that this monitor has been tested for both reliability and validity.

{36} The authors give a good amount of detail (which I have abridged) concerning the validation and use of the monitor. As always, you cannot assume that your readers are familiar with the device you plan to use or that they will make the assumption that you will conduct the necessary validation procedures (there will be analogous issues for most physiological measures). As always, put yourself in the place of your reader and assume you don't know much about this device. What information would you require? Then, assume that you, as the reader, *do* know a good deal about the device. What will you be looking for?

It is worth noting that one section I cut here concerned data editing. Your narrative should, for example, address what algorithms will be in place when outlier readings occur. You are presumably the expert regarding whatever measures you plan to take (or your co-investigators and/or consultants are); you should know—or learn about—the less obvious questions that may arise.

---

### Section D: Research Design and Methods, Example (Continued)

*D15. Data Analysis/Statistics*

*Overview of Approach.* The proposed research is a RCT with an intervention arm, a placebo arm, and a UC arm. The primary aim of this trial is to determine if a guided breathing intervention has a significant and positive effect on lowering SBP, measured with an ABP monitor, after 8 weeks of intervention. {37} Thus, our primary analyses will be based on the intention-to-treat, with results from baseline carried forward for subjects who do not complete the trial. Subsequently, we will examine the long-term effects of device-guided breathing at 12 months. This phase of the study (i.e., involving the 12-month outcomes) will have two treatment arms representing subjects whose use of the device was of standard or extended duration as well as two comparison arms that include the placebo and UC groups. We again propose an intention-to-treat approach in our primary analyses. Our general analytic strategy is, therefore, a one-way ANOVA on the change scores between baseline and 8 weeks (the primary aim) and between baseline and 12 months (the secondary aim). Our power and sample size calculations are based on this analytic strategy. {38}

---

Many researchers do not provide citations for their proposed statistical analyses. Obviously, if the statistics are to be fairly simple (e.g., t-tests, correlations, analyses of variance [ANOVA], regressions, or simple nonparametric tests), you don't need to provide citations. However, when using more complex procedures (e.g., multivariate analysis of variance [MANOVA], simultaneous equation modeling, hierarchical modeling procedures, and so on) or a procedure that is in any way controversial (e.g., contriving a post hoc test to examine differences between groups in a mixed design), provide references to provide validity for your statistical approach.

## Notes: Research Design and Methods Example (Continued)

{37} I have deliberately kept this section as short as possible, because the statistical analyses will differ widely from study to study. In this case, however, the design is a simple and straightforward one (the more so, since I cut some complexities out of the design). Note that the authors give a very brief summary of the study design so as to set up the context for the analyses. You can see that they point out that the analyses will be conducted separately for the 8-week and the 12-month outcomes.

{38} Note that, before launching into the specific statistical methods, the authors have provided a clear statement that recaps the design and provides a context for the specifics. The use of the main analytic procedure (a mixed-design ANOVA) is justified; the computation of the within-subjects changes are explained (i.e., the difference in the outcome between the 12-month follow-up and the baseline measurements); the two different phases of the study (8 weeks vs. 12 months) are again touched upon; and the data analyses are tied to the power analyses. The next paragraph continues on in this vein, but this time focusing on what are meant to be the secondary analyses, concerning the mechanisms (or, possibly, moderators).

Unless your design is very simple and requires only t-tests, chi-squares, or simple ANOVAs, I would describe the statistical models, using the appropriate Greek symbols, and provide details concerning any nontrivial part of the analysis.

### Section D: Research Design and Methods, Example (Continued)

In the process of addressing these aims, we also will be able to explore a number of other secondary questions, including mechanisms that may underlie the effect of guided breathing on SBP and the possible moderating or conditional effects of other variables on the results. For these analyses, we will use multiple regression/correlation approaches to take advantage of the continuous nature of many of the proposed mediating or moderating variables. Although motivated by prior research and scholarship, we recognize the exploratory nature of these analyses in the context of this treatment-outcome study. We will be appropriately cautious in our inference strategies (e.g., adjustment of probability levels for claims of statistical significance), and we have focused our analyses and power on the primary aim. {39} More specifically, we intend to test the possibility that the effect of guided breathing on SBP change will be mediated by the effect of guided breathing on the baroreflex. And we intend to test the moderating effect of adherence on the treatment group–SBP change relation, with the specific prediction that increased adherence will enhance the treatment effect. {40}

## Notes: Research Design and Methods Example (Continued)

{39} Labeling a particular analysis as "exploratory" does not relieve the investigator of the responsibility to explain how you are going to control for Type I error (the probability of rejecting your null hypothesis when it is true). In the unlikely event you are not intimately acquainted with the issues of Type I and Type II errors, I advise you to learn about them before you submit your proposal. The reviewers will be well versed in them, and will be looking for instances in which your results may capitalize on chance. Here, the authors explain that they are aware that these analyses are exploratory, but they also explain (albeit possibly in too little detail) how they plan to correct for the increased Type I error due to the increased number of separate exploratory (i.e., no a priori hypotheses) analyses.

A reviewer will jump all over a proposal that looks as though it seeks to capitalize on chance—that looks like a "fishing expedition." To the extent that a hypothesis is strongly justified on the basis of theory and prior results, Type I error is less of an issue (but it is always an issue). Thus, I have seen proposals in which "cardiovascular change" is given as the outcome, measured as systolic and diastolic blood pressure, heart rate, heart rate variability (of which there can be three or four measures), and hemodynamic pattern (i.e., peripheral resistance, cardiac output, and several other measures). If you have multiple outcome measures, you should be prepared to make specific predictions for each of them separately. If, say, only one or two of those measures show the predicted effect, is that sufficient to say that a hypothesis concerning the omnibus construct, cardiovascular change was supported? If you do not have specific hypotheses about *each* individual outcome, you should be prepared to use statistical controls of some sort to protect against Type I error. And this is an even greater problem when you are analyzing research questions or exploratory hypotheses rather than your primary, well-grounded study hypotheses.

{40} The authors could have gone into more detail concerning the statistical models they plan to use: for example, the equations that underlie the procedures. In the present example, however, the design is very straightforward and so are the analyses. It is worth noting, though, that the first ANOVA they plan involves the three study arms, but they do not mention what they plan to do subsequently if the ANOVA is significant. That is, do they propose planned orthogonal comparisons (which would be legitimate in the present case) or more conservative post hoc analyses? In any case, it should have been discussed.

---

**Section D: Research Design and Methods, Example (Continued)**

*Data Management.* In the past two years, we have changed from having subjects hand-enter data, which then requires data (double) entry into a computer, to instead using a system in which data are entered both by the RA and the subject directly into a tablet PC with a touch-sensitive screen. Data are then directly entered, via an interface that our programmer has designed, to a central database; the interface also allows the other electronic data collected in the proposed study (from ABP monitors and holter monitors) to be directly entered into the same database. This minimizes the time spent entering and checking data, and fewer errors result from these procedures. {41}

*Preliminary Analyses and Data Preparation.* Prior to conducting the main analyses, all variables will be screened for inconsistent or abnormal values, and continuous measures will be assessed for skewness and outliers. Transformations to reduce heteroscedasticity and/or the effect of extreme values on the statistical analyses will be used, if necessary. We will also use exploratory graphical methods to assess the effect of these transformations on the linearity of the data.

   Missing data rates and patterns will be assessed; in particular, missing data rates by treatment group will be studied. For the primary analyses, we will use intent-to-treat approaches and carry observations forward. However, for the secondary measures, including questionnaires, we will consider several approaches to handling missing data: maximum likelihood estimation of scattered missing responses, assessment of correlates of missingness, and complete case analysis. Reasons for withdrawal from the study and loss to follow-up will be tabulated by experimental group. {42}

---

## Notes: Research Design and Methods Example (Continued)

{41} It is not always necessary to explain your data management strategy, depending on how complex your database is likely to be. In smaller experiments, it is not necessary; however, if you are conducting a large study or trial involving several waves of data, many different types of measures, and so on, you would do well to discuss who will manage the data and how. It contributes to the reviewers' confidence that you have the capability to successfully carry out the proposed work.

{42} Missing data are almost always an issue in a study, and I have noticed that many researchers do not provide information on what they plan to do in the event data is missing. These authors address two issues here: (1) the imputation techniques they will use in the event of missing data and (2) an analytic strategy that will allow statements to be made concerning the comparability of data from those who withdraw from the study and those who continue. Missing data issues are always important, but if you do not address them in a clinical trial, it will probably be regarded by the reviewers as an important omission.

*D16. Dissemination of Results {43}*

We will disseminate results at conferences and in peer-reviewed journals on the following schedule:

End of Year 1: We will submit a methods/baseline paper to *Controlled Clinical Trials*.

End of Year 2: We will present preliminary findings at a national conference.

End of Year 3: We will present interim findings at a national conference and publish the findings.

End of Year 5: We will present the first set of basic results at a national conference and publish the findings.

Middle of Year 6: We shall present at a national conference and publish more extensive findings concerning both the clinical outcomes and mechanisms.

*D17. Limitations {44}*

*Potential Confounding Due to Changes in Medication, Especially in the Control Condition.* In an intervention in which the experimental group is predicted to show an improvement in the outcome measure, and participants in the control condition are predicted to show no change, there is always a concern that the attending physician may use other methods to control the illness, making it difficult to interpret the results. To minimize this possibility, we shall take the following steps: At screening, potential participants (i.e., those found to be hypertensive) will be informed that their BP is higher than recommended levels, and the RA will suggest that they see a physician. They will be told that if, as a result of the screening, they do plan to see a physician for possible treatment, they will not be admitted to the study immediately, but only after they have seen their physicians; if no new treatment has been prescribed at that physician visit, they may then be admitted to the study; if new treatment has started (either new medications or increased

{43} Dissemination of results is an important feature of the project that is often overlooked in the proposal. One assumes that the authors, once they have data in hand, will plan to present at conferences and to write papers. However, when you consider that the talks and papers are the only product produced in return for large sums of money NIH has invested in you, make your dissemination intentions specific. (And *don't* forget to thank the I/C and NIH and to mention the grant number in your presentations and publications.) The authors have provided a clear list giving the approximate times in the course of the study that they will publicize their findings, and I think that is an excellent idea. It also, incidentally, helps to justify the travel money you will be requesting (see Chapter 7).

{44} The authors have discussed the limitations both in the narrative and, to an extent, toward the beginning of the Research Design and Methods section. They mention them here, as well, as some potentially problematic issues may still exist. Even if you do not have issues not previously addressed in the narrative, provide a limitations section. Reviewers tend to look for it, and it is a useful place to describe your logic concerning potential pitfalls. In the limitations section, you should

- Discuss potential weaknesses in the proposed procedures, especially those that may interfere with a clean interpretation of the data.
- Describe alternative approaches you have considered and why you chose not to use them (it is often the case that there are a limited set of approaches you can take concerning a specific issue, and whichever one you choose is associated with some weakness).
- Specifically note that the case you plan to make is not compromised by the weakness in design.

dosages of medications the participant is already taking), the participant will be told that after two months, he or she may be rescreened (to allow the change in treatment to take effect and stabilize), and, depending on the results, may then be admitted to the study. {45}

*Monitoring and Promotion of Adherence.* We will ask participants in the standard intervention and placebo conditions to use their device 4 days/week for 8 weeks; we will ask those in the extended duration condition to use their device 4 days/week for 12 months. Finally, we will ask all participants to take their BP on 2 days/week for 12 months (3 readings each time). This obviously represents a large burden, especially for those in the extended duration condition. We will know precisely when and for how often the guided breathing and placebo devices are used, as the devices automatically record the date, time, and duration of the sessions, as well as other statistics regarding performance of breathing in the < 10 breath/minute range. Similarly, the home BP device also stores the readings with the dates and times of measurement. The data from the guided breathing and the placebo devices will be used in subanalyses to examine the effects of amount of practice on change in BP (and HRV and baroreflex sensitivity). {46}

*D18. Review Criteria {47}*

*1. Significance.* The proposed study addresses an important public health problem {48}—the excess morbidity, mortality, and economic burden due to uncontrolled HTN. If the aims of the application are achieved, the scientific gains include a better understanding of the role of characteristic breathing patterns and the RSA play in BP regulation; and of the role that non-pharmacological approaches to HTN treatment may play as a supplement and, when necessary, an alternative to pharmacological therapy.

{45} I have included this lengthy paragraph to demonstrate the high level of detail that the authors have included in a well-ordered and readable paragraph. Although they are describing a complicated response to an important problem, the reader, once having read the paragraph, understands completely how the investigators plan to address it. Notice that they first explain the problem clearly, taking the reviewers' point of view, and then provide their solution.

{46} Participant compliance to the study protocol absolutely must be addressed. People, even those who have volunteered for your study and who have agreed to comply with the study requirements, will routinely violate one or another part of the protocol, which leads to missing data or worse, poor-quality data. If there is a differential in compliance between your conditions (i.e., participants are less compliant in one condition than in others), you begin to lose the power of your random assignment, as subjects are self-selecting out of some portions of the data. It is common for applicants to lose points on this issue.

{47} The following section comprises the five criteria that NIH reviewers use to evaluate each application. Each criterion is addressed without false modesty and, at the same time, without unjustified crowing. Make your argument matter-of-factly, but don't hesitate to highlight your strengths.

{48} Note the authors' reference to a public health problem. You should tie the research to the public health considerations as often as you can justify it. This is true whether your research takes place in a test tube, in an animal model, or in a community sample. Ultimately, as far as the NIH is concerned, there is no reason to do the research if it will not (eventually) have implications for treatment.

*2. Approach.* We have proposed the use of a RCT, a powerful design that provides important scientific information concerning the causal relation between the intervention and the outcome and about the feasibility and utility of the proposed intervention. {49} The proposed measures are based on the assessment in the current literature of the most useful, cutting-edge techniques: for example, ambulatory assessment of BP and respiration. The proposed statistical analyses use cutting-edge techniques as well. {50} Alternative research strategies and the rationales for methodological decisions have been described, as in the case of the design (we considered, for example, a crossover design) and control conditions. {51}

*3. Innovation.* The proposed study represents an innovative treatment intervention that is a departure from the traditional manner in which HTN treatment is usually considered, and that represents a potentially important advancement in public health.

*4. Investigators.* This research team has done much of the seminal work in the areas of BP measurement, psychosocial causes of essential HTN, and behavioral interventions for the treatment of HTN. They also have a great deal of experience in the conduct of behavioral clinical trials.

*5. Environment.* NYMC has provided strong support for the research of this group over the past several years. The group itself has the resources necessary to successfully carry out the research in terms of research space, computer and Internet resources, clinical needs including ABP monitors, holter monitors, and ambulatory respiratory assessment monitors. The patient population at NYMC is diverse and composed, to a large degree, of economically disadvantaged patients who are especially in need of nonpharmacological treatments. The outpatient clinic has a substantial patient load, and a large proportion of the patients seen there are minorities with poorly controlled HTN. {52}

{49} Note that the authors have commented on both the scientific and the practical aspects of their approach. Remember, both are equally important in the eyes of the NIH. No matter how strong the methodological approach, if you cannot convince the reviewers that you have the ability to carry out the study, your score will suffer.

{50} Don't forget to comment on your statistical, as well as your experimental, methods.

{51} The authors here provide a couple of specifics to remind the reviewer of what the strengths of their design are. You should do this, as appropriate, rather than simply noting that you used the best techniques available.

{52} Access to particular patient populations that are of interest to the NIH for one reason or another (e.g., because they are underserved, understudied, economically disadvantaged, or culturally diverse) is an important resource in which the reviewers will absolutely be interested.

Remember, the reviewer wants to award you a good score; the point of addressing the five review criteria is to give the reviewer justification for doing so!

## COMMON REVIEWERS' CRITICISMS

In Chapter 9 (Table 9.2), I set out common reviewers' criticisms of proposals. They are provided there rather than here because Chapter 9 is where I discuss the feedback you will receive on the summary sheets and the resubmission process. However, it would obviously be just as well to have these common criticisms in mind while you are writing the original draft, so please consult the table as you are developing the proposal.

# SECTIONS G THROUGH K

You've made it through Sections A through D, and those are the tough ones; however, you're not quite finished. Let's zip through the remaining ones. One important thing to remember: You are given 25 pages for sections A through D; the following sections *do not* count in the 25-page limit. Please also note that once the new SF424 forms are used rather than the current PHS398 forms, the following sections (E through K) will not exist as such. Instead, you will provide the data in response to questions on the electronic SF424 forms. However, Sections A through D will remain in the same format; you will simply turn them into a PDF document and upload them in the appropriate section of the electronic form.

## Sections E and F: Ethical Concerns and Vertebrate Animals

Sections E and F are so important I gave them their own chapter (Chapter 6). Note that, as I will continue to use the guided breathing study as an example in these sections, Section F (Vertebrate Animals) will not be applicable. Section E is, however, and the next chapter will explore that portion of the sample proposal.

## Section G: Literature Cited

You know what the Literature Cited section is, and so you won't see this section in the example; it would not be useful to you. One comment, however: Although you are not constrained in terms of the length of this section, don't go crazy. Cite what you need to, and no more. If you have a possibly controversial point or one that you feel may require convincing evidence, then cite four or five references—or even more, if you have to. For most points, however, you should not need to cite so many items. There is no "correct" number of references; the list should be as long as it has to be—and no longer.

> Find out who will be on the NIH study section that you hope will be evaluating your application (I discuss this in Chapter 8), and find out if any of them have done similar work to that which you are proposing (you should probably know this anyhow!). Don't stretch to cite their work, but *do* cite them if their work is relevant.

## Section H: Consortium/Contractual Arrangements

I explain consortia and contractual arrangements in Chapter 7.

## Section I: Consultants

Consultants will be discussed in Chapter 7 along with the budget justification. In Chapter 7, I will also discuss why and when to use consultants, whom to choose as consultants, how to decide how much to pay them, and what the difference is between *consultants* and *personnel*. In Section I of your proposal, just list the consultants, if any, and refer the reader to the budget justification for more details.

## Section J: Discussion of Anticipated Results

The anticipated results, as well as the analyses and interpretation of the data, should be described in detail in Section D (Research Design and Methods), where they can be understood in the proper context to the research questions and procedures. To briefly recapitulate how the authors in the sample handled this, they said that they anticipate observing significant differences in ambulatory blood pressure change at 8 weeks between the intervention conditions (which do not differ up to that point) and the placebo and usual care conditions, and observing significant differences at 12 months between the standard duration and the extended duration intervention conditions.

## Section K: Significance

In this section, provide just a couple of lines about the significance of the study. Keep it short. In the sample proposal, the authors explained in the Significance section that medication therapy has fallen short of its goal—having all treated hypertensives achieve blood pressures under the recommended limits; their proposed study tests a nonpharmaceutical intervention, guided breathing, that has promise for serving as a useful adjunct to medication therapy.

## Appendices

You are allowed to submit an appendix with your application. The appendix generally contains the PI's or other investigators' relevant publications or materials that should be regarded as supplementary (e.g., self-report instruments). Do *not* use appendices as a means of sneaking in materials to circumvent the 25-page limit imposed on Sections A–D, because appendices may not be seen by the reviewers. I suggest you do not use appendices for other materials unless you don't care too much if the reviewers don't read it, as they often do not.

# ADDITIONAL INFORMATION REQUIRED FOR MENTORED NRSA AWARDS

If you plan to apply for a mentored award (see Section 4 of the PHS 398 instructions to identify which are the mentored awards), there are additional sections you must provide in your proposal. The PHS 398 instructions do a pretty good job of explaining what you will need, so, as usual, I will limit myself to hints that are not contained in the instructions, except for a couple of particularly important sections. Note that, in the new SF 424 forms that are slowly supplanting the PHS 398, this is not an issue, as the application package you download for any particular mechanism will automatically have only the appropriate forms in it.

## Statements by the Sponsor, Co-Sponsors, Consultants, and Contributors

You must get a rave review from your sponsor—don't ask for a letter if you suspect that you will not receive such a response. One extraordinarily useful thing you can do is to offer to write the letter yourself, and send it to your sponsor to edit and sign. This sounds presumptive, but I know that my colleagues and I appreciate it—but *only from persons who have excellent reason to assume that these letters will be raves*. If you don't or can't expect such a positive review, don't offer to draft the letter—but then, if you can't expect a rave, you shouldn't be asking that person for a reference. Assuming the sponsor accepts your offer, you will be faced with a tough proposition: writing about what an outstanding scientist you are and your strong potential to make outstanding contributions to your field. This is not a time to be modest; I suggest to my trainees that they pretend they are writing a letter about someone else who happens to have their exact background. When you write about your prospective training plan, if that is part of your application, be extremely detailed. A common criticism is that the training plans are too ambiguous. Look up the courses you might take, and include course numbers, meeting times, and a brief description of the material to be covered. Include seminars, attendance, and anticipated presentations at conferences, ethics training, and anticipated publications over the course of the funded period.

Also include details concerning the sponsor's experience as a mentor, listing pre- and postdoctoral students as well as previous stints as mentor on career awards, and the career outcomes of the mentees.

Part IV of the PHS 398 instructions provides other details that should be included in the statements. These come up automatically in the new SF 424 applications.

## Environment and Institutional Commitment to the Candidate

*Description of Institutional Environment.* You must also provide a letter signed by the relevant official at your institution. Who this is differs from institution to institution; it may be the department chair, the division chief, or someone in the dean's office, so check to make sure. Again, the letter must be quite detailed; both the PHS 398 and SF 424 instructions describe the areas that must be covered (e.g., names of key faculty members relevant to candidate's proposed developmental plan). The point of this document is to show that the institution will support the candidate's research and career development by providing necessary resources not necessarily paid for by the award, such as laboratory facilities, statistical consultation, and office space. This commitment should be reinforced by the information on the PHS 398 and/or SF 424 forms.

*Institutional Commitment to the Candidate's Research Career Development.* In addition to the items described in the previous paragraph, the NIH dictates that the statement of institutional commitment should include an agreement "to provide adequate time and support for the candidate to devote the proposed protected time to research and career development for the entire period of the proposed award." Moreover, "the institution should provide the equipment, facilities, and resources necessary for a structured career development experience. It is essential to document the institution's commitment to the retention, development, and advancement of the candidate during the period of the award."

The PHS 398 and SF 424 instructions go on to say that, "because of the diverse types of K awards, applicants should contact the appropriate awarding component program director listed in the specific PA or RFA to determine the level of commitment required for this application."

The specific agreement is provided in the instructions. However, the required institutional commitment may vary from one award mechanism to the next, so make sure to investigate carefully depending on what type of award you are going for.

*Research Plan.* The research plan for K awards is similar to the one for the R01; however, it tends to be somewhat less detailed and, depending on the grant mechanism, shorter. Make sure the research plan is consistent with the proposed research development in that you, the candidate, will learn and utilize the skills described in the development plan.

**Table 5.1**       Suggested Writing Timetable

|  | 12 Months | 16 Weeks | 14 Weeks | 12 Weeks | 10 Weeks | 6 Weeks | 4 Weeks |
|---|---|---|---|---|---|---|---|
| Develop initial conceptualization | X | | | | | | |
| Begin collecting pilot data | X | | | | | | |
| Contact PO | X | | | | | | |
| Compile research team | | X | | | | | |
| Obtain application forms | | X | | | | | |
| Begin Specific Aims section | | X | | | | | |
| Begin budget | | X | | | | | |
| Begin Research Design and Methods section | | | X | | | | |
| Begin IRB application | | | X | | | | |
| Determine potential reviewers | | | | X | | | |
| Begin Preliminary Studies section | | | | X | | | |
| Enlist consultants | | | | X | | | |
| Finalize budget | | | | | X | | |
| Obtain letters of support | | | | | X | | |
| Finalize Specific Aims section | | | | | X | | |
| Finalize Research Design and Methods section | | | | | | X | |
| Finalize Preliminary Studies section | | | | | | X | |
| Finalize sections E–K | | | | | | X | |
| Send to colleagues for review | | | | | | X | |
| Write abstract | | | | | | | X |
| Send for budget review and departmental signatures | | | | | | | X |
| Revise up until deadline | | | | | | | X |

## PROPOSAL DEVELOPMENT TIMELINE

Allow yourself sufficient time to write any proposal you plan to submit to the NIH—or any other funding agency. I have seen otherwise competent scientists begin their proposals two or three weeks before the deadline. Can you get it done in that amount of time? Sure. Probably. Maybe. Will it get funded? You should have a pretty good sense by now that the answer is, "Not likely." I suggest you begin writing your specific aims *at least* three months before the deadline. In fact, Table 5.1 shows a possible timeline for some of the major aspects of the development of the proposal. Note that I regard three months as a *minimum*; you may decide you require more time.

You will need to send your proposal to your institution's grants office or comparable office for budget approval and then for necessary signatures (from the department chair or dean). Usually, those responsible for budget approval and signatures want the proposal in their hands at least two weeks before the deadline, sometimes more; find out what your internal deadline is, and then do what your institution requires. The institutional representatives will want the full proposal, including the science; but you may wish you still had those extra two weeks for revisions! I send a "cosmetic" version of the science; that is, the version I send could pass as the final draft, but it's not. Then, I can keep working on the science for another couple of weeks. Don't just send whatever files you happen to have handy, however, because I've had administrators who read sections A–D, don't ask me why. Note, however, that as more and more universities go to on-line submission internally, the option to continue modifying the text after submission no longer exists. Thus, you must consider your institution's due date as the deadline for the entire application (so June 1, for example, becomes May 15 or thereabouts).

## REVISE, REVISE, REVISE, PROOFREAD, PROOFREAD, . . .

To revise and proofread you proposal may seem obvious, but two things tend to happen that interfere. First, you start coming down to the wire, and haven't left yourself enough time. Second, there does arrive a point at which you just can't look at the damn thing another time. I know that there is a point at which I hit a wall, and my eyes slip off the text without being able to process it. These are both great excuses, but they will not provide a lot of comfort if you don't get funded. So, what to do? This is obvious, too, and I've made the point as strongly as possible in other parts of this book. Start early. Start earlier than you would have guessed, because your deadline should *not* be the NIH submission date, but should be *at least* a month earlier. That will take care of the running out of time problem. It will also take care of the other problem, because the obvious solution is that you need to take a few days, even a week, off from the process so that you can approach the writing afresh.

*I absolutely guarantee that if you do this, you will find problems in the text that passed you by on all previous readings!* At the least, you will find places in which you have been redundant and can word things more clearly and efficiently. Myself, I will have read the entire proposal through 30 or more times before submission. There are things you cannot control: whether the reviewers will like your idea, whether NIH funding levels are up or down, and so on; but as a professional, you want to control everything that you can. No typographical errors, no inconsistencies in numbers, no mismatch between section numbers, no inappropriate paragraphs left in from when you cut and paste from someone else's proposal or your most recent publication. . . . Such mistakes do more than annoy the reviewers; they also reflect badly on you in general.

## NOTES

1. The Resources for Grant Applicants page can be found at http://grants1.nih.gov/grants/resources.htm.

2. The full set of formatting instructions can be found at http://grants1.nih.gov/grants/forms.htm.

3. The revised criteria can be found at http://grants.nih.gov/grants/guide/notice-files/NOT-OD-05-002.html.

## 6

# Writing the Application, Part II

## *Human and Animal Concerns*

A large part of the effort in writing an application for the NIH will involve the procedures for the protection of human and animal subjects. You must satisfy both the NIH and your home institution concerning these issues, and parts of your application will be devoted to the protection of human subjects; Section F would be used if you were studying animals.

## A NOTE CONCERNING JUST-IN-TIME PROCEDURES

I have discussed this elsewhere, but it is very important with respect to your institutional review board (IRB) approvals. It used to be the case that the NIH wanted to know that your IRB had approved your protocol at the same time, or within 60 days after, your application went in. Now, you do not send these assurances until requested. This happens when your application receives a priority score that puts it into the *likely* (but not *definite*) funding range. This delayed request for certain documents is known as the "just-in-time" procedure. The elements of the application that are subject to the just-in-time policy are:

- IRB human subjects certification
- Institutional animal care and use committee, vertebrate animals certification
- Current investigator salary support from other sources (see Chapter 7)
- Human subjects education certification

The rationale for the just-in-time policy is to ensure that this information is as up to date as possible; also, there is no point in having the investigators submit materials to the IRB if the application is not going to be funded. This is good news, because you'll have plenty to do just getting the application ready. However, I advise you to begin the IRB process as soon as possible, because you really don't know how long it will take, considering there are almost always revisions.

In addition to the procedures involved in writing and submitting a proposal, your own institution will have *its* own set of procedures as well. It is occasionally the case that your institution's policies and requirements are considerably more exacting than those of the NIH. There are usually two main segments of the home institution policies. First, you have to satisfy the IRB. Second, you will have to satisfy your grants office, which has to sign off on the budget and other aspects of the application. This second part will be discussed in Chapter 7. In the current chapter, we will discuss the IRB requirements, as well as other aspects of protection of both human and animal subjects.

> Each IRB has its own way of doing things, its own forms, its own requirements. One IRB might okay a procedure that receives a thumbs-down at another institution. You may get a consent form rejected because of a typographical error. Get frustrated all you want, but you have to pass the IRB, so it pays to learn its ways. I also suggest going to the committee and asking questions personally. Be nice; if the committee isn't happy, it can fix it so that your grant never gets funded.

## A BRIEF DISCUSSION OF ETHICS AND ACCOUNTABILITY

The ethics that I shall discuss are those regarding the treatment of your subjects, animal and human. When you systematically collect data, you take on the responsibility for the safety and well-being of the persons or animals who serve as your research participants. "Well-being" includes dignity. Thus, in research involving humans, you may be in a position in which you have to keep them ignorant of certain aspects of the study, or perhaps even have to lie to them for the sake of blinding. This may be acceptable in and of itself to your IRB, but you have the ethical responsibility to debrief that person when the study ends in a manner that does not make this person, who collaborated with you for the sake of your research, feel like a fool. If you have animal subjects, you are obligated to ensure their well-being by specifying how they will be maintained (e.g., will there be more than one animal in a cage? what will the feeding schedule be? And so on). If the animals are to be sacrificed, there are various methods by which this may be accomplished, some more humane than others.

## REQUIRED EDUCATION IN THE PROTECTION OF HUMAN RESEARCH PARTICIPANTS

Every person on the application listed as *key personnel* (we will discuss this in Chapter 7), as well as any other personnel who will have any contact with the subjects or with the *data*, must pass a test to demonstrate mastery of the basic information regarding ethical conduct with respect to research participants. However, if persons—key personnel or not—are not involved in the design or conduct of human subjects research, they do not need to comply with this requirement. The test is not difficult and most often is available through your institution (check their web page). The official statement on required education can be found on the NIH Web site.[1]

The NIH does not endorse any specific educational programs. Instead, they leave the program to your institution. The "NIH Bioethics Resources on the Web" lists several courses that institutions may direct key personnel involved in human subjects research to complete.[2]

## What, Precisely, Is a "Human Subject"?

What is a "human subject"? You think you knew this already, eh? *Human subject,* as defined by the NIH, means "a living individual about whom an investigator (whether professional or student) conducting research obtains: (1) data through intervention or interaction with the individual, or (2) identifiable private information."

Even if you are not working with human subjects, but are working with tissues or specimens from human sources, it is advisable to get the educational certification. Research using human specimens, tissues, or data that are unidentifiable may not be considered human subjects research.[3] You may be involved in human subjects research that is exempt from IRB review and approval, but you must still comply with the education requirement.

For most applications, you won't need to include documentation of human subjects education until just prior to receiving the award (see the discussion of just-in-time procedures at the beginning of this chapter). However, if you do not provide the required documentation when requested, your reward may be delayed.

*Background of the Ethics Codes.* If you are interested in the background and history of the NIH ethics codes, there are two documents you should look at, one regarding the Belmont Report, the other regarding the Declaration of Helsinki. Both are available online.[4] Definitely read the NIH's "Human Subjects Ethical Guidelines," as well as the federal policy for the protection of human subjects, "Basic HHS [Department of Health and Human Services] Policy for Protection of Human Research Subjects."[5]

## SECTION E: ETHICAL CONCERNS

You will recall from Chapter 5 that we covered Sections A through D and F through K. Let's continue the example now as to what a typical Ethical Concerns section should look like. Note that, in the PHS 398 forms, this is Section E; in the new SF 424 forms, you provide this information in the Other Project Information section.

First, however, let me jump ahead just for a moment to something we will cover in more detail in Chapter 7. If you are studying human subjects, you must indicate so in Item 4 on the Cover Page of the PHS 398 application (if you are using the SF 424 forms, you do not indicate this until you come to the Other Project Information form). Figure 6.1 shows you what this portion of the PHS 398 Cover Page looks like, and Figure 6.2 shows you the relevant portion of the SF 424 form. You will check the "yes" box in Item 4 of the PHS 398 or Item 1 in the SF 424. In some instances, you may be granted an exemption from having to obtain informed consent from your research participants; the conditions under which you may request an exemption are described later in this chapter (if you are given an exemption by your IRB, they will provide an exemption number). Your institution will have a Human Subjects Assurance Number; most institutions have a Web page that provides information needed for grant submission, or else ask your grants office. Note that most of you will *not* be submitting an application for a Phase III clinical trial. The following definitions will help you determine which type of clinical trial you are proposing.

## Clinical Trial Phases

*Phase I.* Phase I clinical trials are done to test a new biomedical or behavioral intervention in a small group of people—say, between 20 and 80 subjects—for the first time, to evaluate safety (e.g., determine a safe dosage range, identify side effects, etc.).

*Phase II.* Clinical trials that study the biomedical or behavioral intervention in a larger group—several hundred people—to determine efficacy and to further evaluate its safety are known as Phase II trials.

| 4. HUMAN SUBJECTS RESEARCH ☐ No ☐ Yes | 4a. Research Exempt.        ☐ No        ☐ Yes | |
|---|---|---|
| | If "Yes," Exemption No        ▬▬▬▬ | |
| | 4b. Human Subjects Assurance No. ▬▬▬▬ | 4c. NIH-defined Phase III Clinical Trial        ☐ No |

**Figure 6.1**        Item 4 From the PHS 398 Application Cover Page

---

**RESEARCH & RELATED Other Project Information**

1. * Are Human Subjects Involved?        ☐ Yes        ☐ No

1a.   if YES to Human Subjects

Is the IRB review Pending?        ☐ Yes        ☐ No

IRB Approval Date: [                    ]

Exemption Number:   ☐ 1   ☐ 2   ☐ 3   ☐ 4   ☐ 5   ☐ 6

Human Subject Assurance Number: [                    ]

---

**Figure 6.2**        Human Subjects Items From the SF 424 Other Project Information Form Page

*Phase III.* Phase III studies are done to study the efficacy of a biomedical or behavioral intervention in large groups of human subjects, ranging from several hundred to several thousand participants, by comparing the intervention to other standard or experimental interventions; such studies also monitor adverse effects and collect information that will allow the intervention to be used safely.

*Phase IV.* The final type of clinical trial, Phase IV studies, are done after an intervention has been marketed. These studies are designed to monitor the effectiveness of the approved intervention in the general population and to collect information about any adverse effects associated with widespread use.

*NIH-Defined Phase III Clinical Trial.* According to the "Human Subjects Ethical Guidelines," an NIH-defined Phase III clinical trial is a broadly based prospective Phase III clinical investigation, usually involving several hundred or more human subjects, for the purpose of evaluating an experimental intervention in comparison with a standard or control intervention or comparing two or more existing treatments. Often, the aim of such investigation is to provide a scientific basis for the consideration of a change in health policy or standard of care. The definition includes pharmacologic, nonpharmacologic, and behavioral interventions given for disease prevention, prophylaxis, diagnosis, or therapy. Community trials and other population-based intervention trials are also included.

Please note: I have used a somewhat different format for the sample Ethical Concerns section than for the samples of Sections A–D, because the annotations here are not always brief notes, but may also be rather longer discussions. Thus, in the Notes sections, I will either comment briefly or refer you to a particular section of this chapter. The example is in the format of the PHS 398 forms; however, the items shown are identical to the ones used in the SF 424 forms, which are written using your word processor and then uploaded. Thus, the sections written for either the PHS 398 or the SF 424 are identical. The section on the SF 424 forms in Chapter 7 provides additional information.

### Section E: Ethical Concerns, Example

*E1. Risks to the Subjects*

*E1a. Human Subjects Involvement and Characteristics*

Proposed involvement of human subjects, consisting of hypertensive volunteers, in the work will include the following:

- Participants will be randomly assigned to the standard duration intervention condition, the extended duration intervention condition, placebo, or UC. Study duration is 12 months, and there are 5 patient visits: one at the beginning of the study, one at 8 weeks, one at 6 months, one at 9 months, and one at 12 months.
- Patients assigned to the intervention conditions will engage in the following activities, following informed consent: Their blood pressures will be assessed at baseline and follow-up visits using 24-hour ABP. They will also be given questionnaires to complete at the same visits (described in detail in Section D12), and will be given the assessments ($CO_2$, casual BP, ECG, and respiration rate). At the baseline visit, participants' height and weight will be measured. Participants in the intervention conditions will also be given a Respirco Guided Breathing Device or a placebo device. After 8 weeks, participants in the standard duration intervention condition and the placebo condition will return their Respirco devices. {1}
- Patients assigned to the placebo condition will be treated in the identical manner to those in the standard duration intervention condition, except that their Respirco devices will play musical tones, as will the devices in the intervention conditions, but they will not guide the breathing into the 6–10 breaths/minute range. {2}
- Patients assigned to the UC condition will be treated in the identical manner to intervention and placebo participants, except they will not be given a device.
- Patients' charts will provide a great deal of the data; examination of the charts will be in accordance with Institutional Review Board (IRB) guidelines and the Health Insurance Portability and Accountability Act (HIPAA). {3}

*Characteristics of the Subject Population.* We will screen 1,960 adults, to end with a complete sample of 400 (100/condition). Based on our previous experience, we anticipate that approximately 40% of participants will identify themselves as African American, 30% as Hispanic, and 5% as Asian. Age range is 18 years or older, and health status is generally healthy. {4}

## Notes: Ethical Concerns Example

{1} Give the important details, abstracted from Section D (Research Design and Methods), that the study will entail for each participant. Do so for any type of study, not just clinical trials; this includes animal studies as well.

{2} You must describe the manipulation and different conditions.

{3} Note the reference to HIPAA compliance; see the discussion later in this chapter of the HIPAA requirements.

{4} Provide the characteristics of your study population, including a breakdown by ethnicity. See the section on Inclusion of Women and Minorities in Research, below, for a discussion of requirements concerning minority representation.

Eligibility criteria for participation in this study are outlined below.

Inclusion criteria: {5}

- Age 18 years or older
- Screening SBP of 140 *or* DBP of 90; in patients with documented heart disease or diabetes, SBP of 130 *or* DBP of 80
- Fluency in English or Spanish

Exclusion criteria:

- Being deemed unable to comply with the protocol (either self-selected or by indicating during screening an inability to complete all requested tasks)
- Having a significant uncorrected hearing or visual impairment that would make it impossible to correctly use the intervention and BP monitoring devices
- Having an arm circumference of > 47 cm (oscillometric BP cuffs do not give accurate readings for arms of this size)
- Participation in any other HTN-related clinical trial.

{5} The eligibility criteria listed here should be identical to those provided in your Research Design and Methods section; just copy and paste.

### Section E: Ethical Concerns, Example (Continued)

*E1b. Sources of Materials*

Data sources will include noninvasive BP, ECG, respiratory, and $CO_2$ measurements; paper-and-pencil questionnaires; and patient chart data. In addition, we will collect blood specimens. All data will be used specifically for research purposes.

*E1c. Potential Risks*

The only potential risk to the patient concerns the possible violation of the patient's privacy, since patient records will be used as a source of data. In addition, ABP monitoring may result in some skin irritation. {6}

*E2. Adequacy of Protection Against Risks*

*E2a. Recruitment*

BP screenings will be held in public areas of the hospital; persons who have an SBP of 140+ mm Hg or DBP of 90+ mm Hg and who have never been diagnosed with diabetes will be given a brief description of the study procedures and asked if they wish to participate. {7} If the answer is

## Notes: Ethical Concerns Example (Continued)

{6} To assess potential risks, you must carefully analyze every single aspect of the study in which participants (human or animal) are exposed to your study procedures, both directly and indirectly. For example, are your subjects at risk in any way because of the type of data collected or because of the way in which the data are handled and stored? You may not be capable of judging the risks unless you have had sufficient experience; you should absolutely make sure to confer with others who *do* have experience with the procedures you are proposing, as well as with persons from your IRB.

{7} Be specific in your proposal and state that the subjects will be "asked if they wish to participate."

affirmative, an appointment will be made so that the study can be described in detail, consent given, and a screening ABP taken. A $2.50 transit card is given to persons who participate in the screening.

*Consent.* **{8}** The protocol and consent will be approved by the NYMC IRB. When the participant arrives, the RA will give a full description of the study, including the study conditions, in clear, easy-to-understand language; the RA will also explain the possibility that the patient may be assigned to the UC or placebo condition and that the participant will only be asked to participate in the remaining phases of the study if the ABP is in the hypertensive range 135↑ mm Hg SBP or 85↑ mm HG DBP. (Diagnosis of HTN using ABP monitoring uses lower levels than diagnosis using clinic pressures, which are 140+ mm Hg SBP or 90+ mm Hg DBP, because clinic pressures tend to be higher, possibly due to the White Coat effect. The RA will also explain the schedule of reimbursement for the patient's travel costs and effort: $35 for the current appointment; $30 for the second part of the baseline visit 1–2 weeks later; $60 for the 8-week visit, which involves a second 24-hour ABP measurement; and $100 for the 12-month visit, which requires a third ABP monitoring. **{9}**

If the patient remains interested in participating, **{10}** the RA will provide a copy of the consent form; if the patient asks for help or evinces a problem in reading the consent, the RA will read the consent to the patient. If the patient desires to participate, he or she then signs the informed consent, and the RA co-signs.

**{8}** Consult the section on Informed Consent later in this chapter concerning consent procedures and the development of the consent form. A checklist of what must be included in the consent form is provided there. Also, see this chapter's discussions of conditions under which signed consent may be waived and under which you may request an expedited review of consent procedures.

**{9}** You have to be careful about how much you plan to reimburse your subjects—and note that the term is no longer "pay" but rather "reimburse." The concern is that, if your offer of reimbursement is too high, it may be perceived as coercion, an irresistible carrot, especially for those who find themselves in more economically challenged circumstances. There is no set standard; reimbursement levels depend largely on what you are asking people to do. Also, rates should be somewhat higher in parts of the country with a higher cost of living. Ask your colleagues what amounts they have used that were approved by your IRB, or ask guidance from the IRB itself.

**{10}** Again, note that the authors use qualifying language: "*if* the patient remains interested in participating, . . ."

### Section E: Ethical Concerns, Example (Continued)

*E2b. Protection Against Risk*

The physical risks of the studies are minimal. **{11}** As part of the process involved in obtaining written informed consent, all participants will be reminded that their responses are confidential, that they may refuse to participate in the project or withdraw at any time without explanation, and that such an action will in no way affect their future interactions with the NYMC. To ensure confidentiality, data will be associated with an individual participant only by an assigned identification number, the code for which will be kept in a locked drawer.

## Notes: Ethical Concerns Example (Continued)

**{11}** *Minimal risk* means that the probability and magnitude of harm or discomfort anticipated in the research is not greater in and of itself than that ordinarily encountered in daily life or during the performance of routine physical or psychological examinations or tests.

As a safety check, the participants in all conditions will have clinic BPs checked at each of the 3 visits over the 12-month study period. If at any time a participant's average clinic BP reading exceeds 165/95, he or she will be directed to see a physician as soon as possible, with the BP readings sent to the physician's office. {12}

There may be direct benefits to the participants in the intervention condition in terms of hypothesized BP control; in addition, the research will provide important information about an intervention strategy for control of high BP. In light of the anticipated knowledge to be derived from the study, the minimal risks to participants appear reasonable. {13}

*E3. Potential Benefits of the Proposed Research to the Subjects and Others*

The intervention is expected to benefit the patients by increasing their BP control, reducing their cardiovascular risk profile, and increasing their role as active participants in the management of their HTN. {14}

*E4. Importance of the Knowledge to Be Gained*

Although drug therapy has proved effective for the BP control of many hypertensives, current estimates indicate that the BP of approximately 50% of persons on antihypertensive drug therapy remains uncontrolled. This increases risk for target organ damage, cardiovascular events, and mortality. The present study tests a behavioral intervention that has been shown to reduce BP in several small trials, and that thus may represent a useful treatment that will supplement or, in some cases, even supplant drug therapy.

*E5. Women and Minority Inclusion in Clinical Research* {15}

*E5a. Inclusion of Women*

We shall enroll 70% women and 30% men in the study, as our previous studies show that women in this population tend to be more likely to volunteer.

*E5b. Inclusion of Minorities*

At least 50% of the sample we will recruit will comprise minority participants, approximately 30% Black and 20% Hispanic.

*E5c. Inclusion of Children* {16}

Children aged 18 years to 21 years will be included in the present study. However, those less than 18 years will not be included, because HTN is extremely rare in this age group.

{12} Note the specificity with which the authors spell out the level at which a blood pressure level is considered risky and the precise steps that will be taken in the event that such levels occur.

{13} Use this phrasing, "The minimal risks to participants appear reasonable," or something very similar.

{14} You may find that the answer to the question of what potential benefits the study has for it subjects is "none." That's okay; just say as much. Remember, the question refers to the *benefit to the individual patient*, not to the more general benefit to the science or to the patient population as a whole. I would not include reimbursement in this paragraph, as it is supposed to be only to compensate research participants for their time and effort, not as an income subsidy.

{15} Again, see the fuller discussion later in this chapter of the inclusion of women and minorities in research and give particular note to the conditions under which you may exclude either women or minorities.

{16} This chapter contains a detailed discussion concerning the inclusion of children in research. In particular, you should note the definition of *children* as "persons who have not attained the legal age for consent to treatments or procedures involved in the research, under the applicable law of the jurisdiction in which the research will be conducted." Also of importance are the conditions under which you may exclude children from your study.

## Section E: Ethical Concerns, Example (Continued)

*E6. Data and Safety Monitoring Plan* {17}

In compliance with NIH requirements, we will form a Data and Safety Monitoring Board (DSMB). The purpose of the DSMB is to ensure the safety of participants and the validity and integrity of the data. Personnel involved in the monitoring activities will include the following:

- The PI on this application
- A designated medical monitor: a physician in our program who will provide consultation on medical risks and who will review adverse events
- An internal committee, consisting of the PI and the co-investigators on the present proposal
- The DSMB (details follow)
- The IRB

The DSMB will comprise professionals in the field who are willing to participate and who have no conflict with serving on such a board. We shall include the following: {18}

- An expert in the conduct of clinical trials
- Two professionals with substantive expertise in the area of HTN and BP control: one a physician, one a PhD
- A biostatistician with expertise in clinical trials

The data and safety monitoring plan will comprise the following elements:

- *Reporting of adverse events to the IRB and to NIH trials:* Adverse events will be reported to the NYMC IRB, as well as to the chair of the DSMB. The DSMB has the authority to halt the trial if it perceives that harm is occurring due to the intervention. Summaries of adverse events reports will be made to the NIH in the yearly progress or report or, at the end of Year 5, in the final report, unless the nature of a particular event is such that it bears reporting to NIH immediately.
- *A detailed plan to deal with serious events that may arise:* The plan will address serious events, such as BPs that indicate a hypertensive emergency, that may occur during the baseline and follow-up periods—the only times that any of our personnel will take such measurements—and will include a step-by-step algorithm to deal with such events.
- *An annual review of adverse events:* The DSMB will meet with the PI and the co-investigators yearly for a review of any adverse event reports and patient complaints and of dropout rates. Data will be provided at those meetings by the investigators on key variables that may indicate harm, including changes in BP and cardiovascular risk profile, anxiety, and self-reported adherence to medication regimen. The DSMB biostatistician will evaluate the confidentiality and integrity of the database and the procedures for recording and storing confidential files. The DSMB will also review the elements of the plan to deal with emergencies.

## Notes: Ethical Concerns Example (Continued)

{17} Data and safety monitoring is discussed in detail later in this chapter. *It is only relevant if you are conducting a clinical trial!*

{18} You may not require an actual Data and Safety Monitoring Board; you may only need to submit a data and safety monitoring plan as part of your proposal, depending on the intrusiveness or invasiveness of the proposed intervention and the importance of the outcome measures (e.g., patient satisfaction or possible death). Your NIH program officer will tell you this, and the Data and Safety Monitoring section of this chapter will also give you additional guidance. In the event you *are* required to have a DSMB, you may be allowed to develop one yourself, as is the case here, or the NIH may appoint one for you, again, depending on the nature of the intervention and outcomes. The DSMB composition described for the trial in this example may not be the same as that for a different trial.

The DSMB will perform the following activities:

- Review the research protocol and plans for data and safety monitoring.
- Evaluate the progress of the interventional trial, including periodic assessments of data quality and timeliness, participant recruitment, accrual and retention, participant risk versus benefit, performance of trial sites, and other factors that can affect study outcome.
- When interpreting the data, consider factors external to the study, such as scientific or therapeutic developments, that may have an impact on the safety of the participants or the ethics of the study: for example, a systematic trend showing poorer, rather than increased, BP control or cardiovascular risk profile, in the intervention vs. the control condition.
- Make recommendations to the IRB and investigators concerning continuation or conclusion of the trial.
- Protect the confidentiality of the trial data and the results of monitoring.

# HUMAN SUBJECTS CONCERNS

The Office of Human Research Protections (OHRP) has set out the regulations for addressing human subjects concerns in a document referred to as 45 CFR 46. You may see the document in its entirety on the Department of Health and Human Services (HHS) Web site.[6] I shall be referring to various subsections of that document so that, in the event you want or need to check the source, you will be able to. However, I have provided all the material you will need, most of the time, in the following sections.

The first question you will need to ask is, "Does my proposed research involve human subjects?" The answer to this question is not as obvious as it seems, and I refer you to an excellent chart on the HHS site that will shepherd you through this decision.[7] This HHS page, as you will see, contains a set of flow charts designed to help you make various decisions concerning human subjects. Chart 1 helps to answer the question of whether your research actually does involve human subjects.

Safety issues, of course, must be specified within the context of each study, and it is incumbent on you, the researcher, to ascertain what forms harm might take. Let us use the guided breathing example we have been looking at. Certainly, the intervention seems benign enough, asking people to slow down their breathing to 6–10 breaths a minute for 15 minutes from a typical average of 16 or so breaths per minute. It is possible, however, that some people are particularly sensitive to the reduction in oxygen that this change will bring about in their blood. The application includes the description of a procedure to measure the effect of the breathing device on ventilation and $CO_2$ balance. The authors anticipated a safety issue and took steps to address it, thus allaying in advance a reviewer's potential concern. Presumably, their IRB forms will mention this safety concern as well.

What other safety issues might one see in the guided breathing example? The participants will wear 24-hour ambulatory blood pressure arm cuffs; it seems possible that abrasions might result from this extended period. It also seems likely that the participants' sleep will be disrupted. Finally, the researchers propose to give a self-report anxiety measure to participants. Is it possible that such a measure will actually cause anxiety in and of itself? You may think these concerns are trivial, but your IRB may not. You will have to submit the forms—which, by the way, include the consent form you will ask the participant to sign—and see on which issues the IRB focuses.

The sample proposal involved no invasive measures. If the IRB might be worried about irritation from the arm cuff, imagine what they might worry about if you are giving medications, or, for that matter, *withholding* medications or removing tissue. You have to be ethical, but you should also be strategic, in the sense that you anticipate potential threats and state, in your proposal and in your IRB application, how you will deal with these.

# INFORMED CONSENT

Although for some studies you will be able to have consent waived (see the discussion below on waivers), most studies involving human subjects are going to require that participants sign a consent form before engaging in any of the study procedures. Your IRB will likely have its own consent form, and you will have to follow it faithfully to get their approval. If your IRB does *not* have its own form, obtain one (via the Web) from a large medical school, then submit it (blank) to your IRB and ask if they will accept it. The consent must describe the procedures of the study so that participants understand them; use simple language, not jargon. You must describe the conditions of the study—for example, that the participant may be randomized to a control condition. (A useful strategy in an intervention trial is to explain to patients that if they end up in the control condition, they will be provided the option of availing themselves of the intervention after they have completed the trial.) You want the subjects to be blind to the study hypotheses, yet you have to tell them about your manipulation; that can be a problem. Use language that is general, and do not highlight this point to the extent you can appropriately avoid it. Note that the remainder of this section assumes that your research is *not* for a waiver of consent.

## Developing a Consent Procedure

The OHRP provides a set of tips concerning the development of your consent procedure. I have abstracted the salient points here, but you can see the entire document on the HHS Web site.[8]

*Informed consent is a process, not just a form.* Information must be presented to enable persons to voluntarily decide whether or not to participate as a research subject. The consent process is a fundamental mechanism to ensure respect for persons through the provision of thoughtful consent for a voluntary act. The procedures used in obtaining informed consent should be designed to educate the subject population in terms that they can understand. Therefore, informed consent language and its documentation (especially the explanation of the study's purpose, duration, experimental procedures, alternatives, risks, and benefits) must be written in lay language; that is, it must be understandable to the people being asked to participate. The written presentation of information is used to document the basis for consent and for the subjects' future reference. The consent document should be revised when deficiencies are noted or when additional information will improve the consent process.

*Think of the document primarily as a teaching tool, not as a legal instrument.* Use of the first person voice (e.g., "I understand that . . .") can be interpreted as suggestive, may be relied upon as a substitute for sufficient factual information, and can constitute coercive influence over a subject and so should be avoided. Similarly, the use of scientific jargon and legalese is not appropriate in the consent process.

*Describe the overall experience that will be encountered.* Explain the research activity, how it is experimental (e.g., it involves a new drug, extra tests, separate research records, or nonstandard means of management). Inform the human subjects of the reasonably foreseeable harms, discomforts, inconvenience, and risks that are associated with the research activity. If additional risks are identified during the course of the research, the consent process and documentation will require revisions to inform subjects as they are recontacted or newly contacted.

*Describe the benefits that subjects may reasonably expect to encounter.* There may be benefits other than a sense of helping the public at large. If payment is given to defray the incurred expense for participation, it must not be coercive in amount or method of distribution.

*Describe any alternatives to participating in the research project.* For example, in drug studies the medications may be available through a family doctor or clinic without the need to volunteer for the research activity.

*Tell subjects about the study's confidentiality policy.* Regulations insist that the subjects be told the extent to which their personally identifiable private information will be held in confidence. For example, some studies require disclosure of information to other parties; other studies inherently are in need of a Certificate of Confidentiality (see the discussion below), which protects the investigator from involuntary release (e.g., by subpoena) of the names or other identifying characteristics of research subjects. The IRB will determine the level of adequate requirements for confidentiality in light of its mandate to ensure the minimization of risk and its determination that the residual risks warrant involvement of subjects.

*Discuss compensation for research-related injury.* If research-related injury—physical, psychological, social, financial, or otherwise—is possible in research, that constitutes more than minimal risk (see the OHRP regulations, 45 CFR 46.102[g]) and an explanation must be given of whatever voluntary compensation and treatment will be provided for such injury. *Note that the regulations do not limit injury to "physical injury."* This is a common misinterpretation.

The regulations prohibit waiving or appearing to waive any legal rights of subjects. Therefore, consent language must be carefully selected that deals with what the institution is voluntarily willing to do under various circumstances, such as providing for compensation beyond the provision of immediate or therapeutic intervention in response to a research-related injury. In short, subjects should not be given the impression that they have agreed to and are without recourse to seek satisfaction beyond the institution's voluntarily chosen limits.

*Identify people qualified to provide answers to participants' questions.* The OHRP regulations require that you identify contact persons who would be knowledgeable enough to answer questions about the research, participants' rights as research subjects, and research-related injuries. These three areas must be explicitly named and addressed in the consent process and documentation. Furthermore, a single contact person is not likely to be appropriate to answer questions in all areas because of potential conflicts of interest or the appearance of such. Questions about the research are frequently best answered by the investigators. However, questions about the rights of research subjects or research-related injuries may best be referred to those not on the research team. These questions could be addressed to the IRB, an ombudsman, an ethics committee, or another informed administrative body. Therefore, each consent document can be expected to have at least two names, with local telephone numbers, to act as contacts to answer questions in these specified areas.

*The statement regarding voluntary participation and the right to withdraw at any time can be taken almost verbatim from the OHRP regulations (45 CFR 46.116[a][8]).* It is important not to overlook the need to point out that no penalty or loss of benefits will occur as a result of either not participating or withdrawing at any time. It is equally important to alert potential subjects to any foreseeable consequences to them should they unilaterally withdraw while dependent on some intervention to maintain normal function.

*Ensure provision for appropriate* additional requirements *that concern consent.* Some of these requirements can be found in the OHRP regulations (45 CFR parts 46.116[b], 46.205[a][2], 46.207[b], 46.208[b], 46.209[d], 46.305[a][5–6], 46.408[c], and 46.409[b]). The IRB may impose additional requirements that are not specifically listed in the regulations to ensure that adequate information is presented in accordance with institutional policy and local law.

In addition to these helpful tips, the OHRP has also provided a checklist of items that must be included in the consent. This checklist can be found on the HHS site and is also included in Appendix C.[9]

## Consent Form Checklist

The basic elements of the consent form are

- A statement that the study involves research.
- An explanation of the purposes of the research.
- The expected duration of the subject's participation.
- A description of the procedures to be followed.
- Identification of any procedures that are experimental.
- A description of any reasonably foreseeable risks or discomforts to the subject.
- A description of any benefits to the subject or to others that may reasonably be expected from the research.
- A disclosure of appropriate alternative procedures or courses of treatment, if any, that might be advantageous to the subject.
- A statement describing the extent, if any, to which confidentiality of records identifying the subject will be maintained.
- For research involving more than minimal risk, an explanation as to whether any compensation will be offered as well as an explanation as to whether any medical treatments will be available if injury occurs and, if so, what they will consist of or where further information may be obtained.
- An explanation of whom to contact for answers to pertinent questions about the research and research subjects' rights, and whom to contact in the event of a research-related injury to the subject.
- A statement that participation is voluntary, that refusal to participate will involve no penalty or loss of benefits to which the subject is otherwise entitled, and that the subject may discontinue participation at any time without penalty or loss of benefits to which the subject is otherwise entitled.

Additional elements of the consent, as appropriate, include

- A statement that the particular treatment or procedure may involve risks to the subject (or to the embryo or fetus, if the subject is or may become pregnant), which are currently unforeseeable.
- Anticipated circumstances under which the subject's participation may be terminated by the investigator without regard to the subject's consent.
- Any additional costs to the subject that may result from participation in the research.
- The consequences of a subject's decision to withdraw from the research and procedures for orderly termination of participation by the subject.
- A statement that significant new findings developed during the course of the research, which may relate to the subject's willingness to continue participation, will be provided to the subject.
- The approximate number of subjects involved in the study.

## IRB Latitude

The IRB has the latitude to approve a consent procedure that alters or waives some or all of the elements of consent. According to the OHRP requirements (45 CFR 46.116), the IRB may do so under the following conditions:

C:1 The research or demonstration project is to be conducted by, or subject to the approval of, state or local government officials, and is designed to study, evaluate, or otherwise examine: (1) public benefit or service programs; (2) procedures for obtaining benefits or services under those programs; (3) possible changes in or alternatives to those programs or procedures; or (4) possible changes in methods or levels of payment for benefits or services under those programs; and

C:2 The research could not practicably be carried out without the waiver or alteration.

D:1 The research involves no more than minimal risk to the subjects;

D:2 The waiver or alteration will not adversely affect the rights and welfare of the subjects;

D:3 The research could not practicably be carried out without the waiver or alteration; and

D:4 Whenever appropriate, the subjects will be provided with additional pertinent information after participation.

# EXPEDITED REVIEW

The OHRP notes that an expedited review procedure consists of a review of research involving human subjects by the IRB chairperson or by one or more experienced reviewers designated by the chairperson from among members of the IRB (45 CFR 46.110). If your study is eligible for an expedited review, this can save you time in terms of how long it takes to get your study approved. The criteria, as set out by OHRP, are as follows.[10]

## Research Categories Open to Expedited Review

Categories of research that may receive an expedited review by the IRB include research activities that (a) represent no more than a minimal risk to human subjects, *and* (b) involve only procedures specifically listed as exempted from a full review by the OHRP guidelines (see the Procedures Open to Expedited Review section, below, for the full list). Note that the activities listed should not be deemed to be of minimal risk simply because they are included on this list, and classified research involving human subjects *is not* open to expedited review. Furthermore, the expedited review may not be used where identification of the participants or their responses would reasonably subject them to criminal or civil liability or might endanger them in other ways, such as financially or socially, unless reasonable and appropriate protections will be implemented to minimize the risks related to invasion of privacy and breach of confidentiality.

Finally, the standard requirements for informed consent, or its waiver, alteration, or exception, apply regardless of the type of review utilized by the IRB.

## Procedures Open to Expedited Review

Research studies that involve only the following types activities are open to expedited review by your IRB, *but only when the research represents no more than a minimal risk to human subjects:*

1. Clinical studies of drugs and medical devices, but only when the research poses no more than a minimal risk to the human subjects.

2. Research on drugs for which an investigational new drug application (21 CFR 312) is not required. However, research on marketed drugs that significantly increases the risks or decreases the acceptability of the risks associated with the use of the product is not eligible for expedited review.

3. Research on medical devices for which (a) an investigational device exemption application (21 CFR 812) is not required; or (b) the medical device is cleared or approved for marketing and the medical device is being used in accordance with its approved labeling.

4. Collection of blood samples by finger stick, heel stick, ear stick, or venipuncture from (a) healthy, nonpregnant adults who weigh at least 110 pounds (the amounts drawn may not exceed 550 ml in an 8-week period and collection may not occur more than 2 times per week), or (b) from other adults and children, considering the age, weight, and health of the subjects, the collection procedure, the amount of blood to be collected, and the frequency with which it will be collected (for these subjects, the amount drawn may not exceed the lesser of 50 ml or 3 ml per kg in an 8-week period and collection may not occur more than 2 times per week).

5. Prospective collection of biological specimens for research purposes by noninvasive means (e.g., hair and nail clippings in a nondisfiguring manner; deciduous teeth at time of exfoliation or if routine patient care indicates a need for extraction; excreta and external secretions, including sweat; mucosal and skin cells collected by buccal scraping or swab; or sputum collected).

6. Collection of data through noninvasive procedures that do not involve general anesthesia or sedation and that are routinely employed in clinical practice (excluding procedures involving x-rays or microwaves). Where medical devices are employed, they must be cleared or approved for marketing.

7. Research involving materials (data, documents, records, or specimens) that have been collected, or will be collected solely for nonresearch purposes (such as medical treatment or diagnosis). Some research in this category may be exempt from the HHS regulations for the protection of human subjects (45 CFR 46.101[b][4]).

8. Collection of data from voice, video, digital, or image recordings made for research purposes.

9. Research on individual or group characteristics or behavior, including but not limited to research on perception, cognition, motivation, identity, language, communication, cultural beliefs or practices, and social behavior; or research employing survey, interview, oral history, focus group, program evaluation, human factors evaluation, or quality assurance methodologies. Some research in this category may be exempt from the HHS regulations for the protection of human subjects (45 CFR 46.101[b][2] and [b][3]).

10. Continuing review of research previously approved by the convened IRB (a) where the research is permanently closed to the enrollment of new subjects, all subjects have completed all research-related interventions, *and* the research remains active only for long-term follow-up of subjects; (b) where no subjects have been enrolled and no additional risks have been identified; or (c) where the remaining research activities are limited to data analysis.

11. Continuing review of research, not conducted under an investigational new drug application or investigational device exemption where items 2 through 8 (above) do not apply but the IRB has determined and documented at a convened meeting that the research involves no greater than minimal risk and no additional risks have been identified.

Please note that items 1 through 7 pertain to both initial and continuing IRB review. If you require additional guidance as to whether your application may be eligible for expedited review by your IRB, the HHS Web site offers a decision tree to help you make your determination.[11]

## WAIVER OF THE REQUIREMENT FOR A SIGNED CONSENT FORM

In some cases, an IRB may waive the requirement for the investigator to obtain a signed consent form for some or all subjects. The OHRP notes that this may be true if the IRB finds either of the following conditions:

- That the only record linking the subject and the research would be the consent document, and the *principal risk* would be potential harm resulting from a breach of confidentiality. Each subject will be asked whether he or she wants documentation linking him or her with the research, and the subject's wishes will govern.
- That the research presents *no more than minimal risk* of harm to subjects and involves no procedures for which written consent is normally required outside of the research context.

In cases in which the documentation requirement is waived, the IRB may require the investigator to provide subjects with a written statement regarding the research.

If you have doubts about whether or not you may need a waiver, I once again refer you to the set of decision charts available on the HHS Web site: In this case, you will want Chart 2.[12]

### Informed Consent Exemptions

There are six conditions under which your study may be exempt from informed consent procedures. The exemptions, quoted from the HHS/OHRP Web site, follow.

1. Research conducted in established or commonly accepted educational settings, involving normal educational practices, such as (i) research on regular and special education instructional strategies, or (ii) research on the effectiveness of or the comparison among instructional techniques, curricula, or classroom management methods.

2. Research involving the use of educational tests (cognitive, diagnostic, aptitude, achievement), survey procedures, interview procedures, or observation of public behavior, unless (i) information obtained is recorded in such a manner that human subjects can be identified, directly or through identifiers linked to the subjects; and (ii) any disclosure of the human subjects' responses outside the research could reasonably place the subjects at risk of criminal or civil liability or be damaging to the subjects' financial standing, employability, or reputation.

3. Research involving the use of educational tests (cognitive, diagnostic, aptitude, achievement), survey procedures, interview procedures, or observation of public behavior that is not otherwise exempt [see Chart 4 on the HHS/OHRP Web site], if (i) the human subjects are elected or appointed public officials or candidates for public office; or (ii) Federal statute(s) require(s) without exception that the confidentiality of the personally identifiable information will be maintained throughout the research and thereafter.

4. Research involving the collection or study of existing data, documents, records, pathological specimens, or diagnostic specimens, if these sources are publicly available or if the information is recorded by the investigator in such a manner that subjects cannot be identified, directly or through identifiers linked to the subjects.

5. Research and demonstration projects which are conducted by or subject to the approval of Department or Agency heads, and which are designed to study, evaluate, or otherwise examine (i) public benefit or service programs; (ii) procedures for obtaining benefits or services under those programs; (iii) possible changes in or alternatives to those programs or procedures; or (iv) possible changes in methods or levels of payment for benefits or services under those programs.

6. Taste and food quality evaluation and consumer acceptance studies, (i) if wholesome foods without additives are consumed or (ii) if a food is consumed that contains a food ingredient at or below the level and for a use found to be safe, or agricultural chemical or environmental contaminant at or below the level found to be safe, by the Food and Drug Administration or approved by the Environmental Protection Agency or the Food Safety and Inspection Service of the U.S. Department of Agriculture.

I think these six conditions under which you may request an exemption are self-explanatory. However, check with someone at your institution's IRB concerning your specific research scenario.

Get in the habit of personally delivering documents to and asking questions of IRB personnel; this way, you will get to know them, and you will find that you learn considerably more about what you may and may not do than if you always send an assistant or ask questions by e-mail.

## Refusers

You are obligated to tell the prospective participant about all the procedures (for example, you can't wait until the end of the study to tell them they have to have a blood draw). Will this lead to nonparticipation? Sure. And, as you saw in Chapter 5, you should estimate (based on pretesting, if possible) the refusal rate, so you know how many participants you will have to approach to end with the required number. Also, there is the issue of generalizability: If a substantial proportion refuses, what does that say about the persons who agree? How are they different from those who refused? The IRB won't necessarily care about this, but the reviewers will. One strategy is to prepare a second consent form, for refusers, to allow you to ask them some demographic questions and perhaps give them a few personality question-naires. It is useful to be able to say that differences on key variables were compared between refusers and agreers, and that they didn't differ (you hope).

The consent form is not a minor matter. If you haven't created one before, ask colleagues who have successfully been approved by your IRB if you can see a couple of theirs that passed muster. In many cases, the consent form will contain language that you must use (e.g., in informing patients that their medical care will in no way be affected if they decide not to participate). This language will appear in your colleagues' forms.

## Revisions

Often, your IRB application will be returned to you, denied. The IRB will tell you why. The reason may be trivial and easily fixed, such as a typographical error (no kidding), a small omission, or an inconsistency (perhaps you said you would pay the subjects one amount in one place, but a different amount in another). If this is the case, revise your appli-cation quickly and resubmit it to the IRB. Sometimes, the objection can be so great that there may be no way around it. If that is the case, you had better know it immediately, before you begin writing the proposal. Thus, if you anticipate that your application will meet with serious objections, ask the IRB immediately, before you invest time and energy in the proposal.

# INCLUSION OF CHILDREN IN RESEARCH

Two areas you must address in your NIH proposal are the inclusion of children and the inclusion of women and minorities (discussed below) in your research.

Children are defined in the HHS regulations as "persons who have not attained the legal age for consent to treatments or procedures involved in the research, under the applicable law of the jurisdiction in which the research will be conducted" (45 CFR 46.402[a]).

The NIH provides a flow diagram to help you determine if children can or cannot participate in research, which I have reproduced in Figure 6.3.

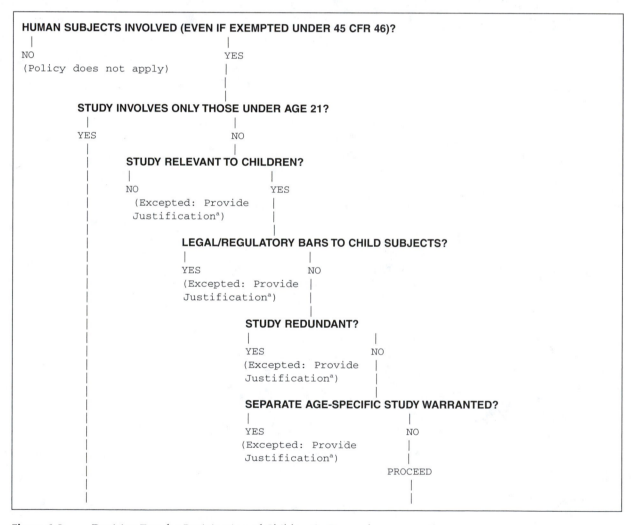

**Figure 6.3**     Decision Tree for Participation of Children in Research

SOURCE: http://grants.nih.gov/grants/funding/children/pol_children_decision_tree.htm.

a. Exceptions will be granted with a clear and compelling rationale and justification establishing that inclusion would be inappropriate according to the above-delineated decision tree.

The application should describe plans to include children, justifying the age range of children chosen for inclusion as well as outlining the expertise of the investigative team for dealing with children of the ages included, the appropriateness of the available facilities to accommodate the children, and the inclusion of a sufficient number of children to contribute to a meaningful analysis, relative to the purpose of the study.

The following Web sites will prove helpful if you are planning to either include, or to exclude, children:

"Inclusion of Children Policy Implementation": http://grants2.nih.gov/grants/funding/children/children.htm

"Inclusion of Women and Minorities as Participants in Research Involving Human Subjects": http://grants.nih.gov/grants/funding/women_min/women_min.htm

The NIH also provides two similarly named Web pages to answer frequently asked questions and to address common NIH concerns:

"OER Human Subjects Web site: Frequently Asked Questions From Applicants": http://grants1.nih.gov/grants/policy/hs/faqs_applicants.htm

"OER Human Subjects Web Site: Frequently Asked Questions": http://grants1.nih.gov/grants/policy/hs/faqs_concerns.htm

You may also find it useful to look at the revised policy for IRB review of human subjects protocols in grant applications, which is available at http://grants2.nih.gov/grants/guide/notice-files/NOT-OD-00-031.html.

## Research Categories Involving Children

For any protocol involving children, the IRB must determine which of the four following categories of research apply to that study, if any. The HHS regulations (45 CFR 46[d]) permit IRBs to approve three categories of research involving children as subjects:

1. *Research not involving greater than minimal risk to the children.* To approve this category of research, the IRB must make the following determinations: (a) The research presents no greater than minimal risk to the children and (b) adequate provisions are made for soliciting the assent of the children and the permission of their parents or guardians (45 CFR 46.404).

2. *Research involving greater than minimal risk but presenting the prospect of direct benefit to the individual child subjects involved in the research.* To approve research in this category, the IRB must determine that (a) the risk is justified by the anticipated benefits to the subjects; (b) the relation of the anticipated benefit to the risk presented by the study is at least as favorable to the subjects as that provided by available alternative approaches; and (c) adequate provisions are made for soliciting the assent of the children and the permission of their parents or guardians (45 CFR 46.405).

3. *Research involving greater than minimal risk and no prospect of direct benefit to the individual child subjects involved in the research, but likely to yield generalizable knowledge*

*about the subject's disorder or condition.* To approve research in this category, the IRB must make the following determinations: (a) The risk of the research represents a minor increase over minimal risk; (b) the intervention or procedure presents experiences to the child subjects that are reasonably commensurate with those inherent in their actual or expected medical, dental, psychological, social, or educational situations; (c) the intervention or procedure is likely to yield generalizable knowledge about the subject's disorder or condition that is of vital importance for the understanding or amelioration of the disorder or condition; and (d) adequate provisions are made for soliciting the assent of the children and the permission of their parents or guardians (45 CFR 46.406).

A fourth category of research requires a special level of HHS review beyond that provided by the IRB:

*4. Research that the IRB believes does not meet the conditions outlined in the three previous categories, but finds that the research presents a reasonable opportunity to further the understanding, prevention, or alleviation of a serious problem affecting the health or welfare of children.* In this case, the IRB may refer the protocol to the HHS for review (45 CFR 46.407).

The research may proceed only if the secretary of Health and Human Services, or his or her designee, after consulting with a panel of experts in pertinent disciplines (e.g., science, medicine, education, ethics, law) and following an opportunity for public review and comment, determines either (a) that the research in fact satisfies the conditions discussed above or (b) the following:

- The research presents a reasonable opportunity to further the understanding, prevention, or alleviation of a serious problem affecting the health or welfare of children.
- The research will be conducted in accordance with sound ethical principles.
- Adequate provisions are made for soliciting the assent of children and the permission of their parents or guardians, as set forth in HHS regulations at 45 CFR 46.408.

For more information on the HHS review process, see "Office for Human Research Protections [OHRP]; Special Protections for Children as Research Subjects: Guidance on the HHS 45 CFR 46.407 ("407") Review Process," which is available online.[13]

There are more conditional statements to address special requirements; if you need to go further, I refer you to the various Web sites referenced earlier in this section. It is important that you understand that the *exclusion* of children must be strongly justified. You might want to look again at the caveat provided by the NIH at the end of the decision tree reproduced in Figure 6.3:

Exceptions will be granted with a clear and compelling rationale and justification establishing that inclusion would be inappropriate according to the above-delineated decision tree.

Remember: Children are persons under age 18 (i.e., of legal age); if you are planning to exclude persons from, say, age 18 to 21, this is not an issue. However, even if excluding children under age 18, I suggest you give your reasons. A common and legitimate justification for the exclusion of children is that the illness or outcome you are studying does not affect that population. Thus, for example, in studies in which persons with hypertension are the focus, I typically would set my inclusion age at 18 (there is the occasional 18-year-old with high blood pressure), but would not examine persons younger than that—nor would the reviewers expect me to.

*Special Requirements.* The HHS imposes additional protections for children involved as subjects in research in 45 CFR 46(d). These protections require that the IRB determine whether adequate provisions are made for soliciting the assent of the children:

> The IRB shall determine that adequate provisions are made for soliciting the assent of the children, when in the judgment of the IRB the children are capable of providing assent. If the IRB determines that the capability of some or all of the children is so limited that they cannot reasonably be consulted, or that the intervention or procedure involved in the research holds out a prospect of direct benefit that is important to the health or well-being of the children, and is available only in the context of the research, the assent of the children is not a necessary condition for proceeding with the research. Even where the IRB determines that the subjects are capable of assenting, the IRB may still waive the assent requirement under circumstances, in which consent may be waived in accord with [45 CFR 46.116(a)].

# INCLUSION OF WOMEN AND MINORITIES IN RESEARCH

The NIH has made a major push over the past several years to gain fair representation of women and minorities in medical research. The NIH Web site provides links to several pages that explain and clarify the NIH's policy on the inclusion of women and minorities. I have abstracted the main points below, but I do recommend you consult the NIH policy statements.[14]

## Inclusion of Women and Minorities as Subjects in Clinical Research

The "NIH Policy and Guidelines on the Inclusion of Women and Minorities as Subjects in Clinical Research" reads as follows:

> It is the policy of the NIH that women and members of minority groups and their subpopulations must be included in all NIH-funded clinical research, unless a clear and compelling rationale and justification establishes to the satisfaction of the relevant Institute/Center director that inclusion is inappropriate with respect to the health of the subjects or the purpose of the research. Exclusion under other circumstances may be made by the director of the NIH, upon the recommendation of an Institute/Center director *based on a compelling rationale and justification.* Cost is not an acceptable reason for exclusion except when the study would duplicate data from other sources. (italics added)

Women of childbearing potential should not be routinely excluded from participation in clinical research. This policy applies to research subjects of all ages in all NIH-supported clinical research studies.

The inclusion of women and members of minority groups and their subpopulations must be addressed in developing a research plan (for a grant application) or proposal (for a contract solicitation) appropriate to the scientific objectives of the study. The research plan or proposal should describe the composition of the proposed study population in terms of sex/gender and racial/ethnic group, and provide a rationale for selection of such subjects. Such a plan should contain a description of the proposed outreach programs for recruiting women and minorities as participants.

### NIH-Defined Phase III Clinical Trials: Planning, Conducting, and Reporting of Analyses for Sex/Gender and Race/Ethnicity Differences

The "NIH Policy and Guidelines on the Inclusion of Women and Minorities as Subjects in Clinical Research" reads as follows:

> When an NIH-defined Phase III clinical trial is proposed, evidence must be reviewed to show whether or not clinically important sex/gender and race/ethnicity differences in the intervention effect are to be expected. This evidence may include, but is not limited to, data derived from prior animal studies, clinical observations, metabolic studies, genetic studies, pharmacology studies, and observational, natural history, epidemiology and other relevant studies.

> Investigators must consider the following when planning, conducting, analyzing, and reporting an NIH-Defined Phase III clinical trial. Based on prior studies, one of . . . three situations . . . will apply.

*1. Prior Studies Support the Existence of Significant Differences.* If the data from prior studies strongly support the existence of significant differences of clinical or public health importance in intervention effect based on sex/gender, racial/ethnic, and relevant subpopulation comparisons, the primary questions to be addressed by the proposed NIH-defined Phase III clinical trial and *the design of that trial must specifically accommodate this*). For example, if men and women are thought to respond differently to an intervention, then the Phase III clinical trial must be designed to answer two separate primary questions, one for men and the other for women, with adequate sample size for each.

The research plan or contract proposal must include a description of plans to conduct analyses to detect significant differences in intervention effect by sex/gender, racial/ethnic groups, and relevant subpopulations, if applicable. The final protocols approved by the IRB must include these plans for analysis. If an award is granted, you will be required, for each funded protocol, to report annually on cumulative subject accrual and progress in conducting analyses for sex/gender and race/ethnicity differences. If your final analyses are not available when you submit the final progress report or an application for a grant continuation, then a justification and plan ensuring completion and reporting of the analyses will be required. If final analyses are required as part of a contract award, these analyses must be included as part of the deliverables. These requirements will be cited in the terms and conditions of all awards for grants, cooperative agreements, and contracts supporting NIH-defined Phase III clinical trials.

Please note that the NIH strongly encourages the inclusion of the results of sex/gender, race/ethnicity, and relevant subpopulations analyses in all publication submissions that result from an NIH-supported study. If these analyses reveal no differences, a brief statement to that effect, indicating the groups and/or subgroups analyzed, will suffice.

*2. Prior Studies Support No Significant Differences.* If the data from prior studies strongly support no significant differences of clinical or public health importance in intervention effect based on sex/gender, racial/ethnic, or relevant subpopulation comparisons, then sex/gender and race/ethnicity will not be required as subject selection criteria. However, the inclusion and analysis of sex/gender and racial/ethnic subgroups is still strongly encouraged.

*3. Prior Studies Neither Support Nor Negate Significant Differences.* If the data from prior studies neither strongly support nor strongly negate the existence of significant differences based on sex/gender, racial/ethnic, and relevant subpopulation comparisons, then the NIH-defined Phase III clinical trial will be required to include sufficient and appropriate entry of sex/gender and racial/ethnic participants, so that you can perform a valid analysis of the intervention effects. However, you will not be required to provide high statistical power for these comparisons.

As described above in situation 1, your research plan or contract proposal must include a description of plans to conduct valid analysis by gender and race, and the IRB-approved final protocols must include these plans. You will also be required, if awarded a grant or contract, to report annually on cumulative subject accrual and progress in conducting analyses for gender and race differences. If your final analyses are not available when you submit your final progress report or application for grant continuation, then you must submit a justification and plan ensuring completion and reporting of the analyses. If final analyses are required as part of a contract award, these analyses must be included as part of the deliverables. These requirements will be cited in the terms and conditions of all awards for grants, cooperative agreements, and contracts supporting NIH-defined Phase III clinical trials.

Again, remember that the NIH strongly encourages the inclusion of the results of sex/gender, race/ethnicity, and relevant subpopulations analyses in all publication submissions that result from an NIH-supported trial. If these analyses reveal no differences, a brief statement to that effect, indicating the groups and/or subgroups analyzed, will suffice.

Also, please note that, *for all three situations, cost is not an acceptable reason for exclusion of women and minorities from clinical trials.*

You must show the NIH how you plan to sample in terms of sex and minority status using a Targeted/Planned Enrollment Table, which is shown and discussed in Chapter 7.

## Specific Questions

The NIH provides the following important additional information, which is taken from the "Outreach Notebook: Frequently Asked Questions Regarding the NIH Guidelines on the Inclusion of Women and Minorities in Clinical Research."[15]

• *What should you do if you are located in a geographic area that does not offer a study population with the diversity required by the policy on the inclusion of women and minorities in clinical research studies?*

In your proposal, you must provide a clear and compelling description and rationale for your proposed study population and its appropriateness for the purpose of your research. When there is limited representation of women or members of racial/ethnic groups in your study population, you must also provide a satisfactory rationale for the lack of that diversity based on the health of the participants and the scientific needs of the research being proposed. If you are aware of similar research completed or underway employing populations complementary to those available in your locale, you can present this as a rationale for limited representation. If the appropriate diversity cannot be achieved in your geographic area, you must address the feasibility of making collaborative or other arrangements to include greater diversity (e.g., you might seek collaborators in other geographic areas where there is access to more diverse populations).

• *Is increased cost an acceptable justification for not including women, minorities, and subpopulations in clinical research studies?*

No. The legislation states that the cost associated with increasing the diversity of a clinical research study population is *not* an acceptable justification for excluding any group.

• *In multicenter clinical research studies, does each study site have to meet the inclusion requirements separately?*

No. When multicenter clinical research studies are proposed, the inclusion requirements may be met by *combining* recruitment from the multiple sites. However, each clinical site must still describe its planned recruitment, retention, and outreach plans, which will be evaluated as part of the initial review of the proposal. As part of its funding plan, the NIH may select recruitment sites with high minority or relevant subpopulation enrollments for inclusion in multicenter studies to achieve inclusion of the most diverse study population.

- *What if my new proposal involves analyzing secondary data in which the race and ethnicity categories do not comply with the new guidelines?*

If you are using secondary data sets that do not conform to the current guidelines and if you do not plan to collect any new or additional data from the subjects, this should be noted in your proposal. In this circumstance, you should complete a Targeted/Planned Enrollment Table (see Chapter 7) if you are submitting a new application, or, if the data allow, the Inclusion Enrollment Report if you are submitting a continuation application, competing supplement applications, and or annual Grant Progress Report. However, if the existing data do not allow accurate correspondence with the new categories in the Inclusion Enrollment Report, then you should report the information using the prior categories and use the April 1998 version of the Inclusion Table.

- *Can more detailed questions about ethnicity and race be asked than current guidelines indicate?*

The Office of Management and Budget (OMB) guidelines provide minimal standards for data collection. Indeed, you are encouraged to explore collecting additional types of information on race and ethnicity that will provide additional insights into the relationships between race and ethnicity and health. For example, after asking the required questions about ethnicity and race, you may opt to ask study participants who choose multiple race/ethnicity categories to identify the group with which they primarily identify. Further questions identifying membership in racial or ethnic subpopulations may also be considered: For example, you may want to ask individuals who select American Indian or Alaskan Native to identify the name of the enrolled or principal tribe. Or, you may want to ask about identification with specific subpopulations within specific ethnic or racial categories (e.g., Puerto Rican, Cuban, Chinese, Japanese, etc.). The scientific question being addressed in the study should guide your decisions regarding the collection of any additional information. You can report information on subpopulations by listing it in an attachment to the required reporting table.

- *What ethnic and racial categories should be used to estimate race and ethnicity?*

You should use the categories described in the PHS 398 or the SF 424 instructions (depending on which forms you are using) and listed in the Targeted/Planned Enrollment Table (see Chapter 7).

- *Where can I find examples of questions for collecting data on ethnicity and race that I could use in my research?*

There are several federal data instruments in the public domain that include questions on ethnicity and race. One is the "Ethnic Origin and Race" section of the Personal Data form in the PHS 398, which is available on the NIH Web site.[16] This data form includes questions that meet the minimum OMB standards by asking the individual first about ethnicity, followed by a question that provides the option of selecting more than one racial designation. That form will soon become obsolete, as you must now provide that information on the NIH eRA Commons Web page, which contains your personal information. (All grant applicants must register with the eRA Commons site.)

You also may want to explore collecting additional types of information on race and ethnicity to provide greater insights into the relationships between race, ethnicity, and health, as discussed above. Examples of federal data instruments that include more detailed questions about ethnicity and race can be found through the U.S. Census Bureau and the Demographics Information collected in the Sample Person Questionnaire of the National Health and Nutrition Examination Survey (NHANES).[17]

- *What will NIH reviewers look for in applications regarding the inclusion of women and minorities in clinical research?*

Peer reviewers will be asked to evaluate whether the research plan in the application complies with the policy to include women and minorities in clinical research studies. Specifically, they will evaluate whether the plan is acceptable or unacceptable. Reviewers are instructed that their assessment of the applicant's plan should be factored into the score for scientific and technical merit and that they should provide a narrative text to answer each of the following questions:

- Does the applicant propose a plan for the inclusion of minorities and both sexes for appropriate representation?

- Does the applicant propose justification when representation is limited or absent?

- Does the applicant propose exclusion of minorities and women on the basis that a requirement for inclusion is inappropriate with respect to the health of the subjects and/or with respect to the purpose of the research?

- Does the applicant propose plans for recruitment, outreach, and retention of study participants, and are those plans appropriate and acceptable?

- For ongoing research projects, is the accrual data adequate in relation to target data?

- *Are there additional elements that reviewers will look for when an NIH-defined Phase III clinical trial is proposed?*

Yes. In addition to the questions listed above, when an NIH-defined Phase III clinical trial is proposed, the reviewers will evaluate the study design and analysis plan using the following two questions as a guide:

- Has evidence been adequately evaluated in terms of whether clinically important sex/gender and racial/ethnic differences in the intervention effect are to be expected?

- Has the planned trial been designed to take into account these clinically important sex/gender and/or racial/ethnic differences so that appropriate numbers from each group are planned to be included in the study, including the need to (a) detect significant differences when available evidence strongly indicates significant sex/gender and/or racial/ethnic differences; or, (b) permit valid analyses when there is no clear-cut scientific evidence to rule out significant differences between sex/gender and/or racial/ethnic groups in intervention effect?

- *Will the criteria for addressing the inclusion of women and minorities in my research plan affect the assigned score for scientific and technical merit?*

Yes. The scientific review groups (SRGs) will treat the evaluation of the representation of women and minorities and their subpopulations in a manner consistent with the evaluation of all other factors that contribute to the overall priority score. Later in this chapter, we will discuss the reviewers' coding scheme used to characterize proposals in terms of their scientific acceptability regarding the inclusion of women and minorities.

> • *How will conformance to the policy for inclusion of women and minorities in clinical research affect funding of grants and cooperative agreements?*

Regardless of the priority score your proposal receives, its percentile ranking, or the program relevance of the proposed research, the NIH funding components *will not award grants or contracts that do not comply with this policy*. If your application is selected for funding but was considered by the review group to have an unacceptable level of gender or minority inclusion, you will need to provide a corrective plan to address the deficiencies prior to the actual award.

> • *What reports need to be prepared using the data on inclusion of women and minorities?*

For all clinical research studies, you will need to provide information in your application, proposal, and progress reports using the following summary format for the Inclusion Enrollment Table for planned enrollment of women and minorities. For ongoing studies, you will need to report annually on the cumulative enrollment of the approved project: Using the same format, provide the number of subjects enrolled in each study. If you are reporting on more than one study or contract, you must provide a separate table for each study. Actual accrual will be compared to the targets for inclusion that are found in the original application/proposal.

# NIH CODING SCHEME FOR ACCEPTABILITY REGARDING INCLUSION OF WOMEN AND MINORITIES

NIH reviewers are provided with a coding scheme to help them characterize proposals in terms of the inclusion of women and minorities. Below are the codes assigned to each application for both sex/gender and minority groups. Being given an unacceptable code ("U") results in a bar to funding, and you must be resolve the inclusion problems before the study can or will be funded.

## Codes for Sex/Gender Inclusion

G1A    Includes both genders, scientifically acceptable

G2A    Includes only women, scientifically acceptable

G3A    Includes only men, scientifically acceptable

G4A    Gender representation unknown, scientifically acceptable

G1U    Includes both genders, scientifically unacceptable

G2U    Includes only women, scientifically unacceptable

G3U    Includes only men, scientifically unacceptable

G4U    Gender representation unknown, scientifically unacceptable

## Codes for Minority Inclusion

M1A    Includes minorities and nonminorities, scientifically acceptable

M2A    Includes only minorities, scientifically acceptable

**M3A**    Includes only nonminorities, scientifically acceptable

**M4A**    Minority representation unknown, scientifically acceptable

**M5A**    Includes only foreign subjects, scientifically acceptable

**M1U**    Includes minorities and nonminorities, scientifically unacceptable

**M2U**    Includes only minorities, scientifically unacceptable

**M3U**    Includes only nonminorities, scientifically unacceptable

**M4U**    Minority representation unknown, scientifically unacceptable

**M5U**    Includes only foreign subjects, scientifically unacceptable

# THE HEALTH INSURANCE PORTABILITY AND ACCOUNTABILITY ACT

The Health Insurance Portability and Accountability Act (HIPAA) Privacy Rule is the first comprehensive federal protection for the privacy of personal health information. Research organizations and researchers may or may not be covered by the HIPAA Privacy Rule.

The HHS Web site provides the full text of the information on the Privacy Rule.[18] Most of this document is geared for health organizations, so a special document on the Privacy Rule's impact on researchers has been made available on the NIH Web site.[19] This document is quite extensive, so I have abstracted the main points here. However, you may want to check out the complete document.

## Why Should Researchers Be Aware of the HIPAA Privacy Rule?

Researchers should be aware of the Privacy Rule because it establishes the conditions under which covered entities can use or disclose protected health information (PHI). Although not all researchers will have to comply with the Privacy Rule, the manner in which the rule protects PHI could affect certain aspects of research.

It is important to understand that many research organizations that handle individually identifiable health information will *not* have to comply with the Privacy Rule because they will not be covered entities (i.e., will not be subject to the Privacy Rule). The Privacy Rule will not directly regulate researchers who are engaged in research within organizations that are not covered entities even though these researchers may gather, generate, access, and share personal health information. For instance, entities that sponsor health research or create and/or maintain health information databases may not themselves be covered entities, and thus may not directly be subject to the Privacy Rule. However, researchers may rely on covered entities for research support or as sources of individually identifiable health information included in research repositories or research databases. The Privacy Rule may affect such independent researchers, as it will affect their relationships with covered entities.

*If you are not sure if your institution is covered by the HIPAA requirements, check with your grants office or your IRB.*

The Privacy Rule recognizes that the research community has legitimate needs to use, access, and disclose individually identifiable health information to carry out a wide range of health research protocols and projects. In the course of conducting research, researchers may create, use, and disclose individually identifiable health information. The Privacy Rule protects the privacy of such information when held by a covered entity but also provides various ways in which researchers can access and use the information for research.

*Certificates of Confidentiality* offer an important protection for the privacy of research study participants by protecting identifiable research information from forced disclosure (e.g., through a subpoena or court order). This topic will be discussed further in the next section of this chapter.

## Health Information Is Protected by the Privacy Rule

To understand the possible impact of the Privacy Rule on your work, you will need to understand what individually identifiable health information is and is not protected under the rule.

The Privacy Rule defines PHI as "individually identifiable health information, held or maintained by a covered entity or its business associates acting for the covered entity, that is transmitted or maintained in any form or medium (including the individually identifiable health information of non-U.S. citizens)." This includes identifiable demographic and other information relating (a) to the past, present, or future physical or mental health or condition of an individual, or (b) to the provision or payment of health care to an individual that is created or received by a health care provider, health plan, employer, or health care clearinghouse. For purposes of the Privacy Rule, genetic information is considered to be health information.

There are, however, instances when individually identifiable health information held by a covered entity is not protected by the Privacy Rule. The rule excludes from the definition of PHI individually identifiable health information that is maintained in education records and employment records held by a covered entity in its role as an employer.

*Don't ever assume that such information is* not *covered by HIPAA. If you are embarking on a study involving such records, check first with your IRB.*

A critical point of the Privacy Rule is that it applies only to information held or maintained *by a covered entity or its business associate acting for the covered entity.* Individually identifiable health information that is held by anyone other than a covered entity, including an independent researcher who is not a covered entity, is *not* protected by the Privacy Rule and may be used or disclosed without regard to the rule. There may, however, be other federal and state protections covering the information held by these noncovered entities that limit its use or disclosure.

In contrast to HIPAA, the HHS Protection of Human Subjects Regulations describe *private information* as including information about behavior that occurs in a context in which an individual can reasonably expect that no observation or recording is taking place, and information which has been provided for specific purposes by an individual and which the individual can reasonably expect will not be made public (for example, a medical record). Under the HHS Protection of Human Subjects Regulations, private information must be individually identifiable (i.e., the identity of the subject is or may readily be ascertained by the investigator or is associated with the information) in order for obtaining the information to constitute research involving human subjects (of course, obtaining data through direct intervention or interaction with the individual also constitutes human subjects research under HHS regulations).

## Acceptable Use and Disclosure of PHI

PHI may be used and disclosed for research with an individual's written permission in the form of an authorization. In addition, PHI may be used and disclosed for research *without* an authorization in limited circumstances. For example, PHI can be used or disclosed for research if a covered entity obtains documentation showing that an IRB or Privacy Board has waived the requirement for authorization or allowed an alteration. The rule also allows a covered entity to enter into a data-use agreement for sharing a limited data set. There are also separate provisions for how PHI can be used or disclosed for activities preparatory to research and for research on decedents' information.

It is important to note that there are circumstances in which health information maintained by a covered entity is *not* protected by the Privacy Rule. PHI excludes health information that is de-identified—that is, information from which all identifying markers have been stripped—according to specific standards. (For a listing of the specific information that must be de-identified before PHI can be released, consult the NIH page on the Privacy Rule.)[20] Health information that is de-identified can be used and disclosed by a covered entity, including a researcher who is a covered entity, without authorization or any other permission specified in the Privacy Rule. Under the Privacy Rule, covered entities may determine that health information is not individually identifiable in either of two ways. These are described below.

*Authorization for Research Uses and Disclosures.* One way the Privacy Rule protects the privacy of PHI is by generally giving individuals the opportunity to agree to the uses and disclosures of their PHI not otherwise permitted by the rule by signing an authorization form. The Privacy Rule establishes the right of an individual, such as a research subject, to authorize a covered entity to use and disclose his/her PHI for research purposes. The use of the authorization is in addition to the informed consent to participate in research required under the HHS Protection of Human Subjects Regulations and other applicable federal and state laws.

Please note that HIPAA is quite specific about what needs to be done to obtain authorization. Again, consult the NIH document on the Privacy Rule for details.

*Research on Decedents' Protected Health Information.* To use or disclose PHI of a deceased person for research, covered entities are *not* required to obtain authorization from the personal representative or next of kin, a waiver or an alteration of the authorization, or a data use agreement. However, the covered entity must obtain from the researcher who is seeking access to decedents' PHI (a) oral or written representations that the use and disclosure is sought solely for research on the PHI of decedents, (b) oral or written representations that the PHI for which use or disclosure is sought is necessary for the research purposes, and (c) documentation, at the request of the covered entity, of the death of the individuals whose PHI is sought by the researchers.

## Access to PHI

With few exceptions, the Privacy Rule guarantees individuals access to their medical records and other types of health information maintained by the covered entity or its business associate within what is known as a *designated record set*. Research records may be part of a designated record set if, for example, they are medically related or are used to make decisions about research participants.

In most cases, patients or research subjects can have access to their health information in a designated record set at a convenient time and place. However, during a clinical trial, an individual's right of access can be suspended while the research is in progress if, in consenting to participate in the trial, the individual agreed to the temporary denial of access. The covered entity, however, must inform participating individuals that their right to access health records in the designated record set will be restored upon conclusion of the clinical trial.

## Conclusion

The Privacy Rule was not intended to impede research. Rather, it provides ways to access vital information needed for research in a manner that protects the privacy of the research subject. The Privacy Rule describes methods to de-identify health information such that it is no longer PHI or governed by the Rule. If de-identified health information cannot be used for research, covered entities can obtain individuals' written permission for the research in an authorization document that describes the research uses, disclosures of PHI, and the rights of the research subject. When obtaining the authorization form is not practicable, an IRB or Privacy Board could waive or alter the authorization requirement. The Privacy Rule also provides alternatives to obtaining an authorization, waiver, or alteration of this requirement, such as allowing for the use of limited data sets. The Privacy Rule also contains a provision that grandfathers in ongoing research.

Many researchers are accustomed to complying with federal and state regulations that protect participants from research risks; some of these regulations require, as applicable, a researcher to describe privacy and confidentiality protections in an informed consent. While the Privacy Rule may add to these privacy protections, researchers are aware of the importance of protecting research subjects from foreseeable research risks, including risks to privacy. Understanding how and why the Privacy Rule protects the privacy of identifiable health information is an important step in understanding how covered entities implement the Privacy Rule's standards.

Researchers with questions regarding the Privacy Rule or the handling of PHI are encouraged to contact their IRB, counsel, or privacy officer to learn more about how the Privacy Rule affects their work and their institution. Researchers are also encouraged to send questions and comments about the Privacy Rule to HHS's Office for Civil Rights (OCR) at ocrprivacy@hhs.gov. Several other federal agencies are also prepared to assist researchers with questions about the Privacy Rule. Information can be found at the sites listed below:

- Text of the HIPAA Privacy Rule: http://www.hhs.gov/ocr/hipaa
- HHS, OCR: http://www.hhs.gov/ocr/hipaa
- Agency for Healthcare Research and Quality (AHRQ): http://www.hrq.gov/
- Centers for Disease Control and Prevention (CDC): http://www.cdc.gov/nip/registry/hipaa7.htm
- Food and Drug Administration (FDA): http://www.fda.gov/
- Indian Health Services (IHS): http://www.ihs.gov/AdminMngrResources/HIPAA/index.cfm
- NIH: http://privacyruleandresearch.nih.gov/
- HHS, OHRP: http://ohrp.osophs.dhhs.gov/
- Substance Abuse and Mental Health Services Administration (SAMHSA): http://www.hipaa.samhsa.gov/

## Final Note on HIPAA

This was a long and not particularly exciting section. As you can tell, most of the language was taken directly from the HHS Web site and, believe it or not, I cut out most of the original text. However, it is extremely important that you be familiar with the HIPAA restrictions and the exceptions, which are well summarized in the Conclusions section above. Finally, I have provided the URLs connected with the government agencies with which HIPAA is concerned; however, many nongovernmental institutions have slide presentations and other ancillary information you may find helpful. Type "HIPAA" or "HIPAA research" into your search engine to find some of these.

## CERTIFICATES OF CONFIDENTIALITY

Certificates of confidentiality constitute an important tool to protect the privacy of research study participants. Thus, the NIH encourages their appropriate use. The NIH makes information widely available to investigators working on sensitive biomedical, behavioral, clinical, or other types of research at the Certificate Kiosk.[21] Note that information is added to this site periodically, so you are encouraged to check back. There are various sources of information at this kiosk, including a slide presentation, that you will find helpful.

The NIH issues certificates of confidentiality to protect identifiable research information from forced disclosure. They allow the investigator and others who have access to research records to refuse to disclose identifying information on research participants in any civil, criminal, administrative, legislative, or other proceeding, whether at the federal, state, or local level. Certificates of confidentiality may be granted for studies collecting information that, if disclosed, could have adverse consequences for subjects or damage their financial standing, employability, insurability, or reputation. By protecting researchers and institutions from being compelled to disclose information that would identify research subjects, certificates of confidentiality help achieve the research objectives and promote participation in studies by assuring confidentiality and privacy to participants.

HIPAA's Privacy Rule does not protect against all forced disclosure, since it permits disclosures required by law, for example. Certificates of confidentiality are legal protections that *do* protect against forced disclosure by giving their holders a legal basis for refusing to disclose information, which, absent the certificate, they would be obliged to disclose.

## DATA AND SAFETY MONITORING

Please note that the following discussion of data and safety monitoring is relevant *only* if you are conducting clinical trials. There is a great deal to know about developing and working with a Data and Safety Monitoring Board (DSMB), and I cannot recount it all here. I will provide a few basics, and then provide URLs that will help you.

The NIH writes,

> DSMBs play an essential role in protecting the safety of participants, and assuring integrity of the study. They accomplish the former by being familiar with the protocol, proposing appropriate analyses, and periodically reviewing the developing outcome and safety data. They accomplish the latter by reviewing data on such aspects as participant enrollment, site visits, study procedures, forms completion, data quality, losses to follow-up, and other measures of adherence to protocol. The Board makes recommendations based on those data, regarding appropriate protocol and operational changes. DSMBs (and the investigators) monitor toxicity and discuss any concern in this regard. The DSMB monitoring function is above and beyond the oversight traditionally provided by IRBs and as such is particularly important for multicenter trials.

Professor Janet Wittes is an expert in data and safety monitoring, having served on the DSMBs of several of the major trials that have been conducted over the past several years.[22] DSMBs are necessary entities, according to Dr. Wittes, and that necessity

> stems from the ethical imperative to dissociate the treating physician from the accruing data in order to maintain a legitimate "state of equipoise" regarding the therapies being studied and to remove those with vested interest in specific treatment from deciding whether the trial should continue.[23]

"Equipoise" is the perception or belief that uncertainty exists concerning the effectiveness of available treatments, including the treatment to be investigated.

## Why a DSMB?

According to the NIH "Policy for Data Safety and Monitoring," published June 10, 1998, each I/C "should have a system for the appropriate oversight and monitoring of the conduct of clinical trials to ensure the safety of participants and the validity and integrity of the data for all NIH-supported or conducted clinical trials." Moreover, "The establishment of the [DSMBs] is required for multi-site clinical trials involving interventions that entail potential risk to the participants."

The NIH issued further guidance June 5, 2000, indicating that for Phase I and Phase II clinical trials, "a DSMB may be appropriate if the studies have multiple clinical sites, are blinded (masked), or employ particularly high-risk interventions or vulnerable populations."

DSMBs are particularly important when

- Effects on morbidity and mortality are expected
- Risks associated with treatment are unknown (new therapy, genetic)
- Risks of severe side effects are high (e.g., chemotherapy)
- Vulnerable populations are involved (e.g., comatose patients, children)
- The study involves a High-impact trial, or when controversial or high–public health impact is expected
- The study is a large or multicenter trial (i.e., when there are management or quality control issues)

The NIH has become considerably more conservative concerning the conduct of clinical trials just in the past few years. It used to be that if the conceivable risks were fairly minimal (e.g., those related to the guided breathing intervention I've been using as an example), you would not have to worry about a DSMB. That has changed now: If you are conducting a clinical trial, you must at least submit a data and safety monitoring plan, and you will likely be told by your program officer to either put together a DSMB yourself (in lower-risk trials) or to work with the NIH, who will develop a DSMB for your trial.

## Principles of Monitoring Data and Safety

All clinical trials require monitoring. Data and safety monitoring is required for all types of clinical trials, including physiologic, toxicity, and dose-finding studies (Phase I); efficacy studies (Phase II); efficacy, effectiveness, and comparative trials (Phase III); and so forth.

Monitoring should be commensurate with risks. The method and degree of monitoring needed is related to the degree of risk involved in the study. A monitoring committee is usually required to determine safe and effective conduct and to recommend conclusion of the trial when significant benefits or risks have developed or the trial is unlikely to be concluded successfully. Risk associated with participation in research must be minimized to the extent practical.

Monitoring should also be commensurate with size and complexity. Monitoring may be conducted in various ways or by various individuals or groups, depending on the size and scope of the research effort. These ways of conducting monitoring exist on a continuum from monitoring by the principal investigator or NIH program staff in a small Phase I study to the establishment of an independent DSMB for a large Phase III clinical trial.

## Practical and Implementation Issues

*Performance of Data and Safety Monitoring.* Monitoring activities should be conducted by experts in all scientific disciplines needed to interpret the data and ensure patient safety.

Clinical trial experts, biostatisticians, bioethicists, and clinicians knowledgeable about the disease and treatment under study should be part of the monitoring group or be available, if their presence is warranted.

Ideally, those monitoring outcomes of a trial are in no way associated with the trial. For trials that are conducted as part of a cooperative group, a majority of the individuals monitoring outcome data should be external to the group.

Generally, DSMBs meet first in open session, attended by selected trial investigators, NIH program staff or program officers, and perhaps industry representatives, and then in closed session where they review emerging trial data. When masked data are presented or discussed, no one with a proprietary interest in the outcome should be allowed to participate. Participants in the review of masked or confidential data and discussions regarding continuance or stoppage of the study should have no conflict of interest with or financial stake in the research outcome. However, if there is an open session, they could be present.

An important part of the DSMB concerns what are known as *stopping rules*, the algorithms that describe the conditions under which the DSMB must consider terminating the trial prematurely. Not surprisingly, if the intervention is causing measurable harm to the participants, more so than would be expected and more so than occurs in the control arms, this must be considered. The DSMB will provide guidance concerning which variables should be the focus of interim data analyses. These certainly will include events such as death, if the population is at high risk; however, it may also involve intermediate variables, such as depression. You will want to think carefully about the model under which you are planning to operate; that is, what are the potential mediators of outcomes, and is there any chance that the intervention will affect these? You must think creatively about this. For example, you might not consider that your intervention has anything to do with medication adherence, but if your intervention might have an effect on depression (and the data show that depression has a negative impact on adherence), you might need to provide analyses of both depression and of medication adherence.

You also should consider stopping rules in the event that your intervention is so powerful and efficacious that you see an obvious positive effect on the outcome you are planning to assess. It is considered abusive to research participants to ask them to participate in a trial if the information their participation will provide is already known. Of course, nobody wants to stop a trial for this reason, because, frankly, it means giving back funds to the NIH. As a taxpayer, I am all in favor of stopping successful trials and returning unused funds. However, you will be torn if this happens to you, because you and others were probably counting on the salary support for the period of the original award. At the least, the DSMB will want to see a very large effect before it is forced to consider shutting down for this reason; and while it can happen, presumably you have gone into this with a reasonable idea of what effect size you should expect, based on your, or others', pilot data.

Confidentiality must be maintained during all phases of the trial, including monitoring, preparation of interim results, review, and response to monitoring recommendations. Besides selected NIH program staff, other key NIH staff, and trial biostatisticians, usually only voting members of the DSMB should see interim analyses of outcome data. Exceptions may be made under circumstances where there are serious adverse events (discussed below) or whenever the DSMB deems it appropriate.

Individuals or groups monitoring data and safety of interventional trials will perform the following activities:

- Review the research protocol and plans for data and safety monitoring.
- Evaluate the progress of interventional trials, including periodic assessments of data quality and timeliness, participant recruitment, accrual and retention, participant risk versus benefit, performance of trial sites, and other factors that can affect study outcome. Monitoring should also consider factors external to the study when interpreting the data, such as scientific or therapeutic developments that may have an impact on the safety of the participants or the ethics of the study.
- Make recommendations to the I/C, IRB, and investigators concerning continuation or conclusion of the trials.
- Protect the confidentiality of the trial data and the results of monitoring.

*Adverse Event.* An *adverse event* is defined by the NIH as the occurrence of an adverse effect occurring during a clinical study. An *adverse effect* is an unanticipated problem or unfavorable symptom or disease occurring during a clinical study, though not necessarily caused by the study treatment, that harms subjects or others: For example, a loss of research records, drug overdose, serious symptom, or death would be an adverse effect.

Let me go a step further so that you fully understand the nature of adverse events. If your subject comes into your laboratory, or clinic, or wherever participants are being seen for your trial, and comments that her hay fever has been acting up lately, you must record it as an adverse event. You must fill out an adverse event report, and send it to your IRB and, possibly, to your DSMB, depending on the severity of the event. That is, you will *eventually* provide the DSMB will all adverse event reports, but unless the event is considered serious, you can provide the report at the DSMB meeting rather than sending it immediately. How is *serious* defined? That should be discussed at your initial DSMB meeting.

Adverse event reporting policy is laid out by the NIH and can be accessed online.[24]

*Web Resources.* Much of the information about DSMBs on the Web is found in either downloadable documents, which often don't have their own URLs (at least as far as I can tell) but which are easily found when you enter "DSMB" in a search engine. For example, an excellent presentation by Dr. Peter Kaufmann of the National Heart, Lung, and Blood Institute (NHLBI) can be found that way. Official NIH pages can be found at the following URLs:

- http://grants.nih.gov/grants/guide/notice-files/not98-084.html
- http://grants2.nih.gov/grants/guide/notice-files/not99-107.html

Many I/C Web pages provide useful information. In particular, you might look at the pages for the NHLBI and the National Institute of Neurological Disorders and Stroke (NINDS):

- http://www.nhlbi.nih.gov/funding/policies/dsmb_est.htm
- http://www.ninds.nih.gov/funding/research/clinical_research/dsm_guidelines.htm

*Last Note.* If you are proposing a Phase I, Phase II, or Phase III clinical trial, you almost certainly will have to submit a data and safety monitoring plan and/or establish a DSMB. Contact your NIH program officer for advice.

## HUMANE CARE AND USE OF LABORATORY ANIMALS

As you will have noticed in Section F of the proposal example shown in Chapter 5, there is a heading entitled "Vertebrate Animals." In that particular example, "not applicable" appeared next to the heading because the proposal used in the example applied only to humans. However, in the event you are working with animals, you are responsible for their welfare, and the standards for this are laid out by the NIH. Presumably, your institution will have an Institutional Animal Care and Use Committee (IACUC), which is in charge of ensuring that these standards are met.

Figure 6.4 shows an excerpt from the PHS 398 Cover Page (addressed in detail in Chapter 7), which pertains to animal use in a proposed study. If you plan to use laboratory animals in your study, check the "yes" box; your institution will probably have a Web page that provides information needed for grant submission, including assurance numbers and approval dates; otherwise, contact your institution's grants office. Figure 6.5 shows items from the SF 424 Other Project Information form that pertain to the use of animal subjects.

There are several Web pages that provide very specific information about how to care for laboratory animals. Three that might be of particular use are

- Animal Welfare Act: http://www.nal.usda.gov/awic/legislat/awa.htm
- Guide for the Care and Use of Laboratory Animals: http://www.nap.edu/readingroom/books/labrats/
- Office of Laboratory Animal Welfare, "Public Health Service Policy on Humane Care and Use of Laboratory Animals": http://grants.nih.gov/grants/olaw/references/phspol.htm

This last document outlines, in Section C, the policy on research projects conducted or supported by the PHS. Specifically, it states that,

In order to approve proposed research projects or proposed significant changes in ongoing research projects, the IACUC shall conduct a review of those components related to the care and use of animals and determine that the proposed research projects are in accordance with this Policy. In making this determination, the IACUC shall confirm that the research project will be conducted in accordance with the Animal Welfare Act insofar as it applies to the research project, and that the research project

| 5. VERTEBRATE ANIMALS | ☐ No | ☐ Yes |
|---|---|---|
| 5a. If "Yes", IACUC Approval Date | 5b. Animal welfare assurance no. | |

**Figure 6.4**     Item 5 From the PHS 398 Application Cover Page

| RESEARCH & RELATED Other Project Information | | |
|---|---|---|
| 2. * Are Vertebrate Animals Used? | ☐ Yes | ☐ No |
| 1a. if YES to Vertebrate Animals | | |
| Is the IACUC Review Pending | ☐ Yes | ☐ No |
| IACUC Approval Date: | | |
| Animal Welfare Assurance Number | | |

**Figure 6.5**     Animal Subjects Items From the SF 424 Other Project Information Form

is consistent with the ["Guide for the Care and Use of Laboratory Animals"[25]] unless acceptable justification for a departure is presented. Further, the IACUC shall determine that the research project conforms with the institution's assurance and meets the following requirements:

a. Procedures with animals will avoid or minimize discomfort, distress, and pain to the animals, consistent with sound research design.

b. Procedures that may cause more than momentary or slight pain or distress to the animals will be performed with appropriate sedation, analgesia, or anesthesia, unless the procedure is justified for scientific reasons in writing by the investigator.

c. Animals that would otherwise experience severe or chronic pain or distress that cannot be relieved will be painlessly killed at the end of the procedure or, if appropriate, during the procedure.

d. The living conditions of animals will be appropriate for their species and contribute to their health and comfort. The housing, feeding, and nonmedical care of the animals will be directed by a veterinarian or other scientist trained and experienced in the proper care, handling, and use of the species being maintained or studied.

e. Medical care for animals will be available and provided as necessary by a qualified veterinarian.

f. Personnel conducting procedures on the species being maintained or studied will be appropriately qualified and trained in those procedures.

g. Methods of euthanasia used will be consistent with the recommendations of the American Veterinary Medical Association (AVMA) Panel on Euthanasia (PDF), unless a deviation is justified for scientific reasons in writing by the investigator.

## CONCLUSION

The rules concerning human and animal subjects will no doubt cause you a great deal of work and occasional headaches. However, you will be best served by taking the attitude that your research participants are partners, not merely subjects, in your studies. Allow yourself plenty of lead time if you are planning to study human subjects or animals, as the IRB rarely accepts new proposals without demanding revisions. This can draw the process out for *months*, so it is in your interest to be an expert on the ethical concerns involved in your proposed research. Rather than regarding the IRB process as an impediment to your research efforts, the most productive attitude you can take is that it is as much a part of developing your proposal and conducting your studies as the research design, the planned statistical analyses, or any other key component of the research.

## NOTES

1. The NIH policy on required education for those involved in the design or conduct of human subjects research can be found at http://grants.nih.gov/grants/guide/notice-files/NOT-OD-00-039.html.

2. The "NIH Bioethics Resources on the Web" can be accessed at http://www.nih.gov/sigs/bioethics/specific.html.

3. Guidance on what constitutes human subjects research can be found at http://www.hhs.gov/ohrp/humansubjects/guidance/cdebiol.pdf.

4. The Belmont Report is available at http://www.hhs.gov/ohrp/humansubjects/guidance/belmont.htm and the Declaration of Helsinki is at http://www.wma.net/e/policy/b3.htm.

5. The "Human Subjects Ethical Guidelines" are at http://grants1.nih.gov/grants/policy/hs/regulations.htm#Ethical and the Federal Policy for the Protection of Human Subjects at http://www.hhs.gov/ohrp/humansubjects/guidance/45cfr46.htm.

6. Document 45 CFR part 46 can be accessed at http://www.hhs.gov/ohrp/humansubjects/guidance/45cfr46.htm.

7. The chart is available at http://www.hhs.gov/ohrp/humansubjects/guidance/decisioncharts.htm.

8. OHRP advice on the development of your consent procedure is available at http://www.hhs.gov/ohrp/humansubjects/guidance/ictips.htm.

9. The OHRP checklist can be accessed at http://www.hhs.gov/ohrp/humansubjects/assurance/consentckls.htm.

10. OHRP guidelines on expedited reviews are available at http://www.hhs.gov/ohrp/humansubjects/guidance/expedited98.htm.

11. Consult Chart 8 at http://www.hhs.gov/ohrp/humansubjects/guidance/decisioncharts.htm.

12. Consult Chart 2 at http://www.hhs.gov/ohrp/humansubjects/guidance/decisioncharts.htm.

13. "OHRP Guidance, Children Involved as Subjects in Research" is available at http://www.hhs.gov/ohrp/children/guidance_407process.html.

14. Links to the NIH's policy on the inclusion of women and minorities can be found at http://grants.nih.gov/grants/funding/women_min/women_min.htm.

15. The "Outreach Notebook" is available at http://orwh.od.nih.gov/inclusion/outreachFAQ.pdf.

16. The Personal Data Form from PHS 398 can be downloaded from http://grants.nih.gov/grants/funding/phs398/personal.pdf.

17. For questions used by the U.S. Census Bureau to collect information on race and ethnicity, see http://www.census.gov/dmd/www/2000quest.html. To access the Demographics Information collected through NHANES, see http://www.cdc.gov/nchs/about/major/nhanes/questexam.htm.

18. Information on HIPAA's Privacy Rule can be accessed at http://www.hhs.gov/ocr/hipaa.

19. The NIH document on HIPAA can be accessed at http://privacyruleandresearch.nih.gov/pr_02.asp.

20. See http://privacyruleandresearch.nih.gov/pr_02.asp

21. The NIH Certificate Kiosk can be accessed at http://grants2.nih.gov/grants/policy/coc.

22. I was introduced to the work of Dr. Wittes through a presentation by Dr. Peter Kaufmann, of the National Heart, Lung, and Blood Institute (NHLBI).

23. Wittes, J. (1993). Behind closed doors: The data monitoring board in randomized clinical trials. *Statistics in Medicine, 12,* 419–424.

24. See http://grants1.nih.gov/grants/guide/notice-files/not99-107.html for the NIH policy on adverse event reporting.

25. See http://www.nap.edu/readingroom/books/labrats/ for the "Guide for the Care and Use of Laboratory Animals."

# Writing the Application, Part III

*The PHS 398 and SF 424 Forms Packets*

## 7

This chapter covers a lot of ground—as much ground as the form pages themselves. I'll teach you how to develop a budget, what should go into your project title, how to describe your institution's resources, and so on. The NIH provides you with a comprehensive set of instructions, and I won't repeat these if I can avoid it, except when I want to elaborate or explain. Read the instructions, though; you should know them so well that you practically have them memorized by the time you get done.[1]

## CHANGES IN THE APPLICATION PROCESS

The NIH currently uses two nonoverlapping sets of application forms: the Public Health Service (PHS) 398 forms, and the Standard Form (SF) 424, which is an innovation designed to make things easier and more efficient for both the applicants and NIH staff. At this time, the SF 424 is not available for most applications; the NIH expects it to be online by the end of 2006. The SF 424 (which I will sometimes refer to as the "new" form) is similar in many ways to the PHS 398, in terms of the information you must provide. However, the SF 424 is entirely Web-based, so the format is somewhat different. Several of the attachments for the SF 424 are virtually identical to the PHS 398 forms, and these are completed using your word processor in precisely the same fashion as before. Now, however, there is one extra step: You must convert each file to a PDF format and then attach it in the appropriate field shown in the SF 424.

I begin here with the PHS 398 forms and use the structure that the NIH provides—that is, I will discuss the form pages in the order in which they arise. You should use this chapter as a reference, with your own form pages sitting open on your computer as you fill them out.

To avoid confusion, here is a summary of the application packages:

- PHS 398: The basic package that most applications will use. In the PHS 398 package, some forms may be irrelevant for some applications. Thus, for example, if you are submitting a career (K) application, you would use the PHS 398, but you would use a different Table of Contents page (provided in the PHS 398 package) from the one you would use if applying for a research grant such as the R01. Similarly, if you are applying for a R01 award, there are pages in the PHS 398 package that you would ignore, such as the Career

Development Award Reference Report (Series K), which is relevant only to the career (K) awards.

- PHS 2590: This package is used only for noncompeting renewals (i.e., progress reports) for grants that are already past their initial budget period.

- SF 424: This is a Web-based package that is, at this time, still in the testing stage. It is submitted electronically, unlike the PHS 398 and PHS 2590 packages, which are submitted in paper form. To use the SF 424, you must first select the specific application you are submitting; that is, if you are responding to an RFA, you must provide the RFA identification number, and the appropriate package will become available. The same holds true for investigator-initiated applications, such as the R01. The advantage with the SF 424 is that you do not need to worry about which forms are or are not relevant for your application; only the appropriate forms will be provided when you download the application package. I will explain in detail how to access the SF 424 later in this chapter.

There are additional form packages that serve special purposes. These are all shown on the NIH's Office of Extramural Research (OER) Web page (www.grantsl.nih.gov), along with the PHS 398, PHS 2590, and SF 424 packages. They are similar to the PHS 398 packages, so I will not describe them separately.

Because the NIH is in the midst of a transition from the present forms—the PHS 398 and PHS 2590 packages—to their eventual replacement—the SF 424—I shall describe both in detail, using annotated examples. Note that some sections have a header note saying "PHS 398 only," some say "SF 424 only," and some say "PHS 398 and SF 424." When you read a section that says "PHS 398 only" (for example), this does not mean that the *data* in that section (whether budget numbers or narrative details) are not required for the SF 424, it just means the *format* for the SF 424 is different. Thus, you will see the same information again in a later section, for the appropriate forms package.

## THE FORM PAGES

### The Face Page (PHS 398 Only)

The Cover Page (or *Face Page*) contains a good deal of the administrative data that the NIH requires. Many institutions have a Web page that provides the specific information required to complete this form; it can be called by any number of names. At Columbia University, where I work, the page is called "Proposal Submission Procedures," and contains such information as how long before the grant submission date signatures must be obtained and which offices must see the proposal prior to submission. It also contains a section called "Important Information for Proposal Processing." Consult your institution's Web site; if you don't find something like the Columbia page, ask someone in your grants office for the necessary information.

Figure 7.1 presents a completed sample of the Face Page using data pertaining to the guided breathing proposal I have been using as an example.

*Project Title.* Don't just dash off a title. It is the first detail that will be noted about your proposal, and in 81 characters (including spaces), you want to provide a great deal of information about your proposal. In this sample title, "RCT: Effect of Guided Breathing Intervention on Ambulatory BP in Hypertensives," the authors included

- The major independent and dependent variables (guided breathing intervention and ambulatory blood pressure)
- The study population (hypertensives)
- The design (a randomized controlled trial, or RCT)

An RCT is an extremely powerful research method, and the authors want to note that they are using that design in the title; this will also help to make sure that the proposal goes to the preferred study section (see Chapter 9 for details on how this works). Why prefer one study section over another? It comes down to the question of what sort of experts you want reviewing your proposal. If this proposal went to a study section composed mainly of laboratory experimentalists, they may not be able to appreciate why the authors have made some choices and what the problems are in conducting an RCT, which are very different than those that come up in laboratory studies.

Also, ambulatory blood pressure is accepted in the research community as a superior method of assessment, compared to clinic measurements; it is a better predictor of target organ damage, for example. Thus, it is important to mention it in the title as well.

A couple of other things you should note: Should you use an abbreviation, such as "RCT" or "BP," in the title? In this case, I would say yes. Everyone on the relevant study section will know what the abbreviations mean, and it tells a great deal about what you intend. And, again, make sure to mention your main independent and dependent variables in the title.

> Don't make your title too vague. For example, "Behavioral Intervention for Hypertension" doesn't help NIH staff to guide your proposal to an appropriate study section, and you want the reviewers, right from the start, to have a sense of what the proposal is about. Also, don't waste words in the title: Don't, for example, use phrases like "The Study of. . . . " You have only 81 characters, and you want to make them count.

## Abstract, Performance Sites, Key Personnel, and Human Embryonic Stem Cells (PHS 398 Only)

For those of you who have filled out PHS 398 forms before, you will notice changes from the previous form pages. The second form page underwent one of the most radical makeovers, as it expanded from one to two pages. The first of these pages (Figure 7.2) covers the abstract and performance sites; the second page (Figure 7.3) covers key personnel and human embryonic stem cells. One thing to note: You should number the form pages consecutively throughout the application—do not use suffixes such as *4a, 4b.*

## Table of Contents (TOC; PHS 398 Only)

Figure 7.4 shows a sample Table of Contents (TOC) form. One thing to note: K (career) awards require a different TOC, which will be included in the forms packet for that mechanism.

## Budgets (PHS 398 and SF 424)

As with the other sections, I will try to deal with issues in a chronological order, which means that major issues and minor points may sit side by side. I will assume you have never before developed a budget and are nervous at the prospect. Actually, creating a budget is a very straightforward process and not all that difficult; just stick with me through the details.

*(Text continues on page 162)*

Form Approved Through 09/30/2007                                                    OMB No. 0925-0001

| Department of Health and Human Services Public Health Services | LEAVE BLANK—FOR PHS USE ONLY. | | |
|---|---|---|---|
| **Grant Application** | Type | Activity | Number |
| | Review Group | | Formerly |
| *Do not exceed character length restrictions indicated.* | Council/Board (Month, Year) | | Date Received |

**1.   TITLE OF PROJECT** *(Do not exceed 81 characters, including spaces and punctuation.)* **{1}**
RCT: Effect of Guided Breathing Intervention on Ambulatory BP in Hypertensives

**2.   RESPONSE TO SPECIFIC REQUEST FOR APPLICATIONS OR PROGRAM ANNOUNCEMENT OR SOLICITATION   ☒ NO   ☐ YES**
*(If "Yes," state number and title)*

Number: [ ]            Title: [ ]

| **3.   PRINCIPAL INVESTIGATOR/PROGRAM DIRECTOR** | New Investigator   ☒ No   ☐ Yes {2} | | |
|---|---|---|---|
| 3a. NAME (Last, first, middle) | 3b. DEGREE(S) | | 3h.  eRA Commons User Name {3} |
| Kaoru Okata | M.D. | [ ] | kokata |

| 3c. POSITION TITLE<br>Assistant Professor of Medicine | 3d. MAILING ADDRESS *(Street, city, state, zip code)*<br>New York Medical Center |
|---|---|
| 3e. DEPARTMENT, SERVICE, LABORATORY, OR EQUIVALENT<br>General Medicine | Dept. of General Medicine, Box 383<br>890 125th Street<br>New York, NY 10027 |
| 3f. MAJOR SUBDIVISION<br>Medicine | |
| 3g. TELEPHONE AND FAX *(Area code, number and extension)*<br>Tel:  (212) 555-1234            FAX:  (212) 555-1235 | E-MAIL ADDRESS:<br>kokata@nymc.edu |

| 4.   HUMAN SUBJECTS RESEARCH<br>☐ No  ☒ Yes | 4b.  Human Subjects Assurance No. **{4}**<br>FWA99991234 | | 5.   VERTEBRATE ANIMALS ☒ No ☐ Yes | |
|---|---|---|---|---|
| | 4c.  Clinical Trial<br>☐ No  ☒ Yes | 4d. NIH-defined Phase III<br>Clinical Trial ☒ No ☐ Yes | 5a. If "Yes," IACUC<br>approval Date | 5b. Animal welfare assurance no. **{5}** |
| 4a. Research Exempt<br>☐ No  ☒ Yes | If "Yes," Exemption No. [ ] | | [ ] | A9999-01 |

| 6.   DATES OF PROPOSED PERIOD OF SUPPORT *(month, day, year—MM/DD/YY)* **{6}** | | 7.   COSTS REQUESTED FOR INITIAL BUDGET PERIOD **{7}** | | 8.   COSTS REQUESTED FOR PROPOSED PERIOD OF SUPPORT | |
|---|---|---|---|---|---|
| From | Through | 7a. Direct Costs ($) | 7b. Total Costs ($) | 8a. Direct Costs ($) | 8b. Total Costs ($) |
| 12/1/2003 | 11/30/2008 | 281,814 | 454,075 | 1,514,737 | 2,397,765 |

| 9.   APPLICANT ORGANIZATION **{8}** | | 10. TYPE OF ORGANIZATION | | |
|---|---|---|---|---|
| Name<br>Address | The Trustees of New York Medical Center<br>900 125th Street<br>New York, NY 10027 | Public:      → ☐ Federal      ☐ State      ☐ Local | | |
| | | Private:     → ☒ Private Nonprofit | | |
| | | For-profit:  → ☐ General      ☐ Small Business<br>☐ Woman-owned ☐ Socially and Economically Disadvantaged | | |
| | | 11.   ENTITY IDENTIFICATION NUMBER<br>13-1234567A8 | | |
| | | DUNS NO. | 123456789 | Cong. District | 14 |

| 12.   ADMINISTRATIVE OFFICIAL TO BE NOTIFIED IF AWARD IS MADE | | 13.   OFFICIAL SIGNING FOR APPLICANT ORGANIZATION | |
|---|---|---|---|
| Name | Mr. Allen Birdwell | Name | Ms. Paula Omale |
| Title | Associate Director for Finance | Title | Associate Dean for Sponsored Programs |
| Address | 900 125th Street<br>New York, NY 10027 | Address | 900 125th Street<br>New York, NY 10027 |
| Tel: 212-555-1236   FAX: 212-555-1237 [ ] | | Tel: 212-555-1238   FAX: 212-555-1239 | |
| E-Mail: abirdwell@smc.edu | | E-Mail: pomale@nymc.edu | |

| 14.   PRINCIPAL INVESTIGATOR/PROGRAM DIRECTOR ASSURANCE:<br>I certify that the statements herein are true, complete and accurate to the best of my knowledge. I am aware that any false, fictitious, or fraudulent statements or claims may subject me to criminal, civil, or administrative penalties. I agree to accept responsibility for the scientific conduct of the project and to provide the required progress reports if a grant is awarded as a result of this application. | SIGNATURE OF PI/PD NAMED IN 3a.<br>*(In ink. "Per" signature not acceptable.)* | DATE<br>[ ] |
|---|---|---|
| 15.   APPLICANT ORGANIZATION CERTIFICATION AND ACCEPTANCE:<br>I certify that the statements herein are true, complete and accurate to the best of my knowledge, and accept the obligation to comply with Public Health Services terms and conditions if a grant is awarded as a result of this application. I am aware that any false, fictitious, or fraudulent statements or claims may subject me to criminal, civil, or administrative penalties. | SIGNATURE OF OFFICIAL NAMED IN 13.<br>*(In ink. "Per" signature not acceptable.)* | DATE<br>[ ] |

PHS 398 (Rev. 09/04)                              Face Page                                    **Form Page 1**

**Figure 7.1**     Sample Face Page

NOTES

{1} Note that you are limited to 81 characters here, but do craft a title that provides details about your project. See the discussion in the "Project Title" section.

{2} To ensure fair reviews for new investigators, the NIH has issued instructions to reviewers that all applicants should be evaluated in a manner appropriate for the present stage in their careers. So, if you are eligible to mark yourself as a new investigator, do so—in part because the NIH has recently changed its policy concerning paylines. A new investigator is one who has not previously served as such on any PHS-supported research project other than a small grant (R03), an Academic Research Enhancement Award (AREA, R15), an exploratory/developmental grant (R21), or certain research career awards directed principally to physicians, dentists, or veterinarians at the beginning of their research career (K01, K08, K22, and K23). Current or past recipients of Independent Scientist and other nonmentored career awards (K02 and K04) are not considered new investigators. Recent changes at the NIH mean that new investigators will have a higher payline (see Chapter 9 for an explanation of the payline) than all other investigators: At this time, new investigators will have an advantage of 5%. Thus, if the NHLBI payline were 20%, the payline for new investigators would be 25%, which represents a great advantage.

{3} This is a new line on the form. Log on to the NIH's eRA Commons page (at https://commons.era.nih.gov/commons/), open an account, and note your user name.

{4} See Chapter 6 for a detailed discussion of this section. The Human Subjects Assurance Number is one of those bits of information you will find on your institution's grants information page or by asking someone in your grants office; include it even if you are not studying humans.

{5} This number, too, can be found on your institution's grants information page or by asking someone in your grants office. Include the Animal Welfare Assurance Number even if you are not studying animals.

{6} Chapter 9 will give you an approximate schedule of when things will happen, including, if you are funded, when you will get your money. I tend to assume about a year from the submission date, although new procedures are being instituted that will cut the time period. For example, if I submit in June 2005, I will note in this section that the money will begin on June 1, 2006. It should end one day earlier than it began (if it begins on June 1, it ends on May 31) in the appropriate year (depending on how many years support you requested, and receive).

{7} You can't complete either this box the next—the two sections asking for your direct and total costs—until you complete the budgets and the checklist, which will be discussed in detail later in this chapter.

{8} You can find all the information needed to complete the remaining sections from your institution's grants information page or by asking someone in your grants office.

| Principal Investigator/Program Director (Last, First, Middle): | Okata, K. {1} |
|---|---|

DESCRIPTION: See instructions. State the application's broad, long-term objectives and specific aims, making reference to the health relatedness of the project (i.e., relevance to the **mission of the agency**). Describe concisely the research design and methods for achieving these goals. Describe the rationale and techniques you will use to pursue these goals.

**In addition**, in two or three sentences, describe in plain, lay language the relevance of this research to **public** health. If the application is funded, this description, as is, will become public information. Therefore, do not include proprietary/confidential information. **DO NOT EXCEED THE SPACE PROVIDED.**

Although drug therapies have improved blood pressure (BP) control, 50% of hypertensives on drug treatment have inadequately controlled BP. Device-guided breathing trains patients to slow their breathing to a rate of 5-6 breaths/minute (0.1 Hz) range. It is this range at which respiratory sinus arrhythmia (RSA) has its greatest amplitude, and is associated with maximal heart rate variability (HRV). Several published studies have shown that the intervention has had substantial effects on BP reduction, ranging from reductions in systolic/diastolic BP (SBP/DBP) of 5.5/3.6 to 15.2/10.0 mm Hg. These effects are surprisingly large, considering the relatively brief practice sessions (daily 15-minute sessions for 8 weeks), and may represent an effective, accessible, cost-efficient way to help control BP in hypertensives. However, there are 3 limitations which must be addressed before the Guided Breathing technique can be recommended for widespread use. (1) To what extent are the observed BP changes sustained throughout the day and night? The FDA requires that effective antihypertensive treatment lower the BP over a full 24 hours. So far, only one small study (N=13) has examined the effects on ambulatory BP (ABP), and only daytime BP was measured. (2) Is there anything special about breathing at 6-10 breaths/minute, or is it a non-specific relaxation effect? (3) What is the effect duration? Only one study (6-month duration) has examined the effects of guided breathing on BP for more than 8 weeks. It is possible that the intervention causes some resetting of BP-regulating mechanisms that persists after the intervention is discontinued, or it is possible that the BP will return to the pretreatment level. For example, one would not give anti-HTN medication for 8 weeks and stop, and expect an effect on BP a year later. The development of behavioral interventions needs to take into account methods to sustain long-term effects. The aim of this proposal is to conduct a blinded, randomized controlled trial (RCT) to test the efficacy of a Guided Breathing Intervention in uncontrolled hypertensives to address these issues. (1) We will use 24-hour ABP to examine BP changes. (2) We will include 2 control groups, Usual Care (UC), and a Placebo Condition (using a device that is identical to the guided breathing device, except that it does not slow the breathing rate). (3) We will study the effects of the intervention at both 8 weeks (the duration of the training) and again at 12 months, in both the intervention and placebo arms. {2}

| PERFORMANCE SITE(S) (organization, city, state) |
|---|
| New York Medical Center, New York, NY<br>Bronx Hospital, the Bronx, NY                    {3} |

**Figure 7.2**    Sample Form Page 2: Abstract and Performance Sites

NOTES

{1} Every page, even outside letters, should have the PIs name at the top right.

{2} I have described what should go into the abstract in Chapter 5. The PHS 398 instructions provide a good summary of what should be included in a good abstract.

{3} For the sake of illustration, I am incorporating a second site (Bronx Hospital) so we can illustrate a subcontract, which will be discussed later in this chapter in the section on budgets.

{4} This page will always be page 2 in your (PHS 398) application.

| Principal Investigator/Program Director (Last, First, Middle): | | Okata, Kaoru | |
|---|---|---|---|

KEY PERSONNEL. {1} See instructions. *Use continuation pages as needed* to provide the required information in the format shown below. Start with Principal Investigator. List all other key personnel in alphabetical order, last name first.

| Name | eRA Commons User Name | Organization | Role on Project |
|---|---|---|---|
| K. Okata | okaoru44 | New York Medical Ctr. | PI |
| L. Ruggiero | ruggiero | Bronx Hospital | Co-Inv, Site PI {2} |
| T. Smith | smitht088 | New York Medical Ctr. | Co-Inv |
| Q. McBurney | qmcburn | New York Medical Ctr. | Co-Inv |
| | | | |
| | | | |
| | | | |
| | | | |
| | | | |
| | | | |
| | | | |
| | | | |
| | | | |

OTHER SIGNIFICANT CONTRIBUTORS

| Name | Organization | Role on Project |
|---|---|---|
| K. Lubin | New Jersey Med. Ctr. | Consultant {3} |
| | | |
| | | |
| | | |
| | | |
| | | |
| | | |
| | | |
| | | |
| | | |
| | | |
| | | |

| **Human Embryonic Stem Cells** | ☒ No | ☐ Yes | |
|---|---|---|---|

If the proposed project involves human embryonic stem cells, list below the registration number of the specific cell line(s) from the following list: http://stemcells.nih.gov/registry/index.asp. *Use continuation pages as needed.*

If a specific line cannot be referenced at this time, include a statement that one from the Registry will be used.

**Cell Line**

| |
|---|
| |
| |
| |
| |
| |
| |

| ***Disclosure Permission Statement.*** Applicable to SBIR/STTR Only. See SBIR/STTR instructions. | ☐ Yes | ☒ No |
|---|---|---|

**Figure 7.3**    Sample Form Page 2: Key Personnel and Human Embryonic Stem Cells

NOTES

{1} In addition to the principal investigator (PI), key personnel are defined as individuals who contribute to the scientific development or execution of the project in a substantive, measurable way, whether or not salaries are requested. Typically, these individuals have doctoral or other professional degrees, although individuals at the masters or baccalaureate level, as well as consultants, should be included if their involvement meets the definition. Key personnel must devote measurable effort to the project whether or not salaries are requested—"zero percent" effort or "as needed" are not acceptable levels for those designated as key personnel.

{2} Until now, the NIH has allowed only one PI on a grant; it is now beginning to look as though co-PIs will be allowed, with both individuals being considered the PIs. However, when there is a consortium established through a subcontract, there also must be a PI at the subcontracted site.

{3} We'll discuss what a *consultant* is later in the section on budgets.

| | Page Numbers |
|---|---|
| Principal Investigator/Program Director (Last, First, Middle): Okata, K. | |
| The name of the principal investigator/program director must be provided at the top of each printed page and each continuation page. | |

| | Page Numbers |
|---|---|
| **Face Page** ................................................................................................................................... | 1 |
| **Description, Performance Sites, Key Personnel, Other Significant Contributors, and Human Embryonic Stem Cells**............................................................................................. | {1}   2 |
| **Table of Contents**........................................................................................................ | |
| **Detailed Budget for Initial Budget Period (or Modular Budget)** ................................................. | {2}   5 |
| **Budget for Entire Proposed Period of Support (not applicable with Modular Budget)** ........................... | 6 |
| **Budgets Pertaining to Consortium/Contractual Arrangements (not applicable with Modular Budget)** | {3}   7 |
| **Biographical Sketch** – Principal Investigator/Program Director (Not to exceed four pages) ........................... | 8 |
| **Other Biographical Sketches** (Not to exceed four pages for each – See instructions) ...................... | 9 |
| **Resources** .............................................................................................................................. | |
| **Research Plan** ....................................................................................................................... | |
| Introduction to Revised Application (Not to exceed 3 pages) ......................................................... | |
| Introduction to Supplemental Application (Not to exceed one page) ......................................................... | |
|     A.  Specific Aims ........................................................................................................ | |
|     B.  Background and Significance ........................................................................... | |
|     C.  Preliminary Studies/Progress Report/ (Items A-D: not to exceed 25 pages*) ........... | |
|         Phase I Progress Report (SBIR/STTR Phase II ONLY) * SBIR/STTR Phase I: Items A-D limited to 15 pages. ......................... | |
|     D.  Research Design and Methods ......................................................................... | |
|     E.  Human Subjects Research ................................................................................ | |
|         Protection of Human Subjects (Required if Item 4 on the Face Page is marked "Yes") ................... | |
|         Data and Safety Monitoring Plan (Required if Item 4 on the Face Page is marked "Yes" **and** a Phase I, II, or III clinical trial is proposed) ...................... | |
|         Inclusion of Women and Minorities (Required if Item 4 on the Face Page is marked "Yes" and is Clinical Research) ...................... | |
|         Targeted/Planned Enrollment Table (for new and continuing clinical research studies) ................... | |
|         Inclusion of Children (Required if Item 4 on the Face Page is marked "Yes") ................... | |
|     F.  Vertebrate Animals ............................................................................................ | |
|     G.  Literature Cited ................................................................................................ | |
|     H.  Consortium/Contractual Arrangements ........................................................ | |
|     I.  Resource Sharing ............................................................................................. | |
|     J.  Letters of Support (e.g., Consultants) ........................................................... | |
| Commercialization Plan (SBIR/STTR Phase II and Fast-Track ONLY) ......................................................... | |
| **Checklist** .................................................................................................................................... | |
| **Appendix** (Five collated sets. No page numbering necessary for Appendix.) <br><br> Appendices NOT PERMITTED for Phase I SBIR/STTR unless specifically solicited. .......................☒ {4} | Check if Appendix is Included |
| Number of publications and manuscripts accepted for publication (not to exceed 10) | |
| Other items (list): | |

**Figure 7.4**     Sample Table of Contents Form

NOTES

{1} Remember that the PHS 398 description (abstract) now takes two pages (pages 2 and 3).

{2} We'll get to the difference between a detailed budget and a modular budget later in the chapter.

{3} In the budgets section, we'll talk about subcontracts.

{4} Provide relevant published or in-press papers in the appendix.

{5} The TOC will almost always be page 4 in the PHS 398 forms package.

As long as I'm on the topic of budgets, allow me to give you some advice. Twenty years ago, things were different. The NIH did not keep such close tabs on your activities, and neither did your home institution. Skirting the rules was common. Things have changed dramatically, and I urge you to find out what the rules are, both from the NIH and your home institution, and to follow them to the letter. Don't mess about. The NIH conducts audits of institutions that receive their grants (remember—it is not *your* grant, it is not *your* money; it is your *institution's* money). The NIH also has the right to conduct a site visit to your lab and to look at consent forms, the way data are maintained, and anything else they might want to see. If your records are not in perfect order and the finances don't match up, you can find yourself in big trouble.

*What is a budget?* A budget is the portion of the proposal in which you provide details to the sponsors about how you plan to spend their money in order to accomplish the goals of the study. An NIH *grants* budget (I am not going to talk about NIH contract budgets, which are an entirely different matter) requires less detail than many other sponsors would request. You must find the correct level of detail. Thus, rather than merely requesting funds for "office supplies," you might note that you plan to purchase photocopy paper, toner cartridges, and blank CD-ROMs for data storage. On the other hand, you do not need to explain that you plan to purchase a package of 12 pencils at 49 cents each. I have tried to provide examples of what you are apt to come up against, and I suggest you use the example as a template. I cannot foresee every contingency, so you will have to use your imagination and, it is to be hoped, the advice of senior colleagues who have successfully submitted NIH budgets before.

You may be surprised to hear that reviewers who have been around long enough to have seen several proposals and budgets will usually have a pretty good idea of how much a proposed study should cost, even before they have seen the budget. The reviewers are not supposed to consider the budget in their evaluation of your proposal, but they often do anyhow. In a proposal that can run several hundred thousand dollars per year, and a couple of million dollars over five years, most reviewers could, I would guess, estimate the total budget within $100,000 per year of what it should cost. So, don't pad your budget, but also don't underfund yourself.

Don't try to show the NIH what a bargain you are giving them. The reviewers not only will not be impressed, but they will also chalk it up to inexperience and reduce your priority score. Also, while you're writing the proposal, you'll be willing to say almost anything to get the money, figuring you'll work out the details once you are funded. The fact is, you really do not want to *get* a grant that is underfunded. If you do, you will spend the duration of the funding period frantically trying to keep up with your commitments, and you'll be miserable.

The NIH expects you to hold up your end of the bargain; these days, they will send you a recruitment plan, based on your sample size and planned timeline, noting not only the number of subjects that you need to consent in each three-month period, but how many of them should be female, how many minorities, and so on. You will have to sign and return this plan, thus, in effect, establishing a contract. They will then require quarterly reports describing actual recruitment. If, in any particular quarter, you fail to make at least 80% of your established quota, they have the right and wherewithal to terminate your grant. They won't do it the first time it happens, but once it does, your program officer will be keeping an eye on your quarterly reports.

How do you come up with an estimate of your costs? Let's go to the PHS 398 budget forms and look at them item by item. Again, I shall not duplicate items covered in the PHS 398 instructions, unless I wish to expand or clarify.

A simple spreadsheet can help you plan your costs as you begin thinking about your budget. Consider that you have two broad categories of costs to consider: fixed costs (costs that are independent of the number of subjects or animals or test tubes you plan to study) and non-fixed costs (costs that vary with the number of subjects). The PI's salary is a fixed cost: You will want to receive whatever percentage of your salary you have budgeted, regardless of the number of subjects. Costs associated with subjects (such as subject payments) are not fixed: So, if you are studying twice the number in Year 2 as in year 1, presumably the non–fixed costs in Year 2 will be twice those for Year 1.

Use a spreadsheet program to work out your non-fixed costs. Let us assume you plan to study the change in catecholamine levels, from baseline to one-year follow-up in 60 patients over a period of three years. Your non-fixed expenses are subject payments, syringes, and serum assays. This is most likely a far simpler scenario than you are likely to undertake, but it serves as a useful illustration. First, provide a reference table showing the number of patient visits. As it is a one-year follow-up, in Year 1 there are no follow-up visits; Year 2, however, has both baseline and follow-up visits, and Year 3 has only follow-up visits. Your spreadsheet might look something like this:

Year 1, Baseline $N = 20$; Follow-up $N = 0$
Year 2, Baseline $N = 40$; Follow-up $N = 20$
Year 3, Baseline $N = 0$; Follow-up $N = 0$

| Baseline | Year 1 | Year 2 | Year 3 | Total |
|---|---|---|---|---|
| Subject payment @$50 | $1,000 | $2,000 | $0 | $3,000 |
| Syringes/Vials @$4 | $80 | $160 | $0 | $240 |
| Assays @$60 | $1,200 | $2,400 | $0 | $3,600 |
| | | | | |
| *Follow-Up* | *Year 1* | *Year 2* | *Year 3* | *Total* |
| Subject payment @$80 | $0 | $1,600 | $3,200 | $4,800 |
| Syringes/Vials @$4 | $0 | $80 | $160 | $240 |
| Assays @$60 | $0 | $1,200 | $2,400 | $3,600 |
| | | | | |
| **TOTAL** | **$2,280** | **$7,440** | **$5,760** | **$15,480** |

The very bottom line of this table is of most concern to you for budget purposes. By using this procedure, you can easily see what you will need to budget for your non-fixed costs. Note that the NIH *does not* want to see this worksheet; however, it should help you develop your budget pages and your budget justification.

## Budget Pages (PHS 398 Only)

There are two form pages for the detailed budget in the PHS 398 packet; they are called FP4 and FP5 (FP for *form page*). The first page is the detailed budget page for the *initial year* of the proposed period. The top of the second page is somewhat less detailed and covers all the years of the proposed period, up to the maximum of five years. The bottom half of the second page is the *justification,* and we'll talk about that later in the chapter. Figures 7.5 and 7.6 show you the two budget form pages.

A couple of general points: First, you use FP4 and FP5 only when requesting more than $250,000 per year; if you are requesting less, you use a *modular budget,* which will be discussed in a later section. (Note: SBIR and STTR applications do not use the modular format, no matter the direct costs.) Second, some requests for applications (RFAs) may specify that you are to use the detailed budget page (FP4) even if the award is less than $250,000. Finally, all items listed in the budget must appear in the budget justification, which is discussed later in this chapter.

| Principal Investigator/Program Director (Last, First, Middle): | | | | Okata. K. {1} | | | |
|---|---|---|---|---|---|---|---|
| **DETAILED BUDGET FOR INITIAL BUDGET PERIOD DIRECT COSTS ONLY {2}** | | | | | FROM 9/1/06 | THROUGH 8/31/07 {3} | |

| PERSONNEL (Applicant organization only) | | TYPE APPT. (months) | % EFFORT ON PROJ. | INST. BASE SALARY | DOLLAR AMOUNT REQUESTED (omit cents) | | |
|---|---|---|---|---|---|---|---|
| NAME | ROLE ON PROJECT | | | | SALARY REQUESTED | FRINGE BENEFITS | TOTAL |
| K. Okata {4} | {5} Principal Investigator | {6} 12 | {7} 25 | {8} 80,000 | 20,000 | {9} 5,000 | 25,000 |
| T. Smith | Co-Inv | 12 | 10 | {10} 180,100 | 18,010 | 4,502 | 22,512 |
| Q. McBurney | Co-Inv | 12 | 20 | 164,000 | 32,800 | 8,200 | 41,000 |
| TBN {11} | ABP Tech | 12 | 10 | 48,000 | 4,800 | 1,200 | 6,000 |
| B. Serrana | Nurse | 12 | 10 | 90,000 | 9,000 | 2,250 | 11,250 |
| R. Butler | Res Coord | 12 | 40 | 48,000 | 19,200 | 4,800 | 24,000 |
| TBN | Res Asst | 12 | 100 | 40,000 | 40,000 | 10,000 | 50,000 |
| **SUBTOTALS** ⟶ | | | | | 143,810 | 35,952 | 179,762 |

| | |
|---|---|
| CONSULTANT COSTS<br>K. Lubin, Ph.D. 10 days @$500/day=$5,000 {12} | 5,000 |
| EQUIPMENT (Itemize)<br>1-Medico Model A243 $CO_2$ monitor @$8,500 {13} | 8,500 |
| SUPPLIES (Itemize by category)<br>Office supplies (toner cartridges, CD-ROMs, copy paper, etc.) @$100/month=$1,200 {14}<br>99 Spirometry tubes for $CO_2$ monitor @$6.00=$594<br>1-HiTec Desktop Computer @$800 {15}<br>80-Respirco Guided Breathing devices @$200=$16,000 | 18,594 |
| TRAVEL<br>Local travel between NYMC and Bronx Hospital @$100/month=$1,200 {16} | 1,200 |

| PATIENT CARE COSTS {17} | INPATIENT | | |
|---|---|---|---|
| | OUTPATIENT | | |

| | |
|---|---|
| ALTERATIONS AND RENOVATIONS (Itemize by category) | |
| OTHER EXPENSES (Itemize by category)<br>Screening: 576 @$2.50=$1,440<br>Subject payment: Visit 1: 66@$65=$4,290; Visit 2: 33 @$60=$1,980 {18}<br>DSMB members reimbursement: 4 members@$1,000=$4,000<br>Communications (conf calls, tel): $1,000 {19} | 12,710 |

| CONSORTIUM/CONTRACTUAL COSTS {20} | DIRECT COSTS | 56,048 |
|---|---|---|
| **SUBTOTAL DIRECT COSTS FOR INITIAL BUDGET PERIOD** (Item 7a, Face Page) {21} | | $ 281,814 |
| CONSORTIUM/CONTRACTUAL COSTS | FACILITIES AND ADMINISTRATIVE COSTS | 26,902 |
| **TOTAL DIRECT COSTS FOR INITIAL BUDGET PERIOD** | | $ 308,716 |
| **SBIR/STTR Only: FEE REQUESTED** | | |

**Figure 7.5**    Sample FP5: Initial Budget Period

NOTES

{1} Every page in the application should have the PI's name in the top right corner.

{2} Direct and indirect costs are explained in the "Facilities and Administrative Costs" section later in this chapter.

{3} Be careful to enter the correct year: Remember, this page is for the *first* year of your budget only.

{4} The first name will always be that of the PI. Co-investigators, if there are any, should come next, followed by other professionals and staff.

{5} The PI label appears in the form; you must fill in titles for all other personnel listed in this section.

{6} The number you enter in the "Type Appt." column refers to the portion of the year that the employee *works for that institution*. A "12" here means the person works 12 months per year (i.e., he or she is fully employed at that institution); "3" would indicate that the person works three months/year (e.g., for the summer).

{7} Estimate the effort that each person will contribute by asking the following: How much time in a five-day week, on average, will this person need to devote to this project? One day a week equals 20%. For example, why did the authors put only 10% for the ABP technician? The timeline (see Chapter 5) calls for 33 subjects to be recruited per quarter, or 11 per month; no more than 10% effort ($\frac{1}{2}$ day per week) should be necessary to accomplish this.

{8} Find out your institution's base salary for each person. In most cases, you cannot arbitrarily change this without discussion with your grants office; someone from that office has to sign off on the budget, and may refuse to do so if the base salary listed is different from the institution's number for that person.

{9} The fringe rate pays for medical and retirement benefits. It is charged over and above the base salary. For the example, I've used a fringe rate of 25%. Multiply the fringe rate by the salary requested (listed in the previous column): In the example, this results in a fringe benefit figure of $5,000. Find out your institution's rate for the current budget period; this information will be given on your institution's Web site, or you can obtain it by asking someone in the grants office. The fringe rate can change, so check you institution's Web site or talk with the grants office whenever you are establishing a budget.

{10} The NIH places a cap on the amount of base salary you can request; the cap is currently $180,100, but by the time you read this it has undoubtedly changed, so check.

> It is a little complicated to figure out the correct fringe dollars across the years if the rate varies, especially so if the timing of the increase does not occur on the first day that your grant began. What you must do is use your spreadsheet program to show a worktable on a separate "page," but linked to your main budget, that calculates the fringe dollars for each individual listed in "Personnel," separately for each year of the grant. This allows you to put in a different fringe rate from one year to the next. In the event the rate change does not match your start date (e.g., it begins 5 months into your year), you would add a "weighting" column for each fringe rate for each year; in this example, it would be 7/12 multiplied by the previous rate, plus 5/12 multiplied by the new rate.

{11} Sometimes, you may recognize that you will need a person in a particular position, but the actual person is as yet unknown; write "TBN" (To Be Named) in the name box, and fill in the appropriate information on the rest of the line (i.e., appropriate base salary, etc.).

{12} A consultant cannot be hired from your own institution; that person would have to be listed as personnel. However, if you formed a consortium and established a subcontract, that person *could* be listed as personnel *with his or her home institution*. The reasons to list a person as a consultant as opposed to as personnel on a sub-contract are discussed later in this chapter.

{13} The NIH notes that equipment is an item that costs at least $5,000. Your institution may set a different limit, however. Knowing what constitutes equipment is important because indirect costs (or facilities and administrative [F&A] costs) do not cover equipment, but do get paid on personnel, supplies, consultant costs, travel, and other expenses. F&A costs are discussed later in this chapter.

{14} The NIH does not require that you itemize items that cost less than $1,000; however, give at least some information. You're going to give more detail in the budget justification.

{15} You can justify a computer if, and only if, it is to be used on the project. (Some grants contain an "administrative core," and computers that are not directly used for the conduct of the funded study may, in some cases, be allowed.) Don't forget to include computers, but don't overdo it. And note that the computer is listed in the "Supplies" category, not in "Equipment."

{16} The authors of the sample proposal included "local travel" between the two sites in their budget; they will also ask for funds for travel to national conferences, but not until Year 2. You should have something to present if you're going to ask for reimbursement for travel to a conference, but in Year 1, you won't yet have anything to present.

{17} See the PHS 398 instructions for information on patient care costs and alterations and renovations.

{18} Note that the authors have worked out how many subjects will be screened and seen in Year 1 using the timeline given in the Research Design and Methods section (Section D) of the proposal.

{19} Don't forget to include expenses such as warrantees, communications costs (e.g., phone bills), postage, and photocopy charges.

{20} See the consortium budget page and the "Consortia and Subcontracts" section of this chapter to see where these figures come from.

{21} Once you have the subtotal for direct costs, you can fill in box 7a on the Face Page. If you are submitting an R01 application, you are allowed to ask for up to $499,999 per year (*not* $500,000) for up to five years. If the need arises for more than that, consult your program officer.

## General Hints Regarding Budgets (PHS 398 and SF 424)

### General Hints Regarding Budgets

You may find that your budget is $500,000 or more in one or more years, but less than that in other years. Move items that can be paid in other years to those in which you have room to ask for more money: For example, you might buy all of your lab supplies in Year 1. If you are still over budget in one or more years, and have money in Years 1 or 2, you can budget costs that will be spent in later years (such as subject payments) in the early years and explain that you plan to carry over the funds until they are needed.

*How do you decide if a particular person should be listed as a co-investigator?* First, any person listed as a co-investigator should be key to the science in some way, either in terms of the thinking or in terms of the doing (i.e., conducting a portion of the research). There are other considerations, as well. Will having the person listed as a co-investigator, because of his or her ability in some key area, make the proposal more attractive to reviewers? (As compared to listing her or him as a "consultant," which generally implies a less central role.) Is the person someone in your lab who will be offended or angry if *not* listed as a co-investigator, and if so, should you be concerned?

*How do you determine how much effort is appropriate for the PI?* First, the PI must put in at least 20% effort. Second, you want to cover all your available effort. If you are listed on someone else's grant as providing 20% effort, you would have 80% effort left; however, you can't put that much effort on an R01 for the PI. You are supposed to be *managing* this project, and that includes delegating jobs to others, who get paid less. I would say 30% is pretty close to the maximum amount of effort one can justify on an R01; you might push it to 40% if you can justify playing a large role in the conduct of the study. Note that K awards are quite different in regard to the amount of effort required of the PI.

*Am I allowed to stretch my budget to cover expenses on other projects?* You may only pay for effort that is to be used *directly* on the project from which it is paid. There are strict rules about things for which you may not use these funds (e.g., you may not hire yourself a general assistant and call that person a *research* assistant; you may not use grant funds to pay for food for staff meetings), and you must not violate them. It may be tempting to stretch the rules, but in these troubled and litigious times, I have to recommend staying on the straight and narrow.

*Can personnel be listed as an "in-kind" contribution?* The short answer is a qualified yes. "In-kind" means that, for some reason, a particular person cannot receive or does not want to ask for money, although he or she is still listed as putting in effort. It may be, for example, that your budget is tight and a colleague is willing to help by being listed as "in-kind." It might also be that this person is already 100% funded and doesn't have any effort to spare. The problem with this last possibility is that one can only contribute 100% of one's effort. Of late, the "in-kind" designation has come under scrutiny. Your grants office may not allow you to do this; check with them first (you may be allowed to list someone, however, as "as needed").

*How do I know how many personnel I will need?* Think through the personnel you will require to competently run the project. It is important to provide sufficient resources in your budget for this; don't try to look like a good value by underbudgeting! Note that in Figure 7.5 the research coordinator in this sample budget is listed at 40% effort and the research assistant (RA) at 100%. This shows that the authors are thinking about the management of the study; that they have estimated they will need a full-time RA to conduct the procedures (something described in more detail in the budget justification), but that the RA's supervisor—the research coordinator—is only needed for 40% of the time (remember, 40% means, on average, two days a week). Moreover, as you will see on the five-year budget page (Figure 7.6), the effort of the ambulatory blood pressure (ABP) technician, which begins at 10% in Year 1, when there are relatively few subject visits, is increased to 20% in the remaining years, when there are more subject visits. This change in effort is explained in the budget justification.

You might notice that the ABP technician's effort was not reduced in Year 5, when there are, once again, fewer subject visits: This may be an oversight on the part of the authors, or it may have been that the technician will need that 20% to pay the rent, as there may not be other active grants at that time to take up the slack, and the authors guessed that they would not be faulted for it. Notice also that in Year 5, the research coordinator and the RA also will not be needed as much to see subjects, since there will be fewer visits then; however, as the budget justification explains, their duties in that year will be shifted to data entry.

*How do I account for cost-of-living increases over the full budget period?* The NIH allows you up to a 3% increase per year in wages, consultant costs, supplies, travel, and other expenses.

*Should I always request five years of support?* Not necessarily. Obviously, you want as many years as you can justify; however, if you can run a study in three years but stretch it out to cover five, you may show yourself studying too few subjects per year, and this will cause concern among the reviewers. It is better to ask for what you really need to do the study, which will lead to a better likelihood of being funded.

## Facilities and Administrative Costs (PHS 398 and SF 424)

You're a scientist, not an administrator or, for that matter, a businessman or -woman, but you have to know about administrative and business matters if you're going to put together a proposal and run a grant. The budget is a large part of this, and although you may have help from colleagues or staff in your grants office, it still is up to you to develop most of it. When you are fortunate enough to be given an award by the NIH, the funds available to you to spend are the *direct costs*—the amount you requested (less any cuts that the NIH chooses to make) to actually run the grant. This may include some of your salary and those of co-investigators, colleagues, and staff who will be helping you. It can also include equipment, supplies, subject payments, and so on.

What you do *not* see are the overhead expenses, also called *indirect costs* or *facilities and administrative* (F&A) costs. These are monies that go directly to your university, your department in the medical school, or, sometimes, directly to the deanery. In theory, these monies are used to pay for various costs, such as your rent (i.e., the office and lab space you occupy), your electricity bill, and the salaries of the people in the grants office who tell you how you can and cannot spend grant funds. The amount of the indirect costs increases as your direct costs increase, but as some direct costs (such as equipment, among many other costs) do not incur overhead, the association is not perfect.

Your institution most likely has an overhead or indirect costs rate that it has negotiated with the NIH. To find out your institution's F&A rate (as you can see, I use the three terms interchangeably), consult your institution's Web site or ask someone in your grants office. (If you are submitting an SBIR or STTR and do not have a negotiated rate, see the discussion, below, of budgets for those grant mechanisms.) The rate for Columbia University Medical Center, for example, is currently 61%. That means that, if I receive $100,000 from the NIH to run a study, it actually costs the NIH in the neighborhood of $161,000. I say "in the neighborhood," because F&A is not paid on every item in the direct costs, including equipment, patient care costs, renovations and alterations, and consortia.

In many institutions, there is more than one F&A rate. F&A rates for different funding agencies may differ; moreover, there is often more than one F&A rate for NIH grants, depending on whether the work is to be done on or off campus (where the rates are lower). The point of all of this is that you need to know your institution's guidelines and policies. Staff at your institution may give seminars and probably can provide a manual; use all the resources you can.

This is just bookkeeping, so why should it concern you? For one thing, your importance to your institution may rest, to some extent, on the amount of indirect costs that you bring in, so you would like these to be as great as possible.

| Principal Investigator/Program Director (Last, First, Middle): | Okata, K. |
|---|---|

## BUDGET FOR ENTIRE PROPOSED PROJECT PERIOD DIRECT COSTS ONLY

| BUDGET CATEGORY TOTALS | | INITIAL BUDGET PERIOD *(from Form Page 4)* | ADDITIONAL YEARS OF SUPPORT REQUESTED | | | |
|---|---|---|---|---|---|---|
| | | | 2nd | 3rd | 4th | 5th |
| PERSONNEL: *Salary and fringe benefits. Applicant organization only.* | | {1}     179,762 | 190,098 | 195,800 | 201,674 | 207,724 |
| CONSULTANT COSTS | | 5,000 | 3,090 | 3,182 | 3,277 | 3,375 |
| EQUIPMENT | | 8,500 | 0 | 0 | 0 | 0 |
| SUPPLIES | | 18,594 | 27,616 | 21,249 | 5,893 | 1,746 |
| TRAVEL | | 1,200 | 4,200 | 4,200 | 4,200 | 5,700 |
| PATIENT CARE COSTS | INPATIENT | 0 | 0 | 0 | 0 | 0 |
| | OUTPATIENT | 0 | 0 | 0 | 0 | 0 |
| ALTERATIONS AND RENOVATIONS | | 0 | 0 | 0 | 0 | 0 |
| OTHER EXPENSES | | 12,710 | 30,140 | 36,864 | 29,281 | 12,102 |
| CONSORTIUM/ CONTRACTUAL COSTS | DIRECT | 56,048 | 57,729 | 59,460 | 61,243 | 63,080 |
| **SUBTOTAL DIRECT COSTS** *(Sum = Item 8a, Face Page)* {2} | | 281,814 | 312,873 | 320,755 | 305,568 | 293,727 |
| CONSORTIUM/ CONTRACTUAL COSTS | F&A | 26,902 | 27,709 | 28,540 | 29,396 | 30,278 |
| **TOTAL DIRECT COSTS** | | 308,716 | 340,582 | 349,295 | 334,964 | 324,005 |
| **TOTAL DIRECT COSTS FOR ENTIRE PROPOSED PROJECT PERIOD** | | | | | | $ 1,657,562 |
| **SBIR/STTR Only Fee Requested {3}** | | | | | | |
| **SBIR/STTR Only: Total Fee Requested for Entire Proposed Project Period** (Add Total Fee amount to "Total direct costs for entire proposed project period" above and Total F&A/indirect costs from Checklist Form Page, and enter these as "Costs Requested for Proposed Period of Support" on Face Page, Item 8b.) | | | | | | $ |

JUSTIFICATION. Follow the budget justification instructions exactly. Use continuation pages as needed. {4}
SEE CONTINUATION PAGES.

**Figure 7.6**     Sample FP5: Budget for the Entire Project Period

NOTES

{1} Rather than using annotations for each figure in this form, I shall explain how these numbers were arrived at in the Budget Justification (which follows).

{2} As the instructions note, sum this row, and write the sum into box 8a on the Face Page.

{3} The fee is only of concern if you are submitting a SBIR or STTR application, discussed later in the chapter.

{4} Don't begin the budget justification here; just write "see continuation pages" so reviewers know where to find it.

## THE BUDGET JUSTIFICATION (PHS 398 AND SF 424)

The budget justification provides the explicit rationale for the role and percentage of effort of all study personnel and for all study expenses listed in the budget. It must be consistent with the specific aims you have listed in you Specific Aims section and with your Research Design and Methods section. You should be very explicit in the justification; use the example below as a guide to the level of detail you are expected to provide. Be sure to provide justification for each budget year of the proposed study. The reviewers may look at this section if they have concerns about a particular budget item, so be thorough.

---

### Budget Justification, Example

*Budget Justification: New York Medical Center* {1}

*Personnel*

**Note:** We have allocated funds to allow a 3% increase per year in Years 2–5, as allowed by NIH policy (except for any salary that is at the current NIH cap of $180,100).

Fringe benefit rate at NYMC is 25%.

**Kaoru Okata, MD (PI: 25% effort)** {2} is Assistant Professor of Medicine in the Department of General Medicine at NYMC. He has extensive experience in the conduct of clinical trials and has specialized in behavioral interventions to reduce BP in hypertensives. He currently is the site-PI on an NHLBI-funded R01 that focuses on a stress-management intervention in hypertensive patients, and is a co-investigator on Dr. Smith's NHLBI-funded R01, which focuses on mechanisms by which medication adherence may be affected. Dr. Okata has worked with Drs. Smith and McBurney for the past five years; thus, this is a well-established collaboration, {3} and Dr. Okata is highly qualified in terms of both the science and the experience in administration of an R01-level award. Dr. Okata will be responsible for the design of the study and the collaboration with Dr. Ruggiero in terms of data collection, and will also hold primary responsibility for manuscript preparation. {4}

**Theresa Smith, MD (Co-Inv: 10% effort)** is Professor of Medicine at NYMC. She has extensive experience in the causes and treatment of HTN, and has published extensively in the area of BP measurement. She is an expert in the area of ABP assessment, and has helped develop the American Heart Association (AHA) evidence-based guidelines for use of these monitors in clinical practice. Dr. Smith will collaborate with Dr. Okata on the design of the study and will work with Drs. Okata and Ruggiero in the supervision of the collection of the BP data. She will be responsible for all BP and ambulatory assessment procedures, will assist with data analysis, and will participate in manuscripts. {5}

---

## Notes: Budget Justification Example

{1} There is no NIH form for the budget justification in the PHS 398 forms; either put it on plain paper (with the PI's name in the upper right corner of every page) or on the continuation pages you will find in the PHS 398 packet. Provide general information, including the 3% per year increase (which the NIH allows), noting that salaries at the current NIH cap are excluded. Also, provide your fringe rate.

{2} Begin with the PI. He is requesting 25% effort here, which means that he plans to devote approximately 1¼ days per week on this project. This is a reasonable amount of time. The NIH will want to see that you are devoting at least 20% effort to the proposed project. Of course, you might like to ask for more percentage effort, if your salary is not already fully covered, but don't request more than 30% or 35%; at that level, it begins to look as though you are not delegating work appropriately. Of course, this is not the case if you are submitting a career (K) award, where you may be requesting funds for all or most of your salary.

{3} Note that most of this paragraph is devoted to justifying the qualifications of the PI. Don't be shy about this; however, the reviewers may not read this part of the justification, as you will put much the same information in the Preliminary Studies section of your narrative.

{4} The remainder of this paragraph is devoted to laying out the responsibilities that the PI is delegating to himself.

{5} Because this example involves a quite junior investigator as the PI, the paragraphs devoted to co-investigators are meant to reassure the reviewers that although the PI may be junior, the team as a whole possesses the requisite skills to carry out the project. You must think strategically about how much effort each co-investigator will devote to the project: You do not want it to appear nominal (e.g., 2% effort) or, skills notwithstanding, it will look as though the co-investigator is not going to spend any real time on your project. You do not want to have the co-investigators devote *too much* effort, however, for a few reasons. First, co-investigators are likely to be costly, and you will be surprised how quickly you hit the budget limit. Second, you don't want it to look as though the co-investigator is the real PI and is allowing you to reap the honor of the award. Third, as with the PI, too large a percentage of effort will look like poor management of resources, unless the justification is very strong (such as supervising very complex data collection procedures).

---

### Budget Justification, Example (Continued)

**Quentin McBurney, PhD (Co-Investigator: 20% effort)** is a biostatistician who has worked with this group for the past 12 years. He is an expert in the analysis of hierarchical models, as well as in database management. Dr. McBurney will work with Drs. Okata and Ruggiero to develop a database for the study and will supervise data entry. Dr. McBurney will be responsible for analyzing the data and will assist in manuscript preparation. {6}

**TBN, MA ABP Technician: 10% effort in Year 1; 20% effort in Years 2–5)** {7} will be responsible for training the research coordinator and the RA in ABP monitoring procedures and will be responsible for quality control of the BP measurements. The technician will also supervise the instrumentation of the ABP monitor. The technician is listed at 10% effort in Year 1 because there will not yet be a large number of subject visits; the percentage of effort will be increased to 20% beginning in Year 2, when the subject visits begin to increase in number. {8}

**Beth Serrana, RN (Nurse: 10% effort)** will assist with chart reviews. {9}

**Reina Butler, BS (Research Coordinator: 40% effort)** will supervise the RA; together, they will be responsible for conducting the screenings and, with the ABP technician, will be responsible for consenting and enrolling participants and carrying out the study procedures. Ms. Butler will be supervised by Drs. Okata and Ruggiero. In Year 5, when the flow of research participants has slowed, Ms. Butler will supervise and work with the RA to enter data.

**TBN, BA (Research Assistant: 100% effort)** will work with the research coordinator to conduct the patient visits. In Year 5, the RA will concentrate on data entry.

---

## Notes: Budget Justification Example (Continued)

{6} Recall that I suggested earlier that you have a statistician on your team, unless the statistics are extremely simple and/or the PI or one of the co-investigators already on the project can demonstrate experience in this area.

{7} "TBN" means "To Be Named"; if you don't have someone specific in mind, use this designation.

{8} List technical staff in the personnel section. Be sure to note, on the budget page, their role on the project.

{9} You don't need to provide a whole paragraph if a brief statement sufficiently describes the person's qualifications and responsibilities.

The personnel section of the budget justification should provide enough detail to make it clear why each person is necessary to the project, and exactly what his or her contribution will be. Note that for the ambulatory BP technician, it was explained that she would start at 10% effort in Year 1, and would be increased to 20% in Year 2. Note also that a justification was provided for keeping the research coordinator and RA on at the same effort levels in Year 5, to change over to other duties.

## Budget Justification, Example (Continued)

*Consultant*

**Kenneth Lubin, PhD** is Asst. Professor of Medicine at the New Jersey Medical Center. He is an expert in the development of databases that involve multiple sources of input (in this case, hand-entered data, ABP data, ECG data, and baroreflex data; the latter are downloaded electronically). Dr. Lubin will provide 10 days in Year 1 to develop the database; and 6 days in the remaining years to maintain it. Dr. Lubin's fee will increase by 3% per year. Thus, Dr. Lubin will be paid as follows: {10, 11}

| Year | Fee | Days/Year | Total |
|------|-----|-----------|-------|
| 1 | $500/day | 10 | $5,000 |
| 2 | $515/day | 6 | $3,090 |
| 3 | $530/day | 6 | $3,182 |
| 4 | $546/day | 6 | $3,277 |
| 5 | $563/day | 6 | $3,375 |
| **Total** | | | **$17,924** |

*Supplies*

*Office Supplies.* We have budgeted $100/month for office supplies, including computer storage, media, printer paper, and toner cartridges. {12} The budget will be increased by 3% each succeeding year.

| Year | Supplies |
|------|----------|
| 1 | $1,200 |
| 2 | $1,236 |
| 3 | $1,273 |
| 4 | $1,311 |
| 5 | $1,350 |
| **Total** | **$6,370** |

*Medico Spirometry Tubes.* Spirometry tubes ($6.00/tube) are necessary to calibrate the Medico $CO_2$ monitor at each usage.

| Year | Number | Cost |
|------|--------|------|
| 1 | 99 | $594 |
| 2 | 330 | $1,980 |
| 3 | 396 | $2,376 |
| 4 | 297 | $1,782 |
| 5 | 66 | $396 |
| **Total** | **1,188** | **$7,128** |

*Respirco Guided Breathing Device.* Respirco will modify the necessary number of devices for the placebo condition at no extra charge (see Letters). A total of 300 devices are needed over the first four years of the project.

| Year | Number | Cost |
|---|---|---|
| 1 | 80 | $16,000 |
| 2 | 122 | $24,400 |
| 3 | 88 | $17,600 |
| 4 | 10 | $2,000 |
| **Total** | **300** | **$60,000** |

*Desktop Computers.* We have budgeted funds for two desktop computers to be used for data collection and management for this study, one in Year 1 and one in Year 4.

2 desktop computers @$800 = $1,600 {13}

## Notes: Budget Justification Example (Continued)

{10} Here, we touch upon a very important and somewhat subtle point. Why is Dr. Lubin a consultant, paid by the day or hour, and not listed as a co-investigator on another subcontract? The answer depends on several things. First, a consultant is generally a person who performs a very specific task and who may not be more generally involved with the science. That does seem the case here. However, there are other factors to consider. On the one hand, it is prestigious to be able to list "Co-Investigator on NIH grant" on your cv. Also, as discussed earlier, being a co-investigator brings indirect costs into your own institution. On the other hand, Dr. Lubin may already have 100% of his effort covered. He might step his effort down on one of the awards on which he is listed, freeing up 10% that could be listed on the subcontract.

Let us say that Dr. Lubin's base salary is $100,000 a year. Perhaps you would pay him 5% of his effort (remember, you also have to pay his fringe rate). However, if 100% of Dr. Lubin's salary is already covered on other grants or by his institution, he may prefer to be paid as a consultant because he may do so *over and above* his 100% salary. With the consulting fee you are going to pay him in Year 1, then, he would be earning not $100,000, but $105,000. The NIH policy is peculiar about this point; your percentage of effort may not total to more than 100 (except in special cases); however, you can earn consulting fees from an NIH-sponsored award. You can't and shouldn't abuse this difference by overusing it, but you can see why perhaps Dr. Lubin would prefer to be a consultant. One final reminder: A person from your home institution cannot be a consultant on your grant.

{11} The 3% yearly increase can be applied to any of the expense categories except things such as subject payments, which you will want to hold constant, and other items for which it would not make sense to increase the budget. Whenever you apply the 3% increase, note it in that item's justification.

{12} Notice how the authors have broken out the supplies to a cost per month, rather than just providing a lump yearly sum.

{13} Even though one might think of computers as equipment, each of these machines costs less than the NIH-defined minimum for equipment ($5,000). This difference is important, because F&A does not get charged on equipment, and you want all the F&A you can justify going to your institution.

### Budget Justification, Example (Continued)

*Travel {14}*

*Local Travel.* We have budgeted $100/month for travel between NYMC and Bronx Hospital for meetings among the investigators during each of the five years of the budget period.

*Travel to National Conferences.* We have budgeted $3,000 in Years 2, 3, and 4 for travel for two investigators to one national conference. In Year 5, we budgeted an extra $1,500 to allow three investigators to travel to one national conference.

> Be careful about how much travel money you request; this is a red-flag item for reviewers.

*Other Expenses*

*Screening.* We budgeted $2.50/person to purchase Metro cards to use as incentives for the screenings.

| Year | Number | Cost |
|------|--------|------|
| 1 | 576 | $1,440 |
| 2 | 768 | $1,920 |
| 3 | 768 | $1,920 |
| 4 | 192 | $480 |
| **Total** | **2,304** | **$5,760** |

You are not constrained to buying supplies or paying other expenses to match the number of subjects you plan to see in a given budget period. There are at least two reasons to bunch expenses up in one or more years, and not incur those expenses in others. If, for example, your expenses are higher during the latter years of the budget period, you can front-load expenses in the earlier years to reduce the strain on your budget in those top-heavy years. Another reason to redistribute expenses is that some items come packaged in what may be, for your study, a several-year supply or you may get a better price on some items or services by buying in bulk.

*Subject Reimbursement.* The study comprises 4 visits: Visit 1a (consent), Visit 1b (baseline), Visit 2 (week 8), and Visit 3 (month 12). The reimbursements are as follows: Visit 1a = $30, Visit 1b = $35, Visit 2 = $60, Visit 3 = $100.

| Year | Visits 1a, 1b | Visit 2 | Visit 3 | Cost |
|------|---------------|---------|---------|------|
| 1 | 66 | 33 | 0 | $6,270 |
| 2 | 132 | 132 | 66 | $23,100 |

| 3 | 132 | 132 | 132 | $29,700 |
| 4 | 66 | 99 | 132 | $23,430 |
| 5 | 0 | 0 | 66 | $6,600 |
| **Total** | | | | **$89,100** |

*DSMB.* We have budgeted funds for honoraria to be paid to four persons who will comprise our DSMB. The DSMB will meet at least once/year (on our premises), and will engage in conference calls when necessary. The budget will be increased by 3% each succeeding year. {15}

| Year | Honoraria |
|---|---|
| 1 | $4,000 |
| 2 | $4,120 |
| 3 | $4,244 |
| 4 | $4,371 |
| 5 | $4,502 |
| **Total** | **$21,237** |

*Communications.* We have budgeted $1,000 a month for conference calls, videoconferencing, and other communication expenses.

## Notes: Budget Justification Example (Continued)

{14} You can add the 3% per year increase to travel funds. Note that the authors have broken travel expenses into local and national travel, and have deliberately *not* requested funds for national travel in Year 1, when they would not yet have anything from this project to present.

{15} The need for a data and safety monitoring board (DSMB) was discussed in Chapter 6. Note that you are encouraged to budget honoraria for the members and to figure in the 3% yearly increase.

### Budget Justification, Example (Continued)

*Consortium* {16}

We will form a consortium with Bronx Hospital, which is the home institution of Dr. Ruggiero, a co-investigator on this project. A separate budget is provided (Bronx Hospital F&A = 48%).

## Notes: Budget Justification Example (Continued)

{16} As you can see, only a brief mention of the consortium is made here; however, the consortium provides its own budget and checklist page (the page on which the institution's F&A rates are shown).

## CONSORTIA AND SUBCONTRACTS (PHS 398 AND SF 424)

Sometimes, you may want to avail yourself of resources from another institution (i.e., an institution other than the one from which you plan to submit the application). The resources might be patients or other subjects; that is, you are looking for at another site because you either do not think you will be able to find enough patients at your own institution or for purposes of increasing the generalizability of your results. It might be that there is a piece of equipment at another institution that you need to run your study, and you might be able to come to an agreement with that institution to bring your patients there for that one procedure. It might be that there are one or more persons at this other institution that you would like to have as co-investigators. To accomplish any of these partnerships, you need to set up a *consortium* between this other institution and your own, and your institution will establish a *subcontract* with them to do this. The *primary* contract would exist between the NIH and your home institution; a subcontract will exist between your institution and this other institution (and there can be more than one).

There is a small point I must cover to avoid confusion. In Chapter 3, I mentioned that the NIH sometimes offers *contracts*, as opposed to *grant initiatives*, to promote the conduct of certain studies. One learns about the offering by reading the NIH "Guide for Grants and Contracts" (see Chapter 3), which will show a request for proposals (RFP), which is for research contracts (in contrast to RFAs, which are for research grants). I won't be discussing research contracts in this volume. When I talk here about a "contract" between the NIH and your institution in the context of a grant, this is different than the contracts offered by the RFPs.

How do you go about setting up a subcontract? It really is not difficult. Let's use the example that has been running through this book. New York Medical Center (NYMC) plans to establish a consortium with Bronx Hospital (BH). All the NYMC wants from BH is the services, for a small part of the time, of Dr. Ruggiero, who is a co-investigator on this project. Think about it this way: Drs. Okata (the PI, at NYMC), Smith (at NYMC), and Ruggiero (at BH) are long-time colleagues, and have decided they would like to submit this application together; Dr. Okata, of NYMC, is going to be the PI; thus the proposal must be submitted from NYMC. However, Dr. Ruggiero is paid by BH, so they propose a subcontract between NYMC and BH. The subcontract is not actually enacted at the time of submission; if the project is not funded, there may never be a need for it. However, what does need to go into the application are (a) a letter from BH that states its *intention* to form a subcontract (most institutions have a standard form letter, like the one shown later in Figure 7.7); (b) a budget from BH that uses the same form pages that NYMC will use, taken from the PHS 398 packet; and (c) a budget justification (see below).

Take a look at the detailed budget page for BH, shown later in the chapter, and you will see that the direct costs for BH are $56,048. This pays for some of Dr. Ruggiero's time, for some of his assistant's time, and for some office supplies. This will be explained in BH's budget justification.

The indirect rate for BH is 48%. That makes BH's indirect costs $26,902 (remember, these are monies that go directly to BH, not to the investigator). If you go back to the detailed budget pages for NYMC, you'll see where these amounts are entered in the forms, and it should now make sense. Your "Subtotal Direct Costs" include the direct costs from your subcontract (in this case, for your initial budget period, $281,814); the subcontractor's indirect costs ($26,902) get added to that amount, to give you the "Total Direct Costs" (in this case, for your initial budget period, $308,716). These are the calculations that produce the numbers seen on the initial period budget page.

That's it for now. There will be a few more calculations on the checklist page, and we'll get to that in a moment.

Figure 7.7 shows a sample letter of intent to form a consortium; Figures 7.8 and 7.9 show the budget pages that BH would submit with the sample NYMC proposal. I have also included the BH budget justification.

I admit the subcontract stuff is a little tricky, but, all in all, this is a pretty straightforward process when you consider that the authors asked for more than one and a half million dollars, over five years. Actually, for an RCT that proposes to run 400 subjects, that's a small amount of money; in reality, it would cost more.

---

## Budget Samples for Subcontracting Institution

*Budget Justification—Bronx Hospital*

*Personnel*

**Note:** We have allocated funds to allow a 3% increase per year in Years 2–5, as allowed by NIH policy.

The fringe rate at The Bronx Hospital is 22.2%.

**Lawrence Ruggiero, PhD (PI: 15% effort)** is Assoc. Professor in the Department of Psychiatry at The Bronx Hospital. He is a recognized expert in the assessment and interpretation of HRV and baroreflex sensitivity. Dr. Ruggiero has worked with Drs. Smith and Okata for the past six years, and has set up their psychophysiology laboratory at NYMC. He is a co-investigator on an R01 with Dr. Smith (PI), on which his responsibility is to oversee the collection and analysis of ECG data. On the present proposal, his responsibilities would be similar: Dr. Ruggiero would train the research coordinator and the RA in instrumentation techniques for the collection of ECG (for HRV analysis) and for continuous, noninvasive BP (for the baroreflex sensitivity analyses). He will assist in the analysis of the data and in manuscript preparation.

**Nadia Nelin, MS (Research Assistant: 60% effort)** will be responsible for scoring the ECG data for the spectral analysis to assess HRV.

*Supplies*

*Office Supplies.* We have budgeted $50/month for office supplies, including computer storage media, printer paper, and toner cartridges. The budget will be increased by 3% each succeeding year.

| Year | Supplies |
|---|---|
| 1 | $600 |
| 2 | $616 |
| 3 | $636 |
| 4 | $655 |
| 5 | $674 |
| **Total** | **$3,183** |

*(Text continues on page 183)*

# The Bronx Hospital

**1000 Grand Central Parkway, The Bronx, NY 12345**

## STATEMENT OF INTEREST TO FORM A CONSORTIUM

April 3, 2005

Mr. Allen Birdwell
New York Medical Center
Research Administration
900 125th Street
New York, NY 10027

RE:              Proposed consortium with New York Medical Center
Project Title:   RCT: Effect of Guided Breathing Intervention on Ambulatory BP in Hypertensives
PI:              Kaoru Okata, MD

Dear Mr. Birdwell:

The programmatic and administrative personnel of The New York Medical Center and The Bronx Hospital, in accordance with the consortium grant policy established by the National Institutes of Health, are prepared to establish the necessary inter-institutional agreement(s) to form a consortium.

In the event that this proposal is funded, The Bronx Hospital will enter into an inter-institutional agreement with your organization. Award notices or contracts resulting from this submission should be sent to my attention at:

The Bronx Hospital
1000 Grand Central Parkway
The Bronx, NY 12345

Human Assurance # FWA00009999

Any questions or negotiations regarding this submission should be directed to me at (718) 555-3579 or via electronic mail at Asevern@TBH.edu

Sincerely,

Allen Severn

Allen T. Severn, MD
Director, Grants and Contracts Office

---

**Figure 7.7**      Sample Statement of Intent to Form a Consortium

NOTE

The language used in this letter is meant to serve as an example only, and may not satisfy the legal requirements of your institution or any institutions with whom you desire to enter into a consortium arrangement. It is also worth noting that this letter should always appear on the subcontracting institution's letterhead.

| BRONX HOSPITAL SUBCONTRACT {1} | Okata, K. {2} | | | | | | |
|---|---|---|---|---|---|---|---|

| DETAILED BUDGET FOR INITIAL BUDGET PERIOD DIRECT COSTS ONLY | | | | | FROM 9/1/06 | THROUGH 8/31/07 | |
|---|---|---|---|---|---|---|---|
| PERSONNEL (*Applicant organization only*) | | TYPE APPT. (*months*) | % EFFORT ON PROJ. | INST. BASE SALARY | DOLLAR AMOUNT REQUESTED (*omit cents*) | | |
| NAME | ROLE ON PROJECT | | | | SALARY REQUESTED | FRINGE BENEFITS | TOTAL |
| L. Ruggiero | Principal Investigator | 12 | 15 | 136,000 | 20,475 | {3}  4,545 | 25,020 |
| N. Nelin | Res Asst | 12 | 60 | 41,500 | 24,900 | 5,528 | 30,428 |
|  |  |  |  |  |  |  |  |
|  |  |  |  |  |  |  |  |
|  |  |  |  |  |  |  |  |
|  |  |  |  |  |  |  |  |
|  |  |  |  |  |  |  |  |
| | SUBTOTALS ——————————————▶ | | | | | | |
| CONSULTANT COSTS | | | | | | | |
| EQUIPMENT (*Itemize*) | | | | | | | |
| SUPPLIES (*Itemize by category*) Office supplies (toner cartridges, CD-Roms, copy paper, etc.) @ $50/month=$600 | | | | | | | 600 |
| TRAVEL | | | | | | | |
| PATIENT CARE COSTS | INPATIENT | | | | | | |
| | OUTPATIENT | | | | | | |
| ALTERATIONS AND RENOVATIONS (*Itemize by category*) | | | | | | | |
| OTHER EXPENSES (*Itemize by category*) | | | | | | | |
| CONSORTIUM/CONTRACTUAL COSTS | | | DIRECT COSTS | | | | |
| SUBTOTAL DIRECT COSTS FOR INITIAL BUDGET PERIOD (*Item 7a, Face Page*) {21} | | | | | | | $ 56,048 |
| CONSORTIUM/CONTRACTUAL COSTS | | | FACILITIES AND ADMINISTRATIVE COSTS | | | | |
| TOTAL DIRECT COSTS FOR INITIAL BUDGET PERIOD | | | | | | | $ 56,048 |
| SBIR/STTR Only: FEE REQUESTED | | | | | | | |

**Figure 7.8**    Sample Budget Page (Year 1) for a Subcontracting Institution

NOTES

{1} Indicate here that this is a subcontract, so that it is differentiated from the main first-year budget page.

{2} The project PI's name goes here, although this is the Bronx Hospital budget.

{3} The fringe rate for Bronx Hospital is 22.2%.

{4} There *is* no Face Page for the subcontract, so ignore this line in the form. Note also that you *do not* put the subcontract indirect costs anywhere on this page.

| BRONX HOSPITAL SUB-CONTRACT | Okata, K. | | | | |
|---|---|---|---|---|---|

**BUDGET FOR ENTIRE PROPOSED PROJECT PERIOD DIRECT COSTS ONLY**

| BUDGET CATEGORY TOTALS | | INITIAL BUDGET PERIOD *(from Form Page 4)* | ADDITIONAL YEARS OF SUPPORT REQUESTED | | | |
|---|---|---|---|---|---|---|
| | | | 2nd | 3rd | 4th | 5th |
| PERSONNEL: *Salary and fringe benefits. Applicant organization only.* | | 55,448 | 57,110 | 58,823 | 60,587 | 62,405 |
| CONSULTANT COSTS | | | | | | |
| EQUIPMENT | | | | | | |
| SUPPLIES | | 600 | 618 | 637 | 656 | 675 |
| TRAVEL | | | | | | |
| PATIENT CARE COSTS | INPATIENT | | | | | |
| | OUTPATIENT | | | | | |
| ALTERATIONS AND RENOVATIONS | | | | | | |
| OTHER EXPENSES | | | | | | |
| CONSORTIUM/ CONTRACTUAL COSTS | DIRECT | | | | | |
| **SUBTOTAL DIRECT COSTS** *(Sum = Item 8a, Face Page)* | | 56,048 | 57,729 | 59,460 | 61,243 | 63,080 |
| CONSORTIUM/ CONTRACTUAL COSTS | F&A | | | | | |
| **TOTAL DIRECT COSTS** | | 56,048 | 57,729 | 59,460 | 61,243 | 63,080 |
| **TOTAL DIRECT COSTS FOR ENTIRE PROPOSED PROJECT PERIOD** | | | | | | $ 297,560 |
| **SBIR/STTR Only Fee Requested** | | | | | | |

| **SBIR/STTR Only: Total Fee Requested for Entire Proposed Project Period** (Add Total Fee amount to "Total direct costs for entire proposed project period" above and Total F&A/indirect costs from Checklist Form Page, and enter these as "Costs Requested for Proposed Period of Support" on Face Page, Item 8b.) | $ |
|---|---|

JUSTIFICATION. Follow the budget justification instructions exactly. Use continuation pages as needed.

SEE CONTINUATION PAGES

PHS 398 (Rev. 09/04)                                   Page                                      **Form Page 5**

**Figure 7.9**     Sample Budget Page (Full Project Period) for the Subcontracting Institution

## THE CHECKLIST (PHS 398 ONLY)

We're going to go out of order at this point and look at the checklist (which is actually the last page of your application), as it relates to the indirect costs to be computed. Figure 7.10 shows a checklist for the example we have been using. The checklist is fairly straightforward, but there are a couple of details to discuss.

Once you have completed the checklist, you are finally ready to fill in sections 7b and 8b on the Face Page. You have already filled in 7a and 8a; you knew those numbers once you completed the two detailed budget pages. Section 7b is the sum of the "Total Direct Costs" (*not* the "Subtotal Direct Costs") from the Budget for Entire Proposed Project page (Figure 7.6) plus the indirect cost for the initial budget year, which is shown on the checklist (Figure 7.10). Thus, you add $308,716 and $145,359, and fill in the sum ($454,075) in box 7b on the Face Page (Figure 7.1). For box 8b, you add the sum of the "Total Direct Costs" from Figure 7.6 ($1,657,562) with the total indirect costs as they are shown on the checklist ($740,203), which sum to $2,397,765.

## MODULAR BUDGETS (PHS 398 AND SF 424)

Now that you've made it through the detailed budget pages, the modular budgets should be a snap. The idea behind the modular budgets was that reviewers should not focus on small amounts of money in small grants awards (you may not consider $250,000/year small, but in terms of the paperwork burden, the NIH does).

As usual, I'm going to walk you through an example. I would prefer to use the same example I used in the detailed budget, but since a modular budget is used only when the budget is $250,000 or less (unless a particular RFA or other call specifies differently), I have cut out several items to bring down the costs. The subcontract will remain the same.

Before we dive into the sample budget, there are a few things you need to know.

- The NIH has a new policy that kicks in whenever you are concerned about going over a budget limit, including the decision whether to use a modular format (which has a ceiling of $250,000) and whether you need to write a letter to request permission to request $500,000 or more. These ceiling amounts do not include the F&A costs that stem from any subcontracts you might have. Thus, let us say that the box labeled "Subtotal Direct Costs for Initial Budget Period" on the first-year detailed budget page contains the amount $450,000. Let us also say that you have a subcontract, and the indirect costs for that subcontract are $80,000. That means that your totals will come to $530,000. Do you need to request permission to submit this application? No, you do not. Similarly, if the subtotal box contained the amount $225,000 and the F&A from your subcontractor was $50,000 (for a Total Direct of $275,000), you would use the modular format.

- The modular format is applicable only to R01, R03, R15, R21, and R34 applications.

- "Modules" are packets of $25,000. If you are using the modular format, your "Subtotal Direct Costs" will always be a multiple of 25,000. For example, as you will see in our example, we are requesting nine modules ($225,000) in each of the five years. For some reason, the NIH prefers that you keep the modules the same. If, however, you do use different numbers of modules, then provide an additional narrative budget justification for the variation requested.

As you noticed in our detailed budget (Figure 7.6), we vary from year to year by several thousand dollars. How does the NIH want you to keep them the same? You compute the

| Principal Investigator/Program Director (Last, First, Middle): | Okata, K. |
|---|---|

**TYPE OF APPLICATION** *(Check all that apply.)* {1}

☒ NEW application. *(This application is being submitted to the PHS for the first time.)*

☐ REVISION of application number: ▨

*(This application replaces a prior unfunded version of a new, competing continuation, or supplemental application.)*

| ☐ COMPETING CONTINUATION of grant number: ▨ | INVENTIONS AND PATENTS *(Competing continuation appl. and Phase II only)* | |
|---|---|---|
| *(This application is to extend a funded grant beyond its current project period.)* | ☐ No | ☐ Previously reported |
| ☐ SUPPLEMENT to grant number: ▨ | ☐ Yes. If "Yes," | ☐ Not previously reported |

*(This application is for additional funds to supplement a currently funded grant.)*

☐ CHANGE of principal investigator/program director.

  Name of former principal investigator/program director: ▨

☐ CHANGE of Grantee Institution. Name of former institution: ▨

| ☐ FOREIGN application | ☐ Domestic Grant with foreign involvement | List Country(ies) Involved: ▨ |
|---|---|---|
| ☐ SBIR Phase I | ☐ SBIR Phase II: SBIR Phase I Grant No. ▨ | ☐ SBIR Fast Track |
| ☐ STTR Phase I | ☐ STTR Phase II: STTR Phase I Grant No. ▨ | ☐ STTR Fast Track |

**1. PROGRAM INCOME** *(See instructions.)*

All applications must indicate whether program income is anticipated during the period(s) for which grant support is requested. If program income is anticipated, use the format below to reflect the amount and source(s).

| Budget Period | Anticipated Amount | Source(s) |
|---|---|---|
| ▨ {2} | ▨ | ▨ |
| ▨ | ▨ | ▨ |
| ▨ | ▨ | ▨ |

**2. ASSURANCES/CERTIFICATIONS** *(See instructions.)*

In signing the application Face Page, the authorized organizational representative agrees to comply with the following policies, assurances and/or certifications when applicable. Descriptions of individual assurances/certifications are provided in Part III. If unable to certify compliance, where applicable, provide an explanation and place it after this page.
•Human Subjects Research •Research Using Human Embryonic Stem Cells •Research on Transplantation of Human Fetal Tissue •Women and Minority Inclusion Policy •Inclusion of Children Policy •Vertebrate Animals•

•Debarment and Suspension •Drug-Free Workplace *(applicable to new [Type 1] or revised [Type 1] applications only)* •Lobbying •Non-Delinquency on Federal Debt •Research Misconduct •Civil Rights (Form HHS 441 or HHS 690) •Handicapped Individuals (Form HHS 641 or HHS 690) •Sex Discrimination (Form HHS 639-A or HHS 690) •Age Discrimination (Form HHS 680 or HHS 690) •Recombinant DNA Research, Including Human Gene Transfer Research •Financial Conflict of Interest (except Phase I SBIR/STTR) •Smoke-Free Workplace •Prohibited Research •Select Agents and Toxins •STTR ONLY: Certification of Research Institution Participation

**3. FACILITIES AND ADMINSTRATIVE COSTS (F&A)/INDIRECT COSTS.** See specific instructions.

| ☒ DHHS Agreement dated: | 5/1/2004 {3} | ☐ No Facilities and Administrative Costs Requested. | |
|---|---|---|---|
| ☐ DHHS Agreement being negotiated with | ▨ | Regional Office. | |
| ☐ No DHHS Agreement, but rate established with | ▨ | Date | ▨ |

CALCULATION* *(The entire grant application, including the Checklist, will be reproduced and provided to peer reviewers as confidential information.)*

| | | | | | |
|---|---|---|---|---|---|
| a. Initial budget period: | Amount of base $ | {4} 242,266 | x Rate applied | {5} 60.0 % = F&A costs $ | 145,359 |
| b. 02 year | Amount of base $ | 255,144 | x Rate applied | 60.0 % = F&A costs $ | 153,086 |
| c. 03 year | Amount of base $ | 261,295 | x Rate applied | 60.0 % = F&A costs $ | 156,776 |
| d. 04 year | Amount of base $ | 244,325 | x Rate applied | 60.0 % = F&A costs $ | 146,594 |
| e. 05 year | Amount of base $ | 230,647 | x Rate applied | 60.0 % = F&A costs $ | 138,388 |
| | | | | TOTAL F&A Costs $ | 740,203 |

*Check appropriate box(es):

| ☐ Salary and wages base | ☒ Modified total direct cost base {6} | ☐ Other base *(Explain)* |
|---|---|---|

☐ Off-site, other special rate, or more than one rate involved *(Explain)*

Explanation *(Attach separate sheet, if necessary.):*

▨

**Figure 7.10**    Sample Checklist

NOTES

{1} Our example is a new application; that is, it is not a resubmission (we'll talk about resubmissions in Chapter 8), nor is it a competing continuation or any of the other options.

{2} Program income is gross income earned by the applicant organization that is directly generated by a supported activity or earned as a result of the award. Examples include the following:

- Fees earned from services performed under the grant (e.g., resulting from laboratory drug testing)
- Rental or usage fees, such as those earned from fees charged for use of computer equipment purchased with grant funds
- Third-party patient reimbursement for hospital or other medical services, such as insurance payments for patients when such reimbursement occurs because of the grant-supported activity
- Funds generated by the sale of commodities, such as tissue cultures, cell lines, or research animals
- Patent or copyright royalties (exempt from reporting requirements)

{3} Look on your institution's "Information for Grants and Contracts" Web page, if it has one, for this information; if not, ask someone in your grants office.

{4} This is just a tad complicated. First, the *base* salary is not the same as the direct costs. The base is *the amount on which your institution charges indirect costs.* If you look at the Year 1 detailed budget page, you will see a box labeled "Subtotal Direct Costs for Initial Budget Period" ($281,814 in the sample budget page in Figure 7.5). You would subtract this amount from this any costs on which F&A may not be charged. These include equipment, patient care costs, alterations and renovations, and the subcontract amounts. This last is important: The NIH is paying F&A on the subcontract direct costs to the subcontracting institution; you would not expect them to pay twice by allowing your institution to charge F&A on the subcontract direct costs.

In the sample budget (Figure 7.5), we requested $8,500 in equipment in Year 1; thus, the first step in computing the base is to subtract the $8,500 from the $281,814, which leaves $273,314. Next, we subtract the consortium/contractual costs, which in this case is $56,048. But an additional step remains. Although NIH does not wish to pay indirect costs twice, your institution does want some money as a fee for administering the subcontract. Thus, the NIH will allow your institution to charge its indirect rate *on the first $25,000* of the subcontractor's direct costs; thus, in Year 1 (only), we add $25,000 to the amount we have calculated so far, so the total calculation of the base for the initial budget period year is:

$$\$281,814 - \$8,500 - \$56,048 + \$25,000 = \$242,266$$

Not every institution charges their F&A on the first $25,000 of the consortium direct costs, so check with your grants office.

In the remaining four years, as it happens, no funds for equipment, or any of the other categories on which F&A may not be charged, were requested. Thus, in those years, the base is the "Subtotal Direct Costs" minus the "Consortium/Contractual Costs" (see Figure 7.6).

What would happen if the subcontract direct costs are less than $25,000 in Year 1—say they are $15,000? You would add the $15,000 to the base in Year 1; then, in Year 2, you would add the remaining $10,000.

If you have more than one subcontract, does your institution charge $25,000 for each subcontract? You bet. If, for example, you had three different subcontracts, then during Year 1, you would add in $75,000 to the base.

{5} Here, you simply enter your institution's F&A rate (get it from your institution's Web page or ask someone in the grants office), then multiply the base by the rate to get the figure for the final column. Then sum the items in the final column: This is the amount you are asking the NIH to pay in addition to your direct costs to fund your grant.

{6} Ask someone in your grants office which box to check.

total number of modules for all years, and then divide by the number of years. So, in our example, most of the budget goes into the middle years, because that is when we would be having most of our patient visits. Let us say that we would like to request five modules in Year 1, eight in Year 2, ten in Years 3 and 4, and eight in Year 5, for a total of 41 modules. That number, divided by five, would come to nine modules in each year.

- When you use a modular format, you provide a less comprehensive budget justification than when you use the detailed budget format. Specifically, you provide justification for all personnel consultants and for consortia—that's it. Round the total costs (direct costs plus F&A) to the nearest $1,000. List the individuals and organizations with whom consortium arrangements have been made. List all personnel, including percentage of effort and roles on the project. No individual salary information should be provided. Indicate whether the collaborating institution is foreign or domestic. The reason for the more elaborate consortium section on the modular budget justification is that you do not provide a detailed budget or a checklist for the consortium in an application that uses the modular format.

Figure 7.11 shows the budget justification form page for a modular application. As with the other budget pages, indicate that the budget justification itself can be found on the continuation pages. I have included the continuation pages for the sample justification in the next section.

---

### Modular Budget Justification Continuation Pages, Example

*Budget Justification (Continued From Personnel, Modular Budget Format Page)*

**Reina Butler, BS (Research Coordinator: 40% effort)** will supervise the RA. Together, they will be responsible for conducting the screenings, and with the ABP technician, they will be responsible for consenting and enrolling participants and carrying out the study procedures. Ms. Butler will be supervised by Drs. Okata and Ruggiero. In Year 5, when the flow of research participants has slowed, Ms. Butler will supervise and work with the RA to (double) enter data.

**TBN, BA (Research Assistant: 100% effort)** will work with the research coordinator to conduct the patient visits. In Year 5, the RA will concentrate on data entry.

**Kenneth Lubin, PhD (Consultant)** is Asst. Professor of Medicine at the New Jersey Medical Center. He is an expert in the development of databases that involve multiple sources of input (in this case, hand-entered data, ABP data, ECG data, and baroreflex data; the latter are downloaded electronically). Dr. Lubin will provide 10 days in Year 1 to develop the database and 6 days in the remaining years to maintain it. {1}

*Continued From Consortium, Modular Budget Format Page*

Dr. Ruggiero will supervise the assessment of HRV and baroreflex sensitivity. Dr. Ruggiero has worked with Drs. Smith and Okata for the past six years and has set up their psychophysiology laboratory at NYMC. Dr. Ruggiero will train the research coordinator and the RA in instrumentation techniques for the collection of ECG (for HRV analysis) and for continuous, noninvasive BP (for the baroreflex sensitivity analyses). He will assist in the analysis of the data and in manuscript preparation.

**Nadia Nelin, MS (Research Assistant: 60% effort)** will be responsible for scoring the ECG data for the spectral analysis to assess HRV.

---

## Note: Modular Budget Justification Continuation Pages

{1} *Do* include consultants, if you have them, in the modular budget justification.

## Modular Budget Checklist (PHS 398 and SF 424)

Figure 7.12 shows the checklist for the modular budget example. As you can see, everything is identical to the checklist for the detailed budget, except for the amounts of the base and the F&A. The calculations, however, are identical. As before, Year 1 is the only year in which we have a cost on which indirects are not charged: equipment ($8,500). Note, however, that this time, this cost is *not* noted in the budget justification, per NIH instruction. Still, F&A is not charged on equipment, nor is it charged on the consortium direct costs, because NIH is paying F&A costs on those to the subcontracting institution. However, as with the detailed budget, your institution gets to charge the first $25,000 of the consortium direct costs as a fee. So, for Year 1, the base is figured thusly:

$$\$225,000 - \$8,500 - \$56,048 + \$25,000 = \$185,452$$

In the remaining years, it is simpler because no other equipment was budgeted and because you don't have the $25,000 to contend with. Thus, the base for the remaining years is calculated as the "DC Less Consortium F&A" (from Figure 7.11) minus the consortium direct costs for that year. The direct costs for the primary institution (NYMC) don't change from year to year—they are always $225,000—so the calculations are, for Years 2–5 respectively, $225,000 − $57,729 (Year 2), $59,460 (Year 3), $61,243 (Year 4), and $63,080 (Year 5). If you do the math, you'll find that those are the amounts that I plugged into the "Base" column on the previous page; then you multiply the base for each year by the home institution's indirect rate (60%), and you get the F&A for that year.

Next, what goes into boxes 7b and 8b on the Face Page? For the initial budget period, as with the detailed budget, you are going to add the "Total Direct Costs" from the modular budget page (Figure 7.11) for Year 1 ($251,902), plus the indirect cost from the checklist (Figure 7.12) for Year 1 ($111,271) and you get $363,173. Plug that number into box 7b on the Face Page. Next, add the "Total Direct Costs" from the modular budget page for all the years ($1,267,825) and the F&A for all the years ($621,317), and you get $1,899,142. Plug that number into box 8b of the Face Page.

## General Budget Notes (PHS 398 and SF 424)

• You do not include the subcontractor's checklist in your application (whether modular or nonmodular); however, your institution will probably want to see it.

• You do need to submit biosketches from the key personnel on your subcontract on your application (either modular or nonmodular).

• I haven't found specific guidelines saying that you may not submit the subcontractor's Resources page (discussed later in the chapter), so I suggest you submit it.

• As I have said before, your own institution may require documentation over and above that required by the NIH. You should check with your grants office. Columbia University, for example, requires the following:
  – Detailed budget pages and budget justification, even for modular grants.
  – A statement of the work to be provided by the subcontractor(s).
  – A copy of the indirect cost and fringe benefit rate agreement.
  – Other Support pages for all key personnel (including the subcontract key personnel). The NIH doesn't require this immediately (i.e., they use the just-in-time procedure), but your institution may want it up front.
  – Resources page from the subcontractor(s).
  – A checklist from the subcontractor(s).
  – Current institutional review board (IRB) certification and/or Institutional Animal Care and Use Committee (IACUC) approval from the subcontractor(s).

| Principal Investigator/Program Director (Last, First, Middle): | Okata, K. |
|---|---|

## BUDGET JUSTIFICATION PAGE MODULAR RESEARCH GRANT APPLICATION

|  | Initial Period | 2nd | 3rd | 4th | 5th | Sum Total (For Entire Project) |
|---|---|---|---|---|---|---|
| DC less Consortium F&A | {1} 225,000 | 225,000 | 225,000 | 225,000 | 225,000 | 1,125,000 |
|  | (Item 7a, Face Page) |  |  |  |  | (Item 8a, Face Page) |
| Consortium F&A | {2} 26,902 | 27,709 | 28,540 | 29,396 | 30,278 | 142,825 |
| Total Direct Costs | {3} 251,902 | 252,709 | 253,540 | 254,396 | 255,278 | $ 1,267,825 |

### Personnel

Kaoru Okata, M.D. (PI: 25% effort) is Assistant Professor of Medicine in the Department of General Medicine at New York Medical Center. Dr. Okata will be responsible for the design and conduct of the trial, and holds primary responsibility for manuscript preparation. {4}

Theresa Smith, M.D. (Co-Investigator: 10%) is Professor of Medicine at NYMC. Dr. Smith will be responsible for the collection of ambulatory blood pressure data, and will be available to consult on hypertension issues if they arise. She will also participate in manuscript preparation.

Quentin McBurney, Ph.D. (Co-Investigator: 20%) is a quantitative psychologist and biostatistician who has worked with this group for the past 12 years. Dr. McBurney will be responsible for maintaining the data base and for the data analyses.

TBN, M.A. (Ambulatory BP Technician: 10% effort in year 1; 20% effort in years 2-5) will be responsible for training the research coordinator and the research assistant in ambulatory BP monitoring techniques, and will be responsible for quality control of the BP measurements. The technician will devote 10% in year 1 because there will not yet be a large number of subject visits, but will be increased to 20% effort in years 2-5, when the subject visits will be greater in number.

Beth Serrana, R.N. (Nurse: 10% effort) will assist with chart reviews.

SEE FOLLOWING CONTINUATION PAGE

### Consortium

Approximately $88,000 Total Costs per year (48% F&A; $56,048 direct costs) {5}
Consortium with The Bronx Hospital {X} Domestic { } Foreign
Lawrence Ruggiero, Ph.D., will devote 15% effort.

SEE FOLLOWING CONTINUATION PAGE

### Fee (SBIR/STTR Only) {6}

**Figure 7.11**    Sample Modular Budget Justification Page

NOTES

{1} I am not going to show you an entire modular Face Page, because it would be identical to the one shown in Figure 7.1, except for the amounts shown in boxes 7a, 7b, 8a, and 8b. We have to get to the modular checklist before we can discuss boxes 7b and 8b, but you can easily see the amounts that go into boxes 7a ($225,000) and 8a ($1,125,000). I am, however, going to show you a check-list for the modular budget in Figure 7.12.

{2} Consortium F&A costs are figured the same way here as for a detailed budget; look at the checklist in Figure 7.12.

{3} The numbers in this row are simply the sums of the numbers in the two boxes above them.

{4} I tend to make the budget justification briefer and more focused for a modular budget.

{5} This section is *not* laid out this way on the form for you; you have to do that yourself (including the "{X}" part). Just copy the format as I have shown it, using your own information.

{6} We'll discuss the SBIR/STTR fee later in the chapter.

| Principal Investigator/Program Director (Last, First, Middle): | Okata, K. | | |
|---|---|---|---|

**TYPE OF APPLICATION** *(Check all that apply.)*

☒ NEW application. *(This application is being submitted to the PHS for the first time.)*

☐ REVISION of application number: ▓▓▓▓

*(This application replaces a prior unfunded version of a new, competing continuation, or supplemental application.)*

| ☐ COMPETING CONTINUATION of grant number: ▓▓▓▓ | INVENTIONS AND PATENTS *(Competing continuation appl. and Phase II only)* | |
|---|---|---|
| *(This application is to extend a funded grant beyond its current project period.)* | ☐ No | ☐ Previously reported |
| ☐ SUPPLEMENT to grant number: ▓▓▓▓ | ☐ Yes. If "Yes," | ☐ Not previously reported |

*(This application is for additional funds to supplement a currently funded grant.)*

☐ CHANGE of principal investigator/program director.

Name of former principal investigator/program director: ▓▓▓▓

☐ CHANGE of Grantee Institution. Name of former institution: ▓▓▓▓

| ☐ FOREIGN application | ☐ Domestic Grant with foreign involvement | List Country(ies) Involved: ▓▓▓▓ |
|---|---|---|
| ☐ SBIR Phase I | ☐ SBIR Phase II: SBIR Phase I Grant No. ▓▓▓▓ | ☐ SBIR Fast Track |
| ☐ STTR Phase I | ☐ STTR Phase II: STTR Phase I Grant No. ▓▓▓▓ | ☐ STTR Fast Track |

**1. PROGRAM INCOME** *(See instructions.)*

All applications must indicate whether program income is anticipated during the period(s) for which grant support is requested. If program income is anticipated, use the format below to reflect the amount and source(s).

| Budget Period | Anticipated Amount | Source(s) |
|---|---|---|
| ▓▓▓▓ | ▓▓▓▓ | ▓▓▓▓ |
| ▓▓▓▓ | ▓▓▓▓ | ▓▓▓▓ |
| ▓▓▓▓ | ▓▓▓▓ | ▓▓▓▓ |

**2. ASSURANCES/CERTIFICATIONS** *(See instructions.)*

In signing the application Face Page, the authorized organizational representative agrees to comply with the following policies, assurances and/or certifications when applicable. Descriptions of individual assurances/certifications are provided in Part III. If unable to certify compliance, where applicable, provide an explanation and place it after this page.
•Human Subjects Research •Research Using Human Embryonic Stem Cells •Research on Transplantation of Human Fetal Tissue •Women and Minority Inclusion Policy •Inclusion of Children Policy •Vertebrate Animals•

•Debarment and Suspension •Drug-Free Workplace *(applicable to new [Type 1] or revised [Type 1] applications only)* •Lobbying •Non-Delinquency on Federal Debt •Research Misconduct •Civil Rights (Form HHS 441 or HHS 690) •Handicapped Individuals (Form HHS 641 or HHS 690) •Sex Discrimination (Form HHS 639-A or HHS 690) •Age Discrimination (Form HHS 680 or HHS 690) •Recombinant DNA Research, Including Human Gene Transfer Research •Financial Conflict of Interest (except Phase I SBIR/STTR) •Smoke-Free Workplace •Prohibited Research •Select Agents and Toxins •STTR ONLY: Certification of Research Institution Participation

**3. FACILITIES AND ADMINSTRATIVE COSTS (F&A)/ INDIRECT COSTS.** See specific instructions.

| ☒ DHHS Agreement dated: | 5/1/2004 | ☐ No Facilities and Administrative Costs Requested. | |
|---|---|---|---|
| ☐ DHHS Agreement being negotiated with | ▓▓▓▓ | Regional Office. | |
| ☐ No DHHS Agreement, but rate established with | ▓▓▓▓ | Date | ▓▓▓▓ |

CALCULATION* *(The entire grant application, including the Checklist, will be reproduced and provided to peer reviewers as confidential information.)*

| a. Initial budget period: | Amount of base $ | 185,452 | x Rate applied | 60.0 | % = F&A costs $ | 111,271 |
|---|---|---|---|---|---|---|
| b. 02 year | Amount of base $ | 213,791 | x Rate applied | 60.0 | % = F&A costs $ | 128,274 |
| c. 03 year | Amount of base $ | 212,960 | x Rate applied | 60.0 | % = F&A costs $ | 127,776 |
| d. 04 year | Amount of base $ | 212,104 | x Rate applied | 60.0 | % = F&A costs $ | 127,262 |
| e. 05 year | Amount of base $ | 211,222 | x Rate applied | 60.0 | % = F&A costs $ | 126,733 |
| | | | | | TOTAL F&A Costs $ | 621,317 |

*Check appropriate box(es):

| ☐ Salary and wages base | Modified total direct cost base | ☐ Other base *(Explain)* |
|---|---|---|

☐ Off-site, other special rate, or more than one rate involved *(Explain)*

Explanation *(Attach separate sheet, if necessary.):*

▓▓▓▓

**Figure 7.12**    Sample Checklist for Modular Budget

# SBIR/STTR BUDGETS

There are only a few things that I need to mention about SBIR and STTR budgets. First, *modular budgets are not accepted for these applications, no matter what your direct costs are*. You must use the detailed budget pages for Phase I, Phase II, and fast-track applications.

The NIH SBIR Web page provides the complete set of instructions and forms for these applications.[2] I strongly suggest that you download and study them. The budgets are similar, but not identical, to the R01 budget I have been using as an example, and the exceptions are important.

## Budget Exceptions (PHS 398 and SF 424)

*Indirect Costs.* Indirect costs, also occasionally called *overhead,* are to be used for the costs of running the organization that plans to be responsible for conducting the research—in this case, the small business concern. In the SBIR and STTR, these funds go directly to that organization and, unlike the direct costs for a project, may be used for expenses that are not specific to the particular project. For example, the small business may use the funds to help pay the rent, to pay for bookkeeping or office services, or to pay for an administrative assistant. Also, in SBIR/STTR applications, the fringe benefits for personnel paid on the budget usually come from the indirect costs, as opposed to R01 applications, where fringe benefits are a direct cost.

Up until now, we have been assuming that you are submitting from an academic or medical institution, which will already have a negotiated F&A rate with the NIH. However, these are not the type of institutions that submit an SBIR or STTR application; it is the small business concern. If you, as a scientist, plan to collaborate with a small business on an SBIR or STTR application, you may write a subcontract from the small business to your home institution, and this will follow the rules laid out in the section on consortia and subcontracts. However, it is to the small business that the award will go, and *it is also to the small business that the indirect costs will go*; thus, the small business must have an F&A rate. If it already has one, great; if not, the NIH allows the small business concern to set its own rate, within limits, as follows:

- *Phase I Applications.* Small businesses may propose a rate *not to exceed* 40% of the total direct costs. In this event, on the checklist, first, do not mark an "X" in any of the boxes at the top of Section 3. Complete line 3a, *Initial Budget Period.* For a Phase I you will probably not have to complete 3b, because you probably won't be asking for more than one year of support; however, if this is a Phase II application, complete 3b and, if you are requesting more than two years of support, complete lines 3c and so on.

The instructions, which you should be reading, tell you that under "Explanation" (the bottom line of the checklist) insert the phrase: "Estimated F&A costs allocable (applicable) to this project are shown in line 3a (3b, etc.)."

- *Phase II Applications.* Everything in a Phase II application is identical to what I told you for Phase I applications, except for one crucial item: In the Phase II application, you may use an unnegotiated F&A rate up to 25% (not 40%). If you wish to charge a higher rate, you must negotiate that.

- *Negotiation of F&A Costs.* The Division of Financial Advisory Services (DFAS) in the Office of Acquisition Management and Policy at the NIH is the office authorized to negotiate F&A cost rates with small business concerns receiving NIH SBIR/STTR awards. Upon request of DFAS, the applicant small business concern should provide an F&A cost proposal and supporting financial data.

The F&A cost proposal, based on companywide cost data, should be accompanied by the following supporting information:

- Income statement and balance sheet for the applicant organization's most recently completed fiscal year. Certified statements prepared by a certified public accountant engaged to conduct an annual audit should be submitted, if available. The F&A cost proposal should include a reconciliation with the income statement; that is, there should be a cross-referencing from amounts on the income statement to amounts shown in the proposal, and a clear identification of individual elements (labor, materials, other expenses, etc.) of independent (self-sponsored) research and development (IR&D) expenses. Note that IR&D costs and the related F&A costs are not allowable under NIH awards.

- A listing of categories of costs normally classified and claimed as direct costs on federal awards and nonfederally supported projects or activities.

- An explanation of how the organization accounts for paid absences (vacation, holiday, and sick leave).

- Certification of final indirect costs. Go to the NIH Final Certification Web page for directions on how to apply for certification.[3] This certificate is to be completed by an official at a level no lower than a vice president or chief financial officer of the business segment submitting the proposal.

*The Fee.* In addition to the indirect costs, the NIH allows the small business concern to request a fee of up to 7% of the *total costs* (that is, direct costs plus indirect costs). Here is their explanation:

The fee is intended to be a reasonable profit factor available to for-profit organizations, consistent with normal profit margins provided to profit-making firms for research and development work. The fee is not a direct or indirect "cost" item and may be used by the small business concern for any purpose, including additional effort under the SBIR/STTR award. The fee applies solely to the small business concern receiving the award and not to any other participant in the project. However, the grantee may pay a profit/fee to a contractor providing routine goods or services in accordance with normal commercial practice.

You can see that there is a separate line for the fee on the detailed budget pages.

## THE BIOGRAPHICAL SKETCH PAGE (PHS 398 AND SF 424)

There is not too much to say about the Biographical Sketch form. You probably already have such a sketch. Make sure you include one for every person listed as key personnel, including consultants (if and only if they are listed as key personnel), and key personnel on any subcontracts you might have. Do not include conference abstracts in the bibliographies.

## THE RESOURCES PAGE (PHS 398 AND SF 424)

In the PHS 398 forms packet, you will find the Resources page. Give it a fair amount of attention, because reviewers will often look at this to ensure that you will be able to carry out the promised work, especially if they have doubts. Provide more detail about items that specifically pertain to the project you are proposing, not just the general items such as office space. If a category is irrelevant, just mark down *N/A* (not applicable).

Figure 7.13 shows an example of a Resources page based on the guided breathing proposal used throughout the book.

## OTHER SUPPORT (PHS 398 AND SF 424)

The Other Support form is one of the just-in-time forms that we discussed earlier. That means you do not include this form in your application; you wait until you are asked for it, which happens only if you receive a priority score that may be within the funding range from the reviewers (see Chapter 9). If you are asked to send in your Other Support form, make sure you indicate the state of your support *at the time you are asked to send in the form*, not at the time you applied, and remember to include pending support.

You may only put 100% of your effort toward extramural funded applications, no matter who the funding agency is. It is illegal to put more than 100% (although, as discussed in the budgets section, consulting fees are *not* included and are not mentioned in this document). Thus, the Other Support form shows who is paying for your effort, and from which funding source.

An Other Support page is provided in the PHS 398 forms packet; it is a little different from other forms in that you are given an example on the form page, which you presumably will erase (after printing it for your reference), so that you have a blank page. Take a look at it, and also look at the sample presented in Figure 7.14, which continues to make use of the example we have been using.

You must submit a separate Other Support page for each person listed in the personnel section of your detailed budget. If you are using a modular format, you still will be asked for Other Support pages for each person listed in the budget justification. *Do not* include these pages in your application, just as you do not include the detailed budget pages in a modular format application; the NIH may refuse to allow your application to be reviewed if you do.

If you do not have any other support from funding agencies, enter "none" in the appropriate space in the Other Support form.

If you are applying for more than one grant at the same time, point out on your Other Support pages and in your cover letter (see Chapter 8) that there's no overlap between them, and make sure the specific aims of each grant differ. You cannot send the same application to more than one PHS agency at the same time, with few exceptions: Contact your business office for details.

For each source of support, provide the following information:

- Project Number. If applicable, include a code or identifier for the project.
- Project Title.
- Source. Identify the agency, institute, foundation, or other organization that is providing the support.
- Major Goals. Provide a brief statement of the overall objectives of the project, subproject, or subcontract.
- Dates of Approved/Proposed Project. Indicate the inclusive dates of the project as approved/proposed. For example, in the case of NIH support, provide the dates of the approved/proposed competitive segment.
- Annual Direct Costs. In the case of an active project, provide the current year's direct cost budget. For a pending project, provide the proposed direct cost budget for the initial budget period.

| Principal Investigator/Program Director (Last, First, Middle): | Okata, K. |
|---|---|

## RESOURCES

FACILITIES: Specify the facilities to be used for the conduct of the proposed research. Indicate the performance sites and describe capacities, pertinent capabilities, relative proximity, and extent of availability to the project. Under "Other," identify support services such as machine shop, electronics shop, and specify the extent to which they will be available to the project. Use continuation pages if necessary.

Laboratory:

The Behavioral Cardiovascular Center at New York Medical Center, led by Dr. Theresa Smith, occupies 3,000 square feet of offices and laboratory/subject rooms, as well as a sound-proofed psychophysiological laboratory. Interview rooms are available for participant or patient screening, as are conference rooms.

Clinical:

The NYMC is a tertiary-care teaching facility that is fully accredited by the Joint Commission on the Accreditation of Healthcare Organizations. The NYMC draws its patients from the Greater New York Metropolitan area; it contains 1,942 beds with a medical staff of nearly 3,120 physicians. All told, there are 28,944 employees at NYMC. Dedicated exam rooms are available in the Behavioral Cardiovascular Center's space, as well as several research clinical rooms.

Animal:

N/A

Computer:

There are 11 desktop and 4 laptop computers in Dr. Smith's laboratory, as well as three small personal laser printers and one networked laser printer. All computers are equipped with ports to the University network, high speed internet connections, and access to an account on a SUN enterprise 450 with dedicated 1 gigabyte disk drive, Solaris 8 operating system, and licenses for Statsoft v.4.6.

Office:

Each faculty member has his/her own office; the Fellows share two offices, and research assistants are located in one of two large rooms, equipped with carrels; each has his/her own carrel with a desk, and a desktop computer that conncects to the NYMC network.

Other:

In the Behavioral Cardiovascular Center, there is a part-time computer/graphics consultant, two full-time data entry clerks, a full-time grants administrator, and an IRB compliance officer.

MAJOR EQUIPMENT: List the most important equipment items already available for this project, noting the location and pertinent capabilities of each.

We own 16 Acme Model 12345 ambulatory blood pressure monitors; 14 of these are presently being used in other studies, leaving two free (we have requested funding for two more). We own a Nemex 6-lead ECG, and Finapres Model 2300 continuous blood pressure monitor.

**Figure 7.13**    Sample Resources Page

## TARGETED/PLANNED ENROLLMENT TABLE PAGE (PHS 398 AND SF 424)

The NIH added the Targeted/Planned Enrollment Table page to the forms packet only a few years ago. The table is self-explanatory; if you are planning to study human subjects, you will have described in the Research Design and Methods section the racial/ethnic makeup of your sample. Use the estimates you outlined there to arrive at your figures for each category in the table. Figure 7.15 shows a sample Targeted/Planned Enrollment Table and the notes attached to it discuss the difference between ethnic and racial categories.

## LETTERS OF SUPPORT (PHS 398 AND SF 424)

By signing the Cover Page, you and the chief financial officer of your institution are making certain promises. If you have established a consortium with another institution, you and the chief financial officer of the subcontracting institution sign a letter of intent, again implying that you will do what you promise. But sometimes you bring in resources over which you may have little control, and the NIH would like some assurance that you can deliver. For example, we included in the sample budget the services of a consultant, Dr. Lubin, to do database work. The NIH would like to see a letter from Dr. Lubin, written on his institution's stationery, in which he describes what it is he is agreeing to do, for how many days in each year, and for what remuneration. Figure 7.16 shows a sample letter of this sort.

The authors of the sample proposal noted that the manufacturer of the guided breathing devices had agreed to modify a certain number of devices for use in the placebo condition and to sell them at the usual price of $200 per unit. Of course, the authors can—and do—say that in the proposal, but a letter from the manufacturer would provide evidence that this negotiation occurred and the arrangement was agreed to. Figure 7.17 provides this letter.

If you are planning to go into other sites to recruit subjects and gather data, but do not plan to establish a consortium with these sites, the reviewers would like to see a letter from the director of each of those sites agreeing to allow you to use the site and to participate in your study.

All these letters should go into one section of the proposal, following the recruitment goals page.

## PERSONAL INFORMATION ON THE PI (PHS 398 ONLY)

I do not reprint this page as it is self-explanatory. I only wanted to mention that this page does *not* go into the application; you print out one copy and insert it, separately, in the envelope with the applications and any appendices.

## VARIATIONS IN THE FORM PAGES (PHS 398 ONLY)

There are a few exceptions to the form pages for career development awards and for STTR awards. Career development awards call for a substitute Table of Contents page (see Figure 7.18) and some require different references, the guidelines for which are presented in Figure 7.19. Note that these two differences do not pertain to all K awards, just those for career development. The pages are completely self-explanatory, so the figures present the blank form pages.

*(Text continues on page 204)*

**For New and Competing Applications (PHS 398) – DO NOT SUBMIT UNLESS REQUESTED**

**For Non-competing Progress Reports (PHS 2590) – Submit only Active Support for Key Personnel**

**PHS 398/2590 OTHER SUPPORT**

---

Provide active support for all key personnel. **Other Support includes all financial resources, whether Federal, non-Federal, commercial or institutional, available in direct support of an individual's research endeavors, including but not limited to research grants, cooperative agreements, contracts, and/or institutional awards.** Training awards, prizes, or gifts do not need to be included.

There is no "form page" for other support. Information on other support should be provided in the *format* shown below, using continuation pages as necessary. *Include the principal investigator's name at the top and number consecutively with the rest of the application.* The sample below is intended to provide guidance regarding the type and extent of information requested.

For instructions and information pertaining to the use of and policy for other support, see Other Support in the PHS 398 Part III, Policies, Assurances, Definitions, and Other Information.

**Okata, K.**

ACTIVE

> 1 R01 HL 99999-05 (Okata; Site PI)          9/1/2000-8/31/2005                    25%
> NIH/NHLBI                                    $481,079
> RCT: Effect of Stress Management on Ambulatory BP

The major goal of this trial is to test the effectiveness of a behavioral stress management program on ambulatory blood pressure in hypertensive patients.

> 2 R01 CA 00000-02 (Smith)                    3/1/2004-2/28/2009                    10%
> NIH/NCI                                       $296,465
> Physician-Patient Communication as a Function of Race

The major goal of this study is to exam the effects of ethnicity and race on patients' understanding of physicians' instructions for medication regimens in breast cancer patients.

> A4528                                         6/15/2003-6/14/2004                    5%
> Menken Foundation (Smith)                     $50,000
> Depression Effects on Medication Adherence in Post-MI Patients: Pilot Study

The major goal of this study is to examine the effect of clinically-assessed depression on adherence to an 81 Mg daily aspirin regimen for 12 months following release from hospital.

PENDING

> LDB12345                                      10/1/2005-9/30/2006                    5%
> Lorentin Cardiovascular Health Foundation     $120,000
> Lipid Reduction in High-Risk Patients for CVD Using Motivational Interviewing

The major goal of this project is to conduct a pilot trial to test motivational interviewing techniques to reduce LDL levels in patients at high risk for CVD.

OVERLAP: None

---

**Figure 7.14**    Sample Other Support Page

NOTE

You can see that Dr. Okata is presently supported by grants for 40% of his effort; the rest of his support may come from clinical activities or teaching. Had Dr. Okata's effort totaled 100%, the pending grant would have put him over the 100% limit, and he would have had to explain how he would reconcile this. For example, he might have written, "If the Lorentin Cardiovascular Health Foundation application is funded, Dr. Okata will reduce his effort on CA 0000 by 5%."

Principal Investigator/Program Director (Last, First, Middle):        Okata, K.

## Targeted/Planned Enrollment Table {1}

**This report format should NOT be used for data collection from study participants**

**Study Title:** RCT: Effect of Guided Breathing Intervention on BP in Hypertensives

**Total Planned Enrollment:** 400 {2}

| TARGETED/PLANNED ENROLLMENT: Number of Subjects | | | |
|---|---|---|---|
| **Ethnic Category {3}** | **Sex/Gender** | | |
| | **Females** | **Males** | **Total** |
| Hispanic or Latino | 56 | 24 | 80 |
| Not Hispanic or Latino | 224 | 96 | 320 |
| **Ethnic Category: Total of All Subjects*** | **280** | **120** | **400** |
| **Racial Categories** | | | |
| American Indian/Alaska Native | 0 | 0 | 0 |
| Asian | 14 | 6 | 20 |
| Native Hawaiian or Other Pacific Islander | 0 | 0 | 0 |
| Black or African American {4} | 84 | 36 | 120 |
| White | 182 | 78 | 260 |
| **Racial Categories: Total of All Subjects*** | **280** | **120** | **400** |

*The "Ethnic Category: Total of All Subjects" must be equal to the "Racial Categories: Total of All Subjects."

**Figure 7.15**    Sample Targeted/Planned Enrollment Table

NOTES

{1} This page is not listed in the table of contents; I suggest you put it immediately after Section K (Significance; see Chapter 5), and immediately before the Letters section (discussed later in this chapter). (This note is relevant only for the PHS 398 forms.)

{2} Make sure the "Total Planned Enrollment" number agrees with the number you gave in the Research Design and Methods section of the proposal.

{3} The distinction between race and ethnicity might be a little confusing. As you can see, the NIH currently uses two dimensions to describe one's heritage: ethnic category ("Hispanic or Latino" or "not Hispanic or Latino"), and racial category, which comprises the five listed categories. Every subject is described in both dimensions; thus, the totals for both, as you can see, must be equal. It gets a little confusing in racial categories, in which either White or Black/African American could include the subjects listed as Hispanic or Latino in the ethnic category. If you don't collect very specific data, however, you won't know this; all you'll know is that a person is Hispanic, White, Latino, and so forth, in which case you'll have to guess. (Most lump persons who characterize themselves as Hispanic or Latino as White, although this is often not the case.) I suggest using the NIH breakdown as shown to collect data.

{4} Even the NIH breakdown may be insufficient, depending on the focus of your research. Hispanic or Latino, for example, comprises many cultures that differ along many dimensions; Black/African American also, by default, includes Caribbean Blacks, who can be very different from African Americans. If this is important to your research, develop your own, finer-grained categories.

# The New Jersey Medical Center

**89 Paramus Road ✹ Paramus, NJ ✹ Phone: (201) 555-6756 ✹ FAX: (201) 555-6758**

April 4, 2005

Kaoru Okata, MD
New York Medical Center
Dept. of General Medicine, Box 383
890 125th Street
New York, NY 10027

Dear Dr. Okata:

This letter confirms my willingness to serve as a database consultant on your proposed study, "RCT: Effect of Guided Breathing Intervention on Blood Pressure in Hypertensives." As I have worked with your team on several previous occasions and am already familiar with your methods of data collection, I believe I can develop a database that will allow you to easily enter and check data, and to retrieve it for analysis. As we discussed, I will be available for consultation for 10 days in Year 1, and for 6 days in Years 2 through 5, at $500/day in Year 1, with that fee increasing by 3% each succeeding year, in accordance with NIH policy.

I look forward to working with you and your team once again on this exciting project.

Sincerely,

*Kenneth Lubin*

Kenneth Lubin, Ph.D.
Asst. Professor of Psychiatry

**Figure 7.16**    Sample Letter From a Consultant

# Respirco, Inc.

108 Meridian Way
San Diego, CA 91234

March 31, 2005

Kaoru Okata, M.D.
New York Medical Center
Dept. of General Medicine, Box 383
890 125th Street
New York, NY 10027

Dear Dr. Okata:

I am writing in support of your application to the NIH entitled "RCT: Effect of Guided Breathing Intervention on Ambulatory BP in Hypertensives."

I am happy to confirm that Respirco, Inc., is willing and able to provide you with 80 modified Respirco devices for the placebo condition in this proposed trial, in addition to the 220 Respirco devices in the standard configuration that provide feedback on respiration rate and guide the breathing into the 6-10/minute range. We will also provide you with and support the software used to download the data from the devices to monitor participant adherence.

We look forward to working with your group in the instrumentation of this project and I wish you the best in this exciting study.

Best Regards,

*C. Michaels*

Cecelia Michaels
President and CEO

**Figure 7.17**    Sample Letter of Agreement From a Manufacturer

| CDA TOC Substitute Page | Candidate (Last, first, middle): | |
|---|---|---|

Use this substitute page for the Table of Contents of Research Career Development Awards. Type the name of the candidate at the top of each printed page and each continuation page.

**RESEARCH CAREER DEVELOPMENT AWARD TABLE OF CONTENTS (Substitute Page)**

| | Page Numbers |
|---|---|
| **Letters of Reference*** *(attach unopened references to the Face Page)* | |
| **Section I: Basic Administrative Data** | |
| Face Page (Form Page 1)............................................................. | 1 |
| Description, Performance Sites, Key Personnel, Other Significant Contributors, and Human Embryonic Stem Cells (Form Page 2)............................................................. | 2 |
| Table of Contents (this CDA Substitute Form Page 3)............................................................. | |
| Budget for Entire Proposed Period of Support (Form Page 5)............................................................. | |
| Biographical Sketches *(Candidate, Sponsor[s],* Key Personnel and Other Significant Contributors** | |
| *—Biographical Sketch Format page) (Not to exceed four pages)* ............................................................. | |
| Other Support Pages (not for the candidate) ............................................................. | |
| Resources (Resources Format page)............................................................. | |
| **Section II: Specialized Information** ............................................................. | |
| **Introduction to Revised Application*** (Not to exceed 3 pages) ............................................................. | |
| **1. The Candidate** | |
|    A. Candidate's Background............................................................. | |
|    B. Career Goals and Objectives: Scientific Biography ....................*(Items A-D included in 25 page limit)* ....... | |
|    C. Career Development/Training Activities During Award Period ..... | |
|    D. Training in the Responsible Conduct of Research ............................ | |
| **2. Statements by Sponsor, Co-Sponsor(s),* Consultant(s),* and Contributor(s)*** | |
| **3. Environment and Institutional Commitment to Candidate** | |
|    A. Description of Institutional Environment | |
|    B. Institutional Commitment to Candidate's Research Career Development ............................ | |
| **4. Research Plan** | |
|    A. Specific Aims ............................................................. | |
|    B. Background and Significance ..........................*(Items A-D included in 25 page limit)* ........ | |
|    C. Preliminary Studies/Progress Report ............................ | |
|    D. Research Design and Methods ............................ | |
|    E. Human Subjects Research ............................ | |
|    Targeted/Planned Enrollment Table (for new and continuing clinical research studies) ............................ | |
|    F. Vertebrate Animals ............................ | |
|    G. Literature Cited. ............................ | |
|    H. Consortium/Contractual Arrangements* ............................ | |
|    I. Resource Sharing ............................ | |
| **Checklist** ............................................................. | |
| **Appendix** (Five collated sets. No page numbering necessary.) [ ] Check if Appendix is included | |
| Number of publications and manuscripts accepted for publication *(not to exceed 5)* | |
| List of Key Items: | |
| *Note: Font and margin requirements must conform to limits provided in the Specific Instructions.* | |
| *Include these items only when applicable. | |
| **CITIZENSHIP** | |
| ☐ U.S. citizen or noncitizen national    ☐ Permanent resident of U.S. (If a permanent resident of the U.S., a notarized statement must be provided by the time of award.) | |

PHS 398 (Rev. 09/04)                                                                  **CDA TOC Substitute Page**

**Figure 7.18**    Career Development Award Table of Contents Page

**CAREER DEVELOPMENT AWARD REFERENCE REPORT GUIDELINES**
*(Series K)*

**Title of Award:**

**Type of Award:**

**Application Submission Deadline:**

**Name of Candidate (Last, first, middle):**

**Name of Respondent (Last, first, middle):**

The candidate is applying to the National Institutes of Health for a Career Development Award (CDA). The purpose of this award is to develop the research capabilities and career of the applicant. These awards provide up to five years of salary support and guarantee them the ability to devote at least 75–80 percent of their time to research for the duration of the award. Many of these awards also provide funds for research and career development costs. The award is available to persons who have demonstrated considerable potential to become independent researchers, but who need additional supervised research experience in a productive scientific setting.

We would appreciate receiving your evaluation of the above candidate with special reference to:

- potential for conducting research;
- evidence of originality;
- adequacy of scientific background;
- quality of research endeavors or publications to date, if any;
- commitment to health-oriented research; and
- need for further research experience and training.

Any related comments that you may wish to provide would be welcomed. These references will be used by PHS committees of consultants in assessing candidates.

Complete the report in English on 8-1/2 × 11" sheets of paper. Return your reference report to the candidate sealed in the envelope as soon as possible and in sufficient time so that the candidate can meet the application submission deadline. References must be submitted with the application.

We have asked the candidate to provide you with a self-addressed envelope with the following words in the front bottom corner: "DO NOT OPEN—PHS USE ONLY" Candidates are not to open the references. Under the Privacy Act of 1974, CDA candidates may request personal information contained in their records, including this reference. Thank you for your assistance.

PHS 398 (Rev. 09/04) **CDA Reference Guidelines Format Page**

**Figure 7.19** Career Development Award Reference Guidelines

The STTR uses a different initial year budget page for the participating research institution. It is almost identical to the usual initial year budget page, discussed earlier, so I will not extend the example; instead, I show you a blank form page in Figure 7.20.

## ELECTRONIC SUBMISSION AND THE NEW SF 424 FORM

As I mentioned earlier, new procedures are currently being put in place for all government grants, including those destined for the NIH. These procedures involve some new forms and electronic submission. (Only those of you who have photocopied until 3AM and then flown to Bethesda for a last-minute submission will appreciate how happy some of us are about this.) The procedures are so new that, as of October 2005, most grant mechanisms are not yet affected; the schedule of when they will come online can be found in the Introduction to this book, and the final instructions are not yet available. Thus, there may be changes that occur between the time of this writing and your use of this book.

> Whenever I refer to the "manual" regarding the SF 424 forms, I am referring to the Word document you can—and should—download from the NIH's Office of Extramural Research applications page, which you can find at http://grants1.nih .gov/grants/funding/424/index.htm.

At the time of this writing, there are only a few grant mechanisms that are using the new SF 424 forms. This does not include the R01, for example, for which the use of these forms does not commence until October 2006. However, these are the procedures you will follow as the mechanisms in which you are interested come online.

## FINDING RESEARCH OPPORTUNITIES AND DOWNLOADING APPLICATIONS PACKAGES

Finding research opportunities and downloading application packets from the NIH Web site are related because you must identify a specific grant application package, one tied to a particular offering or to an investigator-initiated call, before you can download the package. There is good reason for this: Different packages will require a different subset of the available forms. The package you download, tied as it is to a specific call, will have only the necessary pages. Here are the procedures I follow, and I know they work. The procedures are also given in many other places on the Web, including under the "Customer Support" tab of the Grants.gov home page.[4]

- Go to the Grants.gov home page and select "prepare to apply for grants through Grants.gov."
- Check "Grant Researcher" and select "Go." Then select "Download PureEdge Viewer," which is the software required to download the grants packages. Unfortunately for Mac users, the PureEdge software works only on Windows machines. If you use a Macintosh, you'll have to purchase Windows emulator software.

| STTR Research Institution Budget Additional Page | Principal Investigator/Program Director: (Last, First, Middle) | | | | | |

| BUDGET of RESEARCH INSTITUTION (STTR ONLY) | | | | FROM | THROUGH | |

| NAME AND ADDRESS OF RESEARCH INSTITUTION | | | | | | |

| PERSONNEL | | TYPE APPT. (months) | % EFFORT ON PROJ. | INST. BASE SALARY | DOLLAR AMOUNT REQUESTED (omit cents) | | |
|---|---|---|---|---|---|---|---|
| NAME | ROLE ON PROJECT | | | | SALARY REQUESTED | FRINGE BENEFITS | TOTAL |
| | Principal Investigator | | | | | | |
| | | | | | | | |
| | | | | | | | |
| | | | | | | | |
| | | | | | | | |
| | | | | | | | |
| SUBTOTALS → | | | | | | | |

| CONSULTANT COSTS | |
|---|---|
| EQUIPMENT (Itemize) | |
| SUPPLIES (Itemize by category) | |
| TRAVEL | |

| PATIENT CARE COSTS | INPATIENT | | |
|---|---|---|---|
| | OUTPATIENT | | |

| ALTERATIONS AND RENOVATIONS (Itemize by category) | |
|---|---|

| OTHER EXPENSES (Itemize by category) | |
|---|---|

| TOTAL DIRECT COSTS (also enter as Consortium/Contractual Costs on Budget Page of Small Business Concern) | $ |
|---|---|
| FACILITIES and ADMINISTRATIVE COSTS (show calculation) | $ |

(also enter as Consortium/Contractual Costs on Budget of Small Business Concern)

CERTIFICATION OF RESEARCH INSTITUTION PARTICIPATION. Through the signature below of the duly authorized representative of the research institution on this "Certification of Research Institution" page, and by way of the signature of the official signing for applicant organization (small business concern) on the Face Page of the application, the small business concern and the research institution certify jointly that: (1) the proposed STTR project will be conducted jointly by the small business concern and the research institution in which not less than 40 percent of the work will be performed by the small business concern and not less than 30 percent of the work will be performed by the research institution ("cooperative research and development"); (2) the proposed STTR project is a cooperative research or research and development effort to be conducted jointly by the small business concern and the research institution in which not less than 40 percent of the work will be performed by the small business concern and not less than 30 percent of the work will be performed by the research institution ("performance of research and analytical work"); and (3) regardless of the proportion of the proposed project to be performed by each party, the small business concern will be the primary party that will exercise management direction and control of the performance of the project. If the research institution is a contractor-operated federally funded research and development center, the duly authorized representative of the contractor-operated federally funded research and development center certifies, additionally, that it: (4) is free from organizational conflicts of interests relative to the STTR program; (5) did not use privileged information gained through work performed for an STTR agency or private access to STTR agency personnel in the development of this STTR grant application; and (6) used outside peer review, as appropriate, to evaluate the proposed project and its performance therein.

| Signature of Duly Authorized Representative | Printed Name | Title | Date of Signature |
|---|---|---|---|
| | | | |

**Figure 7.20**    STTR Research Institution Budget Page

- Select "Download and install both the PureEdge Viewer and PureEdge Viewer Upgrade." Then, under "Downloading and Installation," select the URL http://www.grants.gov/PE Viewer/ICSViewer602_grants.exe. Select "Run" and follow the instructions; an "Install Wizard" will come up on your screen. Follow the directions it provides.
- After you select "Finish" in the Wizard, you will see a "Viewer Help" screen. Minimize and/or print it out.
- Under "Downloading and Installation," select the URL http://www.grants.gov/PEViewer/ PureEdgeUpgradeSetup.exe. Then, select "Run." A second Wizard appears. Follow the directions and the necessary software should now be installed on your computer.
- Return to the main Grants.gov Web page and select "Search for Grant Opportunities." You must locate a specific call for proposals, even for investigator-initiated grants, as the application package that comes up will be tailored to the requirements of that particular call. Thus, some fields in the forms will already be populated. As some forms—or different versions of forms—will be irrelevant to some applications, only the appropriate collection of forms will appear in your package.

You are ready now to hunt for a funding opportunity announcement (FOA). You can do this by keyword or by using either a funding opportunity number (FON) or a Catalog of Federal Domestic Assistance (CFDA) number, if you know either one of these from having seen them on a call. You can also browse the funding opportunities: See the options to the left of the vertical line on the "Search for Grant Opportunities" page of Grants.gov.

I suggest, so that you can see how it works, that you select "Posted Grant Opportunities within last 7 days" and then find a Department of Health and Human Services (HHS) offering that interests you (other agencies' offerings are also displayed). Select one, even if you don't see one that interests you, so you can see what it looks like. Find the full FON, including the prefix (e.g., "PA") and the hyphens; then go back to the Grants.gov home page and select "Download an Application Package." Fill in the FON and, on the screen that comes up, select "Download Application Package."

Note that, as of this writing, there are still relatively few funding opportunities that use the new electronic submission procedures, so you may get a message saying, "The application for Funding Opportunity Number [X] has not been posted by the awarding agency for submission through Grants.gov. See the Full Funding Opportunity for application instructions." In that event, try another call until you find one. Assuming that the FON you selected does have an electronic application package, you will see a "Download" option under the blue bar ("Instructions and Application"). Select it; you may also want to download the application instructions. (Most of the available packages at this writing are for SBIR/STTR awards, and the instructions for these awards are different than those for all other awards, so you may not be interested, as part of this exercise, in reading these instructions if they are not awards that truly interest you.) In any event, select "Download Application Package," and in a few moments a new window will appear showing the page displayed in Figure 7.21.

As you can see from the information in Figure 7.21, I selected a program announcement for an SBIR award entitled "Pharmacologic Agents and Drugs for Mental Disorders." The offering agency is the NIH; the CFDA number, description, and FON are provided, as is other information about this particular offering.

Below the program announcement information, there is a space for you to enter the "Application Filing Name" (you can use any name you choose in this box; later in the application process, you will provide an official project title, limited to the usual 81 characters and spaces), and below that are the mandatory and then the optional application documents for you to select.

Contextual help is available on the Grants.gov "Grant Application Package" page. Simply pass your cursor over a field, and an explanation will pop up.

| Submit | Save | Print | Cancel | Check Package for Errors |
|--------|------|-------|--------|--------------------------|

| GRANTS.GOV | **Grant Application Package** |
|------------|------------------------------|

| Opportunity Title: | Pharmacologic Agents and Drugs for Mental Disorders (SBIR) |
|---|---|
| Offering Agency: | National Institutes of Health |
| CFDA Number: | 93.242 |
| CFDA Description: | Mental Health Research Grants |
| Opportunity Number: | PA-06-027 |
| Competition ID: | |
| Opportunity Open Date: | 11/07/2005 |
| Opportunity Close Date: | 04/02/2008 |
| Agency Contact: | GrantsInfo<br>Telephone: (301) 435-0714<br>Email: GrantsInfo@nih.gov |

This opportunity is only open to organizations, applicants who are submitting grant applications on behalf of a company, state, local or tribal government, academia, or other type of organization.

*Application Filing Name: [                                        ]

**Mandatory Documents**

| SF424 (R&R) |
| PHS 398 Research Plan |
| PHS 398 Cover Page Supplement |
| PHS 398 Checklist |
| SBIR/STTR_Information |
| Research & Related Other Project Information |
| Research & Related Documents |

[ Open Form ]

**Optional Documents**

| PHS 398 Cover Letter File |
| Research & Related Subaward Budget |

[ Open Form ]

Move Form to Submission List [ => ]

Move Form to Documents List [ <= ]

**Mandatory Completed Documents for Submission**

Mandatory Documents Mandatory Completed Documents for Submission

[ Open Form ]

Move Form to Submission List [ => ]

Move Form to Documents List [ <= ]

**Optional Completed Documents for Submission**

[ Open Form ]

**Instructions**

( 1 )  Enter a name for the application in the Application Filing Name field.

**Figure 7.21**    Sample Grant Application Package Window on Grants.gov

If you select the first mandatory document—SF424(R&R)—then click the grey "Open Form" button below, a new form will appear (shown in Figure 7.22). We'll go through this form in detail in a moment, but as you can see in Figure 7.22, some of the fields are already populated (e.g., in box 10, the CFDA number will appear).

If you need more help in getting started finding funding opportunities (and funding opportunity packages) and downloading the forms, I suggest you go back to the Grants.gov home page and select the "Customer Support" tab, at the top right of the page. This leads to a manual, a tutorial, and multimedia presentation, all of which contain details on these aspects of the process.

## THE SF 424 FORM

You now know how to get the forms into your computer, so it is time to look at them in detail. For this, I suggest you go to the NIH's Office of Extramural Research (OER) home page,[5] and then select "NIH Forms and Applications." Under "Forms/Applications/Instructions," select the first option—"SF 424 (R&R)." On the Web page that comes up, select the first option—"Grants.gov Application Guide SF424 (R&R)." You can see, by the way, that the *second* option ("Grants.gov SBIR/STTR Application Guide SF424 [R&R]") will bring up the instructions specifically developed for those interested in SBIR and STTR grants. However, I suggest you stick with the first set of instructions for the moment, as it is those that will pertain to the following discussion.

Print out the instructions and highlight the relevant sections. It is worth reading them all the way through; they contain an abundance of details you will need. I will point out the most relevant of these, but this is supplemental; treat the content in the manual as your primary reference.

In the following section, I provide facsimiles of the form pages (and these *are* facsimiles; you will find minor differences in the real forms), completed using the guided breathing example that has been running through this book.

Figures 7.22 through 7.26 continue the example I have been using thus far, as it would look when using the SF 424 (R&R) format.

## Attachments

*Project Summary/Abstract* (Item 6 in the Other Project Information form page). No form is provided for the project summary/abstract. Follow the instructions in the manual and note, noting that you are limited to 30 lines of text, and are to use the specified font, font size, and margins. The abstract should be a single block of text; guidelines for writing it are provided in Chapter 5.

*Project Narrative* (Item 7 in the Other Project Information form page). The Project narrative is not, as the name might imply, the 25 pages of science; it is a new component. The manual says, "For NIH and other PHS agencies applications, this attachment will reflect the second component of the Project Summary [that is, the statement of your project's relevance]. . . . Using no more than two or three sentences, describe the relevance of this research to *public* health. In this section, be succinct and use plain language that can be understood by a general, lay audience." No form is provided; just write it on your word processor, convert it to PDF, and upload it.

*Bibliography and References Cited* (Item 8 in the Other Project Information form page). Place your references in a separate file.

*Facilities & Other Resources* (Item 9 in the Other Project Information form page). From the manual:

> This information [about facilities and other resources] is used to assess the capability of the organizational resources available to perform the effort proposed. Identify the facilities to be used (Laboratory, Animal, Computer, Office, Clinical and Other). If appropriate, indicate their capacities, pertinent capabilities, relative proximity, and extent of availability to the project. Describe only those resources that are directly applicable to the proposed work. Provide any information describing the Other Resources available to the project (e.g., machine shop, electronic shop) and the extent to which they would be available to the project.

Though it is not specifically noted anywhere that I could find it, but I suspect that the intention of the NIH is that you use a facsimile of the current PHS 398 "Resources" page. However, this you should not include equipment in the facsimile, as a separate attachment (described below) is required. (next item).

*Equipment* (Item 10 in the Other Project Information form page). In the equipment attachment, list major items of equipment already available for this project and, if appropriate identify location and pertinent capabilities.

*(Text continues on page 220)*

| APPLICATION FOR FEDERAL ASSISTANCE<br><br>**SF 424 (R&R)**<br><br>1. *TYPE OF SUBMISSION | 2. DATE SUBMITTED<br>02/01/2002 | Applicant Identifier |
|---|---|---|
| | 3. DATE RECEIVED BY STATE<br>02/01/2002    {1} | State Application Identifier |

1. *TYPE OF SUBMISSION

☐ Pre-application  ☒ Application
        ☐ Changed/Corrected Application {2}

| 4. Federal Identifier    {3} |
|---|

**5. APPLICANT INFORMATION**                                 * Organizational DUNS:   123456789    {4}

*Legal Name:    New York Medical Center

Department:    Medicine Cardiology          Division:

* Street 1:    900 West 125th Street          Street 2:

* City:  New York     County:  Manhattan      * State:  NY     * ZIP Code:  10027

* Country:   USA

Person to be contacted on matters involving this application

Prefix:     * First Name:  {4}       Middle Name:            *Last Name:           Suffix:
Mr.         Allen                                            Birdwell

*Phone Number:  (212) 555-1236      Fax Number:  (212) 555-1237      Email:   abirdwell@nymc.edu

| 6. *EMPLOYER IDENTIFICATION *(EIN)* or *(TIN)*: {4}<br>13-1234567A8 | 7. *TYPE OF APPLICANT:<br>Please select one of the following |
|---|---|

**8. *TYPE OF APPLICATION:** ☒ New

☐ Resubmission  ☐ Renewal  ☐ Continuation  ☐ Revision

If Revision, mark appropriate box(es).

☐ A. Increase Award  ☐ B. Decrease Award  ☐ C. Increase Duration

☐ D. Decrease Duration  ☐ E. Other *(specify)*

*Is this application being submitted to other agencies?   Yes ☐   No ☐

What other Agencies?

Other (Specify):

**Small Business Organization Type**

☐ Women Owned      ☐ Socially and Economically Disadvantaged

**9. *NAME OF FEDERAL AGENCY:**

National Institutes of Health

**10. CATALOG OF FEDERAL DOMESTIC ASSISTANCE NUMBER:**
99-999

TITLE:

**11. *DESCRIPTIVE TITLE OF APPLICANT'S PROJECT: {5}**

Effect of Guided Breathing Intervention on Ambulatory BP in Hypertensives

**12. *AREAS AFFECTED BY PROJECT** (cities, counties, states, etc.)*

N/A

| 13. PROPOSED PROJECT:<br>*Start Date {6}      *Ending Date<br>12/01/2003          11/30/2008 | 14. CONGRESSIONAL DISTRICTS OF: {4}<br>a. *Applicant           b. *Project<br>14                    14 |
|---|---|

**15. PROJECT DIRECTOR/PRINCIPAL INVESTIGATOR CONTACT INFORMATION**

Prefix:     *First Name:        Middle Name:         *Last Name:          Suffix:
Dr.         Kaoru                                    Okata

*Position/Title:  Asst. Prof. of Medicine     *Organization:  New York Medical Center

Department:  Medicine Cardiology       Division:

*Street 1:   890 West 125th Street       Street2:

*City:  New York      County:  Manhattan       *State:  NY      *ZIP Code:  10027

*Country:   USA

*Phone Number:  (212) 555-1234     Fax Number:  (212) 555-1235     *Email:   kokata@nymc.edu

OMB Number: 4040-0001
Expiration Date: 04/30/2008

**Figure 7.22**    Sample SF 424 (R&R) Form: Page 1

NOTES

{1} In Figures 7.22–7.23, to differentiate between fields that you must fill in and fields that will already contain material (either entered previously or computed, as in the budget), text in the fields that you must fill in has been highlighted in grey.

{2} Unless specifically noted in a program announcement, NIH and other PHS agencies do not use pre-applications.

{3} This field is completed only if you are submitting a revision (now called "resubmission"), competing continuation (now called "renewal"), or progress report (now called "continuation").

{4} This information is available from your grants office or your institution's grants Web page.

{5} Note the limit of 81 characters, including spaces.

{6} Chapter 9 will give you an approximate schedule of when things will happen, including, if you are funded, when you will get your money. Note that the funding period should end one day earlier than it began (thus, if the award begins on June 1, it ends on May 31) in the appropriate year, depending on how many years' support you requested, and receive.

**SF 424 (R&R)** APPLICATION FOR FEDERAL ASSISTANCE

Page 2

---

**16. ESTIMATED PROJECT FUNDING {1}**

a. * Total Estimated Project Funding    2, 397, 765

b. * Total Federal & Non-Federal Funds    2, 397, 765

c. * Estimated Program Income    N/A

**17. * IS APPLICATION SUBJECT TO REVIEW BY STATE EXECUTIVE ORDER 12372 PROCESS?**

a. YES ☐ THIS PREAPPLICATION/APPLICATION WAS MADE AVAILABLE TO THE STATE EXECUTIVE ORDER 12372 PROCESS FOR REVIEW ON:

DATE:

b. NO ☒ PROGRAM IS NOT COVERED BY E.O. 12372; OR

{2} ☐ PROGRAM HAS NOT BEEN SELECTED BY STATE FOR REVIEW

---

**18. By signing this application, I certify (1) to the statements contained in the list of certifications\* and (2) that the statements herein are true, complete and accurate to the best of my knowledge. I also provide the required assurances \* and agree to comply with any resulting terms if I accept an award. I am aware that any false, fictitious, or fraudulent statements or claims may subject me to criminal, civil, or administrative penalties. (U.S. Code, Title 18, Section 1001)**

☒ * I agree

*\* The list of certifications and assurances, or an internet site where you may obtain this list, is contained in the announcement or agency specific instructions.*

---

**19. Authorized Representative    {3}**

Prefix:    * First Name:    Middle Name:    * Last Name:    Suffix:

Mrs.    Pamela    Meredith    Omale

* Position/Title: Assoc. Dean Spons. Pgms.    * Organization: New York Medical Center

Department: Medicine Cardiology    Division:

* Street 1: 890 West 125th Street    Street 2:

* City: New York    County: Manhattan    * State: NY    * ZIP Code: 10027

* Country: USA

* Phone Number: (212) 555-1238    Fax Number: (212) 555-1239    * Email: pomale@nymc.edu

**\* Signature of Authorized Representative**      **\* Date Signed**

Completed on submission to Grants.gov      Completed on submission to Grants.gov

---

**20. Pre-application** [      ]    [ Add Attachment ]    [ Delete Attachment ]    [ View Attachment ]

OMB Number: 4040-0001
Expiration Date: 04/30/2008

**Figure 7.23**    Sample SF 424 (R&R) Form: Page 2

NOTES

{1} Item 16 asks for the total (total direct costs + indirect costs) over the entire budget period. 16a and 16b will always be the same, unless the FOA specifically addresses this issue. "Program income," in 16c, is the gross income earned by the applicant organization that is directly generated by a supported activity or earned as a result of the award.

{2} Under 17b, check "no," as I have done in the example. This field exists because the SF 424 is a general grant application used by agencies other than the NIH.

{3} You can get the name of your institution's authorized representative from your institution's Web page or from someone in the grants office.

**RESEARCH & RELATED Project/Performance Site Location(s)**

**Project/Performance Site Primary Location**

Organization Name: | New York Medical Center

\* Street1: | 900 West 125th Street          Street 2: |

\* City: | New York          County: | Manhattan          \* State: | NY          \* ZIP Code: | 10027          \* Country: | USA

**Project/Performance Site Location 1**

Organization Name: |

\* Street1: |          Street 2: |

\*City: |          County: |          \*State: |          \*ZIP Code: |          \*Country: |

| Reset Entry |                                                    | Next Site |

Additional Location(s) |          | Add Attachment |          | Delete Attachment |          | View Attachment |

OMB Number: 4040-0001
Expiration Date: 04/30/2008

**Figure 7.24**     Sample SF 424 (R&R) Form: Project/Performance Site Locations

NOTE

This form is quite self-explanatory; the manual tells you exactly how to complete the fields. Note that in the example that I have used, the proposed work is intended to take place at the primary location only; thus, the fields for "Project/Performance Site Location 1" are left empty. I note, however, that I had to think twice about the nomenclature here. The "primary location" may also be "site location 1," in which case "Project/Performance Site Location 1" on the form page actually becomes "Site Location 2," and so on. It is a little confusing, but my reading of the instructions indicates that's how they want it done.

## RESEARCH & RELATED Other Project Information

1. * Are Human Subjects Involved? ☒ Yes  ☐ No

1.a.  If YES to Human Subjects

Is the IRB review Pending? ☐ Yes  ☒ No

IRB Approval Date:  N/A

Exemption Number: ☐ 1  ☐ 2  ☐ 3  ☐ 4  ☐ 5  ☐ 6

Human Subject Assurance Number:  FWA99991234   {1}

2. * Are Vertebrate Animals Used? ☐ Yes  ☒ No

2.a. If YES to Vertebrate Animals

Is the IACUC review Pending ☐ Yes  ☐ No

IACUC Approval Date:  N/A

Animal Welfare Assurance Number  A9999-01   {1, 2}

3. * Is proprietary/privileged information included in this application? ☐ Yes  ☒ No

4.a. * Does this project have an actual or potential impact on the environment? ☐ Yes  ☒ No   {3}

4.b. If yes, please explain:

4.c. If this project has an actual or potential impact on the environment, has an exemption been authorized or an environmental assessment (EA) or environmental impact statement (EIS) been performed? ☐ Yes   No ☒

4.d. If yes, please explain:

5.a. * Does this project involve activities outside the U.S. or partnership with international collaborators? ☐ Yes  ☒ No

5.b. If yes, identify countries:

6. * Project Summary/Abstract   {4, 5}   | Add Attachment | Delete Attachments | View Attachments

7. * Project Narrative   | Add Attachment | Delete Attachments | View Attachments

8. Bibliography and References Cited   | Add Attachment | Delete Attachments | View Attachments

9. Facilities and Other Resources   | Add Attachment | Delete Attachments | View Attachments

10. Equipment   | Add Attachment | Delete Attachments | View Attachments

11. Other Attachments   | Add Attachment | Delete Attachments | View Attachments

OMB Number 4040-0001

**Figure 7.25**    Sample SF 424 (R&R) Form: Other Project Information

NOTES

{1} You can get the Human Subject Assurance Number from your institution's Web page or from someone in the grants office.

{2} Include the Animal Welfare Assurance Number even if you are not studying animals—and include the Human Subjects Assurance Number even if you are not studying humans.

{3} Check "no" unless a specific FOA indicates that the National Environmental Policy Act (NEPA) applies.

{4} Many of the documents you will use are not included in the SF 424; you must complete them separately, convert them to PDF format, and attach them at the appropriate juncture. I'll tell you where to get these, and provide details later in the chapter.

{5} I have described what should go into the abstract in Chapter 5. Also, the manual provides a good summary of what should be included in a good abstract.

## RESEARCH & RELATED Senior/Key Person Profile {1}

---

PROFILE - Project Director/Principal Investigator

| Prefix | * First Name | Middle Name | *Last Name | Suffix |
|---|---|---|---|---|
| Dr. | Kaoru | | Okata | MD |

Position/Title: Asst. Prof. of Medicine        Department: Medicine

Organization Name: New York Medical Center        Division: Cardiology

* Street 1: 890 125th Street        Street 2:

* City: New York        County: Manhattan        *State: NY        *Zip Code 10027        Country USA

* Phone Number: 212-555-1234        Fax Number: 212-555-1235        * E-Mail: kokata@nymc.edu

Credential, e.g., agency login        kokata {2}

* Project Role: PD/PI        Other Project Role Category:

*Attach Biographical Sketch {3}        [ ]    Add Attachment | Delete Attachments | View Attachments

Attach Current & Pending Support        [ ]    Add Attachment | Delete Attachments | View Attachments

---

PROFILE – Senior/Key Person 1

| Prefix | * First Name | Middle Name | *Last Name | Suffix |
|---|---|---|---|---|
| Dr. | Quentin | James | McBurney | |

Position/Title: Assoc. Prof. of Medicine        Department: Medicine

Organization Name: NY Medical Center        Division: Cardiology

* Street 1: 890 125th Street        Street 2:

* City: New York        County: Manhattan        *State: NY        *Zip Code 10027        Country USA

* Phone Number: 212-555-1234        Fax Number: 212-555-1235        * E-Mail: qmcburney@nymc.edu

Credential, e.g., agency login        qmcburn

* Project Role: Co-Investigator        Other Project Role Category:

*Attach Biographical Sketch {3}        [ ]    Add Attachment | Delete Attachments | View Attachments

Attach Current & Pending Support        [ ]    Add Attachment | Delete Attachments | View Attachments

Reset Entry                                                                    Next Person

ADDITIONAL SENIOR/KEY PERSON PROFILE(S)

Additional Biographical Sketch(es)        [ ]    Add Attachment | Delete Attachments | View Attachments
(Senior/Key Person)

Additional Biographical Sketch(es)        [ ]    Add Attachment | Delete Attachments | View Attachments
(Senior/Key Person)

---

**Figure 7.26**    Sample SF 424 (R&R) Form: Senior/Key Person Profile

NOTES

{1} How do you know who to list as "key personnel"? In addition to the PI, key personnel are defined as individuals who contribute to the scientific development or execution of the project in a substantive, measurable way, whether or not salaries are requested. Typically, these individuals have doctoral or other professional degrees, although individuals at the master's or baccalaureate level, as well as consultants, should be included if their involvement meets the definition. Key personnel must devote measurable effort to the project whether or not salaries are requested—"zero percent" effort or "as needed" are not acceptable levels of effort for those designated as key personnel.

Until recently, the NIH allowed only one PI on a grant; it is now beginning to look as though a co-PI title will be allowed. When there is a consortium established through a subcontract, there also must be a PI at the subcontracted site.

{2} This form is pretty straightforward. Note that the fields are already populated with information about the PI, with the exception of the line regarding the credential, which you fill in; you also must fill in all the information for additional profiles. If you do not already have an agency login number, log on to the eRA Commons page (https://commons.era.nih.gov/commons/), open an account, and note your user name (see Chapter 6 for a detailed discussion).

{3} You will upload the biographical sketch form here. The biographical sketch form is virtually identical to the PHS 398 form—and in fact, is still called a PHS 398 form. You will also upload the Other Support form, but this is almost always a just-in-time requirement (see Chapter 6 for a discussion of "just-in-time" procedures). Both forms are discussed in this chapter.

## THE BUDGET COMPONENTS OF THE SF 424 (R&R) FORM

Before looking at the budget forms, please first read the earlier discussions concerning budgets in this chapter, including the section on detailed budgets and modular budgets, as well as explanations of direct and indirect costs.

In the SF 424 forms, you are offered two options: (1) an R&R Budget Component or (2) a PHS 398 Modular Budget Component. Your application will contain one of these (they are listed as "optional," but they are optional only in the sense that you get to choose one or the other). In general, you will use the R&R Budget Component when your yearly budget exceeds $250,000 in any year or when directed to by the FOA; use a Modular Budget when the budget is $250,000 or less in all years. (Note: SBIR/STTR mechanisms do not use the modular format, no matter how small the yearly budget.) Figures 7.27–7.30 show sample R&R Budget forms.

> For those of you who are used to the PHS 398 forms, the procedure has always been to provide a detailed budget only for Year 1, and then a summary budget for the remaining periods. However, the new SF 424 forms differ in that you must submit a detailed form (as in Figure 7.27) for every budget period for which you request funds.

### SF 424 (R&R) Budget Justification

As noted in the Budget Justification section earlier in the chapter, the budget justification provides explicit rationale for the role and percentage effort of all study personnel and for all study expenses listed in the budget. It must be consistent with the specific aims you have listed in and with your Research Design and Methods section.

The SF 424 (R&R) package does not contain a form for the budget justification. You are expected to follow the format I used in the example shown in the Budget Justification section of this chapter. The manual says the following:

> Use the budget justification to provide the additional information requested in each budget category identified above and any other information you wish to submit to support your budget request. Note this is a single justification for all budget years so include all justification information for all years in the same file.

Remember to convert your budget justification to a PDF document before attaching it to Section K of the "Research & Related Budget, Sections F Through K" form page (see Figure 7.29).

## SF 424 (R&R) Subaward (Previously Called the Subcontract)

Sometimes, you may want to avail yourself of resources from an institution other than the one from which you plan to submit the application. We discussed this in some detail in the earlier section on Consortia and Subcontracts, and I encourage you to refer to that section.

A form is provided in the SF 424 (R&R) package that allows you to attach your budget justifications for both the main award and the subaward. Figures 7.31 and 7.32 show the budget pages for an SF 424 (R&R) subward.

*(Text continues on page 234)*

**RESEARCH & RELATED BUDGET – SECTIONS A & B, BUDGET PERIOD 1 {1}**

*ORGANIZATIONAL DUNS: | 123456789    {2}

*BUDGET TYPE: ☒ Project      ☐ Subaward/Consortium     {3}

Enter name of Organization: | New York Medical Center

[Reset Entries]      * Start Date: | 12/01/2003      * End Date: | 11/30/2004      Budget Period: 1

| | Prefix | *First Name | Middle Name | *Last Name | *Project Suffix | Role | {5} Base Salary | {4} Cal. Mos | Acad. Mos | Sum. Mos | {5} *Requested Salary | {6} *Fringe Benefits | *Funds Requested |
|---|---|---|---|---|---|---|---|---|---|---|---|---|---|
| 1. | Dr. | Kaoru | | Okata | MD | D/PI | 80,000 | 12 | | | 20,000 | 5,000 | 25,000 |
| 2. | Dr. | Quentin | James | McBurney | PhD | Co-Inv | 164,000 | 12 | | | 32,800 | 8,200 | 41,000 |
| 3. | Dr. | Theresa | Pincus | Smith | MD | Co-Inv | 180,100 {7} | 12 | | | 18,010 | 4,502 | 22,512 |
| 4. | | | | | | | | | | | | | |

5. Total Funds requested for all Senior Key Persons in the attached file | 88,512

Total Senior/Key Persons | 3

Additional Senior Key Persons: | | [Add Attachment]   [Delete Attachments]   [View Attachments]

B. Other Personnel

| *Number of Personnel | *Project Role | Cal. Mos | Acad. Mos | Sum. Mos | *Requested Salary | *Fringe Benefits | *Funds Requested |
|---|---|---|---|---|---|---|---|
| 0 | Post Doctoral Associates | | | | | | |
| 0 | Graduate Students | | | | | | |
| 0 | Undergraduate Students | | | | | | |
| 0 | Secretarial/Clerical | | | | | | |
| 1 | Ambulatory BP Technician | 12 | | | 4,800 | 1,200 | 6,000 |
| 1 | Research Nurse | 12 | | | 9,000 | 2,250 | 11,250 |
| 1 | Research Coordinator | 12 | | | 19,200 | 4,800 | 24,000 |
| 1 | Research Assistant | 12 | | | 40,000 | 10,000 | 50,000 |

Total Other Personnel | 4

Total Salary, Wages and Fringe Benefits (A&B) | 179,762

**Figure 7.27**    Sample SF 424 (R&R) Form: Research & Related Budget, Sections A and B

NOTES

{1} You must complete this form for each budget period for which you request funds; I have not shown the detailed budget forms for Years 2–5 to save space.

{2} You can get your organization's DUNS number from your institution's Web page or from someone in the grants office.

{3} You would check "Project" here, as this is the budget for the main award, not for the budget for a subcontract—or "subaward." Your institution, which is presumably submitting the grant, is the main contractor. In the event that you establish a consortium with another institution, your two institutions will arrange to have a contract (the subcontract) to establish the scope of work, the financial arrangements, and so forth. (All this is discussed in the section on subcontracts in this chapter.) Using the new forms, you must obtain the subcontractor's information, and then enter it into this form, this time checking "Subaward/Consortium."

{4} The instructions explain the three "months" options listed here. Note that *if effort does not change throughout the year,* use the "calendar months" column. *If effort varies between academic and summer months,* leave the "calendar months" column blank and use only the "academic months" and "summer months" columns.

{5} You arrive at the requested salary by deciding upon the percentage effort each person listed will provide. Do this by asking how much time in a week (on average) this person will need to devote to this project. One day is equal to 20%. Thus, the ambulatory blood pressure technician's requested dollars equals 10% effort, a percentage based on the timeline (Chapter 5), which calls for 33 subjects to be recruited per quarter (or 11 per month); no more than 1/2 day per week (10% effort) should be necessary to accomplish this.

{6} Get the fringe figures/rates from your department's administrator. Make sure they're correct, or you risk a delay in obtaining necessary signatures. The fringe pays for medical and retirement benefits, and is charged over and above the base salary. Find out your institution's rate for the current budget period (I've used 25% here).

{7} The NIH places a cap on the amount of base salary you can request; the cap is currently $180,100, but it changes, so check.

# "Research & Related Budget, Sections C, D, and E" Example

RESEARCH & RELATED BUDGET – SECTIONS C, D, E, BUDGET PERIOD 1

*Organizational DUNS: | 123456789 |

*Budget Type      ☒ Project      ☐ Subaward/Consortium

Enter name of Organization: | New York Medical Center |

| Reset Entries |      * Start Date: | 12/01/2003 |    * End Date: | 11/30/2004 |     Budget Period:  1

C. Equipment Description {1}

Equipment Item *Funds Requested

| | | |
|---|---|---|
| 1. | Medico Model A243 $CO_2$ monitor @$8,500 | 8,500 |
| 2. | | |
| 3. | | |
| 4. | | |
| 5. | Total funds requested for all equipment listed in the attached file | 0 |
| | Total equipment | 8,500 |

Additional Equipment: [          ]    | Add Attachment |    | Delete Attachments |    | View Attachments |

D. Travel                                                                            *Funds Requested

| | |
|---|---|
| 1. Domestic Travel Costs {2} | 1,200 |
| 2. Foreign Travel Costs | 0 |
| Total Travel Cost | 1,200 |

E. Participant/Trainee Support Costs {3}                                              *Funds Requested

| | |
|---|---|
| 1. Tuition/Fees/Health Insurance | 0 |
| 2. Stipends | 0 |
| 3. Travel | 0 |
| 4. Subsistence | 0 |
| 5. Other | 0 |
| [0]  Number of Participants/Trainees Total Participant/Trainee Support Costs | 0 |

---

**Figure 7.28**    Sample SF 424 (R&R) Form: Research & Related Budget, Sections C, D, and E

NOTES

{1} The NIH notes that equipment is an item that costs at least $5,000. Your institution may set a different limit, however. The definition of equipment is important because indirect costs, or F&A, do not cover equipment, though they do get paid on personnel, supplies, consultant costs, travel, and other expenses.

{2} The authors have included local travel between the two sites in this calculation. They also ask for funds for travel to national conferences, but not until Year 2. As I have stated before, you should have something to present if you're going to ask for reimbursement for travel to a conference, and in Year 1, you won't have anything yet.

{3} The example I have been using does not budget funds for trainees; however, you should definitely consider doing this. The NIH likes to see it, and it will benefit you in unforeseen ways.

## RESEARCH & RELATED BUDGET – SECTIONS F-K, BUDGET PERIOD 1    | Next Period |

*Organizational DUNS:  | 123456789 |

*Budget Type    ☒ Project    ☐ Subaward/Consortium

Enter name of Organization:  | New York Medical Center |

| Reset Entries |    * Start Date: | 12/01/2003 |    * End Date: | 11/30/2004 |    Budget Period:   1

F.  Other Direct Costs                                                      *Funds Requested

| 1.  Materials and Supplies {1} | 18,594 |
| 2.  Publication Costs {2} | 0 |
| 3.  Consultant Services {3} | 5,000 |
| 4.  ADP/Computer Services | 0 |
| 5.  Subawards/Consortium/Contractual Costs {4} | 56,048 |
| 6.  Equipment or Facility Rental/User Fees {5} | 0 |
| 7.  Alterations and Renovations {6} | 0 |
| 8.  Subject payments    {7} | 7,710 |
| 9.  Reimbursement for DSMB members    {8} | 4,000 |
| 10.  Communications (conference call services)    {9} | 1,000 |

Total Other Direct Costs:  | 92,352 |

G.    Direct Costs                                                        Funds Requested

Total Direct Costs (A Thru F):  | 281,814 |

H.    Indirect Costs {10}                        {11}

| Indirect Cost Type Rate | (%) | Base ($) | *Funds Requested |
|---|---|---|---|
| 1. Modified Total Direct Costs | 60 | 242,266 | 145,359 |
| 2. | | | |
| 3. | | | |
| 4. | | | |

Total Indirect Costs:  | 145,359 {12} |

{13} Cognizant Federal Agency   | HHS; Ms. Janet Levine; (201) 555-1234 |

(Agency Name, POC Name and POC Phone Number)

I. Total Direct and Indirect Costs                              Funds Requested

Total Direct and Indirect Institutional Costs (G + H):  | 427,173 {14} |

J. Fee {15}                                                  Funds Requested

| 0 |

{16} K. Budget Justification  | | | Add Attachment |  | Delete Attachments |  | View Attachments |

(Only attach one file)

**Figure 7.29**    Sample SF 424 (R&R) Form: Research & Related Budget, Sections F Through K

NOTES

{1} You can justify a computer if it is to be used on the project (but note that it is listed under supplies, not in equipment). Don't forget to include computers, but don't overdo it.

{2} No publication costs were budgeted in this application, but they should have been. The manual explains what sorts of expenses you can charge.

{3} Here, under "Consultant Services," we touch upon a very important and somewhat subtle point. Why is Dr. Lubin a consultant, paid by the day or hour, and not listed as a co-investigator on another subcontract? Please refer to the discussion in the sample Budget Justification earlier in this chapter.

{4} See the consortium budget page in Figure 7.8 and the section on consortia and subcontracts to see where these figures come from. Remember that F&A is not charged on these costs.

{5} Think about things such as photocopier rental. Don't forget such expenses, but only charge what is directly involved in running the proposed study.

{6} See the manual for patient care costs and alterations and renovations. Note that F&A is not charged on these costs.

{7} Note that the authors have worked out how many subjects will be screened and seen in Year 1, using the timeline given in the Research Design and Methods section of the proposal.

{8} If and only if you are conducting a trial, you will need to establish a Data and Safety Monitoring Plan (see Chapter 6).

{9} Don't forget to include expenses such as warrantees, communications costs (e.g., phone bills), postage, and photocopy charges.

{10} Read the discussion earlier in the chapter of indirect costs (also called "F&A" or "overhead"). Ask someone in your grants office which indirect cost type you should use.

{11} See note 4 in Figure 7.10 for a discussion of base salary and an explanation of why it is not the same as the direct costs.

{12} Your institution may have more than one F&A rate, even within the same grant. For example, if you include a training component in your application, the NIH pays a maximum of 8% in indirect costs on those funds, although it will pay your institution's higher rate for nontraining expenses. If you did have costs that were paid with different F&A rates, you would list the costs for each different rate on a different line, and you would sum the "Funds Requested" to arrive at the "Total Indirect Costs." If you are using only one F&A rate, as will often be the case, then the "Funds Requested," shown in line 1, will be the same as those listed in the "Total Indirect Funds" box, as they are here. Note also that this total *does not* include the F&A paid on the subcontract.

{13} For NIH applications, the cognizant federal agency will always be the Department of Health and Human Services (HHS).

{14} Note that the total direct costs, *not the modified base,* is being summed with the indirect costs.

{15} The "fee" does not apply unless you are submitting a SBIR or STTR application.

{16} The budget justification for the SF 424 will be discussed later in the chapter.

## RESEARCH & RELATED BUDGET – Cumulative Budget

|  | | Totals ($) |
|---|---|---|
| **Section A, Senior/Key Person** | | 469,920 |
| **Section B, Other Personnel** | | 505,138 |
| Total Number Other Personnel | 4 | |
| **Total Salary, Wages and Fringe Benefits (A+B)** | | 975,058 |
| **Section C, Equipment** | | 8,500 |
| **Section D, Travel** | | 19,500 |
|   1.  Domestic | 19,500 | |
|   2.  Foreign | 0 | |
| **Section E, Participant/Trainee Support Costs** | | 0 |
|   1.  Tuition/Fees/Health Insurance | 0 | |
|   2.  Stipends | 0 | |
|   3.  Travel | 0 | |
|   4.  Subsistence | 0 | |
|   5.  Other | 0 | |
|   6.  Number of Participants/Trainees | 0 | |
| **Section F, Other Direct Costs** | | 0 |
|   1.  Materials and Supplies | 75,098 | |
|   2.  Publication Costs | 0 | |
|   3.  Consultant Services | 17,924 | |
|   4.  ADP/Computer Services | 0 | |
|   5.  Subawards/Consortium/Contractual Costs | 142,826 | |
|   6.  Equipment or Facility Rental/User Fees | 0 | |
|   7.  Alterations and Renovations | 0 | |
|   8.  Other 1 | 121,097 | |
|   9.  Other 2 | 0 | |
|   10.  Other 3 | 0 | |
| **Section G, Direct Costs (A thru F)** | | 1,514,737 |
| **Section H, Indirect Costs** | | 740,203 |
| **Section I, Total Direct and Indirect Costs (G + H)** | | 2,254,940 |
| **Section J, Fee** | | 0 |

**Figure 7.30**    Sample SF 424 (R&R) Form: Research & Related, Cumulative Budget

NOTE

All fields on this form are completed automatically.

## RESEARCH & RELATED BUDGET – SECTIONS A & B, BUDGET PERIOD 1

*ORGANIZATIONAL DUNS: 321543876

*BUDGET TYPE:  ☐ Project  ☒ Subaward/Consortium    {2}

Enter name of Organization:   Bronx Hospital

[Reset Entries]   * Start Date: 12/01/2003    * End Date: 11/30/2004    Budget Period: 1

A. Senior/Key Personnel

| | Prefix | *First Name | Middle Name | *Last Name | Suffix | *Project Role | Base Salary | Cal. Mos | Acad. Mos | Sum. Mos | *Requested Salary | *Fringe Benefits | *Funds Requested |
|---|---|---|---|---|---|---|---|---|---|---|---|---|---|
| 1. | Dr. | Lawrence | | Ruggiero | Ph.D. | PD/PI | 136,500 | 12 | | | 20,475 | 4,545 | 25,020 |
| 2. | | | | | | | | | | | | | |
| 3. | | | | | | | | | | | | | |
| 4. | | | | | | | | | | | | | |

5. Total Funds requested for all Senior Key Persons in the attached file          25,020

Total Senior/Key Persons  1

Additional Senior Key Persons: _____    [Add Attachment]   [Delete Attachments]   [View Attachments]

B. Other Personnel
*Number of Personnel *Project Role

| | | Cal. Mos | Acad. Mos | Sum. Mos | *Requested Salary | *Fringe Benefits | *Funds Requested |
|---|---|---|---|---|---|---|---|
| 0 | Post Doctoral Associates | | | | | | |
| 0 | Graduate Students | | | | | | |
| 0 | Undergraduate Students | | | | | | |
| 0 | Secretarial/Clerical | | | | | | |
| 1 | Research Assistant | 12 | | | 24,900 | 5,528 | 30,428 |
| | | | | | | | |
| | | | | | | | |
| | | | | | | | |

1                                    Total Other Personnel    30,428

Total Salary, Wages, and Fringe Benefits (A + B)    55,448

---

**Figure 7.31**     Sample SF 424 (R&R) Form: Research & Related Budget Sections A and B for Subaward {1}

NOTES

{1} As you can see on this page and in Figure 7.32, the subcontract budget requests funds for personnel (this page) and for office supplies (Figure 7.32). Because no items on any of the other budget forms are used or affected, I haven't shown them.

{2} On the budget sheet for a subaward, check "Subaward/Consortium," not "Project."

## RESEARCH & RELATED BUDGET – SECTIONS F-K, BUDGET PERIOD 1   | Next Period |

*Organizational DUNS:   | 321543876 |

*Budget Type        ☐ Project   ☒ Subaward/Consortium

Enter name of Organization:   | Bronx Hospital |

| Reset Entries |   * Start Date: | 12/01/2003 |   * End Date: | 11/30/2004 |   Budget Period:   1

F.   Other Direct Costs {1}                                                    *Funds Requested

1.   Materials and Supplies                                                    | 600 |

2.   Publication Costs                                                         | 0 |

3.   Consultant Services                                                       | 0 |

4.   ADP/Computer Services                                                     | 0 |

5.   Subawards/Consortium/Contractual Costs                                    | 0 |

6.   Equipment or Facility Rental/User Fees                                    | 0 |

7.   Alterations and Renovations                                              | 0 |

|                                                    |   |   |
|                                                    |   |   |
|                                                    |   |   |

                                        Total Other Direct Costs: | 600 |

G.  Direct Costs                                                    Funds Requested

                                    Total Direct Costs (A Thru F): | 56,048 |

H.  Indirect Costs                           {2}

| Indirect Cost Type Rate | Rate (%) | Base ($) | *Funds Requested |
|---|---|---|---|
| 1. Modified Total Direct Costs | 48 | 56,048 | 26,902 |
| 2. | | | |
| 3. | | | |
| 4. | | | |

                                        Total Indirect Costs: | 26,902 |

Cognizant Federal Agency   | HHS; Mr. Alan Burrell; (201) 555-1235 |

(Agency Name, POC Name and POC Phone Number)

I. Total Direct and Indirect Costs                                 Funds Requested

        Total Direct and Indirect Institutional Costs (G + H): | 82,951 |

J. Fee                                                             Funds Requested
                                                                   | 0 |

K. Budget Justification   | _____ |   | Add Attachment |   | Delete Attachments |   | View Attachments |

                        (Only attach one file)

**Figure 7.32**    Sample SF 424 (R&R) Form: Research & Related Budget, Sections F Through K for Subaward

NOTES

{1} As you can see, this is a small and uncomplicated budget, with a request only for $600 a year for office supplies.

{2} The F&A rate for Bronx Hospital is 48%.

## SF 424 (R&R) MODULAR BUDGETS

Modular budgets have been discussed at length in the section dealing with the PHS 398 forms. The information presented there applies to the SF 424 forms, as well. Figures 7.33 and 7.34 show you what the modular budget forms in the SF 424 package should look like, and the next section discusses the accompanying modular budget justification.

### SF 424 (R&R) Modular Budget Justification

The R&R modular budget justification, as with all budget justifications, provides an explicit rationale for the role and percentage effort of all study personnel and for all study expenses listed in the budget; must be consistent with the project's specific aims and with your Research Design and Methods section; and should be very explicit.

The SF 424 (R&R) package does not contain a form for the modular budget justification; you are expected to follow the format I used in the example shown in the Budget Justification section of this chapter. Remember to convert the justification to a PDF document before attaching it to Section K of the "Research & Related Budget, Sections F Through K" form page.

When using the SF 424 forms for your modular budget justification, you are asked to break it into three sections, and upload each separately. The sections are as follows.

*Section 1: Personnel.* In the personnel section of your modular budget justification, list all personnel, including names, number of person-months devoted to the project (indicate whether the time is academic, calendar, and/or summer), and roles on the project. *Do not provide individual salary information.* Modules should be a reasonable estimate of allowable costs for the proposed project and you must use the current salary limitation when estimating the number of modules.

*Section 2: Consortium Justification.* In the consortium section of your modular budget justification, provide an estimate of total costs (direct costs plus F&A) for each year, rounded to the nearest $1,000. List the individuals and/or organizations with whom consortium or contractual arrangements have been made, indicating whether the collaborating institution is foreign or domestic, and list all personnel, including their percentage of effort and roles on the project. *Do not provide individual salary information.* While only the direct cost for a consortium/contractual arrangement is factored into eligibility for using the modular budget format, the total consortium/contractual costs must be included in the overall requested modular direct cost amount.

*Section 3: Additional Narrative Justification.* You include this third section if the budget requires additional justification: for instance, if you are varying the number of modules requested per year. If no additional justification is necessary, include a simple statement to that effect, such as, "We have no additional items to include in this section."

The budget justification for the subaward (or subcontract) will look exactly the same as it did for the detailed budget page—the modular format is never used for subcontracts, no matter their size. Use the SF 424 (R&R) budget form, and check "subaward" at the top.

Examples of the three modular budget justification sections follow.

---

### Modular Budget Justification (Personnel), Example

**Kaoru Okata, MD (PI: 3.0 person-months devoted to the project) {1}** is Assistant Professor of Medicine in the Department of General Medicine at NYMC. Dr. Okata will be responsible for the design and conduct of the trial and holds primary responsibility for manuscript preparation.

**Theresa Smith, MD (Co-Investigator: 1.2 person-months devoted to the project)** is Professor of Medicine at NYMC. Dr. Smith will be responsible for the collection of ABP data, and will be available to consult on HTN issues if they arise. She will also participate in manuscript preparation.

**Quentin McBurney, PhD (Co-Investigator: 2.4 person-months devoted to the project)** is a quantitative psychologist and biostatistician who has worked with this group for the past 12 years. Dr. McBurney will be responsible for maintaining the database and for the data analyses. {2}

**TBN, MA (ABP Technician: 1.2 person-months devoted to the project in Year 1; 2.4 person-months devoted to the project in Years 2–5)** will be responsible for training the research coordinator and the RA in ABP monitoring techniques, and will be responsible for quality control of the BP measurements. The technician will devote 10% of his or her time in Year 1 because there will not yet be a large number of subject visits, but will be increased to 20% effort in Years 2–5, when the subject visits will be greater in number.

**Beth Serrana, RN (Nurse: 1.2 person-months devoted to the project)** will assist with chart reviews.

---

## Notes: Modular Budget Justification (Personnel) Example

{1} The new SF 424 system for modular budgets, as near as I can figure it, does not want to be given a percentage effort as the current (PHS 398) system requests. Instead, they request a figure that represents the "person-months" in a given year for which you are requesting funding. Presumably, then, if a person is meant to apply 100% effort to the project, that person would be listed as putting in 12 months per year. Using the same logic, the authors here translated "10% effort" to mean 1.2 person-months (12 months × 0.10).

{2} Note that you do not need to say much about each person. Tell who they are and what they'll be doing on the project.

(Text continues on page 240)

# PHS 398 Modular Budget, Periods 1 and 2

OMB Number: 0925-0001
Expiration Date: 9/30/2007

**Budget Period: 1**

[Reset Entries]     Start Date: 12/01/2003     End Date: 11/30/2004

## A. Direct Costs

|  | * Funds Requested ($) |
|---|---|
| {1} * Direct Cost less Consortium F&A | 225,000 |
| Consortium F&A | 26,902 |
| * Total Direct Costs | 251,902 |

## B. Indirect Costs

| Indirect Cost Type | {2, 3} Indirect Cost Rate (%) | {4} Indirect Cost Base ($) | * Funds Requested ($) |
|---|---|---|---|
| 1. Modified Total Direct Costs {3} | 60 | 185,453 | 111,272 |
| 2. | | | |
| 3. | | | |
| 4. | | | |

Cognizant Agency (Agency Name, POC Name and Phone Number)

HEALTH AND HUMAN SERVICES
Ms. Janet Levine;          {3}
(201) 555-1234

Indirect Cost Rate Agreement Date    05/01/2004   {3}          Total Indirect Costs    111,272

## C. Total Direct and Indirect Costs (A + B)          Funds Requested ($)    363,175

**Budget Period: 2**          {5}

[Reset Entries]     Start Date: 12/01/2004     End Date: 11/30/2005

## A. Direct Costs

|  | * Funds Requested ($) |
|---|---|
| * Direct Cost less Consortium F&A | 225,000 |
| Consortium F&A | 27,709 |
| * Total Direct Costs | 252,709 |

## B. Indirect Costs

| Indirect Cost Type | Indirect Cost Rate (%) | Indirect Cost Base ($) | * Funds Requested ($) |
|---|---|---|---|
| 1. Modified Total Direct Costs | 60 | 162,272 | 100,363 |
| 2. | | | |
| 3. | | | |
| 4. | | | |

Cognizant Agency (Agency Name, POC Name and Phone Number)

HEALTH AND HUMAN SERVICES
Janet Levine
(201) 555-1234

Indirect Cost Rate Agreement Date    05/01/2004          Total Indirect Costs    100,363

## C. Total Direct and Indirect Costs (A + B)          Funds Requested ($)    353,072

**Figure 7.33**   Sample PHS 398 Modular Budget, Periods 1 and 2

NOTES

{1} The direct costs (minus consortium indirect costs) will always be a multiple of $25,000.

{2} The example is still using the 60% indirect rate for the institution.

{3} Get this information from your institution's research Web page or from someone in your grants office.

{4} Figuring out the indirect cost base is only slightly complicated. The base here is not the same as the direct costs: It is the direct costs minus costs associated with items on which no indirects are paid, including equipment ($8,500 in this budget, although it is not shown *because this is a modular budget*), and the subcontract direct costs ($56,048). You deduct the subcontract directs because the NIH will be paying the subcontractor's rate on this amount, and does not wish to pay indirects twice on the same money—with one exception. Many institutions charge a "fee" of their indirect rate on the *first* $25,000 of the subcontract directs for the processing work involved in setting up a consortium. (Remember, the F&A is paid on the first $25,000 of the subcontract direct costs. If the subcontract were only $15,000 in both Years 1 and 2, your institution would charge the NIH its indirect rate on the $15,000 in Year 1, and on the remaining $10,000 in Year 2.) So, that "fee" gets added into the base, because the base is the amount on which the NIH will pay F&A (or indirects).

Here is how you get to the number shown in the form:

$$\$225,000 - \$8,500 - \$56,048 + \$25,000 = \$185,452$$

The remaining years would be simpler, because no other equipment was budgeted and because you don't have the $25,000 "fee" to contend with. Thus, the base for the remaining years is calculated as the direct costs less the consortium F&A and the consortium direct costs for that year. The direct costs don't change from year to year—they are always $225,000—so the calculations are, for Years 2–5, respectively, $225,000 – $27,709 (Year 2), $28,540 (Year 3), $29,396 (Year 4), and $30,278 (Year 5).

{5} Remember to put in the start and end dates for the second budget period.

# PHS 398 Modular Budget, Period 5 and Cumulative

**Budget Period: 5**

| | | |
|---|---|---|
| Reset Entries | Start Date: 12/01/2003 | End Date: 11/30/2004 |

## A. Direct Costs

|  | * Funds Requested ($) |
|---|---|
| * Direct Cost less Consortium F&A | 225,000 |
| Consortium F&A | 30,278 |
| * Total Direct Costs | 255,278 |

## B. Indirect Costs

| Indirect Cost Type | Indirect Cost Rate (%) | Indirect Cost Base ($) | *Funds Requested ($) |
|---|---|---|---|
| 1. Modified Total Direct Costs | 60 | 194,723 | 116,834 |
| 2. | | | |
| 3. | | | |
| 4. | | | |

Cognizant Agency (Agency Name, POC Name and Phone Number)

| Indirect Cost Rate Agreement Date | 05/01/2004 | Total Indirect Costs | 116,834 |
|---|---|---|---|

## C. Total Direct and Indirect Costs (A + B)

| | Funds Requested ($) | 372,112 |
|---|---|---|

---

**Cumulative Budget Information {1}**

### 1. Total Costs, Entire Project Period

| | | |
|---|---|---|
| * Section A, Total Direct Cost less Consortium F&A for Entire Project Period | $ | 1,125,000 |
| Section A, Total Consortium F&A for Entire Project Period | $ | 142,824 |
| * Section A, Total Direct Costs for Entire Project Period | $ | 1,267,826 |
| * Section B, Total Indirect Costs for Entire Project Period | $ | 506,364 |
| * Section C, Total Direct and Indirect Costs (A + B) for Entire Project Period | $ | 1,774,190 |

### 2. Budget Justifications

| | | | | |
|---|---|---|---|---|
| Personnel Justification | | Add Attachment | Delete Attachment | View Attachment |
| Consortium Justification | | Add Attachment | Delete Attachment | View Attachment |
| Additional Narrative Justification | | Add Attachment | Delete Attachment | View Attachment |

**Figure 7.34**    Sample PHS 398 Modular Budget, Period 5 and Cumulative

NOTE

{1} All fields in the "Cumulative Budget Information" section are calculated automatically. I have included it so you can see what it looks like; I have not included modular budgets for Periods 2, 3, and 4, but they are required for each year for which you have requested funds.

## Modular Budget Justification (Personnel), Example (Continued)

**Reina Butler, BS (Research Coordinator: 4.8 person-months devoted to the project)** will supervise the RA; together, they will be responsible for conducting the screenings and, with the ABP technician, will be responsible for consenting and enrolling participants and carrying out the study procedures. Ms. Butler will be supervised by Drs. Okata and Ruggiero. In Year 5, when the flow of research participants has slowed, Ms. Butler will supervise and work with the RA to enter data.

**TBN, BA (Research Assistant: 12 person-months devoted to the project)** will work with the research coordinator to conduct the patient visits. In Year 5, the RA will concentrate on data entry.

**Kenneth Lubin, PhD (Consultant)** is Assistant Professor of Medicine at the New Jersey Medical Center. He is an expert in the development of databases that involve multiple sources of input (in this case, hand-entered data, ABP data, ECG data, and baroreflex data; the latter are downloaded electronically). Dr. Lubin will provide 10 days in Year 1 to develop the database and 6 days in the remaining years to maintain it. {3, 4}

## Notes: Modular Budget Justification (Personnel) Example (Continued)

{3} Do include consultants, if you have them, in the modular budget justification.

{4} I have discussed in the other budget justification examples why Dr. Lubin has been listed as a consultant, paid by the day or hour, and not listed as a co-investigator on another subcontract. The reasons set forth elsewhere apply here as well.

## Modular Budget Justification (Consortium), Example

Consortium with the Bronx Hospital ☑ Domestic ☐ Foreign

Approximately $88,000 Total Costs per year ($56,048 direct costs; 48% F&A = $26,902) {1}

## Note: Modular Budget Justification (Consortium) Example

{1} This is the way one is instructed to lay out this section when using the PHS 398 form. Since the information requested for a modular SF 424 budget justification is identical, I suggest using the same layout (including the foreign/domestic checkbox) when using the SF 424 package.

## Modular Budget Justification (Additional Narrative), Example

We have no additional items to include in this section. {1}

## Note: Modular Budget Justification (Additional Narrative) Example

{1} As I noted earlier, this section of the justification is used if the budget requires additional justification: for instance, if you are varying the number of modules requested per year. If no additional justification is necessary, indicate as much.

## SF 424 (R&R) BIOGRAPHICAL SKETCHES

Please recall that on the SF 424 (R&R) Senior/Key Person Profile form, there was a space to attach a biosketch for each person. That form is available on the NIH grants page,[6] along with the instructions and a sample biosketch. Thankfully, the new SF 424 (R&R) looks pretty much like the current PHS 398 forms, so you don't have to redo your biosketch from scratch. Do notice, however, that you must enter your eRA Commons user name on the form.

Make sure to include a biosketch for every person listed as key personnel; this includes consultants, but only if they are listed as key personnel, and key personnel from any sub-contractor if you are planning to include one or more consortia.

Figure 7.35 shows what the biosketch form looks like.

## RESEARCH PLAN COMPONENT

The Research Plan component form provides fields so that you may attach the various required files (converted to PDFs) that constitute your research plan. As you can see in Figure 7.36, there is a section for the research plan attachments (i.e., Specific Aims, Background and Significance, Preliminary Studies/Progress Report, and Research Design and Methods), as well as places to attach documents relating to human subjects research and other research plan documents (e.g., information on vertebrate animal research, consortium/contractual arrangements, letters of support, and resource sharing plans). Some of these sections will be irrelevant for your application; only upload files for the sections that are relevant.

The manual provides excellent instructions for the sections to be attached to this form, so have it at hand as you write each section. I have provided detail on the writing of the Human Subjects sections in Chapter 6 and on the writing of the research sections in Chapter 5.

### Targeted/Planned Enrollment Table

You attach the Targeted/Planned Enrollment Table in the Human Subjects section of the Research Plan form. The SF 424 (R&R) uses the same table as the PHS 398, which is available on the NIH grants page,[7] and you are encouraged to refer back to the earlier discussion of the table in this chapter.

### Letters of Support

Letters of support were discussed in the context of the PHS 398 form earlier in the chapter, and Figures 7.16 and 7.17 offer sample letters.

## CHECKLIST COMPONENT FOR SF 424 (R&R)

I do not include a sample of the checklist you are to use for the SF 424 (R&R), but you should note that it is not in any way related to the checklist used in the PHS 398, although the SF 424 (R&R) form is also named "PHS 398 Checklist." (Some of the new forms have

# BIOGRAPHICAL SKETCH

Provide the following information for the key personnel and other significant contributors.
Follow this format for each person. **DO NOT EXCEED FOUR PAGES.**

| NAME | POSITION TITLE |
|------|----------------|
| **eRA COMMONS USER NAME** | |

EDUCATION/TRAINING *(Begin with baccalaureate or other initial professional education, such as nursing, and include post-doctoral training.)*

| INSTITUTION AND LOCATION | DEGREE *(if applicable)* | YEAR(s) | FIELD OF STUDY |
|--------------------------|--------------------------|---------|----------------|
|  |  |  |  |
|  |  |  |  |
|  |  |  |  |
|  |  |  |  |
|  |  |  |  |
|  |  |  |  |
|  |  |  |  |
|  |  |  |  |
|  |  |  |  |
|  |  |  |  |
|  |  |  |  |
|  |  |  |  |
|  |  |  |  |
|  |  |  |  |
|  |  |  |  |
|  |  |  |  |
|  |  |  |  |
|  |  |  |  |
|  |  |  |  |
|  |  |  |  |
|  |  |  |  |

**Figure 7.35**     Biographical Sketch Form

OMP Number: 0925-0001
Expiration Date: 9/30/2007

## PHS 398 Research Plan

### 1. Application Type:

From SF 424 (R&R) Cover Page and PHS 398 Checklist. The responses provided on these pages, regarding the type of application being submitted, are repeated for your reference, as you attach the appropriate sections of the research plan.

*Type of Application:

☐ New  ☐ Resubmission  ☐ Renewal  ☐ Continuation  ☐ Revision

### 2. Research Plan Attachments:

Please attach applicable sections of the research plan, below.

1. Introduction to Application | [          ] | Add Attachment | Delete Attachment | View Attachment
(for RESUBMISSION or REVISION only)

2. Specific Aims | [          ] | Add Attachment | Delete Attachment | View Attachment

3. Background and Significance | [          ] | Add Attachment | Delete Attachment | View Attachment

4. Preliminary Studies/Progress Report | [          ] | Add Attachment | Delete Attachment | View Attachment

5. Research Design and Methods | [          ] | Add Attachment | Delete Attachment | View Attachment

Human Subjects Sections

Attachments 6-10 apply only when you have answered "yes" to the question "are human subjects involved" on the R&R Other Project Information Form. In this case, attachments 6-10 may be required, and you are encouraged to consult the Application guide instructions and/or the specific Funding Opportunity Announcement to determine which sections must be submitted with this application.

6. Protection of Human Subjects | [          ] | Add Attachment | Delete Attachment | View Attachment

7. Inclusion of Women and Minorities | [          ] | Add Attachment | Delete Attachment | View Attachment

8. Targeted/Planned Enrollment Table | [          ] | Add Attachment | Delete Attachment | View Attachment

9. Inclusion of Children | [          ] | Add Attachment | Delete Attachment | View Attachment

10. Data and Safety Monitoring Plan | [          ] | Add Attachment | Delete Attachment | View Attachment

Other Research Plan Sections

11. Vertebrate Animals | [          ] | Add Attachment | Delete Attachment | View Attachment

12. Consortium/Contractual Arrangements | [          ] | Add Attachment | Delete Attachment | View Attachment

13. Letters of Support | [          ] | Add Attachment | Delete Attachment | View Attachment

14. Resource Sharing Plan(s) | [          ] | Add Attachment | Delete Attachment | View Attachment

15. Appendix | Add Attachments | Remove Attachments | View Attachments

**Figure 7.36**  Research Plan Form

the "PHS 398" prefix to distinguish them from the SF 424 forms, but they may or may not be identical or even similar to the old PHS 398 forms).

This form is quite straightforward; it allows you to notify the NIH that you are changing the PI, and it provides space, for renewal applications only, to notify the NIH concerning inventions and patents.

## PROGRAM INCOME, ASSURANCES AND CERTIFICATIONS

*Program income* is the gross income earned by the applicant organization that is directly generated by a supported activity or earned as a result of the award. If you anticipate any program income, you use the Program Income, Assurances/Certification form to explain them. This form also provides the assurances, for which you must sign, and, if you cannot comply with assurances, a place for you to attach a document containing an explanation.

The form is self-explanatory, and so I have not included a sample.

## NOTES

1. The NIH instructions for the forms pages can be accessed at http://grants1.nih.gov/grants/funding/phs398/phs398.html.

2. Instructions and forms for SBIR and STTR applications can be found at http://grants1.nih.gov/grants/funding/sbir.htm#sol.

3. The Final Certification application can be accessed at http://ocm.od.nih.gov/dfas/finalcert.htm.

4. See http://www.grants.gov/.

5. The NIH OER home page is accessed at http://grants1.nih.gov/grants/oer.htm.

6. The Senior/Key Person Profile form can be downloaded from http://grants1.nih.gov/grants/forms.htm

7. The Targeted/Planned Enrollment Table form is available at http://grants1.nih.gov/grants/forms.htm.

# Submitting the Application

**8**

**T**here are two methods by which you may submit your application, depending on whether you are using the PHS 398 forms or the new SF 424 forms. The latter are submitted electronically, so there are no issues concerning number of copies, mailing labels, and so on, which will make things vastly more convenient for you. As I have discussed previously, however, the new forms are not yet available for use by the NIH, although the start dates for some grant mechanisms are targeted for 2006. Chapter 7 provides the projected schedule, but you should check the Office of Extramural Research (OER) Web site for updates. Thus, much of the material in this chapter concerns the submission of applications that have used the PHS 398 forms. The differences will be noted, however, as they appear.

## THE ELECTRONIC RESEARCH ADMINISTRATION FOR GRANTS ADMINISTRATION SUPPORT

Whether you are using the PHS 398 or the SF 424 forms, you must register with the Electronic Research Administration (eRA), which provides grants administration support to NIH I/Cs and to all Department of Health and Human Services (HHS) agencies that fund extramural research. The eRA system provides the following features, as described on the eRA Commons Web site.[1]

### Status

The eRA Commons allows principal investigators to review the current status of all their grant applications and review detailed information associated with their grants. Institution officials (i.e., the signing official [SO] or administrative official [AO] associated with the institution) can see a summary view of grant applications, review the Notice of Grant Award, and access the Progress Report face page.

### eSNAP

SNAP is the streamlined noncompeting award process; the should read: the eSNAP feature allows an institution to review noncompeting grant data and submit a progress report *online*.

### Internet-Assisted Review

Internet-assisted review (IAR) allows reviewers to submit critiques and preliminary scores for applications they are reviewing and allows reviewers, scientific review administrators (SRAs), and GTAs to view all critiques in preparation for a meeting. The IAR creates a preliminary summary statement body containing submitted critiques for the SRA or GTA.

### Financial Status Reports

The financial status report (FSR) feature allows for the electronic submission of financial information associated with a grant.

### Administration

The eRA Commons also provides the ability for an institution to create and manage user accounts associated with its institution. Additionally, it allows the institution's SO to maintain the institution information on file at the NIH.

If you do not have an eRA account, I suggest you go to the eRA Commons Web site now and open one.

## THE COVER LETTER

It isn't required, but you should include a cover letter with your application. It will make it easier for the NIH personnel who receive the application to route it appropriately. Include the following information:

a. Your application title.

b. The PA or RFA number, if you are responding to one of these.

c. Names of people who should *not* review your application, such as persons with conflicts of interests (and that might include competitors, if you have such). The process is confidential.

d. Specific disciplines involved in the study, if it is a multidisciplinary proposal.

e. Note if your proposal involves human subjects.

f. Note if the proposal was previously submitted in response to a PA or RFA.

g. Note if you have requested permission to request more than $500,000 and received it, that you have enclosed the required institute approval documentation.

h. Reference, if necessary, any contacts with NIH program officials.

i. A request for assignment and referral of your application to an I/C, Integrated Review Group (IRG), and study section (discussed in detail below).

j. Suggest assignment to multiple I/Cs, if appropriate.

k. You can identify particular expertise needed for the review.

l. I have provided an example of a cover letter in Figure 8.1. The notes in the letter (e.g., {a}) reference the points in this list.

To: NIH Center for Scientific Review

Enclosed please find one signed original, and five (5) copies, of our proposal titled "RCT: Effect of Guided Breathing Intervention on Ambulatory BP in Hypertensives." **{a}** This proposal describes a randomized controlled trial to test the effect of a nonpharmacologic, behaviorally based intervention to improve blood pressure control in hypertensive patients. **{e}**

I have been in contact with Dr. Carl Weathers, a Program Officer at NHLBI, **{h}** who has suggested that NHLBI may be interested in funding this proposal, **{i}** and suggests that it might be directed to the Risk, Prevention, and Health Behavior (RPHB) IRG and to the Behavioral Medicine Interventions and Outcomes study section for review. **{j}** In the event that this application does go to the suggested study section, please note that one of the panel members, Dr. Eleanor Apata, is a consultant on a grant on which I am a co-investigator, which may constitute a conflict of interest for Dr. Apata. **{c}**

One aspect of the proposal concerns the assessment of heart rate variability and of baroreceptor sensitivity; it would be useful if one of the reviewers had experience with the assessment of these measures. **{k}**

Thank you for your consideration.

Sincerely,

**Figure 8.1** Sample Cover Letter

# KNOW YOUR INTEGRATED REVIEW GROUP AND STUDY SECTION

As I mentioned above, you should indicate in your cover letter the I/C, IRG, and study section to which you wish your proposal be sent. Here, then, are some specific considerations you should make.

## Institutes and Centers

The I/C to which you want your proposal sent should be fairly obvious by the time you are ready to submit your proposal. There will almost always be a particular I/C that will be an obvious home to a proposal, and you want to make sure that it goes to that I/C.

## Integrated Review Group

An IRG represents a cluster of study sections around a general scientific area. The Center for Scientific Review (CSR) IRGs are shown in Table 8.1.

---

**Table 8.1    Center for Scientific Review IRGs**

AIDS and Related Research (AARR)

Behavioral and Biobehavioral Processes (BBBP)

Biological Chemistry and Macromolecular Biophysics (BCMB)

Biology of Development and Aging (BDA)

Bioengineering Sciences and Technologies (BST)

Brain Disorders and Clinical Neuroscience (BDCN)

Cell Biology (CB)

Cardiovascular Sciences (CVS)

Digestive Sciences (DIG)

Endocrinology, Metabolism, Nutrition and Reproductive Sciences (EMNR)

Genes, Genomes and Genetics (GGG)

Health of the Population (HOP)

Hematology (HEME)

Immunology (IMM)

Infectious Diseases and Microbiology (IDM)

Integrative, Functional, and Cognitive Neuroscience (IFCN)

Molecular, Cellular, and Developmental Neuroscience (MCDN)

Musculoskeletal, Oral and Skin Sciences (MOSS)

Oncological Sciences (ONC)

Respiratory Sciences (RES)

Risk, Prevention and Health Behavior (RPHB)

Renal and Urological Sciences (RUS)

Surgical Sciences, Biomedical Imaging, and Bioengineering (SBIB)

---

NOTE: See http://www.csr.nih.gov/review/irgdesc.htm for more information on IRGs.

## Study Sections

A study section—also known as a scientific review group (SRG)—is a panel of experts established according to scientific disciplines or current research areas for the primary purpose of evaluating the scientific and technical merit of grant applications.

The study sections within the various IRGs mainly review research project grant applications and a few of the research career award applications. Most National Research Service Award (NRSA) individual fellowship applications are reviewed in special study sections that are designated for these reviews.[2]

Small Business Innovation Research (SBIR) and Small Business Technology Transfer Research (STTR) applications are reviewed in special emphasis panels within the CSR's IRGs. The small business review activities are summarized under the description of each IRG on the NIH Web page and are accessible by clicking on the IRG abbreviation.[3] Thus, for example, if you clicked on the first IRG listed, AIDS and Related Research (AARR), you would see the following study sections:

Molecular and Cellular Biology Study Section (AMCB)

AIDS Immunology and Pathogenesis Study Section (AIP)

AIDS Discovery and Development of Therapeutics Study Section (ADDT)

AIDS-Associated Opportunistic Infections and Cancer Study Section (AOIC)

NeuroAIDS and Other End-Organ Diseases Study Section (NAED)

AIDS Clinical Studies and Epidemiology Study Section (ACE)

Behavioral and Social Science Approaches to Preventing HIV/AIDS Study Section (BSPH)

Behavioral and Social Consequences of HIV/AIDS Study Section (BSCH)

HIV/AIDS Vaccines Study Section (VACC)

AARR Small Business Activities

Small business review panels are assembled on an ad hoc basis for each meeting and are subject to change. Additional information may be found on the NIH Web page entitled "Review of Small Business Applications" and on the page entitled "CSR Study Section Roster Index."[4] To get a listing of the scientific review administrator and membership roster for each study section, click on the study section roster under the study section name within an IRG, or go to the study section index (study sections are listed alphabetically) and click on the specified roster next to the name of the study section.

## Back to the Example . . .

It is important that you become sophisticated about the study sections; you will prefer your application to go to a particular one, and the only way to know which one is to know all the possible relevant ones.

Go to the NIH page that lists IRGs (http://www.csr.nih.gov/review/irgdesc.htm), put the cursor over "Study Section Information," and click on "Integrated Review Groups." Scroll down the page, and you will see a group labeled "RPHB: Risk, Prevention, and Health Behavior." Click on this, and you will see a description of this IRG and the individual study sections that constitute it. I would suggest that, for the sample project on blood pressure and guided breathing, the Behavioral Medicine Interventions and Outcomes (BMIO) IRG is a good match for what is being proposed. Click on this, and it will show you what sorts of studies are reviewed by this group. You have to go pretty far down the list (second to the last), until you see the following:

> Behavioral interventions as primary or adjunctive treatments; studies of behavioral interventions designed to remedy or slow the progression of disease and disorder (e.g., behavior therapy for insomnia, cognitive intervention for early dementia.)

Well, the study we're using in the example has little to do with insomnia or dementia, but the rest looks to be on target. (A cautionary note: The NIH may have changed its format by the time you read this, so you may have to look further than my directions suggest).

Now, go back to the "Behavioral Medicine Interventions and Outcomes" page, and click on "View Roster" at the top of the page. You will see the name of the Scientific Review Administrator (SRA) for this study section, and then you can view the roster of people who sit on this study section. I strongly urge you to go to the Web and look up each of the members and learn their specialties. Try to narrow down who might be one of the three members to review this proposal (this is pretty tough to do), and then go on Medline and find and read some of the published papers for each. What will these guys be looking for in a proposal? It's people who take all this trouble to prepare who end up with the fundable scores.

## SUBMISSION DATES

For R01 applications, there are three submission dates in each year: June 1, October 1, and February 1. For SBIR and STTR applications, the three dates are: April 1, August 1, and December 1. An important thing to watch out for is, if you are responding to an RFA, it may have its own submission date; also, be careful not to confuse due dates for *letters of intent,* when they are required, with the due date for applications. Table 8.2 shows the submission dates, review, and award cycles.

An important thing to know is that, if you are using the PHS 398 application forms (i.e., *not* the SF 424, which may not yet be available), the application does not have to *arrive* at NIH on the due date. It must have been *sent*—postmarked—no later than that date. Page 41 of the PHS 398 instructions reads,

> Applications will be considered on time if they are *sent* on or before the appropriate date listed and a proof of mailing is provided. The critical determination is when the application is *sent,* not when it arrives at NIH. Proof of timely mailing consists of one of the following: A legibly dated U.S. Postal Service postmark or a dated receipt from a commercial carrier or the U.S. Postal Service. *Private metered postmarks are not acceptable.*" (italics added)

## WHERE AND WHAT TO SEND

Sending in your proposal is pretty straightforward from this point on. If you are using the new SF 424 forms, you will simply press the "submit" button online. If you are using the PHS 398 forms, use the NIH provided table of contents to determine the order in which everything in the application goes. Make sure that your page numbers do in fact correspond to the numbers listed in your table of contents! Send five single-sided photocopies of your

**Table 8.2**    Submission Dates, Review, and Award Cycles

| Types of Applications | Cycle I | Cycle II | Cycle III |
|---|---|---|---|
| *Application Submission Dates* | | | |
| Institutional Ruth L. Kirschstein National Research Service Awards[a] (Kirschstein-NRSA)—All new, competing continuation, supplemental, and revised applications | Jan 10 | May 10 | Sep 10 |
| Academic Research Enhancement Award (AREA)—All new, competing continuation, and revised applications *except* those involving AIDS-related research | Jan 25 | May 25 | Sep 25 |
| *New* Research Grants (e.g., R01) and Career Development Awards (K series) | Feb 1 | Jun 1 | Oct 1 |
| Program Project Grants and Center Grants (P series)—All new, competing continuation, supplemental, and revised applications | Feb 1 | Jun 1 | Oct 1 |
| *Competing Continuation, Supplemental,* and *Revised* Research Grants and Career Development Awards[b] | Mar 1 | Jul 1 | Nov 1 |
| Small Business Innovation Research (SBIR) and Small Business Technology Transfer (STTR) Grants—All new, supplemental, and revised applications *except* AIDS and AIDS-related applications | Apr 1 | Aug 1 | Dec 1 |
| Conference Grants and Conference Cooperative Agreements—All new, competing continuation, supplemental, and revised applications | Apr 15 | Aug 15 | Dec 15 |
| AIDS and AIDS-Related Grants—All new, competing continuations, supplemental, and revised applications, *including* AIDS and AIDS-related SBIR/STTR | May 1 | Sep 1 | Jan 2 |
| RFAs and PAs | Special submission dates: Check the specific NIH Guide announcement. | | |
| Review and Award Schedule | | | |
| Scientific Merit Review | Jun–Jul | Oct–Nov | Feb–Mar |
| Advisory Council Review | Sep–Oct | Jan–Feb | May–Jun |
| Earliest Project Start Date[c] | Dec | Apr | Jul |

SOURCE: Information in this table is taken directly from the PHS 398 instructions.

NOTES:

a. Many NIH I/Cs use only one or two of the submission dates for Kirschstein-NRSAs. Please check the program announcement for Institutional Research Training Grants (T32) at http://grants.nih.gov/training/nrsa.htm.

b. Some I/Cs have different submission dates for revised Career Development Award applications. Check with the appropriate I/C.

c. Awarding components may not always be able to honor the requested start date of an application. Therefore, applicants should make no commitments or obligations until confirmation of the start date by the awarding component.

*signed* original, plus the original. If you are sending appendices, send only five copies. Put all of these copies in an envelope or box with your cover letter and your Personal Information sheet (see Chapter 7), and send it out.

In the PHS 398 forms package, you will find a form called "labels.doc" (reproduced at the end of this chapter). This document tells you exactly where to send your package. Note that you may *not* hand-deliver your application; it will not be accepted. Also, note that the zip code differs depending on whether you are using the United States Postal Service (20892–7710) or a courier delivery service (20817). Of course, this information (and the information in the following paragraph) is not relevant if you are using the SF 424 forms, which are submitted electronically.

If you are sending an application in response to an RFA, use the label provided and give the RFA number in the appropriate blank. If you are sending an SBIR or STTR proposal in response to an RFA, use the label provided on the second labels page.

## NOTES

1. https://commons.era.nih.gov/commons/

2. More information about the NRSA Fellowship study sections is available at http://www.csr.nih.gov/events/fellowship_ss/fellow_ss/htm.

3. The linked list of CSR IRGs can be accessed at http://www.csr.nih.gov/review/irgdesc.htm.

4. The "Review of Small Business Applications" page is accessible at http://www.csr.nih.gov/REVIEW/sba.asp and the "CSR Study Section Roster Index" is at http://www.csr.nih.gov/Committees/rosterindex.asp.

# *Mailing address for application*

## *Use this label or a facsimile*

**All applications and other deliveries to the Center for Scientific Review must come either via courier delivery or via the United States Postal Service (USPS). Applications delivered by individuals to the Center for Scientific Review will no longer be accepted.**

**Applications sent via the USPS EXPRESS or REGULAR MAIL should be sent to the following address:**

> **CENTER FOR SCIENTIFIC REVIEW**
> **NATIONAL INSTITUTES OF HEALTH**
> **6701 ROCKLEDGE DRIVE**
> **ROOM 1040 – MSC 7710**
> **BETHESDA, MD 20892-7710**

**NOTE: All applications sent via a courier delivery service (non-USPS) should use this address, but CHANGE THE ZIP CODE TO 20817**

**The telephone number is 301-435-0715. C.O.D. applications will *not* be accepted.**

# *For application in response to RFA*

## *Use this label or a facsimile*

IF THIS APPLICATION IS IN RESPONSE TO AN RFA, be sure to put the RFA number in line 2 of the application face page. In addition, after duplicating copies of the application, cut along the dotted line below and staple the RFA label to the bottom of the face page of the original and place the original on top of your entire package. Failure to use this RFA label could result in delayed processing of your application such that it may not reach the review committee on time for review. ***Do not use*** the label unless the application is in response to a specific RFA. Also, applicants responding to a specific RFA should be sure to follow all special mailing instructions published in the RFA.

RFA No. \_\_\_\_\_ ▢ _____

# *Mailing address for application*

## *Use this label or a facsimile*

**All applications and other deliveries to the Center for Scientific Review must come either via courier delivery or via the USPS. Applications delivered by individuals to the Center for Scientific Review will no longer be accepted.**

Applications sent via the USPS EXPRESS or REGULAR MAIL should be sent to the following address:

**CENTER FOR SCIENTIFIC REVIEW
NATIONAL INSTITUTES OF HEALTH
6701 ROCKLEDGE DRIVE
ROOM 1040 – MSC 7710
BETHESDA, MD 20892-7710**

NOTE: All applications sent via a courier delivery service (non-USPS) should use this address, but **CHANGE THE ZIP CODE TO 20817**

The telephone number is 301-435-0715.  C.O.D. applications will *not* be accepted.

# *For application in response to SBIR/STTR*

## *Use this label or a facsimile*

IF THIS APPLICATION IS IN RESPONSE TO AN SBIR/STTR Solicitation, be sure to put the SBIR/STTR Solicitation number in line 2 of the application face page. In addition, after duplicating copies of the application, cut along the dotted line below and staple the appropriate SBIR or STTR label to the bottom of the face page of the original and place the original on top of your entire package. If this SBIR or STTR application is in response to an RFA, be sure to also include the RFA No. in the space provided below.

## SBIR

RFA No. _____ (if applicable)

## STTR

RFA No. _____ (if applicable)

# The Grant Review and Award Process

## 9

A surprising number of researchers are unfamiliar with the process that is initiated once an application is sent in to the NIH. Understanding the process will allow you to understand the timetables on which you should expect feedback and the sort of feedback to expect. It will provide guidance as to when and why you might want to submit supplementary materials, and it will provide hints as to when it is appropriate to contact NIH staff to ask about progress. Perhaps most important, it provides insight into the criteria used by reviewers to determine your priority score.

Figure 9.1 shows a flow chart adapted from one that appears on the National Institute of Allergy and Infectious Disease (NIAID) Web page. It provides an overview of the application process.

The following is a distillation of an analysis of the process, partly provided by an NIH document entitled "A Straightforward Description of What Happens to Your Research Project Grant Application After It Is Received for Peer Review"[1], and augmented by other important details.

So, what happens once you mail off your application?

1. Your application is received at the Center for Scientific Review (CSR).

2. The application is reviewed by a referral officer, who assigns it to an appropriate Integrated Review Group (IRG), Scientific Review Group (SRG, also known as a study section), and Institute or Center (I/C; this is relevant in the event the application is fundable). In Chapter 8, we discussed what you should say in your cover letter to guide the application to the appropriate study section and I/C.

3. Once your application is assigned, it receives an identification number that conveys a good deal of information about the proposal. For example, the application number *1 R01 HL97865 01* conveys the following:

| Application Type | Activity Code | Administering Organization | Serial Number | Suffix Year |
|---|---|---|---|---|
| 1 | R01 | HL | 97865 | 01 |

Table 9.1 explains in more detail what each of the five parts of the application number indicates.

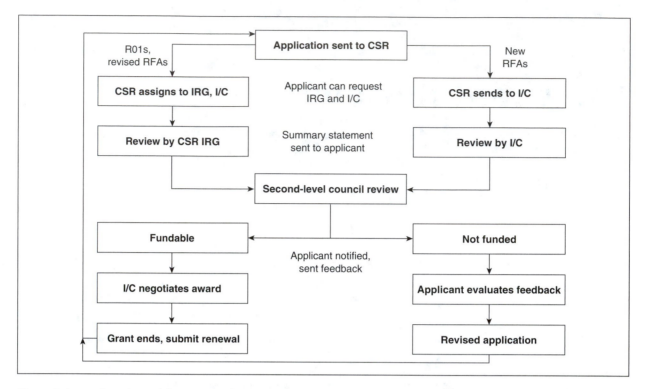

**Figure 9.1**      Overview of the NIH Application Process

**Table 9.1**        Components of the Proposal Identification Number

Application Type    Tells NIH whether your application is new, a renewal, a noncompeting application, or other type.

- Type 1, New: Provides Public Health Service (PHS) support for a new research project grant.
- Type 2, Competing Continuation: Extends a project period that would otherwise expire for one or more grant budget periods; these grant applications are peer reviewed and compete with others for funds.
- Type 3, Supplement: Also called *administrative supplement;* adds funds to a grant without peer review.
- Type 4, Extension: Provides additional time and funds beyond levels originally recommended. Applies only to MERIT and Small Business Innovation  (SBIR) fast-track applications.
- Type 5, Noncompeting Continuation: Continues support in the out years of a grant; does not compete for funds.
- Type 6, Change of Grantee: Transfers an ongoing grant when one organization buys out another, also called *successor of interest.*
- Type 7, Change of Grantee: Transfers an ongoing grant from one grantee institution to another.
- Type 8, Change of NIH I/C: Transfers an ongoing grant from one I/C to another.
- Type 9, Change of I/C: Continues support for an ongoing grant transferred from one I/C to another.

Activity Code       Tells the type of grant for which you've applied.

Administering       This is the code for the I/C to which your application has been assigned (*HL* is for the
Organization        National Heart, Lung, and Blood Institute, or NHLBI).

Serial Number

Suffix Year         Shows the current support year for the grant (a new application will have the suffix "01").

4. Within 10 days, letters will be sent to the applicant and the applicant's sponsored research or grants office, noting the study section and potential funding I/C. At this time, the applicant may question the study section or the I/C assignment by contacting either the Scientific Review Administrator (SRA) for the study section or the referral office (the telephone number is 301-435-0715).

5. The SRA reads through the applications and decides which study section members would be most appropriate as reviewers or discussants. Usually, two or three members are assigned to provide written reviews of each application, and one or two to serve as discussants. Before the SRA sends your application to the review committee, he or she looks at it to make sure it is complete. If you are missing anything, the SRA may contact you. If this happens, make sure you send the missing materials quickly, so the reviewers get the information in time to look at it before the review.

6. The primary and secondary reviewers of the grant present the proposal to the entire group, followed by a 10-to 15-minute discussion by all review group members, most of whom will have focused primarily on the Abstract and Specific Aims sections. If the application ranks in the top 50th percentile, it is assigned a *priority score*. After the discussion of your application has ended, the primary and secondary reviewers each suggest a priority score, ranging between 1.0 (*best*) and 5.0 (*worst*). However, at this point, the score is just a suggestion. When voting, each member marks his or her priority score privately on a scoring sheet. Your priority score is the mean of these scores multiplied by 100. For R01s and some other grant types, the NIH converts the priority score into a percentile, which indicates your application's rank relative to the other applications reviewed by your study section at the last three meetings.

## Who Are the Study Section Members?

Study Section members are active and productive researchers in the medical community who are nominated by the SRA. They serve multiyear terms. The goal is to have the group's combined knowledge span the diversity of the subject matter. The membership is frequently supplemented by temporary members who may augment the group's expertise in a particular area. In some instances, a Special Emphasis Panel (SEP) is formed on an ad hoc basis to review applications that require special expertise or due to special circumstances, such as when a conflict of interest arises.

## Study Section Timetable

Each study section has between 12 and 24 members who review as many as 60 to 100 applications at each meeting. The timetable for the panel members is as follows:

1. The study section meets approximately 20 weeks after the application due date. Because of the interval between submission and review, applicants may wish to submit supplementary materials, such as newly published studies or new preliminary data. However, each study section sets its own policy for acceptance of supplemental materials, for example, page limitations or time of submission. Before submitting supplementary materials, contact the SRA both to alert him or her and to ascertain acceptable content, format, and deadline.

2. Approximately six weeks before the study section meets, the study section members receive packages with their materials. These include a list of the applications on which

they will officially sit as primary, secondary, or tertiary reviewers, as well as a list of applications for which the reviewer has been noted as having a conflict of interest, and therefore on which he or she will not sit and must leave the room during discussion. The first thing members are asked to do is review the applications for which they are listed as a reviewer (there are usually six to eight of these) and inform the SRA of possible conflicts. Although any of the study section members are invited to participate in discussion (except those excluded due to a conflict), it is the official members of the review group for any given application—usually three of them—who will provide a priority score.

3. One week before the study section meets, the SRA solicits, from each member, a list of R01 applications (of those for which the member is officially responsible) believed not to rank in the top 50th percentile for scientific merit. Those applications in the bottom half are considered to be *streamlined*; that is, they are not scored or discussed at the meeting, but written critiques are provided and the applicant may subsequently revise and resubmit the application. Streamlining is not equivalent to disapproval of an application, but rather represents a decision by the study section that the application would not rank in the top half of applications generally reviewed by that study section.

4. In addition to streamlined applications, two other types of applications do not receive a full review, priority score, or summary statement:
   A. *Not recommended for further consideration (NRFC)*: Applications that are unacceptable due to risks or inadequate protection against risks receive a rating of NRFC. These applications cannot be funded.
   B. *Deferred*: If the initial review group cannot determine scientific merit because of inadequate information in the application, it can ask to defer the application to allow the applicant to send in the information. A deferred application is ordinarily reviewed at the next review cycle. However, if the information can be obtained immediately from the applicant, the review can proceed without delay.

5. All regular CSR study section meetings mostly follow the same format. The meetings usually last two days. The chairperson of the study section, who is also a section member, and the SRA are responsible for jointly conducting the meeting. Representatives from the various NIH Institutes are encouraged to attend, but may not participate in the discussions.

6. After the assigned reviewers and discussants provide their evaluations, any outside opinions are read. After general discussion, members mark their priority scores privately on scoring sheets that are collected at the conclusion of the meeting.

7. Within a few days after the study section meets, priority scores and percentiles are mailed to applicants and entered into the application database. Having received your score, you will be anxious to see your *summary statement* (sometimes referred to as the "pink sheets," because they used to be pink), which gives the specific feedback that led to the priority score decisions. Allow approximately six weeks for the summary statement to arrive. The summary statement is described in detail below.

8. Once summary statements are produced, they are transmitted to the appropriate NIH I/C for funding consideration. The SRA's control over the review of these applications ends at this point, and the I/C program officers become the applicant's link to the NIH with regard to interpretation of the reviews and the disposition of the

application. However, your SRA remains *your* link to the process if you have any questions.

9. The NIH National Advisory Council of the potential awarding I/C performs the second-level review. The I/C councils comprise scientists from the extramural research community and public representatives. The councils ensure that the NIH receives advice from a cross section of the U.S. population in the process of its deliberation and decision. The second-level review is based not only on the considerations of scientific merit, as judged by the study sections, but also on the relevance of the proposed study to an I/C's programs and priorities. It looks at the application with an eye toward potential barriers to funding, including human subjects and animal concerns. If you see codes added by the study section about such concerns on your summary statement, resolve them as quickly as possible. The National Advisory Council will not approve application for funding until study section concerns are resolved. Funding approaches vary by I/C, so contact the I/C to which you are applying for specific details. Table 9.2 shows the flow of the review process, repeated cycle after cycle. To use the timetable, determine your submission date (February, June, or October), and follow that row across to determine the approximate timing of the steps. Table 9.2 is based on the current timing of the review and award process; however, please see the note following the Table concerning a new, shorter, timetable that will be in effect once the full conversion to electronic submission (using the SF 424 forms) has been completed.

A simple way to look at it is as follows:

Submit in *February*, and your proposal will be reviewed by the study section in *June*, the council will meet in *September*, and the earliest award date will be in *December*.

Submit in *June*, and your proposal will be reviewed in *October*, the council will meet in *January*, and the earliest award date will be in *April*.

Submit in *October*, and your proposal will be reviewed in *February*, the council will meet in *May*, and the earliest award date will be in *August*.

**Table 9.2**        Cycle-by-Cycle Flow of the Review Process

| Submission Date | Study Date Assigned | Packets Mailed Out | Study Section Convenes | Summary Statement Prepared | Councils Meet | Earliest Award Date |
|---|---|---|---|---|---|---|
| Feb | Mar | Apr | Jun | Aug | Sep | Dec |
| Jun | Jul | Aug | Oct | Dec | Jan | Apr |
| Oct | Nov | Dec | Feb | Apr | May | Aug |

NOTE: Different grant mechanisms and RFAs may have different submission dates. Table 8.2 in shows the dates for all NIH grant mechanisms.

**Last Minute Update:** The following section is abstracted from a notice sent by the NIH in the first week of January, 2006:

As of October 2005, Summary Statements of most reviews will be posted in NIH Commons one month (instead of 2–3 months) after study sections have met. In addition, in February 2006, [the Center for Scientific Review] will begin a pilot study with 40 study sections to cut 1½ months from the review process of R01 applications submitted by new investigators. Specifically, we will: (i) schedule study section meetings up to a month earlier; (ii) provide scientists their study section scores, critiques, and panel discussion summaries within a week after the section meeting; (iii) shave days from the internal steps involved in assigning proposals to study sections; and (iv) extend resubmission deadlines by 3 weeks. If the pilot succeeds, we will seek to expand it. One major step needed before expansion should be completed by October 2006, when all R01 applications must be submitted electronically.

This is an important development for applicants, as it will significantly reduce the duration between submission of the application and the time at which you may *resubmit*. Currently, if you were to submit an application at, say, the February 1 deadline, the soonest you could receive feedback and thus be able to resubmit would be two cycles later—that is, in November, one month after the October deadline (the deadlines for resubmissions are one month after the regular submission date). The new system, however, would make it possible to turn your application around for a July resubmission deadline.

*The Payline.* The payline is a funding cut-off point set by the I/C at the beginning of the fiscal year, which starts on October 1. It is based on the number of grants the I/C expects to fund. The payline is usually set conservatively at the beginning of the fiscal year; thus, those applications whose priority score is within the payline are funded, and others that are near but not within the payline are deferred to later in the year. At year's end, when the I/C has a clearer budget picture, the payline may be raised and several more grants, including some of those that had been deferred, may be funded.

Following National Advisory Council review, there are four possible actions:

1. Approved for funding.

2. Primary responsibility transferred to another I/C that agrees to fund it.

3. Deferred for later funding decision, usually at the end of the fiscal year.

4. Not funded; file is closed.

NIAID provides an excellent question-and-answer dialogue online on how it arrives at its funding decisions.[2]

*Just-In-Time Information.* For applications reviewed by the CSR and scored within a certain fundable range, the NIH requests updated support information, certification of Institutional Review Board (IRB) approval, and human subject education certification. However, these requests are not a guarantee of funding.

## Post-Review Timetable

1. Upon receiving a documentation control form from the program director and verifying selection of funding, an NIH grants management specialist begins the process of developing an award. This involves a cost analysis of the proposed budget, a review for administrative compliance with Department of Health and Human Services (HHS) and NIH policies, and, finally, *negotiations* with the grantee business official and/or the PI. The primary purpose of negotiating an award is to establish the appropriate funding level, resolve identified problems, and agree on specialized terms and condition of the award, if needed. The degree and form of negotiation depend on a variety of factors, such as the dollar amount and complexity of the project and the nature of the problems identified. Negotiation can be done either by phone or through correspondence; however, sometimes an on-site visit may be made to address certain issues or problems in person.

2. Once your application is approved by the I/C's National Advisory Council, you will be contacted within six weeks by the grants management staff to negotiate the award. At the same time, a *notice of grant award* (NGA) is prepared by an NIH grants management officer. The NGA is a legally binding document sent to business offices that establishes funding levels, the period of support, and terms and conditions of the award.

3. The award amount is then forwarded to the NIH's Office of Grants Management (OGM), where it is recorded as an obligation in the NIH official accounting records. The NGA letter is then electronically transmitted to the grantee's business office (or sent by post, if the recipient is does not have e-mail capabilities).

4. How long until your funding begins? The timeframe between the day you mail off your application and the day your grant begins can vary. It takes about four months from submission to get your initial peer review results, and then another three to five months to get your award. That is the *official estimate*. My own experience has been that it takes somewhat longer; I usually set my award period (indicated on the Face Page and the Budget form of the proposal) to begin one year from the submission date. It may come earlier, and that is fine; however, you want to be conservative in your estimates so that you are not counting on funds to begin flowing before they actually do. Part of the variation depends on whether your application qualifies for expedited council review. Applications that qualify for expedited review have a percentile within the payline and no concerns identified by the study section or the National Advisory Council. Another factor is when in the fiscal year it is reviewed. Again, however, this timetable is due to change at some point in 2006, if the transition to electronic submission goes as scheduled.

Payments for grants awarded by the NIH are made through the Division of Payment Management and are primarily made by electronic funds transfer. The grantee can request HHS grant funds by calling the Division of Payment Management to request use of the CASHLINE process or by accessing SMARTLINK II through the Internet. Funds are deposited directly into the recipient's bank account on the next business day. Downloadable forms and payment inquiries can be directed to

Division of Payment Management
P.O. Box 6021
Rockville, MD 20852
(301) 443-1660

or by accessing http://www.dpm.psc.gov/.

If your application is not funded or is deferred for funding, contact your program officer. Ask whether it's worth revising and resubmitting for the next review cycle. The program officer makes the final funding decision, taking into account the advice of peer reviewers and council.

If you are granted an award and want to request additional funds to expand the scope of your project, a competing supplemental application must be submitted according to established deadlines. These applications undergo dual review and compete for funds with all other investigator-initiated competing applications.

If you are not ready to begin running your grant, you can submit a request to the program director at the NIH grants management office to push back the release of funds for up to a year. If you do this, you can draw funds from the Division of Payment Management only when you are ready to run your grant, which avoids premature expiration of your grant support from the awarding I/C. Contact your program director for more information.

You might also want to contact your program officer to clear any doubts about your summary statement, get more feedback from the review, and/or find out the status of your application. To find a program officer, see the staff contact list posted on the I/C's Web site.

If you aren't happy with the outcome of the peer review, you might wonder if there is an appeal process. I take this bit of wisdom from the NIAID site:

> Though you can appeal a review for errors in the review itself—not scientific opinion—
> we strongly advise against it. Appealing wastes time. Even if you win an appeal, in
> most cases you will still have to revise and resubmit your application, which could have
> been done in the first place.

While it is true that one might be inclined to discount some of this advice, considering the source, I suggest that you do avoid an appeal if you possibly can. Bite the bullet and move on to the resubmission process (discussed later in this chapter).

## THE SUMMARY STATEMENT

The summary statement provides a great deal of information: reviewer critiques, a summary of the review discussion, your priority score and percentile, the recommended budget, human and animal subjects codes (which indicate that requirements have or have not been fulfilled), and any administrative comments. The NIH mails it to you with the study section roster, which lists reviewers but does not identify which reviewers were assigned to your application. You, of course, already have known the names on this list for several months, assuming you looked them up at the beginning of the writing of the proposal.

If you have any questions about your summary statement, call the program officer listed in your mailer. Please note that a summary statement is not meant to be an exhaustive critique. Instead, it provides the highlights of the review discussion. You'll use this information to revise the application, if necessary (see the discussion of the resubmission process later in the chapter). However, keep in mind that the summary statement is not meant to be a teaching tool that contains every point reviewers found to be problematic.

## THE PERCENTILE RANK

For unsolicited research applications—but not career (K) award applications—reviewed at the CSR, the NIH turns your priority score into a percentile. A percentile ranks your application relative to the other applications reviewed by your study section at its last three meetings. Since percentiles help indicate the spread of applications in a study section review, you should pay closer attention to the percentile than to the priority score. A percentile roughly translates to the percentage of applications receiving a better priority score during a one-year interval.

Why does the NIH do this? According to the NIAID Web site, about 15 years ago, the NIH began using percentiles to counter a trend called *priority score creep,* in which study sections were increasingly giving applications better priority scores to the point where the scores had little meaning. Percentiles counter this trend by ranking applications relative to others scored by the same study section. Even with percentiling, priority scores continue to cluster in the outstanding range. Reviewers typically give as many as two thirds of their applications priority scores between 100 and 200.

## The Success Rate

*The success rate is not the same as the percentile rank.* A clear explanation of the *success rate* is given by the National Institute of General Medical Science (NIGMS) Web site: The success rate is the total number of grant applications that are funded in a given fiscal year divided by the number of grant applications that were peer reviewed.

The success rate for R01 grants differs from the *percentile ranks* for R01 grants in several ways:

• The percentile ranks are calculated using *all applications* reviewed by the initial review group, including applications assigned to *other* NIH Institutes and Centers. Grants assigned to NIGMS (remember, this information comes from the NIGMS Web site) tend to receive better priority scores than the NIH average. Thus, more than 20% of NIGMS grant applications rank better than the 20th percentile.

• The NIGMS success rate (for example) is typically higher than the percentile ranks of the funded applications. Applications that are amended and resubmitted during the same fiscal year are only counted once in the success rate calculations, whereas all applications, both original and amended versions, are included when the percentiles are calculated. Therefore, funding all applications with ranks better than, say, the 20th percentile will result in a success rate greater than 20% when revised versions of some projects are removed from the success rate base.

Why should this distinction matter to you? The I/C does not rely solely on a percentile cutoff or payline to make its funding decisions. These decisions are based on a number of additional factors, including whether the proposal comes from a new investigator, the level of other funding available to the investigator, the potential of the proposal to have a large impact on science as judged by the I/C scientific staff, and the existence of other grants funded by the I/C or other components of the NIH that cover similar scientific territory. These factors, along with the priority score, the comments on the summary statement, and the advice of the National Advisory Council are considered together to make final funding decisions.

But let's face it: The percentile cutoff exercises a great deal of influence on whether a particular application gets funded or not. However, when trying to estimate the probability of any given application (*your* application) being funded, the odds are usually better than you would be led to believe by the percentile rank.

## THE REVIEW CRITERIA

The NIH provides an excellent summary of the five criteria by which reviewers are instructed to review an application. These were recently revised October 12, 2004, and can be accessed on the NIH Web site.[3]

## Background on the Review Criteria

The goal of the NIH Roadmap initiative is to accelerate and strengthen the behavioral and biomedical research enterprise. During consultation with the extramural scientific community that led to the development of the NIH Roadmap process, it was frequently mentioned that the criteria used to evaluate research grant applications were not placing appropriate emphasis on some important types of biomedical and behavioral research. The Roadmap Trans-NIH Clinical Research Workforce Committee proposed a modification of the NIH peer review criteria for investigator-initiated research grant applications that would better accommodate interdisciplinary, translational, and clinical projects. The updated review criteria were adopted at the August 5, 2004, meeting of the directors of the NIH Institutes and Centers.

## Implementation of the Review Criteria

Since the summer of 2005, reviewers have been instructed to use the review criteria shown below as the basis for evaluating research grant applications and for assigning a single, global score for each scored application. The score reflects the overall impact that the project could have on the advancement of science. The emphasis on each criterion may vary from one application to another, and an application need not be strong in all categories to be judged likely to have a major scientific impact.

Future RFAs and PAs, which will be published in the NIH "Guide for Grants and Contracts," will incorporate and employ these updated criteria as the basis for evaluating all research applications.

## The Criteria

*1. Significance.* Does this study address an important problem? If the aims of the application are achieved, how will scientific knowledge or clinical practice be advanced? What will be the effect of these studies on the concepts, methods, technologies, treatments, services, or preventative interventions that drive this field?

*2. Approach.* Are the conceptual or clinical framework, design, methods, and analyses adequately developed, well integrated, well reasoned, and appropriate to the aims of the project? Does the applicant acknowledge potential problem areas and consider alternative tactics?

> Criteria 1 (Significance) and 2 (Approach) should be addressed in Sections A (Specific Aims) and B (Background and Significance). Alternative methodological approaches should be addressed in Section D (Research Methods).

*3. Innovation.* Is the project original and innovative? For example, does the project challenge existing paradigms or clinical practice? Does it address an innovative hypothesis or critical barrier to progress in the field? Does the project develop or employ novel concepts, approaches, methodologies, tools, or technologies for this area?

> Criterion 3 (Innovation) should be addressed not only in Sections A and B, but in Sections C (Preliminary Studies) *if* innovation in technique plays a major role in the application and, correspondingly, in Section D (Research Design and Methods).

*4. Investigators.* Are the investigators appropriately trained and well suited to carry out this work? Is the work proposed appropriate to the experience level of the principal investigator (PI) and other researchers? If applicable, does the investigative team bring complementary and integrated expertise to the project?

> Criterion 4 (Investigators) will obviously be addressed mostly in Section C (Preliminary Studies), in the beginning, where you describe the research team.

*5. Environment.* Does the scientific environment in which the work will be done contribute to the probability of success? Does the proposed study benefit from unique features of the scientific environment or subject populations? Does it employ useful collaborative arrangements? Is there evidence of institutional support?

> Although you will presumably address Criterion 5 (Environment) on the Resources Page, you also will want to discuss the resources available to you throughout Section D (Research Design and Methods).

I suggest that when you begin drawing up an outline of your research proposal, you review these five criteria, and make sure that you not only address these points, but that you *draw attention* to them. Remember, the reviewers must read several applications and they have the criteria in front of them while they do so. You want them to be able literally to check off each one as satisfied. In addition, I refer you to Chapter 5 and the last section of the sample proposal, where I suggest you provide a summary section to specifically address each of the five criteria.

## Additional Review Criteria

In addition to the above criteria, the following items will continue to be considered in the determination of scientific merit and the priority score.

*Protection of Human Subjects From Research Risk.* The involvement of human subjects and protections from research risk relating to their participation in the proposed research will be assessed.

*Inclusion of Women, Minorities, and Children in Research.* The adequacy of plans to include subjects from both genders, all racial and ethnic groups and subgroups, and children as appropriate for the scientific goals of the research will be assessed. Plans for the recruitment and retention of subjects will also be evaluated.

*Care and Use of Vertebrate Animals in Research.* If vertebrate animals are to be used in the project, the five items described under Section F of the PHS Form 398 research grant application instructions will be assessed.

## Additional Review Considerations

*Budget.* The reasonableness of the proposed budget and the requested period of support in relation to the proposed research will be taken into consideration. However, the priority score should not be affected by the evaluation of the budget. But reviewers, being human, tend to look at the budget, and may penalize you if the budget seems too high—or too low. *If the latter,* they may take that as an indication of inexperience.

*Foreign Applications.* Foreign applications also receive additional consideration. Reviewers rate foreign applications for their ability to bring in talent or resources not available in the United States or to augment U.S. resources. Foreign applications have a good chance of getting funded if either the expertise or resources are not available here (e.g., if they have access to a unique study population). Reviewers will check whether a foreign application proposes research similar to that being done by U.S. investigators and whether there is a need for the research. If similar research is being done, the application will suffer in review.

## SBIR/STTR Review Criteria

The criteria are somewhat different for SBIR and STTR awards, and the NIH Web site outlines the differences.[4] Note that many of the criteria are identical with those described above; I shall only discuss those criteria that are *specific* to the SBIR or STTR.

*1. Significance.* Additional questions concerning the significance of the study include the following:

a. Does the proposed project have commercial potential to lead to a marketable product, process, or service? Does this study address an important problem?

b. What may be the anticipated commercial and societal benefits that may be derived from the proposed research?

c. If the aims of the application are achieved, how will scientific knowledge or clinical practice be advanced? What will be the effect of these studies on the concepts, methods, technologies, treatments, services, or preventative interventions that drive this field?

d. Does the application lead to enabling technologies (e.g., instrumentation, software) for further discoveries?

e. Will the technology have a competitive advantage over existing/alternate technologies that can meet the market needs?

*2. Approach.* Is the proposed plan a sound approach for establishing technical and commercial feasibility? Are the milestones and evaluation procedures appropriate?

*3. Innovation.* There are no differences in the Innovation criterion.

*4. Investigators.* Is the PI appropriately trained and capable of coordinating and managing the proposed SBIR/STTR? Are the relationships of the key personnel to the small business and to other institutions appropriate for the work proposed?

*5. Environment.* Does the scientific and technological environment in which the work will be done contribute to the probability of success?

**Table 9.3**   Approximate Scoring Ranges Corresponding to the Nature of the Critiques

| Range of Priority Scores | Distribution of Scores | Assessed Impact of Research | Overview of Weakness |
|---|---|---|---|
| 1.0 to 1.5 | 10% | High | Few weaknesses |
| 1.5 to 2.0 | 13% | High | Some weaknesses, easily fixed |
| 2.0 to 2.5 | 13% | High | Some moderate weaknesses |
| 2.5 to 3.0 | 13% | Moderate | Some moderate weaknesses and/or several moderate problems |
| Unscored | 50% | Minor | Some moderate weaknesses and/or serious problems |

## SCORING THE APPLICATION

Table 9.3 gives the approximate scoring ranges that will correspond to the nature of the critiques. You already know that applications whose priority scores fall into the bottom 50th percentile will be streamlined. The scores of applications in the top half of the range tend to be relatively evenly distributed, although with fewer at the very top of the distribution, as might be expected. Note that the perceived impact of the proposed research figures heavily into where in the distribution your score will fall, as do the nature of the weaknesses in study design and methodology.

## IF YOUR SCORE IS NOT IN THE FUNDABLE RANGE . . .

There are some tough aspects to being a researcher, the main one being that you send out your best work, and when you do, you open yourself up to criticism and rejection. Most applications submitted to the NIH *do not* get funded. Competition is tougher right now than it has been in the past several years, and that means that fewer applications receive funding. It is somewhat unusual to have an application funded the first time out. In fact, more people succeed on their *second* try than on their first, and still more succeed on their third attempt. More than half of NIH applications eventually get funded.

Still, it will probably rock you when you learn that your proposal did not make the payline. When you get the reviews, the first thing to do is nothing. No kidding. I've been there, and everyone I know who has submitted an NIH application has been there. Take a quick glance at the reviews, and then put them away for a bit. Allow yourself to absorb the shock for a week or so. *Do not* send off an angry e-mail or letter to the study section or SRA.

The next step is revise and resubmit your proposal. The NIH allows you to submit up to three times, including the initial submission and two resubmissions. This is true even if your application was unscored. (However, if you are responding to an RFA, resubmission may not be an option.)

The following section is taken from several sources, including the NIAID Web site and several of my colleagues. It outlines the most common criticisms that reviewers are apt to cite when an application receives an unfundable score.

## Common Reviewer Criticisms and Proposed Solutions

*General*

**Problem:** Lack of new or original ideas.

**Solution:** Is this idea salvageable? It may not be. Discuss this with your program officer and with colleagues in the area.

**Problem:** Poor writing; unclear, difficult to follow arguments.

**Solution:** Get help. There are editors, consultants, and colleagues who can help with this. Often, poor writing indicates that you didn't get the proposal done early enough so that you had time to send it out to colleagues for feedback.

**Problem:** Reviewers are not interested in the subject.

**Solution:** First, let me note that you may have to read between the lines to see if this is what the reviews indicate. Having so concluded, there are two avenues of approach, depending on a critical evaluation of whether it was your presentation made them lose interest, or whether they had no interest in the *subject*. If the former, you have some serious rewriting to do. You are *selling* something in your proposal, whether you like to put it that way or not. You are selling a need for this study; you are selling the contribution that this study will make to this literature. Have you done that? Get colleagues to read your proposal with that question specifically in mind. If you conclude that you have done a credible job of presenting your research question as important and interesting, and your study design as innovative, then you may conclude that the study section did not comprise the proper peers. Resubmit and request a different review group. Go back to Chapter 8 to review the procedures for learning about the study sections; in your resubmission letter, explain the expertise required to review your proposal. There is no guarantee that the study section composition will change, but it may have the desired effect.

*Specific Aims*

**Problem:** Aims are poorly focused, underdeveloped.

**Solution:** Ask yourself the following: If a reader were to look *only* at the aims, without having read any of the other material in this section, would he or she understand what precisely you intend to test in the proposal? If not, you need to hone them so they tell this portion of the story.

**Problem:** Aims are overly ambitious.

**Solution:** One problem here is that, at the point at which you are laying out your aims, you may not have yet begun thinking critically about the particulars of the study design. However, you need to do the two things somewhat simultaneously. Realistically think about the amount of work that the design calls for in any single year of the study period. Is it feasible? If not, you have to cut back. *Do not* figure that you'll go ahead and propose it, and worry about doing the work after you get the money; if your aims are perceived as too ambitious, you will not be funded. And, in the event your proposal is funded, you will have brought untold misery on yourself as you frantically attempt to meet your commitments. If you *fail* to meet them, for example by being unable to recruit research participants on the schedule on which you agreed (and signed off on) with the NIH, they may in fact halt your funding.

*Background and Significance*

**Problem:** Absence of an acceptable scientific rationale.

**Solution:** You are not telling your story well or correctly. You must think of your narrative as building a bridge: Each point of your argument must be supported, as by a sturdy column, by both empirical evidence and biological or psychological plausibility; else the bridge sags.

**Problem:** Uncritical approach.

**Solution:** Have you only cited those articles that help you make your case? At least one of the reviewers is going to be aware of those publications you have failed to cite. Have you pointed out the limitations in your *own* approach? If not, do so, and then explain why you did not choose an alternative. If your explanation doesn't hold water, perhaps you need to revise your approach.

**Problem:** Lack of knowledge of published relevant work.

**Solution:** There is no excuse for this. The Background and Significance section can be laborious to write, but you must satisfy the readers as to your grasp of the area.

**Problem:** The significance of your particular proposed study has not been convincingly stated.

**Solution:** Beef up that portion of the narrative; show importance to the I/C mission as well as to public health. Remember, you have two places where you can discuss this: under Specific Aims (Section A) and Background and Significance (Section B). Do not be modest about this. Provide a heading called "Significance," and then explain *clearly* why it is crucial that your proposed study be conducted.

**Problem:** Provided too much extraneous background information.

**Solution:** Outline the story you want to tell before you write it, and make that outline lean. In an outline, information extraneous to the main thrust of the story will stand out more clearly than in the text. Extraneous information detracts from the nice, linear story I encourage you to tell—and it annoys the reviewers.

*Preliminary Studies/Pilot Work*

**Problem:** The proposed research was not shown to be feasible by the proposed staff, given the resources.

**Solution:** Some researchers focus all their energy on the science and pay too little attention to feasibility. The reviewers, however, are equally concerned with both. Beef up the first part of the Preliminary Studies section (which, in Chapter 5, I suggested you call "Feasibility"). This is the section in which you describe your research team and their accomplishments. If you need more expertise, recruit additional experts, either as co-investigators, other professionals, and/or consultants with the required expertise. However, most of the expertise should reside within your core group.

**Problem:** Preliminary or pilot work was lacking.

**Solution:** There is no reason you should have to wait for the reviewers to tell you this; either you do or do not have adequate pilot data when you set out to write your proposal. The trick is not to kid yourself because you want to get your application in by a particular deadline. Unless the proposal is intended to be exploratory and you are using a mechanism such as the R21 (see Chapter 3), the application will be kicked back to you unless you can convince the reviewers that there is reason to think that (a) you will be able to carry out the proposed work and (b) your hypotheses are on the right track.

Remember, (1) Most proposals are not funded on the first time out, and it takes until the third submission for many; and (2) You only get up to three chances to submit (i.e., the initial submission plus up to two re-submissions, depending on the grant mechanism). Do not waste a submission because you were not adequately prepared (concerning the pilot data or other aspects of the proposal)!

*Research Design and Methods*

**Problem:** Lack of sufficient experimental detail.

**Solution:** This was discussed in Chapter 5, in the section on Research Design and Methods. There is a balance to be struck in your narrative—you must decide how much to tell and how much to leave out. However, the reviewers will expect a great deal of detail in the Research Design and Methods section of your proposal. As you mentally walk through the procedures, for example, what details did you omit that might raise a question for the reviewer? Think beyond what they mentioned in the pink sheets.

**Problem:** Overambitious, unrealistically large amount of work.

**Solution:** This was discussed in the Budgets section in Chapter 7. Obviously, the amount of work you propose bears directly on how much money you are asking for. If the reviewers' assessment is that you are proposing too much work for the money involved, it will reflect poorly on your perceived experience.

**Problem:** Insufficient discussion of obstacles and alternative approaches.

**Solution:** This was addressed at length in Chapter 5. For some reason, many investigators don't simply explain, "Here is why I didn't use approach B." There are two reasons to do this: First, you want to let the reviewers know that you are *aware* of and have *thought about* approach B; and second, you want to present your logic as to why you chose approach A. It will help also if you write what you will do if you get negative results in the trial or an approach doesn't pan out; include a decision tree in your proposal.

The following are specific areas in the Research Design and Methods section in which the reviewers will tend to penalize you:

- Insufficient experience in the proposed methodology
- Methods were underdeveloped
- Inclusion/exclusion criteria were not well justified
- Availability of human research participants not assured
- Inadequate description of instruments or variables and concerns about validity or reliability of the data collection methods
- Concerns about the lack of or inadequate blinding of outcome assessment
- Inadequate description or specification of the outcome measure
- Overambitious proposal; too much work for funds and/or time period
- Concerns about validity or reliability of the outcome

Specific and common criticism about intervention and/or controls (if applicable) are:

- Interventions poorly described
- Interventions unstandardized
- Intervention of questionable potency
- Inadequate description of plans to monitor adherence
- Failure to address contamination or co-intervention in the control group
- Inadequate randomization procedures
- Unblinded administration of the intervention

Common problems in data analysis and sample size calculations for which reviewers tend to fault applicants include the following:

- Insufficient description of the analytic approach
- Lack of an intention-to-treat analytic strategy
- Inadequate control for potential confounders
- Insufficient description of the handling of missing data
- Not enough consideration of attrition

# RESUBMISSION

One of the main predictors of funding is perseverance. I've spoken to many researchers who simply opted out of the process after a rejection or two. The thing is, *everyone* gets a rejection or two (or more). If you have the qualifications, if you have a fundable idea, you should be able to get funded, so stay with it. Resubmit!

Now, you've gotten back the feedback from the study sections, your application was either unscored or scored but not in the funding range, and you plan to resubmit. What are your options? You can

1. Revise the application and resubmit it to the same study section.
2. Revise the application and resubmit it to a different study section.
3. Create a "new" application out of the original one and request a new study section.
4. Create a truly new application.

The NIAID Web site suggests that, to gauge whether an application would be considered "new" or revised, one should use this heuristic: If you revise more than 50%, it's a new application; if less, you must follow the rules for a revised application. Remember, you can revise two times. If your proposal does not get funded on the third try, you can still resubmit, but the proposal must be *substantially* changed so it does not look like a revision. Keep the best parts of the old proposal, and ruthlessly cut away the rest. Give it a new title, of course, as well.

When revising, use the feedback from the study section, painful though it may be to gaze upon. You have advice from three smart people, and you should use it. Rewrite your specific aims as though from scratch; make sure your hypotheses follow smoothly and seamlessly from these. However, if it has been several years since you first submitted, keep in mind that the reviewers' comments may no longer be relevant. Finally, of course, *talk with your program officer*. Any information you can glean will help you focus your revision.

Just as when you revise a manuscript, you must write a letter addressing each of the reviewers' concerns regarding the previous submission, and you have three pages in which to do this. Don't fight with them, and don't be defensive. Be courteous in every regard. If you disagree—and you may—lay out your rationale for sticking with a particular strategy, but choose very carefully the strategies you want to defend—and know that there shouldn't be many of them. The reviewers, particularly when they are the same reviewers (and it often is the case that the same reviewers will see a resubmitted application, although not always), will certainly begin by looking at the reviews of the previous submission and your revision letter. It is wise to make this chore as easy as possible for them. Mark the revised application in some way, using bold-faced type, for example, or arrows in the margin, to make it easy for them to find the revised text, and note the pages of the revised manuscript for every single change. Don't use colored type, because the colors won't photocopy. Do note that the reviewers will certainly be attuned to your degree of responsiveness to the previous critiques; address every single one of them.

Keep in mind that there are no guarantees in this business. When you get a "revise and resubmit" letter from a journal, you'll have noticed that the writer is very careful not to be overly encouraging and offers no guarantees: Think of the proposal resubmission process in the same way. Even if you have the same reviewers, they are not by any means obligated to lower your score (lower is good, remember) because you addressed the previous concerns. They may find new concerns. They will read your entire proposal, not just the fixes you have made, and will evaluate it on its merits. And, of course, there may be new reviewers; they may pay less attention to the criticisms of the previous reviewers and may even disagree with them.

What can you do about this? Do your work better. There is no proposal that cannot be improved, and since you don't have to do all the writing all over again, you now have more time, and some necessary distance, to read the proposal from start to finish. You also have time now to send it out to colleagues for comments. I said there are no guarantees in this business, but I will guarantee that if you take the time and trouble to send it out, you'll be glad you did.

Colleagues will find things that you will be astonished to have missed, having read the damn thing 30 or 40 times. It happens *every time*. The more colleagues you send it to, the better the final result will be. Of course, you should—and may well—have done this for the first submission, but do it again. If you have additional data, be sure to include them in the revision.

Go through the summary with a fine-tooth comb. Read between the lines and try to get a sense of what the reviewers are really saying about the proposal. Is it simply that there is too little pilot data to justify funding at this time? Or (if you can be honest with yourself about it), was the proposal too loose, did it not hang together well enough to convince them of the story you were trying to tell? Get advice not only from colleagues, but from your program officer as well; as I've said before, he or she is there to help you. Your program officer may be able to give you more insight into the discussion at the review meeting.

Finally, if you responded to an RFA or PA and were not funded, you *cannot* resubmit. However, there is no reason you can't submit a new application that is highly similar as an investigator-initiated R01.

## The Introduction to the Revised Application

The letter I've been talking about is actually the introduction to your revised application. You must include it, and it can be no more than three pages in length (those three pages *do not* count toward the application page limit). In addition to responding to the reviewers' criticisms, you can provide a summary of how you have substantially changed the application. You can also summarize any new findings, or note other revisions you have made, in addition to those requested by the reviewers.

## Submission Deadlines for Revised Applications

One last note: The submission deadlines for *revised* applications are one month later than those for *initial* applications. Thus, for an R01 resubmission, the deadlines would be July 1 (rather than June 1), November 1 (rather than October 1), and March 1 (rather than February 1). The PHS 398 instructions and Table 8.2 provide submission dates for all applications.

## Completing the Application

At some point later in the process, you may receive requests for the just-in-time documentation. This may include your list of other support; human subjects assurance; certification of IRB approval of research plan; certification of human subjects education; animal welfare assurance; and/or certification of Institutional Animal Care and Use Committee (IACUC) approval.

It is a little too early to celebrate, however. You will think, "Why would they be requesting this information if they didn't plan to fund me?" but don't go spending the money quite yet. This is a great sign, but no award is official until you receive official word, which comes via the Notice of Grant Award. When *that* arrives, by all means, break out the champagne.

## NOTES

1. You can access "A Straightforward Description of What Happens to Your Research Project Grant Application After It Is Received for Peer Review" at http://www.csr.nih.gov/REVIEW/peerrev.htm.

2. The question-and-answer dialogue can be accessed at http://www.niaid.nih.gov/ncn/qa/funding dec.htm.

3. The five review criteria are available at http://grants.nih.gov/grants/guide/notice-files/NOT-OD-05-002.html. These updated criteria replace those adopted on June 27,1997.

4. SBIR and STTR review criteria can be found at http://grants2.nih.gov/grants/funding/sbirsttr_Reviewcriteria.htm

# Postscript

## *Be Careful What You Wish For . . .*

At this moment, you think, "*Just send me the money, and I'll worry about actually running the project later.*" Well, "later" does arrive, sooner than you expected, and although my intention is not to rain on your parade, I do want to suggest a little caution. I mentioned earlier that you should not be so fixated on getting funded that you misrepresent your capability to actually carry out the research that you have now promised. If you do that, and if you are funded, you can look forward to a certain amount of misery over the funding period while you desperately try to hold up your end of the bargain. Once again, I recommend you look at the National Institute of Allergy and Infectious Disease (NIAID) Web site, which provides a comprehensive description of what happens once you are funded.[1]

Once you have the money, what do you do? First, let's discuss the document that notifies you of your good fortune, the *notice of grant award.*

## NOTICE OF GRANT AWARD

When your notice of grant award (NGA) arrives, so does your big moment: The NIH has now officially notified you that they are going to fund your grant. They may not give you all that you originally requested, but they will give you enough. (If they have really cut you to the point that you feel that you cannot carry out your study, talk to your program officer, who actually may be able to do something about it.)

The NGA contains a good deal of information, and you should read it all. It will tell you the following:

- The amount of funding you will receive for each year of the award.
- The start and end dates of the award.
- The terms and conditions of the award.
- The name and contact information of your *grants management specialist*. This person is not your program officer; the grants management specialist deals with the negotiation, award, and administration of a grant, and also interprets and applies grant policies.
- Restrictions, if any, on your actions until specified requirements have been fulfilled (e.g., for some types of grants, you may need to register with either the Centers for Disease Control and Prevention or the United States Department of Agriculture before you can begin your research).

## MANAGING YOUR GRANT AWARD

The budget that you submitted with your application will have been written at least several months and possibly even a year before the award is actually granted, and some things may have changed in the interim. For example, you may have found that an assay for which you requested funds can be done for free in a colleague's laboratory; at the same time, however, you may find that your institution has given an across-the-board raise to your staff. The NIH is very understanding about the vagaries to which you are exposed, and for that reason does not insist on a line-item budget in which you need to seek special permission for every deviation, no matter how minor.

*However,* things should not change *too* much, because you will eventually have to justify the changes in your yearly progress reports. If, for some reason, things do change a great deal (e.g., if you move to a new institution in the middle of your award period), discuss this with your program officer and with your grants management specialist. Their job is not to hinder you; it is to help. Everyone wants you to be able to conduct your research.

If there have been significant changes, I suggest that you immediately draft a new budget, one that reflects the reality at the time your award begins. Do not simply spend money as you need to without reconciling the expenditures with your balance. Parcel out funds parsimoniously; don't celebrate your new award by treating your staff to new computers, for example, unless they really need them. Unforeseen emergencies tend to arise, and you want to have funds left over that will allow you to deal with them.

On the other hand, if you are not spending your money as planned, this too presents a problem. Have you failed to hire personnel needed to get things rolling? Are you not recruiting enough subjects, so the subject reimbursements are not being spent? Have you failed to bring your consultants in to do whatever was planned, and so the money set aside for them remains unspent? If any of these occur, it suggests that your project is not running on schedule. In addition, there is another, somewhat subtle, consideration. You are a hero to your institution to the extent that, among other things, you bring in indirect costs. However, the indirect costs get awarded to the institution only on funds you have spent; they do not simply just receive the entire amount when the grant is funded. To make your institution love you (even more than it presumably already does), you have to spend the money.

Pace yourself so that most, but not all, of the money is spent at the end of each year of your grant. If you can, give yourself a cushion—say 20%—but remember this: Five years (the longest possible funding period) seems like forever, but the end comes faster than you can ever imagine. The money needs to last you through that period, but also needs to be spent by the end of it. (If the money is not spent *and* if you still have work to do on the project, you may request a no-cost extension; if awarded such an extension, you are granted an additional period during which you can use the unspent funds to complete the project.)

I strongly urge you to conduct the business of your grant award as though you may be audited tomorrow—which might be the case, by the way. The NIH conducts institution-wide audits, and when they arrive at *your* institution, they may well want an accounting of every nickel. They may want to see every consent form, to support your assertion that the money was indeed spent on conducting the study. They may want to conduct a *site visit*, which means that NIH personnel will show up in your lab to ask—or they may request you travel to Bethesda to answer—questions concerning any and every aspect of the science and the finances related to your project. Assume that it will happen tomorrow and conduct business accordingly.

## YEARLY PROGRESS REPORTS

At the end of each budget year in your project, you will have an opportunity to explain changes in the previous year's budget when you submit your progress report. For example, if you had budgeted monies to pay for a procedure that turned out to be superfluous to the main point of your study and decided you needed an additional research assistant to help meet your recruitment goals, you need to lay that out in your progress report. You must also report changes in percentage of effort, especially for the principal investigator (PI). Remember, however, that the PI cannot go below 20% effort nor can the PI reduce his or her effort by 25% or more without NIH permission. Let me elaborate: It is not just that the PI cannot reduce his or her percentage of effort from, say, 50% to 25%, yielding a reduction of 25% in *absolute* terms; the PI cannot reduce his or her effort from, say, 30% to 20%—the absolute reduction of 10% is divided by the 30% to yield a *relative* reduction of 33%.

In addition to the budget changes, the NIH would like to know what you've accomplished during the previous year: conference presentations, publications, and so forth. These reports are not unduly onerous, but take them seriously and complete them in good time. These yearly reports, by the way, are in addition to the *quarterly recruitment reports* you must submit. None of these reports are undoable, as long as you stay on top of them.

## A LAST WORD

It has never been my intention in this book to frighten you or cause you to lose heart. At the same time, I wouldn't be doing my job if I didn't give it to you straight. The NIH represents the big leagues, and of course, it isn't going to be easy to play. However, the NIH funds a lot of grants every year. Many of those go to first-time investigators, and not just in the form of Career Development Awards. If you have a good idea, a good research team, the requisite expertise, and a lot of stamina, download the forms and start thinking of a title.

There is only one reason to remain in an occupation in which you must beg for funds every few years, and that is because you just don't want to do anything else. I know a lot of people who feel that way, and I am lucky to be one myself. However, the saying "Nothing succeeds like success" has never been truer: Go through the process and stay with it even if you aren't funded the first—or second or even the third—time around, and when at last you are funded, I am sure that you'll agree that the effort was worth it, and then some.

## NOTE

1. See http://www.niaid.nih.gov/ncn/grants/manage/index.htm.

**Activity Code.** The three-digit identifier of a specific mechanism or award type (e.g., R01 is a research project grant). Usually, activity codes are grouped together in different budget presentations to form funding mechanisms. Major series of activity codes are as follows:

F—fellowships

K—career development awards

N—research contracts

P—program project and research center grants

R—research project grants

S—research-related programs

T—training grants

U—cooperative agreements

Y—interagency agreements

**Administrative Supplement.** Funds awarded on a noncompeting basis to an existing grant to cover additional expenses within the scope of the existing award. Some examples include

- Additional funds to cover unanticipated, inordinate cost increases that would affect the ability of the PI to carry out the project.
- Funds to cover a time extension period, also known as *bridge funding*.

The request is submitted directly to the awarding I/C at the NIH and funds are awarded "administratively"—in other words, without competitive review by a study section or national advisory council.

**Adverse Effect.** Unanticipated problem or unfavorable symptom or disease occurring during a clinical study, though not necessarily caused by the study treatment, which harms subjects or others: for example, a loss of research records, drug overdose, serious symptom, or death.

**Adverse Event.** Occurrence of an adverse effect occurring during a clinical study.

**Advisory Council.** Chartered NIH I/C advisory committee that performs second-level review, makes funding and policy recommendations, and helps develop research initiatives.

**Animal Welfare Assurance.** Document an institution and all performance sites involving animals in research must have on file with Office of Laboratory Animal Welfare before a Public Health Services agency may award a grant or contract.

**Appendix.** Unessential, supplemental information an applicant may include with a grant application, including publications, manuscripts, abstracts, patents, questionnaires, data collection instruments, and photographs. Peer reviewers are not obligated to review appendixes.

**Asian.** Human subjects term indicating a person having origins in the original peoples of East Asia, Southeast Asia, or the Indian subcontinent including Cambodia, China, India, Japan, Korea, Malaysia, Pakistan, the Philippine Islands, Thailand, or Vietnam.

**Award.** Legally binding document stating the government has obligated funds, including direct costs and facilities and administrative costs.

**Biosketch.** Form in the PHS 398 grant application in which the applicant states employment history, relevant publications, and ongoing and completed research support.

**Black or African American.** Human subjects term indicating a person having origins in the black racial groups of Africa. "Haitian" or "negro" can be used in addition to "Black" or "African American."

**Career Development Award.** Award that supports PhDs and clinicians seeking training to develop a career in biomedical research. Activity codes are K01, K02, K08, K22, K23, K24, and K25.

**Center for Scientific Review.** See *NIH Center for Scientific Review.*

**Child.** Person under legal age for consenting to research treatments or procedures as defined by the law where the research is conducted.

**Clinical Research.** Human subjects term indicating research conducted on human subjects or on material of human origin identifiable with the source person. Policy covers large- and small-scale, exploratory, and observational studies. There are three types: patient-oriented research, epidemiologic and behavioral studies, and outcomes and health services research.

**Clinical Trial.** Human subjects term indicating a prospective study of human subjects designed to answer questions about biomedical or behavioral interventions (e.g., drugs, treatments, devices, or new ways of using known treatments to determine whether they are safe and effective). See also *Phase I, Phase II, Phase III, NIH-Defined Phase III,* and *Phase IV Clinical Trials.*

**Co-Investigator.** An individual involved with the principal investigator in the scientific development or execution of the project. The co-investigator (collaborator) may be employed by, or be affiliated with, the applicant and/or grantee organization or another organization participating in the project under a consortium agreement. This individual would typically devote a specific percentage of effort to the project and would be identified as key personnel.

**Competing Application.** New or competing continuation grant application that must undergo initial peer review.

**Competing Continuation.** Also known as *Type 2, recompeting,* or *renewal* grant whose project period is over and for which an applicant is again seeking NIH support.

**Competing Renewal.** See *Competing Continuation.*

**Computer Retrieval of Information on Scientific Programs.** Also known as *CRISP.* NIH database with descriptions of awarded grants and contracts, including financial data, project abstracts, and indexing terms.

**Consortium Agreement.** A formalized agreement whereby a research project is carried out by the grantee and one or more other organizations that are separate legal entities. Under the agreement, the grantee must perform a substantive role in the conduct of the planned research and not merely serve as a conduit of funds to another party or parties. These agreements typically involve a specific percentage of effort from the consortium organization's principal investigator and a categorical breakdown of costs, such as personnel, supplies, and other allowable expenses, including facilities and administrative costs.

**Consultant.** An individual who provides professional advice or services for a fee, but normally not as an employee of the engaging party. In unusual situations, an individual may be both a consultant and an employee of the same party, receiving compensation for some services as a consultant and for other work as a salaried employee. To prevent apparent or actual conflicts of interest, grantees and consultants must establish written guidelines indicating the conditions of payment of consulting fees. Consultants may also include firms that provide paid professional advice or services.

**Cover Letter.** Letter attached to a grant application or contract proposal that may request a peer review group or I/C or provide other information.

**CRISP.** See *Computer Retrieval of Information on Scientific Programs.*

**CSR.** See *NIH Center for Scientific Review.*

**Data and Safety Monitoring Board.** Also known as *DSMB.* Independent committee that reviews clinical trial progress and safety, and advises the funding I/C whether to continue, modify, or terminate a trial.

**Data Sharing.** Policy requiring researchers requesting more than $500,000 in direct costs in a year to include a data-sharing plan with their grant application or explain why data sharing is not possible.

**Deferred.** Delay in an initial peer review of a grant application by a scientific review group, usually to the next peer review cycle, because of insufficient information. A deferral is also a postponement of a funding decision until after the June or July peer review meetings for applications whose percentiles rank beyond the payline. I/Cs typically fund these applications in percentile order until moneys are used up for that fiscal year.

**Detailed Budget for Initial Budget Period.** Form page 4 in the PHS 398 grant application, used to request a budget over $250,000 for the initial budget period only. See also *Entire Project Period Budget Page.*

**Detailed Budget Page.** See *Detailed Budget for Initial Budget Period* and *Entire Project Period Budget Page.*

**DSMB.** See *Data and Safety Monitoring Board.*

**Dual Assignment.** Assignment of a grant application to two NIH I/Cs simultaneously. The primary I/C manages the application and awards and administers the grant, if it is funded. The secondary I/C assumes this responsibility only if the primary I/C is unable or unwilling to support the application.

**Dual Peer Review.** Peer review process used by the NIH. The first-level, initial peer review, provides a judgment of scientific merit. Generally conducted by an I/C's advisory council, second-level review makes funding recommendations in the context of program priorities and balance. See also *Integrated Review Group* and *Scientific Review Group*.

**Electronic Research Administration.** Also known as *eRA*. Infrastructure in development to allow the NIH to electronically receive, review, and administer grant awards. When completed, it will create an online dialogue between the NIH and its grantees covering the entire life cycle of a grant.

**Entire Project Period Budget Page.** Form page 5 in the PHS 398 grant application. Used to request a budget over $250,000 for a full project period. See also *Detailed Budget for Initial Budget Period*.

**eRA.** See *Electronic Research Administration*.

**Expedited Second-Level Peer Review.** Second-level review of qualifying applications by a subset of members of the I/C Advisory Council after initial peer review. To qualify, an application must be within the payline and have no concerns identified by the study section or council.

**Extramural Research.** Research supported by the NIH through a grant, contract, cooperative agreement, or other funding mechanism to an external organization.

**F&A Cost.** See *Facilities and Administrative Cost*.

**F Awards.** See *Fellowship Awards*.

**Face Page.** Form page 1 in the PHS 398 grant application.

**Facilities and Administrative Cost.** Cost associated with the general operation of an institution and the conduct of its research activities. Formerly known as *indirect costs*. The Department of Health and Human Services supports full reimbursement for facilities and administrative costs for most grant programs. Allowable facilities and administrative costs include the following:

- Depreciation use allowance
- Facilities operations and maintenance
- General administration and expenses
- Departmental administration
- Sponsored project administration
- Libraries

**Fellowship.** Award that provides individual grants to students and scientists at predoctoral, postdoctoral, or senior levels; to minorities and the disabled; and to postdoctoral trainees in the National Institute of Allergy and Infectious Disease (NIAID) Division of Intramural Research to develop careers in biomedical research. Activity codes are F31, F32, F33, and F35.

**Fiscal Year.** Federal budget year: October 1 to September 30.

**Fundable Score.** Percentile or priority score for a grant application that falls within an NIH I/C's percentile rank for funding, called the *payline*.

**Grant Budget Period.** Interval into which a grant project period is divided for funding and reporting purposes, usually 12 months.

**Grant Project Period.** Total period a project has been recommended for support, which may include more than one competitive segment. For example, a project period for a grant begun in 1990 can be divided into competitive segments 1990–1994, 1994–1998, and so forth.

**Grant Start Date.** Official date a grant award begins; same as the first day of the first budget period.

**"Guide for Grants and Contracts."** See NIH *"Guide for Grants and Contracts."*

**Health Disparities.** Differences in the incidence, prevalence, mortality, burden of diseases, and other adverse health conditions that exist among specific population groups in the United States.

**Health Insurance Portability and Accountability Act.** Also known as *HIPAA*. Law from 1996 that amends the Internal Revenue Code to improve portability of health insurance coverage, promote medical savings accounts, improve access to long-term care services and coverage, and simplify administration of health insurance.

**Healthy People 2010.** A statement of national health objectives designed to identify the most significant preventable threats to health and to establish national goals to reduce these threats.

**HIPAA.** See *Health Insurance Portability and Accountability Act.*

**Hispanic or Latino.** Human subjects term indicating a person of Cuban, Mexican, Puerto Rican, South or Central American, or other Spanish culture or origin, regardless of race. "Spanish origin" can also be used.

**Human Subject.** Legally defined term indicating a living person with whom an investigator directly interacts or intervenes, or from whom the investigator obtains identifiable, private information. Regulations apply to human organs, tissues, body fluids, and recorded information from identifiable people.

**Human Subjects Assurance.** See *Institutional Assurance of Protection for Human Subjects.*

**Human Subjects Code.** Number a scientific review group places on a summary statement during initial peer review reflecting the application of human subjects regulations to a project and the inclusion of women, children, and racial and ethnic populations. Some codes indicate a human subjects concern that would result in a bar to award.

**Human Subjects Concern.** Human subjects term indicating any actual or potential unacceptable risk or inadequate protection against risk to human subjects. See also *Human Subjects Code.*

**IACVC.** See *Institutional Animal Care and Use Committee.*

**Indirect Costs.** Formerly used term. See *Facilities and Administrative Cost.*

**Informed Consent.** Person's voluntary agreement, based upon adequate knowledge and understanding, to participate in research or undergo a medical procedure. In giving informed consent, a human subject may not waive legal rights or release or appear to release an investigator or sponsor from liability for negligence.

**Initial Peer Review.** First level of peer review by non-NIH scientific experts, called *peer reviewers,* who assess the scientific merit of research grant applications and contract proposals. The

NIH Center for Scientific Review conducts peer review of investigator-initiated grants. I/Cs review applications and proposals with their own review requirements:

Program projects (P)

Cooperative agreements (U)

Training grants (T)

Career development grants (K)

Contracts (N)

Applications responding to requests for applications and requests for proposals

See also *Dual Peer Review, Integrated Review Group, Scientific Review Group,* and *Study Section.*

**Initial Peer Review Criteria for Grants.** Basis for assessing the scientific merit of NIH research grant applications for initial peer review.

**Initial Review Group.** Formerly used term; see *Integrated Review Group* and *Study Section.*

**Initiative.** Request for applications, request for proposals, or program announcement stating the interest of one or more I/Cs in receiving applications or proposals in a given area because of a programmatic need or scientific opportunity. Requests for applications (RFAs) and requests for proposals (RFPs) generally have monies set aside to fund the research; program announcements (PAs) generally do not. Initiatives are published in the NIH "Guide For Grants and Contracts."

**Institutes and Centers.** Term used by the NIH to denote major NIH organizations: institutes, such as the National Institute of Allergy and Infectious Disease (NIAID), National Heart, Lung, and Blood Institute (NHLBI), and centers, such as the John E. Fogarty International Center (FIC).

**Institutional Animal Care and Use Committee.** Also known as *IACUC.* Committee established by a research institution to ensure that the care and use of animals in research is appropriate and humane. IACUCs independently determine that an institution is meeting requirements to ensure humane care and use of animals and is complying with regulations. They also review and approve protocols.

**Institutional Animal Care and Use Committee Certification.** Approval by an institutional animal care and use committee (IACUC) of a project involving research animals. Grant applications and contract proposals must include verification of IACUC certification before award.

**Institutional Assurance of Protection for Human Subjects.** Human subjects term indicating a document filed with the Office for Human Research Protections, Department of Health and Human Services, formalizing a research institution's commitment to protect human subjects. Institutions can now use an online federal assurance of protection for human subjects.

**Institutional Base Salary.** The annual compensation that the applicant organization pays for an employee's appointment, whether that individual's time is spent on research, teaching, patient care, or other activities. The base salary excludes any income that an individual may be permitted to earn outside of duties to the applicant organization. Base salary may not be increased as a result of replacing institutional salary funds with NIH grant funds.

**Institutional Business Official.** Official designated by a grantee organization for the award and administration of its NIH grants. He or she ensures that the organization complies with the terms and conditions of award and other administrative requirements and is accountable for the use of NIH funds and the performance of the research. He or she may sign an institutional assurance of protection for human subjects and animal welfare assurance, making a commitment on behalf of the institution that policy requirements in those areas will be met.

**Institutional Review Board.** Also known as an *IRB*. Committee set up by a research institution to ensure the protection of rights and welfare of human subjects. IRBs make an independent determination to approve, modify, or disapprove clinical research protocols based on the adequate protection of human subjects, as required by federal regulations and local institutional policy. IRBs must register with the Office for Human Research Protections, Department of Health and Human Services.

**Institutional Review Board Certification of Approval.** Human subjects term indicating that an institutional review board (IRB) has approved a clinical research protocol, consent form (if applicable), monitoring and reporting procedures, and plans for analyzing intervention differences among different groups of human subjects (e.g., women and minorities, ethnic or racial subgroups, and children). IRBs also approve research annually with a noncompeting grant application and any time there are major changes in a research protocol or other procedures. IRBs must also certify approval of results of subset analyses in recompeting grant applications and contract proposals.

**Integrated Review Group.** Also known as an *IRG*. Group of review study sections organized around an area of science that performs initial peer review in the NIH Center for Scientific Review. These study sections share common intellectual and human resources. See also *Dual Peer Review, Peer Review, Scientific Review Group,* and *Study Section.*

**Investigator, New.** See *New Investigator.*

**Investigator-Initiated Research.** Also known as *unsolicited research*. Research funded as a result of an investigator's submitting a research grant application to the NIH. Unsolicited applications are reviewed by chartered Center for Scientific Review scientific review groups. See also *Targeted Research.*

**IRB.** See *Institutional Review Board.*

**IRG.** See *Integrated Review Group.*

**Just-in-Time.** Application timeframe that requires applicants to send some information to the NIH only if an award is likely. Just-in-time is used for other support information and other items, including certification of institutional review board approval, federal assurance, institutional animal care and use committee certification, and a letter stating that key personnel have been trained in protecting human subjects.

**K Awards.** See *Career Development Award.*

**Key Personnel.** In addition to the principal investigator, key personnel are defined as individuals who contribute to the scientific development or execution of the project in a substantive, measurable way, whether or not salaries are requested. Typically, these individuals have doctoral or other professional degrees, although individuals at the master's or baccalaureate level should be included if their involvement meets the definition of key personnel. Consultants should also be included if they meet the definition. Key personnel must devote measurable effort to the project whether or not salaries are requested—"zero percent" effort or "as needed" are not acceptable levels for those designated as key personnel.

**Mechanism.** Budget activity or grouping of related activities that may vary for different budget presentations. Mechanisms usually combine activity codes: for example, the training mechanism includes career (K), fellowship (F), and training (T) activity codes. Other frequently used mechanisms are research project grants, small business grants, and contracts. Often used interchangeably with activity code; however, officially it refers to budget activities.

**Minimal Risk.** Human subjects term indicating that the probability and magnitude of harm or discomfort anticipated in research are not greater than those encountered in daily life or routine tests.

**Minority Group.** Human subjects term indicating a subset of the U.S. population distinguished by either racial, ethnic, or cultural heritage. The categories are American Indian or Alaskan Native, Asian, Black or African American, Hispanic or Latino, and Native Hawaiian and other Pacific Islander. Applications and proposals should describe subgroups to be included in the research. Inclusion should be determined by the scientific questions under examination and their relevance to these racial or ethnic groups. Not every study will include all minority groups or subgroups.

**Misconduct in Science.** Fabrication, falsification, plagiarism, or other practices that seriously deviate from those commonly accepted in the scientific community for conducting or reporting research.

**Modular Budget Justification Page.** Form for modular budget justification in the PHS 398 grant application, used for modular grant budget requests under $250,000. For nonmodular grants, see *Detailed Budget Page*.

**Modular Grant.** Used at the NIH for applications requesting less than $250,000, eliminating the need for budget details. Applicants request budgets in modules of $25,000.

**National Institutes of Health.** Federal agency that conducts and supports biomedical and behavioral research to create fundamental knowledge of living systems and to reduce the burden of illness and disability.

**Native Hawaiian or Other Pacific Islander.** Human subjects term indicating a person having origins in the original peoples of Hawaii, Guam, Samoa, or other Pacific Islands.

**New Application.** NIH grant application that has not received prior funding. Also called a *Type 1* application.

**New Investigator.** Scientist who has never been a principal investigator on a Public Health Services–supported research project other than a small grant (R03), Academic Research Enhancement Award (AREA; R15), exploratory or developmental grant (R21), or career development award except K02 and K04.

**NIH Center for Scientific Review.** Also known as *CSR*. NIH organization that conducts initial peer review of investigator-initiated grant applications for all award types except those reviewed within institutes. It also receives all NIH grant applications and assigns them to I/Cs for administration after award and possibly also review.

**NIH Commons.** Web site where NIH grantees, staff, and the public access and share administrative information about research awards; includes both restricted and public sites.

**NIH-Defined Phase III Clinical Trial.** A broadly based, prospective investigation, including community- and other population-based trials, usually involving several hundred or more people, to evaluate an experimental intervention in comparison with a standard or control, or to compare two or more existing treatments. Often, the aim is to provide evidence for changing policy or standard of care. It includes pharmacologic, nonpharmacologic, and behavioral interventions for disease prevention, prophylaxis, diagnosis, or therapy.

**NIH "Guide for Grants and Contracts."** Weekly NIH publication listing I/C initiatives and policy notices.

**NIH Roadmap Initiative.** Strategic initiatives to be funded under the NIH Roadmap approach to address critical roadblocks and knowledge gap that currently constrain rapid progress in biomedical research.

**Notice of Grant Award.** Legally binding document that notifies a grantee and others that a grant has been funded; contains or references all terms and conditions of an award; and documents the obligation of federal funds. An award notice may be sent electronically or by regular mail.

**Office for Human Research Protections.** Department of Health and Human Services (HHS) office that oversees human subjects protection for HHS-supported research. Formerly the NIH Office of Protection From Research Risks.

**Office of Laboratory Animal Welfare.** NIH office that oversees compliance with the Public Health Services policy on Humane Care and Use of Laboratory Animals.

**Office of Management and Budget.** Also known as the *OMB*. Executive Branch office that assists the president of the United States in preparing the federal budget, evaluating agency programs and policies, and setting funding priorities. In setting policy, the OMB issues government-wide policy directives, called *circulars*, that apply to grants.

**Office of Technology Transfer.** NIH office that manages the NIH invention portfolio and oversees NIH technology transfer. See also *Technology Transfer*.

**OMB.** See *Office of Management and Budget*.

**Other Significant Contributors.** Term that identifies individuals who have committed to contribute to the scientific development or execution of the project but who are not committing any specified measurable effort to the project. These individuals are typically presented at "zero percent" effort or "as needed" (individuals with measurable effort cannot be listed as Other Significant Contributors). Consultants should be included if they meet this definition. This would also be an appropriate designation for mentors on career awards.

**Other Support.** All financial resources—federal, nonfederal, commercial, or institutional—that support a principal investigator's research, including research grants, cooperative agreements, and contracts. Other support must be included in a grant application. Training awards, prizes, or gifts are not included.

**Overlap of Support.** Other support that duplicates research or budgetary items funded by an NIH grant. Overlap of support also occurs when any project-supported personnel has time commitments exceeding 100%.

**PA.** See *Program Announcement.*

**Patient-Oriented Research.** Research into disease mechanisms, therapeutic interventions, clinical trials, or the development of new technologies.

**Payback.** Time and effort that T32 (training) award trainees and fellows must repay the government. During the first year, trainees owe one month of payback for every month of support; then they start paying back one month for every month worked.

**Payline.** Percentile-based funding cutoff point for R01 grant applications, determined at the beginning of a fiscal year by balancing the projected number of grant applications recommended for funding by a scientific review group with the amount of funds available to the I/C. I/Cs tend to fund most R01 applications in percentile order. For other types of grants, for example training and small-business awards, I/Cs may establish a payline based on priority score.

**Peer Review.** System for evaluating research grant applications and contract proposals using non-NIH reviewers who are professional peers of an applicant. The NIH's peer review system comprises both initial peer review and second-level peer review. See also *Dual Peer Review, Human Subjects Code, Integrated Review Group, Scientific Review Administrator, Scientific Review Group,* and *Study Section.*

**Peer Review Criteria.** See *Initial Peer Review Criteria for Grants.*

**Peer Reviewer.** Scientist, usually from academia, who comes to the NIH to review grant applications or contract proposals. Peer reviewers include the scientific review group chair, who leads the discussions. See also *Initial Peer Review, Primary Peer Reviewer, Scientific Review Administrator,* and *Secondary Peer Reviewer.*

**Percentile.** Ranking used by NIH I/Cs to set grant paylines and make funding decisions. A percentile shows the relative position of each application's priority score among all scores assigned by a scientific review group at its last three meetings. The range is from 0.1 to 100.0; lower numbers represent better scores.

**Phase I Clinical Trial.** Tests a new intervention in 20–80 people for an initial evaluation of its safety (e.g., to determine a safe dosage range and identify side effects).

**Phase II Clinical Trial.** Studies an intervention in a larger group of people, usually several hundred, to determine efficacy and further evaluate safety.

**Phase III Clinical Trial.** Studies the efficacy of an intervention in large groups of several hundred to several thousand subjects by comparing it to other standard or experimental interventions while monitoring adverse events and collecting information that will allow safe use.

**Phase IV Clinical Trial.** A study done after an intervention has been marketed to monitor its effectiveness in the general population, and collect information about adverse effects associated with widespread use.

**PHS 2590.** The Public Health Service noncompeting grant progress report. A grantee submits a PHS 2590 to the NIH to report progress and continue funding for the duration of the grant. The form is submitted annually, two months before the beginning of a new budget period. The NIH has a streamlined noncompeting award process (SNAP) for submitting the PHS 2590; award notices identify whether a grant is subject to SNAP.

**PHS 398.** Public Health Service grant application forms and instructions for competing research grants and cooperative agreements.

**Primary Assignment.** Routing of an NIH grant application by the Center for Scientific Review to an I/C, which decides whether to fund it. An I/C may request to change this assignment if the application is more suited to another I/C. See also *Receipt, Referral, and Assignment of Applications* and *Secondary Assignment.*

**Primary Peer Reviewer.** Peer reviewer who reads a grant application thoroughly, writes a critique of it before an initial peer review meeting, and then presents it to the scientific review group for discussion. See also *Secondary Peer Reviewer.*

**Principal Investigator.** Also known as *program director* or *project director*. The one individual designated by the applicant organization to direct the project or program to be supported by the grant. The principal investigator is responsible and accountable to applicant organization officials for the proper conduct of the project or program.

**Principal Investigator, New.** See *New Investigator.*

**Priority Score.** Average of individual ratings of scientific merit given by reviewers of an initial peer review scientific review group. Ratings range from 1.0 (*outstanding*) to 5.0 (*acceptable*). Though scientific review groups use numbers 1.0 to 5.0, scores are listed on a summary statement as 100 to 500.

**Privacy Act.** Law protecting citizens against needless collection or release of personal data.

**Private Information.** Information for which a person can expect that observations or recording are not taking place and that the information will not be made public. Information must be individually identifiable to constitute human subjects research.

**Program Announcement.** Also known as a *PA*. NIH announcement requesting grant applications in stated scientific areas. Generally, money is not set aside to pay for the grants. However, for some PAs, some I/Cs may fund applications with scores beyond the payline. PAs are published in the NIH "Guide for Grants and Contracts."

**Program Director.** See *Principal Investigator.*

**Program Income.** Gross income earned by the applicant organization that is directly generated by a supported activity or earned as a result of the award.

**Program Officer.** Also known as a *program official*. I/C staff member who oversees a scientific program and the progress of grants in his or her portfolio. Program officers work closely with grants management specialists to administer and resolve issues with that I/C's grants.

**Program Official.** See *Program Officer.*

**Program Project Grant.** Grant in the P series that provides an institution with support for a multidisciplinary, long-term research program with an objective or theme involving groups of investigators. Awarded on behalf of a principal investigator, the grant can support projects and shared resources.

**Progress Report for Contract.** Required scheduled report summarizing research progress. It may include technical, fiscal, and invention report information.

**Progress Report for Grants.** See *PHS 2590.*

**Project Costs for Grants.** Total allowable costs, both direct costs and facilities and administrative costs, incurred by a grantee to carry out a grant-supported project. Project costs can include costs charged to a grant and paid by a grantee to satisfy a matching or cost-sharing requirement.

**Project Director.** See *Principal Investigator.*

**Project Period.** See *Grant Project Period.*

**Public Health Service.** Umbrella organization consisting of eight Department of Health and Human Services health agencies, the Office of Public Health and Science, and the Commissioned Corps, a uniformed service of more than 6,000 health professionals.

**R01.** Standard NIH research project grant.

**Racial and Ethnic Categories.** Human subjects terms defined by the Office of Management and Budget and used by the NIH to allow comparisons to national databases.

**Randomized Controlled Trial.** Also known as an *RCT.* A quantitative, comparative, controlled experiment in which a group of investigators study interventions in a series of individuals who receive them in random order.

**Rating Criteria.** See *Initial Peer Review Criteria for Grants.*

**RCT.** See *Randomized Controlled Trial.*

**Receipt Date.** Date grant applications are due to the NIH Center for Scientific Review (CSR). Investigator-initiated applications have three receipt dates, listed on the CSR standard receipt dates Web site. Applications and contract proposals responding to an NIH I/C initiative are due on the date listed in the initiative announcement in the NIH "Guide for Grants and Contracts."

**Receipt, Referral, and Assignment of Applications.** Routing of grant applications arriving at the NIH. The referral section of the Center for Scientific Review (CSR) is the central receipt point for competing applications. CSR referral officers assign each application to an NIH I/Cs and refer it to an integrated review group, notifying applicants of these assignments by mail. Alternatively, the NIH encourages applicants to self-assign.

**Recompeting.** See *Competing Continuation.*

**Renewal.** See *Competing Continuation.*

**Request for Applications.** Also known as an *RFA.* Initiative sponsored by one or more NIH I/C that stimulates research by requesting grant applications in a well-defined scientific area. RFAs have a single application receipt date and are published in the NIH "Guide for Grants and Contracts." They identify funds set aside and the number of awards likely to be made.

**Request for Proposals.** Also known as an *RFP.* Initiative sponsored by an NIH I/C that requests proposals for a contract to meet a specific need, such as the development of an animal model. RFPs have a single proposal receipt date and are published in the NIH "Guide for Grants and Contracts" and on the Federal Business Opportunities (FedBizOpps) Web site.

**Research Plan.** Main part of an NIH grant application describing a principal investigator's proposed research, stating its importance and how it will be conducted. A typical research plan has four main sections: specific aims, background and significance, preliminary studies and progress report, and research design and methods.

**Research Project Grant.** Also known as an *RPG*. Budget term referring to the following grant types: R01, R03, R21, R23, R35, R37, R41, R42, R43, R44, R55, P01, P42, U01, U19, U43, and U44. RPGs are research grants awarded to an institution. R series are single research project grants; P series are multiproject grants. U series cooperative agreements can be either single project (U01, U43, U44) or multiproject (U19). Unlike a multiproject award, a single project award addresses a single research topic even if it involves multiple sites.

**Research Supplement.** Monies that add funds to an existing grant to support and recruit minorities, people with disabilities, and people returning to work from family responsibilities. See also *Administrative Supplement*.

**Research Supplement for Underrepresented Minorities.** See *Research Supplements to Promote Diversity in Health-Related Research*.

**Research Supplements for People With Disabilities.** See *Research Supplements to Promote Diversity in Health-Related Research*.

**Research Supplements for Reentry Into a Research Career.** Monies that add funds to an existing grant to support scientists who have taken time off to care for children or parents or to attend to other family responsibilities.

**Research Supplements to Promote Diversity in Health-Related Research.** Monies that add funds to an existing grant to support disabled and underrepresented minority graduate students, postdoctoral fellows, and faculty.

**Resources Page.** Form page in PHS 398 grant application describing all essential resources in an application.

**Restriction.** Special term and condition in a notice of grant award or article in a contract that limits activities and expenditures for human subjects or animal research. It may be lifted or adjusted after award if requirements are met.

**Resubmission.** The act of sending the NIH a revised investigator-initiated grant application for initial peer review after it has been reviewed one or more times by a scientific review group but did not receive a sufficiently high percentile rank to be funded. Each resubmission is noted in its application identification number (e.g., A1, A2). The NIH limits applicants to two resubmissions. See also *Summary Statement*.

**Review Committee Chairperson.** Member of an NIH initial peer review committee who facilitates discussions of grant applications and contract proposals by the committee.

**Review Criteria.** See *Initial Peer Review Criteria for Grants*.

**Review Cycle.** Time span for one NIH Center for Scientific Review initial peer review round, from the receipt of grant applications to the date of an initial peer review meeting. There are three cycles a year for investigator-initiated grants.

**Reviewer.** See *Peer Reviewer*.

**RFA.** See *Request for Applications*.

**RFP.** See *Request for Proposals.*

**Risk.** Probability of harm or physical, psychological, social, or economic injury resulting from participation in a research study.

**RPG.** See *Research Project Grant.*

**SBIR.** See *Small Business Innovation Research.*

**SBIR Fast Track.** See *Small Business Innovation Research Fast Track.*

**SBIR Phase I.** See *Small Business Innovation Research Phase I.*

**SBIR Phase II.** See *Small Business Innovation Research Phase II.*

**Scientific Review Administrator.** Also known as an *SRA.* Federal scientist who presides over a scientific review group and coordinates and reports the initial peer review of each grant application assigned to it. SRAs act as intermediaries between applicants and reviewers and prepare summary statements for all applications reviewed. See also *Scientific Review Group.*

**Scientific Review Group.** Also known as an *SRG* or *study section.* Chartered committee performing initial peer review in either the NIH Center for Scientific Review or an I/C. Composed of non-NIH scientists, SRGs are managed by a scientific review administrator. I/Cs review grant applications with their own review requirements. See also *Dual Peer Review, Study Section,* and *Integrated Review Group.*

**Scored Application.** Grant application a study section judges to be competitive, generally in the upper half of those being reviewed. It receives a priority score and may be funded by an I/C.

**Second-Level Peer Review.** Peer review to make funding recommendations to the I/C. Generally conducted by an I/C's advisory council, second-level review results in funding recommendations to the I/C director based on program priorities, balance, and policy issues; it does not reassess the science. See also *Expedited Second-Level Peer Review, Initial Peer Review, Integrated Review Group,* and *Scientific Review Group.*

**Secondary Assignment.** Assignment of a grant application by the Center for Scientific Review to an I/C as a backup for funding should the primary I/C decide not to fund it. Either a program officer or an applicant can request secondary assignment. See also *Dual Assignment, Primary Assignment,* and *Receipt, Referral, and Assignment of Applications.*

**Secondary Peer Reviewer.** Peer reviewer who serves as a backup for a primary peer reviewer. Both read a grant application thoroughly before an initial peer review meeting to lend their expertise to the group discussion. The secondary peer reviewer may also write a critique.

**SEP.** See *Special Emphasis Panel.*

**Sex/Gender.** The term *gender* refers to the classification of research subjects into either or both of two categories: women and men. *Sex* refers to biological sex, either male or female.

**Significant Contributor, Other.** See *Other Significant Contributors.*

**Small Business.** Business independently owned and operated and not dominant in its field.

**Small Business Concern.** For-profit business located in the United States, independently owned and operated, not dominant in its field of operation, and qualified as a small business using criteria in 13 CFR part 121.

**Small Business Innovation Research.** Also known as *SBIR*. Government-wide program that promotes research and development with the potential for commercialization at small business concerns.

**Small Business Innovation Research Fast Track.** SBIR award that allows concurrent submission and review of Phase I and Phase II applications to reduce a potential funding gap between the end of Phase I and the start of Phase II.

**Small Business Innovation Research Phase I.** The objective is to establish the technical merit and feasibility of the proposed research/research-and-development efforts and to determine the quality of the performance of the grantee organization prior to providing further federal support in SBIR Phase II.

**Small Business Innovation Research Phase II.** The objective is to continue the research/research-and-development efforts initiated in an SBIR Phase I. Funding in this phase is based on the feasibility results of the Phase I study, scientific and technical merit, and commercial potential of the Phase I application.

**Small Business Technology Transfer.** Also known as *STTR*. Government-wide program that promotes research and development with the potential for commercialization at small business concerns. It differs from Small Business Innovation Research (SBIR) in requiring a formal collaborative relationship with a university or other nonprofit research institution.

**Small Business Technology Transfer Fast Track.** Expedited mechanism incorporating submission and review process in which both Phase I and Phase II of the STTR grant application are submitted and reviewed together.

**Small Business Technology Transfer Phase I.** The objective is to establish the technical merit and feasibility of the proposed research/research-and-development efforts and to determine the quality of the performance of the grantee organization prior to providing further federal support in Phase II.

**Small Business Technology Transfer Phase II.** The objective is to continue the research/research-and-development efforts initiated in the STTR Phase I. Funding in this phase is based on the feasibility results of the Phase I study, scientific and technical merit, and commercial potential of Phase I application.

**Small Disadvantaged Business.** Business that is at least 51% owned and controlled by socially and economically disadvantaged U.S. citizens and that shows potential for success. Companies are certified by the Small Business Administration under Section 8(a) of the Small Business Act.

**Small Disadvantaged Business Concern.** Small business that is at least 51% unconditionally owned, or has at least 51% of its stock unconditionally owned, and is managed by one or more people who are socially and economically disadvantaged.

**SNAP.** See *Streamlined Noncompeting Award Process*.

**Special Emphasis Panel.** Ad hoc initial peer review group with expertise to review a set of research grant applications or contract proposals. See also *Scientific Review Group, Integrated Review Group,* and *Study Section.*

**Specific Aims.** Formal statement of the objectives and milestones of a research project in a grant application.

**SRA.** See *Scientific Review Administrator.*

**SRG.** See *Scientific Review Group* and *Study Section.*

**Streamlined Noncompeting Award Process.** Also called *SNAP.* A streamlined process to continue support of a Public Health Service–supported grant. To continue funding, a grantee sends a PHS 2590 form to the I/C's Grants Management Branch two months before the beginning of a new budget period, following SNAP procedures in the PHS 2590. Under SNAP, financial status reports are due at the end of a competitive segment. A notice of grant award states whether a grant is awarded under SNAP.

**Streamlined Review.** Practice through which grant applications judged by peer reviewers to be in the bottom half of those being reviewed are not discussed and do not receive a priority score. The NIH sends an applicant the primary and secondary reviewers' critiques as feedback. Formerly called *triage.*

**STTR.** See *Small Business Technology Transfer.*

**STTR Fast Track.** See *Small Business Technology Transfer Fast Track.*

**STTR Phase I.** See *Small Business Technology Transfer Phase I.*

**STTR Phase II.** See *Small Business Technology Transfer Phase II.*

**Study Section.** Also called *scientific review group.* Component of an NIH Center for Scientific Review (CSR) integrated review group organized around a scientific area, which conducts initial peer review in that field. Composed of non-NIH scientific experts, study sections are managed by CSR scientific review administrators. See also *Initial Peer Review* and *Dual Peer Review.*

**Subcontract.** Any agreement, other than one involving an employer-employee relationship, entered into by a federal government prime contractor calling for supplies or services required solely for the performance of the prime contract or another subcontract.

**Subject.** Healthy person or patient who participates in a clinical investigation, either as a recipient of an investigational drug or as a control.

**Summary Statement.** Official document showing the outcome of initial peer review and containing priority scores and percentiles, codes for various areas of concern (e.g., human subjects research), and a recommended budget. Summary statements generally have a short synopsis prepared by a scientific review administrator using peer reviewer critiques.

**Supplement.** Monies that add funds to an existing grant. Includes research supplements, administrative supplements, and competing supplements.

**Supplement, Administrative.** See *Administrative Supplement.*

**Supplement, Diversity in Health-Related Research.** See *Research Supplements to Promote Diversity in Health-Related Research.*

**Supplement, Research.** See *Research Supplement.*

**Table of Contents.** Form page 3 in the PHS 398 grant application.

**Targeted/Planned Enrollment Page.** Form in the PHS 398 grant application showing populations included in an application.

**Targeted Research.** Research funded from an NIH I/C set-aside of dollars for a scientific area. I/Cs solicit grant applications using research initiatives: requests for applications and program announcements for grants, and requests for proposals for contracts. Targeted research applications are reviewed by chartered scientific review committees within I/Cs.

**Technology Transfer.** Sharing of knowledge and facilities among federal laboratories, industry, universities, government, and others to make federally generated scientific and technological advances accessible to private industry and state and local governments.

**Total Costs for Grants.** Total allowable costs, both direct and facilities and administrative, incurred by a grantee to carry out a project or activity. These include costs charged to a grant and costs paid by a grantee to satisfy a matching or cost-sharing requirement.

**Training Grant.** Training (T) and fellowship (F) grants.

**Type 1.** See *New Application.*

**Type 2.** See *Competing Continuation.*

**Unscored.** Result of streamlined review for grant applications judged by peer reviewers to be in the bottom half of those being reviewed and therefore unlikely to be funded. A scientific review group generally does not discuss unscored applications, and the applications do not receive priority scores. Unscored applicants receive the primary and secondary reviewers' critiques as a summary statement. Occasionally, an unscored application is funded by a special action of an NIH I/C's advisory council. See also *Streamlined Review.*

**Unsolicited Research.** See *Investigator-Initiated Research.*

**White.** Human subjects term indicating a person having origins in any of the original peoples of Europe, the Middle East, or North Africa.

*Helpful Web Sites*

| | |
|---|---|
| **Animal Welfare Act** | http://www.nal.usda.gov/awic/legislat/awa.htm |
| **Bioethics Resources on the Web** | http://www.nih.gov/sigs/bioethics/specific.html |

*Career (K) Award Mechanisms*

| | |
|---|---|
| K01: Mentored Research Scientist Development Award | http://grants1.nih.gov/grants/guide/pa-files/PA-00-019.html |
| K01: International Research Scientist Development K01 Award | http://grants1.nih.gov/grants/guide/pa-files/PAR-04-058.html |
| K02: Independent Scientist Award | http://grants1.nih.gov/grants/guide/pa-files/PA-00-020.html |
| K05: Senior Scientist Award | http://grants1.nih.gov/grants/guide/pa-files/PA-00-021.html |
| K07: Academic Career Award | http://grants1.nih.gov/grants/guide/pa-files/PA-00-070.html |
| K08: Mentored Clinical Scientist Development Award | http://grants1.nih.gov/grants/guide/pa-files/PA-00-003.html |
| K18: Career Enhancement Award for Stem-Cell Research | http://grants1.nih.gov/grants/guide/pa-files/PAR-02-069.html |
| K23: Mentored Patient-Oriented Research Career Development Award | http://grants1.nih.gov/grants/guide/pa-files/PA-00-004.html |
| K24: Mid-Career Investigator Award in Patient-Oriented Research | http://grants1.nih.gov/grants/guide/pa-files/PA-04-107.html |
| K25: Mentored Quantitative Research Career Development Award | http://grants1.nih.gov/grants/guide/pa-files/PA-02-127.html |
| K26: Midcareer Investigator Award in Mouse Pathobiology Research | http://grants1.nih.gov/grants/guide/pa-files/PAR-99-065.html |
| K30: Clinical Research Curriculum Development | http://grants1.nih.gov/training/K30.htm |
| **Career (K) Awards Kiosk** | http://grants1.nih.gov/training/careerdevelopmentawards.htm |
| **Career (K) Awards Wizard** | http://grants1.nih.gov/training/kwizard/index.htm |

| | |
|---|---|
| Certificates of Confidentiality Kiosk | http://grants2.nih.gov/grants/policy/coc/ |
| CRISP Database | http://crisp.cit.nih.gov/ |
| CSR Study Section Roster Index | http://www.csr.nih.gov/Committees/rosterindex.asp |
| Data and Safety Monitoring (1) | http://grants.nih.gov/grants/guide/notice-files/not98-084.html |
| Data and Safety Monitoring (2) | http://grants2.nih.gov/grants/guide/notice-files/not99-107.html |
| Data and Safety Monitoring: National Heart, Lung, and Blood Institute (NHLBI) | http://www.nhlbi.nih.gov/funding/policies/dsmb_est.htm |
| Data and Safety Monitoring: National Institute of Neurological Disorders and Stroke (NINDS) | http://www.ninds.nih.gov/funding/research/clinical_research/dsm_guidelines.htm |
| Department of Health and Human Services Policy for Protection of Human Research Subjects | http://www.hhs.gov/ohrp/humansubjects/guidance/45cfr46.htm |
| eRA Commons | http://www.commons.era.nih.gov/commons/ |
| Ethics Codes: Belmont Report | http://www.hhs.gov/ohrp/humansubjects/guidance/belmont.htm |
| Ethics Codes: Declaration of Helsinki | http://www.wma.net/e/policy/b3.htm |
| Ethics Codes: Human Subjects | http://grants1.nih.gov/grants/policy/hs/regulations.htm#Ethical |

## Ethnic Origin and Race Data Forms

| | |
|---|---|
| PHS 398 | http://grants.nih.gov/grants/funding/phs398/personal.pdf |
| U.S. Government Census Form | http://www.census.gov/dmd/www/2000quest.html |
| National Health and Nutrition Examination Survey (NHANES) | http://www.cdc.gov/nchs/about/major/nhanes/questexam.htm |

| | |
|---|---|
| **Federal Funding Agencies** | http://www.grants.gov/Health |
| Centers for Medicaid and Medicare Services (CMS) | http://www.cms.hhs.gov/ |
| Administration on Aging (AOA) | http://www.aoa.gov/ |
| Administration for Children and Families (ACF) | http://www.acf.hhs.gov/ |
| Agency for Healthcare Research and Quality (AHRQ) | http://www.ahrq.gov/ |
| Agency for Toxic Substances and Disease Registry (ATSDR) | http://www.atsdr.cdc.gov/ |
| Centers for Disease Control and Prevention (CDC) | http://www.cdc.gov/ |
| Food and Drug Administration (FDA) | http://www.fda.gov/ |
| Health Resources and Services Administration (HSRA) | http://www.hrsa.gov/ |
| Indian Health Service (IHS) | http://www.ihs.gov/ |
| National Institutes of Health (NIH) | http://www.nih.gov/ |
| National Institutes of Occupational Safety and Health (NIOSH) | http://www.cdc.gov/niosh/homepage.html |

| | |
|---|---|
| Office of Minority Health | http://www.cdc.gov/omh/ |
| Substance Abuse & Mental Health Services Administration (SAMHSA) | http://www.samhsa.gov/index.aspx |
| **Fellowship Study Sections** | http://www.csr.nih.gov/events/fellowship_ssfellow_ss/htm |
| **Fiscal Disbursements** | http://grants2.nih.gov/grants/award/trends/distbud03.htm |
| **Grants Management:** National Institute of Allergy and Infectious Disease (NIAID) | http://www.niaid.nih.gov/ncn.grants.manage.index.htm |
| **Guide for the Care and Use of Laboratory Animals** | http://www.nap.edu/readingroom/books/labrats/ |
| **Healthy People 2010** | http://www.healthypeople.gov/default.htm |
| **HIPAA Privacy Rule 1** | http://privacyruleandresearch.nih.gov/pr_02.asp |
| **HIPAA Privacy Rule 2** | http://www.hhs.gov/ocr/hipaa |
| **Human Subjects: FAQs 1** | http://grants1.nih.gov/grants/policy/hs/faqs_applicants.htm |
| **Human Subjects: FAQs 2** | http://grants1.nih.gov/grants/policy/hs/faqs_concerns.htm |
| **Human Subjects Decision Chart** | http://www.hhs.gov/ohrp/humansubjects/guidance/decisioncharts.htm |
| **Human Subjects Regulations 45 CFR Part 46** | http://www.hhs.gov/ohrp/humansubjects/guidance/45cfr46.htm |
| **Human Subjects: Revised Policy for IRB Review** | http://grants2.nih.gov/grants/guide/notice-files/NOT-OD-00-031.html |
| **Human Subjects: Tissues/Specimens** | http://www.hhs.gov/ohrp/humansubjects/guidance/cdebiol.pdf |
| **Inclusion of Children in Research** | http://grants2.nih.gov/grants/funding/children/children.htm |
| **Inclusion of Women/Minorities in Research** | http://grants.nih.gov/grants/funding/women_min/women_min.htm |
| **Institutional Eligibility for R01** | http://grants1.nih.gov/grants/funding/r01.htm |
| **Institutional Research Training (T) Grants** | http://grants.nih.gov/training/nrsa.htm |
| T32 | http://grants1.nih.gov/grants/guide/pa-files/PA-02-109.htm |
| T35 | http://grants1.nih.gov/grants/guide/pa-files/PA-05-117.html |
| **Institutes and Centers** | http://www.nih.gov/icd |
| Clinical Center | http://clinicalcenter.nih.gov/ |
| Center for Scientific Review (CSR) | http://www.csr.nih.gov/ |
| Center for Information Technology (CIT) | http://www.cit.nih.gov/ |
| John E. Fogarty International Center (FIC) | http://www.fic.nih.gov/ |
| National Cancer Institute (NCI) | http://www.nci.nih.gov/ |
| National Center for Complementary and Alternative Medicine (NCCAM) | http://nccam.nih.gov/ |
| National Center for Minority Health and Health Disparities (NCMHD) | http://ncmhd.nih.gov/ |

| | |
|---|---|
| National Center for Research Resources (NCRR) | http://www.ncrr.nih.gov/ |
| National Eye Institute (NEI) | http://www.nei.nih.gov/ |
| National Heart, Lung, and Blood Institute (NHLBI) | http://www.nhlbi.nih.gov/ |
| National Human Genome Research Institute | http://www.genome.gov/ |
| National Institute on Aging (NIA) | http://www.nia.nih.gov/ |
| National Institute on Alcohol Abuse and Alcoholism (NIAAA) | http://www.niaaa.nih.gov/ |
| National Institute of Allergy and Infectious Disease (NIAID) | http://www.niaid.nih.gov/ |
| National Institute of Arthritis and Musculoskeletal and Skin Disease (NIAMS) | http://www.niams.nih.gov/ |
| National Institute of Biomedical Imaging and Bioengineering (NIBIB) | http://www.nibib.nih.gov/ |
| National Institute of Child Health and Human Development (NICHD) | http://www.nichd.nih.gov/ |
| National Institute on Deafness and Other Communication Disorders (NIDCD) | http://www.nidcd.nih.gov/ |
| National Institute of Dental and Craniofacial Research (NIDCR) | http://www.nidcr.nih.gov/ |
| National Institute of Diabetes and Digestive and Kidney Disease (NIDDK) | http://www.niddk.nih.gov/ |
| National Institute on Drug Abuse (NIDA) | http://www.nida.nih.gov/ |
| National Institute of Environmental Health Science (NIEHS) | http://www.niehs.nih.gov/ |
| National Institute of General Medical Science (NIGMS) | http://www.nigms.nih.gov/ |
| National Institute of Mental Health (NIMH) | http://www.nimh.nih.gov/ |
| National Institute of Neurological Disorders and Stroke (NINDS) | http://www.ninds.nih.gov/ |
| National Institute of Nursing Research (NINR) | http://ninr.nih.gov/ninr/ |
| Office of AIDS Research (OAR) | http://www.nih.gov/od/oar/ |
| Office of Behavioral and Social Science Research (OBSSR) | http://obssr.od.nih.gov/ |
| Office of the Director (OD) | http://www.nih.gov/icd/od/ |
| Office of Disease Prevention (ODP) | http://odp.od.nih.gov/ |
| Office of Research on Women's Health (ORWH) | http://www4.od.nih.gov/orwh |

| | |
|---|---|
| **Integrated Review Groups (IRGs)** | http://www.csr.nih.gov/review/irgdesc.htm |
| **Minority Eligibility for Supplements** | http://grants2.nih.gov/grants/guide/pa-files/<br>PA-01-079.html |
| **NIH Home Page** | http://www.nih.gov |
| **National Research Service Awards** | http://grants1.nih.gov/grants/funding/funding_<br>program.htm |
| **National Institute of Allergy and<br>Infectious Disease Q&A:<br>Funding Decisions** | http://www.niad.nih.gov/ncn/qa/fundingdec.htm |
| **NIH Advisory Council** | http://www.csr.nih.gov/roster_proto/nihlist.htm |
| **NIH Basic Fact Sheet** | http://www.nih.gov/about |
| **NIH Grant Mechanisms** | http://grants1.nih.gov/grants/funding/funding_<br>program.htm |
| **NIH Grant Review Criteria** | http://grants.nih.gov/guide/notice-files/<br>NOT-OD-05-002.html |
| **NIH Roadmap Initiative** | http://nihroadmap.nih.gov/ |
| *NIH Training Grant (F) Programs* | |
| F30 | http://grants1.nih.gov/grants/guide/pa-files/<br>PA-05-151.html |
| F31 | http://grants1.nih.gov/grants/guide/pa-files/<br>PA-04-032.html |
| F31 (for minorities/students<br>with disabilities) | http://grants1.nih.gov/grants/funding/funding_<br>program.htm |
| F32 | http://grants1.nih.gov/grants/guide/pa-files/<br>PA-03-067.htm |
| F33 | http://grants1.nih.gov/grants/guide/pa-files/<br>PA-00-131.html |
| **Office for Civil Rights/Department<br>of Health and Human Services** | http://www.hhs.gov/ocr/hipaa |
| **Peer Review Tutorial** | http://www.csr.nih.gov/REVIEW/peerrev.htm |
| **PHS 398 Instructions/Forms** | http://grants1.nih.gov/grants/forms.htm |
| **Resources for Grant Applicants** | http://grants1.nih.gov/grants/resources.htm |
| **Required Education in the<br>Protection of Human<br>Research Participants** | http://grants.nih.gov/grants/guide/notice-files/<br>NOT-OD-00-039.html |
| **Review of Small Business Applications** | http://www.csr.nih.gov/REVIEW/sba.asp |
| *SBIR/STTR* | |
| Award Mechanisms | http://grants2.nih.gov/grants/funding/sbir.htm |
| Award Mechanisms | http://grants2.nih.gov/grants/funding/sbirsttr_<br>programs.htm |
| Differences | http://grants1.nih.gov/grants/funding/sbir.htm |
| Eligibility of Small Business | http://www.sba.gov/size/indexcontacts.html |

| Frequently Asked Questions | http://grants1.nih.gov/grants/funding/sbirsttr_faqs__.doc |
| Immigration Policy | http://grants1.nih.gov/grants/guide/pa-files/PA-00-019.html |
| JoAnne Goodnight Letter | http://grants1.nih.gov/grants/funding/sbir.htm |
| Review Criteria | http://grants2.nih.gov/grants/funding/sbirsttr_Reviewcriteria.htm |
| Tutorial | http://grants1.nih.gov/grants/funding/sbir.htm |
| Unallowable Costs | http://ocm.od.nih.gov/dfas/unallowables.htm |

*Searches for Funded Grants*

| Community of Science | http://fundingopps.cos.com |
| Foundation Center | http://fdncenter.org/ |
| Grantsnet | http://www.grantsnet.org/ |
| Illinois Researcher Information Service (IRIS) | www.library.uiuc.edu/iris/ |

**Small Business Review Activities**          http://www.csr.nih.gov/review/irgdesc.htm

# Appendix C

## *Checklists*

## I. The Science

*Section A. Specific Aims*

Necessary Elements

- Clear statement of the problem or question you plan to investigate
- Background material, to provide context for your proposal
- Why your proposal is innovative, needs to be done
- What you plan to do
- Specific aims or hypotheses

Reminders

- One page or less
- Aims or hypotheses must correspond to hypotheses given in Sections B (Background and Significance) and D (Research Design and Methods)
- Hypotheses must be unambiguous, make clear predictions
- Specific aims should not be overly ambitious

*Section B. Background and Significance*

Necessary Elements

- The problem or question your study will address
- Why that problem or question is important to the NIH
- What others have done to address this problem or question, and why their efforts weren't sufficient
- What you plan to do that is different from previous studies
- Why your plan is novel, cutting edge, and should excite the reader
- An overview of your methodology
- Study hypotheses

Reminders

- Communicate the importance of the problem or research question.
- Strongly justify the need for your particular study and explain the contribution to the field .
- Explain the innovation of the proposed study.
- Do not weigh down the story line with unnecessary information.

### Section C. Preliminary Studies

Necessary Elements

- Description of the team, including prior collaborations and relevant experience
- Studies conducted by the principal investigator (PI) and key personnel that are relevant to proposal
- Pilot data

Reminders

- This section should have two subsections: feasibility and pilot data.
- In the feasibility section, describe the history of collaborations, if any, within the group.
- In the feasibility section, present supporting work by co-investigators and key personnel.
- Use figures and tables to present results.
- In both feasibility and pilot studies sections, make sure the studies are clearly described and their relevance to the project is evident.

### Section D. Research Design and Methods

Necessary Elements

- Overview of methods
- Hypotheses, identical to those given in Sections A (Specific Aims) and B (Background and Significance)
- Study design, including strengths and advantages; also, discuss possible alternatives and your reasons for not using them
- Subjects
- Informed consent procedures
- Recruitment and/or attrition, including a flow chart (see Figure C on page 91)
- Backup plan if recruitment is slower than expected
- Sample size and power calculations; tie these to hypotheses, and address *each* hypothesis, each outcome measure
- Inclusion and exclusion criteria
- Description of manipulation, intervention, independent variables, and control conditions
- Description of outcomes
- Procedures, including quality control measures to ensure high-quality data collection
- Randomization method and considerations (e.g., stratification, matching)
- Study timeline
- Measures used in the study
- Debriefing procedures, if the study involves human subjects
- Data management and missing values
- Statistical analysis
- Dissemination of results
- Potential limitations and solutions

- Summary: Don't repeat methods, but instead, emphasize significance, innovation, strength of the design to address the hypotheses, possible clinical implications of the results, generalizability to other populations, cost-effectiveness of the intervention (if there is one), and correspondence with NIH priorities (e.g., Healthy People 2010, Roadmap Initiative)

Reminders

- Explain design and methodology decisions as needed *as they occur in the text.*
- Clearly show that you have access to your subject population and that enrollment and/or intervention procedures are tested and feasible.
- Justify your inclusion and exclusion criteria.
- Estimate attrition rates and compensate for them in the sample size. Anticipate whether that dropout will be random or systematic, and, if the latter, provide a plan to deal with this.
- Check for biases in subject selection and, if there are biases, discuss what you plan to do to address this problem.
- Explain how you have arranged for research assistants to be blinded to the condition. If you are using a within-subjects design, counterbalance to control for order effects.
- Use tables to show power calculations.
- Describe reliability and validity of test instruments, including both self-report and physiological measurements (if called for).
- If there are several study time points, use a table to show which measures are given at which time points.
- Include procedural details, such as reminder phone calls to subjects.

## II. Administrative Details

*General*

- Every page in the application should have the PI's name in the top right corner.
- The project title should have no more than 81 characters, including spaces.
- Identify the business official at your institution who can sign the cover page of the grant.
- Identify the person in your department or division who can sign off on budgets.
- Carefully measure to ensure that you are not violating any of the formatting dicta (e.g., margin size, type size, etc.).
- Check with your grants office for the latest fringe rates, indirect rates, and salary caps.
- Carefully think out how much work the project will take and budget for research assistants and other personnel accordingly.
- Do not put items costing less than $5,000 under "equipment."
- Include in the budget funds for office supplies, photocopying, communications, postage, leases for photocopy machines, and extended warrantees for equipment, including computers.
- Ask for funds for computers as you anticipate the need (over the years) will arise.
- Batch items to get a better price.
- Triple-check to ensure that subcontracts for facilities and administrative costs are calculated correctly.
- Specify all necessary resources on the Resources form page, including office space and Web access.
- Remember that references *do not* count in the 25-page limit.
- Remember to calculate the *base* correctly on the checklist (i.e., the base does *not* necessarily equal to direct costs).
- Remember that facilities and administrative cost rates are different for training awards than for research grants.

*Budgets*

- Be careful to put in the correct year. Remember, the initial budget page is for the *first* year of your budget only.
- The first name will always be that of the PI. Co-investigators, if there are any, should come next, followed by other professionals and staff.
- Estimate the effort that each person will contribute by asking how much time in a week (on average) will this person need to devote to this project. One full day is 20%. For example, why did the authors of our sample proposal put only 10% for the ambulatory blood pressure technician? The timeline (in Chapter 5) calls for 33 subjects to be recruited per quarter, or 11 per month; therefore, no more than ½ day per week (10% effort) should be necessary.
- Find out your institution's base salary for each person. In most cases, you cannot arbitrarily change this without discussion with your grants office; someone from that office has to sign off on the budget, and may refuse to do so if the base salary listed is different from the institution's number for that person.
- Find out your institution's fringe benefits rate for the current budget period. This information may be given on your institution's "information for grants and contracts" Web page, or you may need to ask someone in the grants office. The fringe rate can change, and if changes are already in the works, they too will be on the Web page or known by your grants office. Multiply the fringe rate by the "salary requested."
- The NIH places a cap on the amount of base salary you can charge; the cap is currently $181,100, but it changes, so check.
- The NIH defines "equipment" as an item that costs at least $5,000. Your institution may set a different limit, however. This possible difference in definition is important, because indirect costs, or facilities and administrative costs, do not cover equipment (though they do get paid on personnel, supplies, consultant costs, travel, and other expenses).
- The NIH does not require that you itemize items that cost less than $1,000; however, give at least some information.
- You can justify a computer (which should be listed in supplies, not in equipment) if it is to be used on the project. Don't forget to include computers, but don't overdo it.
- It is often wise to *not* request travel funds until at least Year 2. You should have something to present if you're going to ask for reimbursement for travel to a conference, and in Year 1, you won't have anything yet.
- Carefully work out the number of subjects that will be screened and run in each year (these numbers should correspond to the timeline) and then budget accordingly.
- Don't forget to include expenses, such as warrantees, communications costs (e.g., phone bills), postage, and photocopy charges.

## Institutional Review Board

*Consent Form*

Basic.

- A statement that the study involves research
- An explanation of the purposes of the research
- The expected duration of the subject's participation
- A description of the procedures to be followed
- Identification of any procedures that are experimental
- A description of any reasonably foreseeable risks or discomforts to the subject
- A description of any benefits to the subject or to others that may reasonably be expected from the research

- A disclosure of appropriate alternative procedures or courses of treatment, if any, that might be advantageous to the subject
- A statement describing the extent, if any, to which confidentiality of records identifying the subject will be maintained
- For research involving more than minimal risk, an explanation as to whether any compensation or any medical treatments will be made available if injury occurs and, if so, what they consist of or where further information may be obtained
- An explanation of whom to contact for answers to pertinent questions about the research and research subjects' rights, and whom to contact in the event of a research-related injury to the subject
- A statement that participation is voluntary, that refusal to participate will involve no penalty or loss of benefits to which the subject is otherwise entitled, and that the subject may discontinue participation at any time without penalty or loss of benefits to which the subject is otherwise entitled

Additional Elements, as Appropriate.

- A statement that the particular treatment or procedure may involve risks to the subject (or to the embryo or fetus, if the subject is or may become pregnant) that are currently unforeseeable
- Anticipated circumstances under which the subject's participation may be terminated by the PI without regard to the subject's consent
- Any additional costs to the subject that may result from participation in the research
- The consequences of a subject's decision to withdraw from the research and procedures for orderly termination of participation by the subject
- A statement that significant new findings developed during the course of the research, which may relate to the subject's willingness to continue participation, will be provided to the subject
- The approximate number of subjects involved in the study

# Index

# About the Author

**William Gerin** received his BA in Psychology from Stanislaus State College in Turlock, California, in 1979, where his specialty was in operant and classical conditioning avoidance models in animals. He then became interested in studying the role of human interactions in emotional regulation and received his PhD in Social Psychology from Columbia University in 1984 under the mentorship of Stanley Schachter. In 1985, he undertook an NIH-sponsored postdoctoral fellowship in cardiovascular epidemiology at the Cornell University Medical Center, where he studied with Thomas G. Pickering, with whom he maintains a close collaborative association. He has now moved his laboratory to Columbia University/New York–Presbyterian Hospital, where he is Director of Experimental Research in the Behavioral Cardiovascular and Hypertension Center. Bill Gerin is currently the principal investigator on two NIH R01 awards and is a co-investigator on several other NIH grants. His current research areas include the role of emotional regulation in the development of hypertension and coronary heart disease; behavioral interventions to improve medication adherence in culturally diverse patient populations; and the role of psychosocial factors in cardiovascular disease. He resides in Manhattan, a block from the Hudson River.